Bouncing Round the Edges

Following the Wind

Edwin Martin

Dedication

To my wife Peta who has been my faithful and loving companion through all the ups and downs of life

Acknowledgements

Many people have been involved in the birth of this book and I am very grateful to all of them. My special thanks to my wife who meticulously examined and edited the text. Simon my older son also spent many hours discussing the presentation of the documents and with editing the text. The book might never have been written apart from the encouragement of my younger son Dominic. I am grateful for the advice of Dr Denis alexander and Chris Aslan Alexander, both of whom are established authors. The advice and suggestions of Rev Peter Crooks a past colleague was invaluable. I am also grateful to Mr David Boydell for his advice on the text.

The whole staff of the AMZ Marketing Hub were always available, knowledgeable, and patient through all the ups and downs of the production of Bouncing Round the Edges. My particular thanks goes to Amber Roy who was my immediate Producer.

About the Author

After escaping from a restrictive religious sect and gaining a first-class honours degree at Cambridge University, Edwin Martin worked in British general practice, providing specialist care for prisoners, the homeless, and drug users alongside his normal general practice work. He served on the management team of the Royal College of General Practitioners. During his time as a student, he embarked on an overland journey to India and back. Edwin has also worked in various countries including India, Fiji, Saudi Arabia, Malta, Uganda, Djibouti, Egypt, and Yemen, often in remote and unstable communities as well as refugee camps. Together with his wife, he has published 32 papers in peer-reviewed journals.

Table of Contents

Preface

Our friends call us medical gypsies. Our sons claimed that we were living through a very prolonged gap year. Our church called us people with a mission. We both came from unusual backgrounds, which possibly aided lateral thinking. We have worked in 10 countries and lived in 7. We worked for the British General Practice service, universities and colleges, overseas governments, the Saudi military, Anglican dioceses, and Christian missions. Usually, we worked with fragile communities such as the poor, the homeless, drug users, refugees, and prisoners, as well as with undergraduate and postgraduate medical students. Some of the communities we lived in were among the most remote in the world, and some were unstable, with nascent violence later leading to war. Our skills, when working in areas of great poverty, have been discovering ways of finding people who can be trained to do complex tasks efficiently despite a low level of education. Our training aim in very resource-deprived environments was to enable medics and paramedics to work effectively in the place where they found themselves, and not to hanker after the scanners and technical kit of the West. We have worked in areas where we were the only trained medical professionals for tens of thousands of sick people. Our further aim has been to identify small steps in reliably sourcing supplies and training to alleviate desperate situations slowly and effectively.

This memoir does not claim to be a definitive record of what happened. However, where possible, we have checked our facts with ex-colleagues. The book is about me (Edwin) more than my wife, Peta. This is because I am reliably informed that Peta is writing her own book. I await this with impatience, sure it will be a nobler tome than this one.

A War Baby and Beyond

It was wartime. I was born by caesarean section ten days before the Dunkirk evacuation, and the headline in the Daily Telegraph on the day of my birth read, “Invasion imminent.” I don’t think that they were referring to my arrival! There were moments of anxious talk, and rationing was a constant presence until I turned 15. However, as a very young boy, life seemed relatively secure if you had known nothing else. The sun shone in the summer, and the snow fell in the winter, and if one was sad, one went and talked to the chickens. Sometimes when the bombers came across, it was very noisy, and Mum and Dad got anxious. One extremely noisy night, Mum woke us up and urged us to pray. My older sister, Janet, complained, saying, "I've already asked, 'Please, Jesus, look after Mummy and Daddy and Edwin and me and keep us safe tonight.'" She added, "Jesus isn't deaf, so I don't need to repeat it." With that, she promptly went back to sleep under the table.

We were very lucky in Rugby in having very little bomb damage during the war, while towns around us were badly damaged. It was also reinforced by the fact that we considered ourselves to be very special individuals, or at least that's what our church, which went by the rather unoriginal name of "the Meeting," told us. We belonged to an ultra-strict sect of the exclusive Plymouth Brethren. Apparently, in the Meeting, we had all taken a good look at all around us and had been so shocked at what we saw that having searched the Bible thoroughly, we chose one verse to be the whole basis of our faith: “Come ye out from among them and be ye separate!”. I remember feeling a bit puzzled about who exactly "them" referred to, but eventually concluded it meant all my friends and anyone remotely interesting. Also, there seemed to be some doubt about what one did when one was separated. So here was a dilemma! Clearly, the status of being very special seemed a good idea, with perhaps God redirecting the bombs away from the family. So, I decided to subscribe to a slightly reformed faith summarised by "Give the impression of coming out from among them and being separate." It just meant that the radio, newspaper, and cinema tickets, all totally forbidden, were hidden upstairs, and your friends snuck in by the back door.

The war came to an end, and VE and then VJ Day came and went. Everybody had a huge party with lots of celebration. There was no celebration in the Meeting, nor were there any parties. I suppose all part of being separate, even giving the impression of being separate, but it seemed a bit of a pity.

Almost immediately after the war, one day, my parents packed up all my clothes, put me in the car, which was just about back on the road and used up some of the precious petrol rations to take me to Coventry. There I was deposited with Aunt Edith and her husband. I was given no explanation. I stayed there for about 2 months and had my first experience of school while I was there. As I remember, it was quite a good experience. Then I was taken home to find a baby in my place on my mother's knee. Again, I was given no explanation. The baby was my younger sister Ruth and she, not surprisingly, usurped all my privileges from then on. It took me years to recognise her very many talents. My only ally at that time, it seemed, was my older sister, Janet, who used to come and sit with me and have conversations in the middle of a large rhododendron bush in our front garden.

September arrived, and I joined the infant section of the school, where I was to be a pupil until I was eleven. Our classroom was a separate building with a large coke stove surrounded by a metal grill at one end. Outside in the playground, there were 3 large and now unused air raid shelters. One of the lasting memories of my first year was when one small boy messed his pants when we were lining up to go to school. The mistress in charge chose to publicly shame the boy, calling him out and causing a mess all over the place. She exclaimed, "Oh dear, oh dear, I don't know if I want to be a teacher in a school where boys go around messing their pants." Somewhere in my brain, this episode was stored under the heading, "If one has a truly horrible teacher and wants to get rid of them, the most effective way may well be to wait until she is supervising line up and then mess one's pants." It did strike me that this process might not be effective on the first application and might need to be repeated. Happily, I never needed to carry out this original piece of research.

I have remarkably few other memories of the infant school apart from the fact that if one did particularly badly in a spelling test, and I was dyslexic, one was sent to the gaffer, the headmaster. He gave the boy or girl 10 words whose spellings one had to learn. The next day he tested them, turning the bottom of their shorts up and smacking their thighs if they made a mistake. Even at this tender age, I wondered why he did that.

As with all schools and schoolboys, there were good times and bad. At eleven years, there was a flurry of intelligence tests (It was galling many years later to find that my son had higher intelligence than I had) and then the dreaded eleven-plus exam. I was told by all concerned that in 1951, in a country that was half bankrupt after the war, this determined my choice of schools and jobs. What was on offer was a good, well-funded school or a poorly funded, ill-taught one and the choice of an interesting job or one involving boredom, grind, and poverty. I do not remember any gloss at all being put on all this; people were blunt, and one coped with the facts one was given, or one did not. In the event, I passed and went to a voluntary aided grammar school, the Lawrence Sherriff School at Rugby. Apparently, this school was partly funded by Rugby School to bypass a clause in its foundation that aimed to educate the sons of the poor. As we, the less fortunate students, were partially funded by this prestigious school, it was deemed acceptable for the rest of the foundation's investments to be spent on the sons of the affluent, the future governors of the country, industry leaders, and military generals.

I duly turned up on the first day of term at my new school and thus started a very enjoyable part of my education. The teachers were talented, though there were some timeservers as in all schools. The curriculum was challenging and interesting, and the school library was excellent. I was a member of a school class including people from a wide range of social classes and backgrounds who got on remarkably well with an excellent team spirit. The only major fly in the ointment was games, or more accurately, the game. Obviously, we were in Rugby, so we played rugby football. What was not at all obvious was why we should only and always play rugby football. We played rugby in the Michaelmas term, in the Easter term, and in the summer term, there was pressure to train for rugby. In fairness, there were cricket pitches, and quite a few boys played cricket well, but it was made very clear we were a rugby-football school. We had heard rumours that soccer was played at Secondary Modern schools; for us, soccer was a sort of an Old Testament to our new and shiny New Testament of a resurrected football called rugby. Once you agreed with that doctrine, you were recognised as one of us. But - speak it softly and not in public, please - I hated rugby football with a deep and permanent loathing, which I suppose was my initiation into the whole concept of a personal commitment to an idea that was otherwise unacceptable.

However, one can find a way around most things with a little ingenuity. We had a biology master, Mr. King, whose two pet hates were alcohol and the smell boys made when they passed wind. These were relatively easy challenges for us to meet (particularly the latter one). There was a competition each week about who could produce the foulest smell. The first matter concerning alcohol was more difficult, particularly as Billy, as Mr King was commonly known, was quite an evangelical abolitionist. He set up an experiment involving two tanks of tadpoles. Into one tank, he poured a measure of alcohol, but the other was left free of such toxic substances just to prove how poisonous alcohol was and how the tadpoles in the treated tank withered and died. However, the boys used to bring small pieces of meat to school and dangle them into the tank on pieces of cotton where the alcohol-treated tadpoles lived. We had no idea what tadpoles ate, and it was amazing that we did not kill them. However, day by day, the alcohol-treated tadpoles grew larger and larger until they were double the size of those without the privilege of such treatment. Day by day, a worried Billy peered at the two tanks, and after a while, both tanks disappeared. Nothing more was said about that experiment.

So, it was evident that even though there was very little interest in Biology felt by most of the boys, Billy was much valued as a teacher for his entertainment value. Here I must confess that I diverged from the settled view of my peers. I loved Biology and all things relating to the natural world, particularly ecology. How did animals and plants live with each other, and what led to patterns of life and landscapes, particularly in woodlands? I discussed this at length with Billy, who seemed to think that he had found an English version of Joan of Arc who would fight for him against the uncivilised hordes massing on all sides. These not only had no interest in nature but in acts of wanton destruction, used to do dreadful things like picking flowers. When I heard of such people, it affected me deeply, and I started looking at my classmates with deep suspicion, or that is what I told Billy. It was only a short step from that to pointing out to him that if I were able to avoid anything to do with rugby and any thought of the game, I would have much more time to do highly instructive surveys of various habitats in nearby woods in the four seasons of the year. Billy apparently went along to the school authorities and told them that I was a very precious natural scientist in the making who, in years to come, could well save the planet (yes, even in those days) and making me play games of any sort would be a dereliction of their duty to the world in general and the school. The net result was that when everybody else trooped off to the games field, I mounted my bike, cycled off to the local woods and carried out a series of ecological research, which (though I say it myself) were quite professionally done and won me several prizes.

The academic level of our school was demanding to say the least, which could either put people off or could be accepted as a challenge. The years passed, O levels came and went, and I was able to choose to do Biology, Physics and Chemistry as my main subjects at A levels and something called Scholarship levels, a sort of supercharged A level, with a clue in its name that if you did well you might get a scholarship to university. By dint of some very hard work, I managed to achieve over 90% in all three A levels and Chemistry and Biology S levels. Following this, I was advised to apply for Cambridge and to take the entrance exams during the next year instead of taking up a place at Birmingham University. The exam was taken, and a place was secured in Medicine at Emmanuel College, Cambridge in December. I then found that it was possible to take one of the first-year Cambridge exams before I matriculated, that is, joined the college. I duly studied at my old school, teaching myself from books. The school kindly gave me the annex to the headmaster's study to work in. I have often wondered what the headmaster's secretary who normally worked there did. Did she work in a classroom or a broom cupboard, I wonder? Of one thing I am sure, my school pulled out all the stops for a pupil who showed some promise. I passed the exam that Easter!

One thing that stood out during my time in the sixth form was a visit to Coventry Cathedral arranged by the school. It was only 12 years after the end of the war, and the bishop, Cuthbert Bardsley, received us in his bombed and burned-out cathedral. The new cathedral had not yet been finished. We sat in the cathedral's ruins, and he talked with us about evil and destruction, grief and mourning and flattened cities, Dresden as well as Coventry. He talked about injured and dead children, lost husbands and wives and deforming injuries. He also talked about forgiveness and remorse, repentance and finding a new way, though hard. Finally, he talked about a God who had come directly into experiences like that instead of standing outside them. He talked about how God in the person of Jesus had done right and, as a result, was scorned and rejected. Finally, he had been killed, and in that death had taken the consequences of all the evil and destruction of the world. Being God, death could not hold him, and he was raised from the dead to offer us the chance to have Him live with us and in us and change us if we would accept what he had done for us. Then the bishop left it at that, and we said goodbye. None of the group from our school was particularly godly, but there was silence as we sat through what he was saying in the setting where this had happened. Quietly and slowly, that changed the form I was in. Boys became more reflective, and a number of them developed a faith in different settings and ways, one becoming a vicar. I often wonder if Bishop Cuthbert ever knew the effect of his talk, or perhaps things like that happened all the time with him.

After passing the Cambridge exam, I faced what to do with the summer term and holiday before going to Cambridge. As with any young person leaving home, my main concern was whether I would have enough money to live in the way I hoped to become accustomed to. This was helped to a degree as I was awarded a State Scholarship by the Department of Education and a Ben scholarship by my school. I have no idea who Ben was, but I was duly grateful to him. After reflection, I decided that this might not be enough, and I looked for jobs. I finally found a job as a hospital porter at the local hospital, the Hospital of St Cross. This was enjoyable but not very paying. However, it came to my notice that a very well-paid job was coming up in the mortuary. This consisted of sewing up corpses after they had had a post-mortem examination to give them some semblance of the form of the human body. I became quite rich as a young student, but unable to explain where my wealth came from, and thus was regarded with some suspicion. It gave me a very good introduction to anatomy as I tried to put the bodies back into some semblance of a human form. And so, I came to the time to leave school and home after a generally stimulating and enjoyable period. However, throughout this time, there was one huge damper on life, on making friends and on becoming a secure part of society. That was our membership of the Meeting. Their aim was that all their members should be "separate from the world," and they succeeded remarkably despite all efforts to bypass the rules. You just didn't belong in the real world!

Cambridge

So eventually, after having passed my first Cambridge University exam at school, having pushed people to all corners of the St Cross Hospital at Rugby as a porter and having sewn up many corpses, and earning a lot of money doing this, I found myself on a platform waiting for a train to Cambridge. At this time, I was still a member of the brethren, so of course, I had to clock in at the Cambridge Meeting so that they could keep a leery eye on any student misbehaviour that I might get up to, which was not in keeping with my exalted standing as a member of the elect group to which I had been called. If I were to do this, of course, it would be their duty by hook or threats to draw me back into the truly separate group I had the privilege of belonging to. Also, being a member of the brethren, I had to live with other brethren members as these were the only people I was allowed to be around or eat with. I lived in the attic of a couple of maiden sisters who ran a hat shop. Apart from the fact that the loft was completely uninsulated and freezing cold, this was a delight. The two sisters were motherly figures who would do anything to make you feel loved and cared for. They seemed to be a throwback into the pre-first world war community and would have been recognised and warmly welcomed into the society of "Cranford" by Mrs. Gaskell. They were fussily dressed; their house was fussily decorated; the trimmings of their hats were fussily made, and all the people who came into their shop were fussily attired copies of the two sisters. I felt I was living in a film set and found myself in a microcosm that I never knew existed. The first breakfast I had with my hostesses; they gave me fishcakes. Being a polite young man, I said how much I enjoyed them and thereafter got fishcakes for breakfast three times a week for the year I lived with them.

Starting at Emmanuel College itself was somewhat daunting. Firstly, one had to find the college, entering through the somewhat imposing gate into a large courtyard largely taken up by a lawn with the portico of the Wren chapel on the other side. There one met the porters and the bulldogs. Any idea one had that Cambridge was a town of dreaming towers (or was that Oxford?), where the air was charged with the emanations and declarations of learned and revered academics, was immediately dispelled. Cambridge was ruled by the porters and the "bulldogs." They "helped" distribute the rooms in college for one year of your stay in Cambridge and could help with finding accommodation in the town for the other two. Whether one had a smooth or bumpy ride largely depended on one's relationship with the porters. The Bulldogs were all very athletic gentlemen whose job it was to make sure that you behaved yourself both in college and in the town. For instance, if you were found not wearing your gown in town, you were arrested by a bulldog from your college and then invited to sherry with the senior tutor of your college, who would tell you off and charge you a small fine. Some people who were to be arrested had the audacity to take off and try and escape. This is where the athletic prowess of the bulldogs came in; they would chase after you through the shopping crowds of the town, a sight to be savoured, and try and catch you. Even if you escaped, all was not necessarily well. If the bulldog could not keep up with you but recognised you, he would cut back to your college and be at the gate waiting for you. Under these circumstances, the fine was higher, and you could get gated, which is kept in college without being let out for a day or two.

However, on the first day, the staff gave us all sorts of instructions and advice, how and where to get a gown (the hand-torn ones were more expensive!), the lockdown times for the college (one had to be in by 11.30 pm or be initiated into the skill of climbing over the wall) and then there was the most important bit of information. This was, of course, that the only people who were allowed to walk on the quadrangle lawn were ducks and fellows. I vowed to walk on that lawn before I left in three years, which was difficult as the lawn was just in front of the porters' windows. In fact, I did walk on the lawn in my third year when I was made a junior scholar, and apparently could do this legally, which was a bit of a comedown.

The first week of term was fresher's week which meant that all the various clubs and organisations in the university set up stalls, and the members were there yelling about the great times that could be had by joining their club. If you looked undecided, you were unceremoniously grabbed and hauled to the stall where you were lectured about the benefits of being perhaps a Soroptimist. Still, it appeared that you could only be a Soroptimist if you were a woman, which was a relief at the time, or perhaps a thespian, though nobody could coherently tell me what a thespian was. Finally, I joined the India Society, since I had always been fascinated by India, the Cambridge Expeditions Society, as they seemed to help organise trips to weird and wonderful places, and finally, the Christian Union. Now, joining the India Society and the Cambridge Expeditions Society was a great and terrible betrayal of the noble brethren's cause and was not promoting being separate. But the greatest betrayal of all, leading to the possibility of immediate excommunication and other less-defined disasters, was associating with the Christian Union. This group of charlatans claimed to know Jesus and claimed to be doing His will by loving their neighbours and telling people the gospel of God's love. To add insult to injury, they said that after their deaths, they would be going to heaven. Any self-respecting Christian knew in their heart of hearts that only the Brethren were truly separate from the world, and only they would have access to the presence of the good Lord in heaven. Any other message came directly from the devil. At first, I had some trepidation associating with the Christian Union. Still, there I found people who knew Jesus and talked to Him daily, reflected His love, told of His gospel and who knew and obeyed the Bible with joy. They were really involved with people who were sad, in trouble, and with problems and would spend hours trying to help. It all seemed rather odd for a while.

And then, of course, there were the courses: Anatomy, Physiology, Pharmacology, Biochemistry, Microbiology, and the rest. Some lecturers were brilliant, and some produced utter and illogical stodge. The lectures started about 9.00 am at the Downing Street site, about 90 seconds from the college. This meant that you could leap out of bed in your digs at about 8.30 am, run to the college, have breakfast in the dining hall, and be sitting on a bench in the relevant lecture room nursing a bout of exercise-induced dyspepsia by 9.02 am before the majority of the lecturers arrived. Judging from the number of burps one heard, it was clear that most of the other students had a morning culture similar to mine. A man visiting from Mars would have been very impressed with the dedicated attitude to morning exercise shown by many of the Cambridge medical students. I say medical students mainly because we were following the only course where the students seemed to make the connection between the university putting on a lecture programme and the necessity of the students attending these lectures. I am sad to say that this had nothing to do with the medical students having a universally noble trait in their characters. It was all the fault of the General Medical Council (GMC), who had the odd attitude that they would not accredit any medical education for registration as a doctor unless the students attended that education and signed in at every course session. It did seem odd that people seemed concerned about whether the GMC would register them at some future date. At most of the lectures, if one looked down the signatures, it seemed that Anthony Armstrong Jones had attended about 11 times at each lecture. This was just before he married Princess Margaret, and shortly after being sent down from Cambridge for carrying out too much personal and real-time reproductive experimentation. The student body considered that this action on the part of the university was an infringement of academic freedom.

One of the practical courses was the dissection of a corpse. On reflection, I suppose it was important for budding doctors to know where everything was inside the body. I approached this matter with great aplomb, having spent most of my time dealing with dead bodies in the last six months. However, to my cost, I very rapidly found that trying to put everything back together again so that it looked semi-normal when somebody had finished a post-mortem examination was considerably different from excising with delicacy and care the obturator nerve of the lower leg to make sure you knew where it was and did not cut it when operating on a person with a fracture.

As well as the lectures and the practical sessions, we had the privilege of having tutorial sessions where we had sessions in groups of up to four students in each subject, usually with a junior fellow or postdoctoral student. The university organised the main teaching sessions, and the tutorial system was arranged by the colleges. We had regular viva voce exams from university staff and, more often, written tests from our tutors and exams each semester. It was not only the tutorial system that was stimulating about being in Cambridge. It was also a time when one rethought or even thought about one's habits, beliefs, and world view for the first time. Coming from my background, to sit in the evenings with fellow students and talk about what they believed and what their hopes for the future were and why, and to be asked to justify what one said was a new experience. People listened, usually politely, however bizarre, odd, outrageous, or just unacceptable your views were, and you were asked to justify what you said. We had people proposing Nazi views, communist views, male dominance views, pacifist views, Green views, and Christian views, and all these people and more were asked to justify what they were saying and the consequences of their views. I never heard anybody mocked or reviled for their views. There was no de-platforming. Nobody wanted the student life to be made "safe" by censoring what people said or thought. The only thing that counted as totally unacceptable was to refuse to discuss and justify one's views and to refuse to be flexible in the face of evidence contrary to one's belief. This was exciting, liberating, and dangerous for a brethren sect member.

At the end of a working day, one had work to do for the university courses, and then dinner was in the Great Hall of the college. This was a very formal occasion. All the students were dressed in gowns and sat at long refectory tables and benches in the grand hall with carved wood, paintings, and stained glass. The faculty came in after a sherry aperitif and sat across the end of the Hall. Grace was said in Latin by one of the scholars, and then the meal was served to all and sundry and was usually edible, which could not be said of all colleges. One could order wine or beer from the buttery, and this would be brought to you. After dinner, if one had finished one's daily quota of work to keep up with the lectures and practical sessions, one might go to a meeting of one of the associations or perhaps go out on the town. There was considerable rivalry between the youth of the town and those of the gown (the university). Occasionally this could overflow into scuffles if tipsy groups from the two sides met, but this was not a major problem. The main problem with the university was women - the lack of them. There were only three women's colleges in 1959-1962, Newnham, Girton, and New Hall, which was tiny. It was always said that the women of Girton were easily recognisable. They all had enormous thighs because they had to cycle the 4 miles to and from the village of Girton several times a day. One of the major dangers on the road around Cambridge was being run down by some super-fit woman from Girton College who was marginally late for a lecture and unwilling to give way for anything, including the one pair of traffic lights I remember. These were counted as advisory street furniture rather than compulsory traffic indicators by Girton girls.

Much of my free time was spent in the context of CICCU (The Cambridge Intercollegiate Christian Union). Most of the members seemed to be kind, were genuinely interested in engaging in meaningful conversations, possessed a good sense of humour, and had a remarkable tolerance towards differing perspectives. But that was not their chief characteristic. The main way they were different was that they seemed to know the person I knew about. Not only did they know Jesus and seemed to talk to Him with great ease, but they also seemed to be like Him. They took a lot of time helping or supporting people who were underprivileged both in the university, the town, and wider afield. I found myself attending several meals and other fund-raising activities supporting work in inner cities and Africa. They also felt that they were extremely fortunate to have been introduced to God Almighty as a warm and loving Father. They believed that everybody was cut off from God because of the evil they had done. Their God was a god of justice who could not tolerate evil, whether that was an abuse of children or women or our much more mundane selfishness, arrogance, and me-first attitude. The consequences of this had to be accounted for and put right. It was their belief and eventually became my belief that Jesus is God that He came down to earth from heaven to re-establish our relationship with God. The bitterness, damage, and broken relationships, consequences of our mindset and actions, were borne by Jesus when He died on the cross, taking our place and penalty. He then promised that He would come and live in us and help us to act in His way.

Having taken this step of becoming a follower of Jesus, there were, of course, all sorts of issues that one had to address if one is going to remain intellectually honest. What evidence is there that there is a God? What evidence is there for the story of Jesus, what he did, and for him being God? Why should God be just and demand just action for wrong? Why should I agree to be accountable to anybody other than myself? I have taken a lifetime working out some of the answers to some of those problems, and I am still unwilling to blindly believe patently untrue things. Books that have helped me along the way, some of them written long after my student times, are The Language of God, by Francis Collins, director of the human Genome project, The Reason for God by Timothy Keller, and God's Undertaker by John Lennox, professor of Maths at Oxford University and reader in the philosophy of science at Green College Oxford.

Most of the time I spent with my friends in CICCU were social occasions, Bible studies, prayer meetings, meetings organising an explanation of the gospel to people who had never considered it, and times when we together specifically met God to talk to him and enjoy time with Him. That's called worship. At times I reflected on the amount of time I spent in this activity. Still, it seemed to me to be eminently logical that if somebody had changed the whole direction of my life, I would want to spend time with him, look at the source document about Him (the Bible) and talk with him (prayer), and do what he did in supporting and loving others. This whole process made me a far more stable personality. I was no longer trying to keep many rules made by somebody else and rules that separated me from others. My whole life was based on relationships both with God and with other people, of whom a minority was of the same persuasion as me. I was a far happier person, somebody with an intellectually satisfying reason for my life, a reasonable plan to move forward, and a reasonable goal to aim at. My friends called the motivation for all this a work of the Holy Spirit, as I do now.

My first year seemed to pass quickly, and I approached the long summer break with glee. During the latter part of the term, a friend and I noticed an advertisement from the Scott Polar Research Institute, which was (and is) based in Cambridge, offering a scholarship for two students who were going to carry out a project in the UK which would test their resilience and sense of adventure. Dick Habershon and I put together a project in which we proposed to climb all the Cuillin Hills on the Isle of Skye and go from peak to peak along the ridge trail. We would camp in a small ridge tent on the mountainside taking everything on our back. We would not use a car or public transport to get there or return. We would cook on a primus stove and buy the food locally. The project lasted six weeks and it rained on all but two days of that period. We fulfilled our aims and found the time extremely enjoyable. It was made much better because we made our base camp high on a hillside, beside a stream above a Youth Hostel at Glenbrittle, and the Hostel manager allowed us to dry our clothes beside the hostel boiler.

During the remaining six weeks of the vacation, I took a part-time job driving ambulances. By this time, my relationships with the brethren were frayed, to say the least. Rumours of my connection with CICCU in Cambridge seemed to have been relayed to the Rugby Meeting. I was greeted with disapproving looks and somewhat cold-shouldered. The ambulance driving job turned out to be very useful as the brethren seemed to feel that ambulance driving was a necessary occupation. I just had to arrange to be on duty every Sunday and often in the evenings to have an excuse to see very little of this disapproving group of people. In fact, I made my point forcibly by always giving a bit of a push on the emergency bell (yes, they were bells in those days) and driving rather fast when passing somebody I recognised as a brother or sister. This seemed to confuse the patients a bit as they did not see the reason to be transported by an ambulance with its bell ringing when they were being taken home from an operation on their right large toenail. The holiday passed, and I returned to Cambridge a little richer with my earnings.

The second year was a time of change for all sorts of reasons. I had to decide whether to take the second part of my Bachelor degree, which would lead to my clinical training in 3 years, or whether to cram it into two years and spend the third year doing some sort of introduction to research. By this time, I was quite heavily involved with the Cambridge India Society, and one of the friends whom I made at society meetings was a person called Chandra, the son of the Minister of Tourism of India. A group of friends and I decided that we would try to drive overland to India via Iran and Afghanistan in our last year. Because of this, we decided to cram all our studies for the second part of our degree into the second year and spend the third-year planning and getting the resources for the trip to India. So academically, the next year was very hard work indeed.

The second problem I encountered was with the brethren. For over a year now, I had been becoming increasingly dissatisfied with the teaching of this organisation. I had the privilege of meeting with student friends who had a faith in a living Lord and led a liberated and joyful life. The separation from ordinary people, the judgmental attitude, and the demands to follow a system of rules for which I could find no justification were becoming increasingly irksome and seemed to have less and less relevance to everyday life. The brethren had also tumbled to the fact that I was meeting with other Christians and that I was starting to question their dictates. The normal reaction from my student friends on hearing this would be to advise me to leave and be done with them. However, I had been brought up from birth in this system, as had my parents. We were taught to regard the world outside the walls of the sect as evil, dangerous, and polluting. It was accepted in some families that one could lie to protect the brethren's organisation and their teaching, so being economical with the truth has been a problem that I have had to fight against all my life. The only people we had ever been allowed to be near to were brethren, and leaving the sect meant leaving everything we had known or felt we had a place in. Happily, a break with this group was taken out of my hands and made inevitable. The powers in the sect decided that to be a member of a professional organisation or put oneself into a situation where one was in any way governed by an ethic outside of the edicts of the Brethren was unacceptable. This was not true separation from the world. A doctor had to be a member of the General Medical Council registered list, and one had to follow the guidance and ethic of this council. Therefore, all medics were told that they had to leave any training to be a doctor, and all qualified doctors had to take themselves off the GMC list and resign from their jobs. I refused point blank. I had felt a calling to go into medicine, and would not allow a bunch of misguided, judgmental, joyless people to dictate how I would lead my life. They did not reflect the love of God to me.

This, of course, had consequences for me. Life was already fraught with trying to cram two years' work into one. However, a representative of every family in the Meeting came to my room in college, told me how evil I was to take this stand, told me how I was committing myself to the devil, and meanwhile hungrily devoured the chocolate biscuits and drank the coffee I served them. I think that that was the thing that riled me most. None of them offered me a packet of biscuits. I talked to them about how Jesus ate with publicans and sinners, how He came to seek and save the lost, how I was a sinner, a saved sinner, and so were they. They took offence at that! In due course, everybody had had their turn informing me how evil I was, and there was a subdued glow in the Meeting, which I continued to attend. They had taken a clear stand against a wicked renegade. I decided that they would reject me, not me them, so I turned up with considerable nonchalance each week and went around asking how they were and if the rheumatism was still troubling old Mr. Jones, the most senior brother.

Eventually, I was summoned to a special meeting of the whole group, which happened to take place on November 5th in the brethren meeting room. This was a purpose-built room in a poorer part of town. The brethren were not popular with those who lived nearby as these people had been studiously ignored for many years. I was placed at the front of the meeting facing the gathering, and all the "evil" they had learned about me over the past few weeks was recounted. Finally, the most senior brother, Mr Jones, stood up to declare judgement on me. He was a very serious old man and decidedly wobbly. He said, "Although it broke his heart, the only thing left for the assembly to do for our young brother Edwin was….." and there was an enormous bang. Mr. Jones sat down hard and looked shocked. Apparently, what had happened was that the youth of the area had chosen that time to attack the meeting room with fireworks. Mr Jones tried again to read me out. When a rocket hit the large window and burst into a multicoloured shower, he was in full flow. Mr Jones sat down heavily again. At this point, a student who had been my friend leaned across and said, "It would be kind Edwin if you just got up and left," which is what I did.

However, in many ways, the result of what happened on that evening was profound. Until I was 21, the whole of my history had been within the tight confines of the brethren. The whole of my social life, such as it was, was within those high and threatening walls, and despite having somewhat enlightened parents, the consequences of leaving the sect were painted in the darkest colours. After I left my last meeting with the brethren's authorities, I was "committed to Satan," which meant that it was declared that I would be going to hell. No contact was allowed between me and anybody I had known in the sect. Even my closest friends would cross the road to avoid meeting me. I no longer existed for my uncles and aunts, and they would put the phone down on me. During this period, I had my first severe depression and was treated by student health services. Happily, my older sister, her husband, and my parents left the sect at the same time as me. My father, at 60, took the job of churchwarden at the largest Anglican church in Rugby within a year of leaving the sect, a great self-reinvention by him! I decided that I needed to reinvent myself, so I went off and bought myself a half share in a punt which was moored on the Queen's College frontage on the River Cam.

It was a typical spring day with the average traffic in town, with shoppers, tourists, and students in groups, often talking loudly. The punt was securely moored against the quay upstream from the Queens College Mathematical Bridge. I had the cushions with me, although I was alone. I often preferred it that way, just me, the boat, and the river. There was a fair current on the river, but not so much that it would cause too much work getting back. There were a few punts around being propelled inexpertly in a desultory manner by young men showing off to their girlfriends. One could ignore them: after a few yards, they would turn back, afraid of arriving late to the punt hiring company and being charged a surcharge. One thrust on the quant pole, we were off downstream, through Coe Fen and Sheep's Green and into an empty river. There was a chilly wind, but the sun came out, shining through the willows lining the river, and in any case, usually, one is not cold when punting. The only sound was the pole plop with each thrust and the dripping from the pole between times. In the distance and soon left behind was the growling of the traffic on Fen causeway. A blackbird was singing, and a linnet joined in making a duet. A crow raucously told them to shut up, and the blackbird flew away. I decided to moor the boat under an overhanging tree and sat in the boat on the cushions I had bought with me. I had not brought a book. I like looking and listening and thinking and occasionally falling asleep. College, work, and all the trouble of the brethren seemed a long way off. A duck arrived to see who was invading its territory. A fish rose and caught a fly. A water rat on the opposite bank came out of its hole and looked around, then dived and disappeared. Three boatloads of raucous tourists came down the river and woke me up. The tranquillity was shattered, the remaining birds flew off, and the duck went to beg for scraps—time to go home. The current was against me, but they say it is all exercise and good for the health. The punt was moored, and I returned to something people call normal life.

At Cambridge, my new family, and friends from CICCU, my college, and the India Society rapidly closed ranks around me, offering me friendship, warmth, and acceptance, all unconditionally, which was something completely new. I became a full member of CICCU and took a full part in arranging the university mission at my college Emmanuel. The aim of the mission was to explain in as open a way as possible to people in the university what it meant to be a committed Christian. My best friend at Emmanuel was a medic in the same year as me, David Hanson. I had met him on my first day at the college, we remained lifelong friends and were each other's best men when we married two weeks apart. When we first met, he presented as an arrogant and dominating character who, as a student, drank a great deal of alcohol. David had been the only person ever to pass the 11+ exam and go to a grammar school from his school in a Derbyshire village and then the only person ever to get a place at Oxbridge from this grammar school. He had been told how wonderful he was, and he believed it. After spending some time as a student, he got to know another medical student in our college called Mike Church. Mike was the son of missionaries working in Ruanda in quite primitive conditions in the countryside.

Mike had spent a large part of his life in Africa and learned to play the guitar, write music and paint. He was a retiring man but passionate about his music, painting, and Jesus Christ. David was drawn to him because of his creativity. He also was intrigued because this man was different. He was loving, accepting of all and sundry, warm and caring, and very happy to talk about the best friend he lived with, Jesus Christ. David found something he had never met before in his life. He accepted Jesus as his Saviour, friend, and the director of his life. This completely changed him. He lost his arrogance and aggressiveness and became a warm, loving person from whom people sought help.

The change over some months was dramatic, and people noticed it. David also worked hard with the preparations for the university mission and was very much looking forward to taking his friends to the meetings to introduce them to the person who had made such a change in his life. However, he became seriously ill with a kidney infection and was in hospital throughout the mission. He was devastated. What he did not know was that 15 of the members of our college had been so struck by the change in this man's life after he became a Christian that they made their own way to the mission meetings to find out what all this was about. A number of them became committed Christians, and most have continued in their faith.

Eventually, this busy year ended, and during the holiday, I went with Hedley, a Cambridge friend of mine, to Spain to visit and stay with some Spanish Christian friends of his, Jamie and Mercedes, and their daughter Amelie. At that time, protestant Christians in Spain were a threatened minority who found access to work, and particularly Christian literature, difficult. When he was working in Spain, my father used to smuggle Spanish Bibles into the country, and we similarly took several Spanish Bibles into the country with us. I was amazed at Spain's poverty, particularly among the protestant Christian population. A good meal for Jamie and Mercedes would be boiled potatoes, olive oil, garlic, and parsley, and some fruits. They very rarely ate meat, and beans were added to their diet a few times a week. This was my first visit abroad, and I revelled in the heat, the dust, the music, and the Mediterranean culture. Other than this trip, I again took up my part-time job driving Ambulances in Rugby. Of course, there was no contact at all with the brethren there, who were diligent in their project of sending me to the devil.

And so, to the third year, which turned out to be a memorable time in my life. Firstly, having spent the last year living in the college, this year I was in digs again in New Square in an exceedingly ancient college-owned cottage. The last time it had been renovated in any way was about the time of the Napoleonic wars. There was a certain charm in this as well as certain disadvantages. One night when in bed, I sneezed with some gusto and, to my alarm, found that the legs of the bed had gone through a rotten floorboard. The major advantage of this residence was that my landlord was the wine waiter at the college. Almost every evening, he would sidle up behind me at college dinner and put a bottle of beer and a glass beside me. I did not complain, particularly because I was never charged for the beer.

The main task of the year was preparing for the trip to India. We were a group of 8 medics, theologians, engineers, and one chap called Tim, who nobody, least of all him, could seem to work out what he was doing at the university. We clearly could not afford to pay for the two Land Rovers we needed for the journey all the way to India and back, so we had somehow to persuade other people to pay for our trip. The priority was to find something that would enthuse people enough to support us. Happily, several members of the team had useful connections. One had a cousin working for a Christian surgical hospital involved in rehabilitating people with leprosy in a town called Narsapur in Andhra Pradesh in India. This was useful to us later as our base when we arrived in India. However, one of our number who had a friend who worked in the Medical Research Council (MRC) was of much more use to us immediately. Apparently, there were two small projects on their books, neither of them important enough to arrange a fully funded project. The first project was to determine the prevalence of anaemia in the tribal peoples in the jungles of the Eastern and Western Ghats hills of south India using random blood tests. The second project was more interesting. Apparently, whether you have hair on the back of the middle phalanx of your fingers is inherited strictly in Mendelian fashion. I wonder who got their doctorate for discovering that relatively useless piece of information. Whoever it was, we had some good news for them. This was going to be vital in a piece of medical research. There was an area in the Western Ghats hills with a very high level of background radiation. The MRC wanted to find out how this affected this population's mutations. By examining families in these areas, one should be able to predict who would have hair on their fingers and who didn't. If one found somebody where this prediction did not work, hey presto, one had found a mutation (that is, if the person concerned did not come from an alliance with the milkman, though I do not remember that possibility being raised in the planning phase).

We had found a project which would be of use to all concerned. The MRC would get their surveys done. They would give us all the equipment to do all the tests, including a kerosene mobile fridge and record books, but they would not give us any money. We had a hugely important task to do, or that was what we told everybody who would listen. With this backing, we could go to the Cambridge Expeditions Association and ask for their accreditation and to donors and ask for money and supplies. In due time, we made an appointment with a professor in microbiology who was an adjudicator for the Cambridge Expeditions Committee for those who sought its backing. He seemed to approve of the tasks we had set ourselves and the fact that we had gained the backing of the Medical Research Council. However, when we told him that we proposed to drive through Europe, Turkey, Iran, Afghanistan, Pakistan, and India, he told us that we were mad and that if we came to harm somewhere in east Iran or Afghanistan, there would be no chance of getting competent help. Also, several areas of the route were bandit-ridden, and driving two Land Rovers, which we proposed to do, would make us prime targets. We argued our case strongly with the usual conviction of young people who believe that nothing bad can ever happen to them. Eventually, our professor recommended that the Cambridge University Expeditions Society adopt our project as one of its approved expeditions with the strict proviso that if we ran into trouble, it would be no responsibility of the Society to provide us with any aid. His parting shot was, "If one of you gets eaten by a bear, don't come to me for help." Within two weeks of our leaving the UK at the start of the expedition, the poor chap was dead of streptococcal meningitis. All of us returned to continue our careers.

Our next job was to garner support for the expedition. We had headed note paper printed and produced a folder explaining the research we planned to do and the vital need for this information to be established. We had to think long and hard to make a convincing case! We also wrote an excellent description of why the Medical Research Council could not itself carry out this research because they were fully occupied with funding research into heart attacks, strokes, and cancer, subjects that were marginally more important than finding the prevalence of anaemia and the prevalence of hairiness on the middle digits of the hands of tribal people in the jungle communities of South India. Our great dread was to be asked why we needed to travel halfway around the world through some of the wildest territories in Asia to do this work. Happily, that question was never asked. My job was to write to every relevant charity and every company in the Federation of British Industries' handbook to ask for either cash support or support in kind. I spent many a happy hour in the university library doing this. Perhaps surprisingly, we received several thousand pounds in financial aid and a considerable amount of food to take with us.

With some of the money, we bought two second-hand Land Rovers. Our group's engineers took the vehicles, strengthened their springs, and fitted welded roof racks. Extra petrol tanks were fitted as we would be going through areas where petrol stations were few and far between. The theologians in the group planned the route as it was felt that many people in their source book, the Bible, undertook very long and perilous journeys, so they had some insight into this sort of matter. Tim, the member whom nobody quite knew what he was doing at the university, got the visas and paperwork to import and export the Land Rovers for all the countries we were going through. We thought he might be flexible enough to deal with inscrutable border forces from remote Central Asian countries. Our planning meetings were a very good excuse for us all to go out for a curry once a week. All went well—that was, until the goods that various companies had donated started arriving in large lorries carrying enormous cardboard boxes. What do you do with 400 Mars bars (and they were full-sized Mars bars in those days)? It also crossed our minds that we would have to eat all 400 of them before arriving in the Middle East in the middle of summer. The 500 tins of sardines were in a smaller package but were much heavier. There was no hope that I could store all these large packages in my tiny sitting room and smaller bedroom in the cottage I was staying in, and most members of the group had the same predicament. Happily, my best friend shared accommodation with a friend in the master's lodge at Emmanuel College. It was a huge set of rooms, with David and Rick having their own bedrooms. They agreed to share one bedroom leaving a very large space for us to keep our stores in. Large parcels kept arriving at our college, and from time to time, the porters asked us where all this stuff was going. We said it was all going to the Master's Lodge, which seemed to satisfy them.

Throughout all this time, I still had to attend some lectures and produce work for my tutors. I had passed enough exams to enable me to pass on the next stage of my medical training, but I still needed to take my degree exams. At that time, one took a bachelor's degree in Natural Science for Medicine at Cambridge, which gave one a Bachelor of Arts (!) degree. I then had to find a London teaching hospital which was willing to take me for clinical training. My tutor had told me that I would be accepted at any of the London Teaching Hospitals, so I applied for the Middlesex Hospital in Mortimer Street in London, where many of my friends were going, and thought no more about it. Time passed, and everybody seemed to be getting confirmation of their places at medical schools, and I heard nothing. I wrote to the admissions tutor of the hospital, and still there was silence. Eventually, I found somebody who knew the private number of the admissions tutor and phoned her up. It turned out that this lady had a very unpleasant cancer and had been ill. Her work had naturally suffered, which was why I had not heard. Instead of being angry, she poured out all her fear and frustration to me, and over the next three years, we became very friendly. I was offered a place.

The term progressed, and the pace of life sped up. At the end of the term, we were all taking our Tripos exams (the Cambridge degree exams), and we planned to leave for India the day after the last exam.

Everybody was tying up loose ends for the trip. Evenings were spent poring over books, sometimes into the early morning hours. Two weeks before the exam, I got fed up with all the stress and decided that if, after three years, I did not know enough to get my degree, then I would not be able to put that right in the next two weeks. So, I made sandwiches every morning and took off down the river on my punt. In many ways, those weeks were the best in my life. I was at peace about my academic work and was looking forward to a great adventure.

The exams came and went, and on 14th June, we set out from Jesus College Cambridge, where the Land Rovers had been parked and prepared, and the adventure had started.

India

As we embarked on our journey towards India, there was a sense of the end of an epoch in our lives. It was the end of our time at Cambridge for all of us and for the aspiring doctors among us, a brief intermission before delving into the realm of hands-on clinical medicine. This milestone was the fruit of a year of unwavering dedication, hard work, planning and remarkably harmonious teamwork. No more exams or obtuse letters from the Afghani consulate about visas; the die was cast, and there was a sense of freedom. We boarded the ferry to Belgium, and soon we were cruising along the autobahns of Germany. However, our idea of cruising was dispelled by a remarkable number of traffic jams. The Land Rovers were loaded to the gunnels and well down on their springs. There were items stored everywhere, on the roof racks, under all the seats, and in all the pockets, nooks and crannies in the cabs. We went to the extent of moving the spare tyre from the back and mounted it on the bonnet. There were four people in each Land Rover: three along the seats at the front of the vehicle and one lying on an old car bench seat across the back. The back of the vehicles was covered with tarpaulin, providing a somewhat breezy but sheltered experience for the person in the back. On one uncluttered area of the route, we had just overtaken a lorry and drawn in again to the slow lane when the lorry in front of us braked very hard and abruptly. We braked and avoided colliding with the lorry, but the lorry behind us hit us hard, turning us over on our side.

We all scrambled out quickly as we had recently filled up with petrol, and the main tank and the auxiliary tank were both completely full. Our first concern was what had happened to the person lying across the back of the vehicle. Fortunately, Land Rovers in those days were extremely heavily built, and only the outside offside corner of the vehicle had been pushed in. Despite the noticeable damage to the car's outer corner, the person named Mike, who was seated in the back, remained unharmed and unaffected. Mike, a remarkably calm individual, later embarked on a missionary career in remote regions of Argentina. We had been the second of the two Land Rovers, and as the other Land Rover returned to locate us, we were eventually towed off the autobahn. When we pointed out that we were on our way to India, the German police gave us an odd look and told us that, as it was the weekend, nothing could be done until Monday. When they asked about our weekend accommodation, and when we told them about our plan to stay in the vehicles, the police gave us an odder look and deposited us on a flat grassy area We moved the vehicles, so they were back-to-back and fixed up a tarpaulin between the vehicles to form a rudimentary tent. One person slept along the front seats of each vehicle, and another person slept at the back on the old car seats; the rest of us slept on camp beds under the tarpaulin. We had a small river nearby for water for washing, and there was a tap within about 100 yards. The meals were the first of many, with canned food to start with and a Mars Bar or two for dessert. We manfully started on the task of finishing all those 400 Mars bars before we reached the part of our journey where they would melt with the heat into a gooey mess. Mike dryly remarked that it was all a bit annoying, and we couldn't help but concur with his assessment.

Monday arrived, and the damaged Land Rover was taken along to the local agency, where we were greeted by a mechanic clad in a pristine white overalls, which somehow didn't seem to fit into our mental image of a mechanic. After about an hour of examining the damage, he told us that the damage was extensive and that the repairs would take at least several weeks. Curious about the specific areas affected, we asked whether the chassis had suffered major deformation or if the axles were damaged. The mechanic clarified that while the chassis and axles remained intact, there was considerable panel work damage, and new panels would need to be ordered. We then told him that we were going to India, which was rather a long way away, and we had to be back by September, so we could not afford the time to wait for the full repairs. At this point, he lost patience with us and passed us on to a younger junior mechanic, who turned out to be absolute gold. Fuelled by enthusiasm for our project, the young mechanic eventually agreed that if we carefully detached the damaged bodywork from the wheels, it wouldn't render the vehicle unfit for the road. Surprisingly, after receiving confirmation from our accommodating mechanics and their assurance of roadworthiness, our insurance company agreed to continue coverage. The work was done by Wednesday, and on Thursday morning, we were off bowling down the autobahn again after very cordial goodbyes from our mechanic. The gentleman in the white overalls did not appear again.

The accident had set us back nearly a week and our journey and work were hanging in the balance. Determined to make up for lost time and return in time to resume our medical studies or other commitments, we made the decision to drive 24 hours a day to catch up. We had a rotating system. Each person would drive for a two-hour shift, then move to the middle seat next to the driver, taking on the role of pilot and map reader. Another important task for the pilot was to keep the driver awake. Several methods of carrying out this task were devised, such as chatting, telling weak jokes, and recounting interesting episodes in their past lives. All of these fell flat, and people resorted to the occasional rib-poking to jolt any nodding driver back to full attention. After this duty, the person on pilot duty moved to the outside left seat and was allowed to sleep. Finally, this person moved to the bench at the back of the vehicle and was again allowed to sleep. Every evening we stopped for a couple of hours, reviewed the day, cooked a meal, and, if necessary, repacked things that had come loose. For some unknown reason, Tim always seemed to find himself standing on the top of the cab shouting instructions to everybody, most of which were ignored. Still, it seemed to make him happy, and he did not get in anybody's way.

Our journey took us through a series of diverse landscapes and regions, beginning with Austria, then traversing Yugoslavia (as it was known at that time), Bulgaria, and finally arriving in Turkey. It was very noticeable that when we entered the eastern part of Austria, which had been under the control of the Soviet Union until 7 years before, the roads were much worse and the houses poorer and in a bad state of repair. The roads were still worse when we were behind the Iron Curtain, and there was a considerable amount of horse-drawn traffic and carts pulled by oxen. Driving through Yugoslavia, it seemed that they had a motorway building programme. We would be driving along what resembled a winding country lane in the Western countries, only to suddenly find ourselves on a newly constructed dual carriageway motorway. Usually, there was nobody else on the road apart from us. Then after about 20 miles, just as suddenly, the motorway stopped. The only sign that this was about to happen was a cut-out figure of a man with his hands held out sideways. If one missed this, which was especially easy to do at night, one would find oneself unexpectedly in the middle of a ploughed field, surrounded by agricultural terrain. From the end of the motorway, one followed a dirt track to rejoin the country lane. We never once saw anybody working on any of these little chunks of motorway, and we wondered what the thinking was, if any, for putting these little bits of good road in the middle of the countryside. One episode that amused us was when we were driving through Bulgaria. People were very welcoming, and all the children would come and wave to a couple of Jeeps from the West. The whole situation seemed to have a rather pleasing amateurish feel about it. During our travels, we found ourselves behind an ox-drawn cart on a bend, with a speed limit sign indicating a maximum of 60 kilometres per hour. We were able to see that the road ahead was clear because the cart was moving at a leisurely pace of approximately 2 miles per hour. We decided to overtake the slow-moving cart and accelerated past it. However, to our surprise, a very fat policeman with a fancy peaked hat, nearly as tall as he was, jumped out from behind a bush where he had been waiting for some such occurrence as this. We braked, ground to a halt about 30 yards down the road, and waited for the policeman, who came running after us. The policeman, red-faced and breathless, chased after us, shouting. He approached the left-hand door and forcefully yanked it open, only to find neither a steering wheel nor a driver. He scratched his head, came round to the right-hand side, pulled the door open, and resumed his shouting. We looked as dumb as possible and made signs indicating we could not understand him. This only made him more vocally agitated, and he started jabbing his finger at the speedometer, calibrated in miles per hour. Suddenly he stopped shouting, peered at the speedometer again, and waived us on. In those days, the speedometers of Land Rovers only went up to 60 miles per hour!

Eventually, we made it to the border with Turkey. We got the impression that Bulgaria and Turkey were not best friends. We passed the Bulgarian border post to be faced by a track that could have been made by a tank driving across a ploughed field. There was no scrap of tarmac, and huge potholes were everywhere, many of which were full of water. We were not the only people crossing; several lorries were also carefully making their way through. The experienced lorry drivers, well-versed in this route, skilfully weaved along the road in a serpentine fashion, avoiding the most hazardous sections of the track. At the Turkish border, we were welcomed with open arms. "What did you think of the crossing?" a border force official asked us. Without hesitation, he continued, "Of course, it is the responsibility of the Bulgarians to maintain the road. The fact that they don't simply show what a poor and ignorant people they are." Little did he know that he was repeating nearly word for word what the Bulgarian officials had said about the Turks.

Our next stop of note was in Istanbul. Firstly, one had to brave the traffic. Some people say that the traffic is worse in Cairo, Beirut or Riyadh, but having spent time in each of these cities, I can confidently vouch for the fact that Istanbul's traffic is worse. This did not put us in a good mood. Additionally, after being on the road for 24 hours a day and having to share one canvas camping wash basin among eight people, relying on water begged, borrowed, or stolen from those around us for over a week, we were not very pleasant to be with. So, we stopped and had a conference about what to do. One person had a brilliant idea: we should go to the Istanbul Hilton, which we did. Two rather dirty Land Rovers, one of them severely dented and both with overloaded roof racks, drove up the curving driveway of the Istanbul Hilton, parked in the car park directly outside the main entrance and eight hirsute, smelly, disreputable-looking men in shorts dismounted and went as a group into the lobby. There we found soft music playing, porters in impeccable uniforms standing around, and a few wealthy-looking guests. We asked one of the porters where the toilets were, and he directed us to the other side of the lobby without batting an eyelid and with great aplomb. We entered a spacious toilet block as a group and arranged ourselves around the basins and toilets. We all had a full wash, shaved, changed our underclothes, and washed our dirty ones. Eight men left the toilet block after about half an hour, still looking disreputable but shaven and smelling much more acceptable. We thanked the porters sincerely, who, in turn, treated us as honoured guests wishing us well and telling us that they hoped to see us all before too long. We were staggered. We had thought we would be thrown out as soon as we arrived. I have no idea whether this level of service was usual in Hilton Hotels in those days, but we all agreed that when we were rich, Hilton Hotels would be the ones to head for.

Being on a bit of a high, we decided to leave the Land Rovers where they were as they were probably safer there under the eye of our friends, the porters, and we walked into town. I was wandering around Taksim Square in a desultory way when I felt a clap on my shoulder. To my surprise, it was Ibrahim, a fellow resident from the same staircase at Emmanuel College in Cambridge. He was Turkish and just happened to be visiting Istanbul on that day. He also told me that the Cambridge Tripos results were out yesterday, and if I could buy an airmail copy of the Telegraph, the results would be within it. I duly found one and took it back to the Land Rovers, where we were all meeting, and we all pored over the papers draped over the bonnets. I found the results of the Natural Sciences for Medicine exams and scanned the results, starting at the 2:1 honours grade and continuing through to the bare pass results. My name was not there. The shock of potentially failing hit me. This would have meant leaving the expedition and making my way back to England. One of my friends pointed out that the page did not contain the complete list. I looked over the page to find I had gained a first-class honours degree. For the second time that day, I was left utterly staggered. Everybody gave me a slap on the back, and then I decided it was time to move on. Otherwise, somebody would have thought I had to treat everybody to a drink.

And so we entered Asia, crossing a very crowded Bosphorus bridge, designed and built by somebody who lives in our home village of Biddenham. We travelled east along the road through Ankara, Sivas Erzurum and into Iran and Tabriz. When we were in Istanbul and, to a lesser extent, in Ankara, one could almost believe one was somewhere in southern or eastern Europe, but not after that. There were many more mosques, and they were much better frequented. More women covered their heads with a hijab scarf. The communities were poorer, and we often saw tractors with trailers full of women wearing the baggy trousers called Harem skirts, who were going off to harvest the aubergines, peppers or tomatoes. The villages had markets with stalls full of the most beautiful vegetables and fruit.

We received a warm welcome everywhere we went and were often invited to take tea with people when we stopped. However, by this stage of the journey, the excitement and novelty of the journey had worn off. Also, we were very tired as we had been driving through many nights trying to make up for the time lost in the accident. We lived in a very uncomfortable vehicle, often driving over bumpy roads. Tempers started getting frayed, and rows broke out over the most trivial matters. The leader of the expedition was a man who was intelligent, forceful, with a great deal of energy, but with absolutely no emotional intelligence at all. He had no insight into how people were feeling, and once he determined what needed to be done, he would simply make an announcement regarding the course of action.

Finally, things got to a state where a change had to happen. We were very blessed in our group in having Salim, a Palestinian Arab and Mike, the phlegmatic chap who had been in the back of the Land

Rover when we had our crash. Both were peacemakers. The issues were defined and looked at. The people travelling in the two vehicles were rearranged according to people with personalities who would get on with each other. We realised that it was impractical to drive day and night continuously, so we implemented a schedule where we alternated between driving at night and resting. Also, Mike travelled in one Land Rover and Salim in the other. In effect, they became the leaders of the expedition, though the original leader remained the nominal head. It is amazing how quickly one comes to an arrangement if you come to what seems an insoluble impasse parked at the side of a semi-desert road in a far country. All the members of the expedition were Christian men, but this did not stop (and never has stopped) problems from occurring. Perhaps it made resolving the problems easier. We rarely prayed together on the trip, and I think this was a mistake I learned from. We were careful to pray during the many times when later in my life, I found myself in remote and threatening environments.

One of our team members had an introduction to a family in Tehran, so we made for the capital once we crossed into Iran. This was the time of the Shah, so Iran presented itself as very Western with relatively little evidence of its Islamic culture except among the poor people. The women were often unveiled without any head covering. There were many mosques, but they seemed almost deserted in many cases, which was a big contrast with Eastern Turkey. As we approached Tehran, much like any capital city, there were straggling suburbs and heavy traffic. It was nighttime, and there were few streetlights. Suddenly the streets were no longer surrounded by buildings, and there was open countryside around us. We decided to stop for the night and contact our hosts in the morning, so as always, we backed the two vehicles together and arranged the tarpaulin to make a tent. Two people slept across the front seats of the Land Rovers, and the rest of us slept on camp beds under the tarpaulin. We slept well until about 6 am when a loud noise and the sounds of several cars awakened us. The police had arrived and were hitting on the tarpaulin and shouting. Startled, we got up and looked around. What we had thought was the countryside turned out to be a large park surrounded by some of the largest houses in Tehran. The police seemed highly amused at the sight of two battered Land Rovers and eight grubby men making a bivouac in one of the most select areas of the city. There was much handshaking all around. The police told us to take our time, have breakfast and then move off, which we did.

Eventually, we found our hosts in an area nearly as select as the one we had camped in the previous night. We were entertained in a large, beautifully furnished villa with a swimming pool, immaculate garden, and large European cars in the drive. The family had servants, gardeners, and chauffeurs. We sat on a terrace looking at the mountains surrounding Tehran and sipped cold white wine. Life seemed good, but we had seen great poverty on our way to Tehran, and this lifestyle somehow seemed unsustainable, even perhaps unethical. The family were great supporters of the scout movement and talked at length about their involvement with the international scout movement. As we listened, it became clear that this movement was greatly respected in Iran, but to belong, it seemed one had to be a member of the elite and super-rich people living within a bubble. Our hosts were extremely hospitable and really put themselves out to give us a good time. When evening arrived, we moved off to the permanent scout camp and had what was probably the most luxurious nights camping of our whole journey.

By now, the temperature was very high, up to 40-45 degrees C, and the landscape to the west of Tehran was arid with large stretches of desert. The roads were poor, often with several parallel tracks over the desert. There was evidence that the road had been tarmacked at one time, but this was all broken up, and it was wise to avoid these areas as they often had big lumps of broken concrete and tarmac strewn around. The surface of the road was often deeply corrugated. The corrugated surface we encountered on the road was a result of the heavy lorries traversing over the uneven terrain, causing a bouncing effect on their springs. It was very uncomfortable to drive over this surface, and this caused considerable wear on our springs, so the reasonable reaction was to slow down. In fact, this was exactly the wrong way to drive. Instead, accelerating to around 40-45 miles per hour, depending on the vehicle's load, allowed us to ride over the corrugations. Of course, driving over desert terrain, one left a huge and long dust cloud behind one, which was very unpleasant for the vehicle behind. For this reason, we tended to drive side by side over these sections. It struck me that we must have looked like one of the scenes of a charge across the desert in the Arab wars shown in the film, The Seven Pillars of Wisdom. At times one came upon a dried-up river, and the road tended to follow the path of the river.

It was evening, and we found ourselves in a wadi, a dried-up riverbed. We set up camp, as always, backing the Land Rovers towards each other and setting up the tarpaulin between them. We were careful not to stop anywhere near the base of the wadi as sudden rainstorms, even from far away, could transform the dry riverbed into a dangerous torrent. Many people had been killed by being caught in such a situation. Even in the middle of a desert like this, one can find bits and bobs of flammable material from thorn bushes. A fire was lit. A tin was opened, and the meal was cooked, eaten, and washed up. We used some of our precious water sparingly from a jerry can to wash and clean our teeth. The sky changed from a burned-out light blue to a darker blue and indigo. A hurricane lantern was lit. The stars came out with seemingly brilliant specs all over the sky. They seemed so close one could almost touch them.

There was no light pollution for miles around. I took my camp bed about 100 yards out into the desert to be alone. The murmuring from the camp lessened and then stopped, then silence. Absolute silence is a luxury after a day of dust, driving, jolting, noise, and busyness. Sleep! We woke with the light of a new day and found it was cold. We were not alone: a local person with two camels had stopped about 300 yards away and was making breakfast as we were. The sun appeared, and suddenly things changed. The heat arrived, and the sky went from blue to a burned-out, worn-out blue.

We had breakfast and climbed inside the tin boxes with wheels which were our homes. Once again, it was scorching hot! The vehicles were repacked, and we squeezed ourselves into our sardine cans and were off. However, our journey came to an abrupt halt after a mere 500 yards. There in the middle of a desert, was a pipe spouting water. We could see why the camel owner had camped a little further along the wadi from us. Where on earth does one find a source of water like this in the middle of a desert? Where the water fell from the pipe, there was a tiny oasis with bushes, plants, flowers and a whole community of little bugs and insects. Ten yards away, there was nothing, just arid earth. We filled a jerry can, took off our T-shirts, placed them under the water flow until they were sodden and then put them back on while still dripping. Back in the Land Rovers, we drove off and opened the flaps at the bottom of the windscreen wide so that air flowed directly over us. This is the best and cheapest form of cooling ever found in a hot and dusty place, the latent heat of evaporation of water cooling us almost until we shivered.

And so, via Mashad to the border with Afghanistan. Mashad has a huge and beautiful shrine dedicated to Imam Reza, one of the early leaders of the Shia sect of Islam, but the town did not seem a happy place. Many very old men were in ancient flowing robes, all bearing grumpy faces. There seemed to be a lot of sheep around. As usual in the Middle East, there were hundreds of little shops and workshops, but the usual chatter and banter seemed absent. So, we did not linger and made for the border post. When we arrived, it was not impressive. It was toward the middle of the day. It did not seem that there was a thriving trade between Iran and Afghanistan - we were the only vehicle waiting to cross. There was a pole across the road and a rather sad torn flag flying from a flagpole. The road shimmered under a heat haze, and there were dust flurries in a slight breeze. We collected the passports, visas and the laisse-passer for the vehicles and went to the border post.

The room had a bare wood floor, and the surrounds had been painted blue long ago. It was now a dirty bluish brown. There was a desk of bare wood and one chair. The only thing moving was a fly with a loud buzz that continually flew around us as though apologising for being the only living thing around. We tried calling out in English, then in French, yet we were met with silence. Salim then called out in Arabic, although this puzzled us since Farsi, not Arabic, is the language spoken by Iranians. Silence! We left the room and walked round the back of the building where to our delight, we found a toilet. The smell warned us of what we would find inside, a squat toilet overflowing with all sorts of unspeakable material and maggots. We decided to use the desert as it was evident everybody else had done for the past while.

We returned to the vehicles and considered just lifting the pole and driving through but decided that we would probably get shot if we did so. So, we sat for about two hours on the shady side of the vehicles and dozed and chatted. After about an hour, we got fed up and had another go at shouting in all the languages we could muster. That made us feel better, even if it had little effect. We then continually sounded the horns of the two vehicles. They had a different tone and produced a pleasing cacophony. Eventually, a rather overweight man in a rather dirty uniform arrived and grumpily asked us what we wanted. That puzzled us slightly. If one is a border guard and finds 8 men in two Land Rovers pointing towards the next country at the border, we reckoned that it was a good bet that they wanted to cross the border. With the little patience we had left, we explained that we wanted to go to Afghanistan. Once the guard got over his surprise, he stamped all our documents and lifted the pole, and we left Iran.

The Afghan border post was efficient and friendly, and we drove off happily into this country not reputed for its security and headed for Herat. It was a beautiful city, noted for its fruits and gardens, but sadly we did not have the time to linger. We were heading for Kandahar and took the road south that bypassed the large town of Farah and skirted the huge internal desert of Afghanistan. To our amazement, we found ourselves driving along a well-constructed tarmac road with properly built hard edges where one could safely draw off the road. In their wisdom, the Afghani government had asked the Americans to build the western half of this long road and the Chinese to build the eastern half and to meet up in the middle. There appeared to be a problem. The Americans and the Chinese were not talking to each other and not communicating in any other way. The roads were being built to completely different specifications, and the two sides had not even agreed on the final route of the road. The meeting up of the two parts of the road appeared to be in some doubt!

We drove on, thankful for a good road for the first time since we were in western Iran and for very light traffic. Many vehicles were very old pickups and lorries, gaudily painted with verses of the Quran and scenes from everyday life. There were more passengers inside than the vehicle was built for, and people were all over the outside. People were sitting on top of the cabs sitting on the load at the back, and sometimes hanging on to the sides. Night came, and we turned off the road and drove a few hundred yards behind a small hill. The silence was only disturbed by the hum in the background of the infrequent passing of a truck. As usual, we backed the Land Rovers together and set up camp.

Surrounded by desert mountains, many of which were marked with streaks of red, black, and gold from the minerals in the soil, we lit a fire. Slowly the sun set and lit up the mountains in a surreal light, almost like a film set. All the colours in the mountains were accentuated. Suddenly the sun disappeared, and just as suddenly, it was cold. Everybody searched for sweaters or jackets and huddled around the fire to seek warmth in the growing cold. The sky was clear, so that and the light of the fire was enough, and we did not need to light the lamps. We were sitting down on the rocks waiting for the meal to cook when suddenly, out of the dark, a young man appeared and sat on a rock and said nothing. He looked around and seemed interested but did not try in any way to communicate. When we tried to communicate with him in whatever language we had and in sign language, he did not respond in any way. Four other young men appeared singly and sat down. They neither talked to us nor each other. We shared our food with them, and they ate but remained silent. At the end of the meal, we offered them a sweet each which had been given to us by some business enterprise before we left. They all accepted, and then they spat them out with clear facial evidence that they thought them disgusting. Then they disappeared as silently and as suddenly as they appeared. We were concerned about what this was all about and whether they were casing the joint to raid us later. The fact that they had accepted food from us and eaten it made that unlikely, as to do this would break the hospitality rules of desert people. However, that night we slept on camp beds, one each across the front and rear of the vehicles and three people on each side. We had an untroubled night.

And so, back to the road, the routine of the desert, and passing lorries and pickups. One day in the early afternoon, the road stopped. One moment we were bowling along the road, then nothing, just a bit of a bump and the vast desert. We had noticed that the traffic on the road had diminished to nil over the past few hours. Now there was just us, a road behind us and the desert in front. Off to the right was a series of low huts where we found a handful of people with whom we had no means of communication and who showed no interest in us. We returned to the end of the road and noticed three tracks that went off in different directions through the desert. We chose the one that seemed the most used and set off across the sand and rocks. The track kept branching, leaving us with the dilemma of choosing one. Eventually, we found ourselves on an ill-marked track passing over very rough, rocky terrain. There was nobody in sight, no sign of habitation and utter silence. We knew our compass was unreliable as the mountains around us contained magnetic rock. We were well and truly lost in the middle of the Afghani desert with no idea where to go and with low stocks of water. With night descending upon us, we ventured into the desert and decided to pray, seeking guidance and hope in our dire circumstances.

We rose from our prayers, and to our astonishment, a battered 1940s Bedford lorry full of wild looking tribesmen, emerged from the desert, directly heading towards us. Our immediate reaction was, "Thank you, Lord. We did ask for help, but we are not sure we meant this lot!" We were concerned that these could be bandits that we knew existed all over Afghanistan and that they might kill us all and take our vehicles and everything in them. The tribesmen, clearly Pashtuns, engaged in rapid conversations in Pashto. To our relief, their conversation was filled with back-slapping and laughter. They seemed genuinely puzzled to encounter a group of young Englishmen wandering about in the middle of the desert, far from any established road. Eventually, Tim, the rather chaotic member of our team, proved his worth by going into the desert and pointing in one direction and shouting "Kandahar?" at the top of his voice. He then turned 90 degrees and shouted Kandahar and so on through all the points of the compass. The tribesmen rapidly tagged on that we were headed for the city of Kandahar, which by happy coincidence or by the Lord's providence, they were going to as well. One tribesman came and sat in the middle seat of the front of each Land Rover, and the person sitting there joined the man in the back of the vehicle. I was driving our vehicle, and it was by far the wildest journey I have ever experienced in my life.

We set off into the night in the direction shown by our guide and rapidly lost the other Land Rover. We were driving by our headlights directly across the desert with no sign of a track and desperately trying to avoid the larger rocks. The tribesman was all the time trying to get me to drive faster. After about two hours, a herd of small desert gazelles crossed our path. Our friend with the Pashtun hat and the flowing robes grabbed the steering wheel and indicated that we should give chase. He drew his dagger, and if he thought I was driving too slowly, he bashed it on the dashboard, which was made of steel. The marks of his activity raised a few eyebrows when we returned to England. Happily, we soon lost the gazelles, and our friendly tribesman was not quite so friendly for half an hour or so to this wimp, who, by his incompetent driving, had lost a wonderful chance of a good meat meal. After about three more hours of driving through the wild country in Helmand province, we regained an apology for a road and finally made it to the city of Kandahar. We never found the Chinese part of the road and wondered whether it existed. On the outskirts of the city, we met up with the other Land Rover, who seemed to have had a rather less colourful character to guide them than we had. We said a very big thank you to our friends and gave them some of our food, which they seemed pleased with but not as pleased as if we had caught a gazelle. There was much backslapping all around, and the old Bedford lorry took off in a cloud of black smoke.

We decided to spend a few hours looking around Kandahar and drove into the centre. It was a typical central Asian town with many narrow streets. Overhead, a tangled web of electric wires crisscrossed the roads with little rhyme or reason. The streets were lined with numerous small shops and workshops, many of which offered similar products or services. In the heart of the city, we encountered a few larger shops and some notable municipal buildings. However, the aspect which struck us most was the conspicuous absence of women. There were occasional sightings of women wearing burkhas, presumably concealing their identities, but even these were few and far between.

We were walking down a street, just absorbing the ambience, and chatting with each other, when we were approached by a man in his mid-40s who spoke impeccable English. It turned out that he was the senior obstetrician and gynaecologist in the local hospital. It surprised us that a man was allowed to do this work in a strictly Islamic country, but most of the women would not have been allowed enough education to become doctors. He invited us into his department, and we were surprised to find wards and operating theatres which seemed much like those in the UK. The Afghani doctor had been trained in India and had also done some training in the USA. We spent a very pleasant hour being shown around and chatting. At one point, I said that I was thirsty, and our newfound friend kindly offered me a glass of water. Initially hesitant, I declined, saying that we never drank water that had not been sterilised. The doctor agreed that this was wise but said that this was sterilised water he used to scrub up before an operation, and I drank it. I decided to drink it, unaware of the consequences I would soon face.

We returned to the Land Rovers and headed towards Spin Buldak near the Pakistani border on a gravel, corrugated road. By this time, the land Rovers had both been driven over the open desert, many gravel-potholed and corrugated roads and very few tarmacked roads. The signs of wear and tear were becoming evident. As we drove through some soft sand, one of the rear wheels suddenly sheared off. This was probably because the wheel nuts had not been sufficiently tightened after repairing a puncture several days before. We took the wheel off with great difficulty because of the soft sand and found that we could tighten the nuts on four of the five bolts, but the thread had been completely stripped on the fifth. We limped into the next small town and went to a hole-in-the-wall garage. To our amazement, we found somebody to translate for us and asked where we could get a new wheel bolt. We were told that a new bolt could only be got from a Land Rover agency, and the nearest one was in Delhi. The mechanic asked us why we would bother to get another bolt, as this type of problem was common in the area. He assured us that many of the trucks had wheels held on by fewer than the regulation numbers of bolts. We decided to continue our journey, knowing we had no other choice. In fact, we drove all the way back to the UK with a wheel only attached by four nuts. The very next day, we were driving down a particularly corrugated road with potholes to add to the problems when the rear main spring broke on one of the vehicles. Again, we visited a workshop in a hole in the wall of a small town. The mechanic did not seem phased at all by this problem. He simply found a metal strip of the right size and forged it into a new spring. This also lasted for the whole of the remaining journey.

In the late afternoon, we arrived at Spin Buldak, the border town between Afghanistan and Pakistan, and went on to the hamlet just before the border post. It seemed a town reminiscent of the American

Wild West. The buildings were in poor repair; many very heavily armed young men were standing around doing nothing apart from looking at us and what we were carrying. There were no signs of any agents of the army or police, and there was a distinct sense of menace. We stopped, filled the tanks and spare tanks with petrol, and asked the way to the border post. The young men stood around, peering inside the vehicles, and just looking. We were told that it was far too late to pass into Pakistan. Between the Afghan and Pakistani border posts, there lay a treacherous high pass spanning around 20 miles, known to be infested with bandits. Travelling through this pass at night would have put us at great risk of being stopped, robbed, or even killed. As we surveyed the surroundings and the people standing there, we decided to take our chances and proceed.

The road was of gravel and very badly maintained. It passed over a high mountain pass with many steep gradients and hairpin bends. We drove as fast as possible and kept the two vehicles as close as possible together. This was difficult, particularly as we were driving by headlights due to the large plume of dust one leaves behind driving on roads like this. It was not an easy or safe drive, but eventually, we arrived at the Pakistani border post. There we met two Pakistani soldiers who were doing a posting as border guards. One spoke good English and told us we must have been mad to drive through this border pass at night, and we were lucky to be alive. The official border force personnel would not be present until morning, so the friendly soldiers offered us a secure parking area to rest. In their care, we finally felt a sense of security and settled down for the night.

The next morning our papers were processed rapidly and smoothly, and we set off for the border town of Chaman and then through the Khojak mountain pass to Quetta. In 1962, this was a city of 100,000. It now has more than one million inhabitants. We had received an invitation to visit and stay for a couple of nights at a CMS mission hospital with the director, who had the unfortunate name of Dr Donald Duck. We arrived and were welcomed by Dr Duck, his wife, and children at a large though sparsely furnished bungalow. A meal was produced, and we talked at length about the joys and trials of living and working in an isolated and, even at that stage, unstable part of the world. Apparently, one of the most difficult problems was caring for the children. They had to be home-schooled using material that took weeks to arrive by post and sometimes did not arrive at all. They had a large garden, but the children were not safe to play in it because of the number of venomous snakes that the whole of the city seemed to be infested with.

Dr Duck worked with local health personnel in the hospital. There were very few fully trained doctors at that stage in the town, and Dr Duck had the attitude of many mission doctors at that time. He kept his basic skills up to date by spending much of his leave time when he returned to the UK in attending training courses. Then if he met a problem that he had never dealt with before and there was nobody else more competent than him to deal with it, he read up on what to do and did it. He had a remarkable success rate! While we were at the hospital, he took us to see one of the few smallpox cases remaining in Pakistan. However, it was to take until 1974 to eradicate the disease in this country fully. It was during our stay in Quetta that I started feeling vaguely unwell. We had fallen behind our schedule by stopping in Quetta again, so we started driving 24 hours a day again through Pakistan. The only incident of note I can remember during this journey was driving around a corner on a gravel, graded road and nearly colliding with an English-registered bus coming at speed in the opposite direction. This seemed bizarre, so we asked about it at the next town we passed through. Everybody there told us that this was the weekly bus which ran from Delhi to London via Pakistan and Afghanistan and was a well-established and regular service. I have often tried to find out details of this service after returning to the UK and have universally drawn a blank. Eventually, we reached Lahore, where we crossed into India.

We found Indian roads quite a challenge. The roads were about the same width as a country road in England except for the bridges. The bridges were single-track, and there were many of them. There was quite a heavy lorry traffic and a lot of overtaking, but the real excitement started on the approach to the bridges. One could see the lorries aligning themselves so that they could be the ones who went across first under all circumstances. This led to overtaking on the approaches and racing if one saw a lorry coming from the opposite direction. Not infrequently, this led to head-on collisions on the bridges. All good fun unless one got caught up in the middle of a pile-up.

In many places, the roads were lined by small tea houses, restaurants, and numerous Indians who seemed to be permanently asleep on rickety beds at whatever time of day one arrived. That is unless they felt the call to pass a bowel motion. In this case, it seemed there was a specific ridge that one went to where one squatted in full view of everybody and with a line of other people occupied in the same activity. One performed the necessary while often having lengthy and enthusiastic conversations about many subjects with one's neighbours on the ridge, particularly about politics. Toward evening we used to draw off the main road and stop in a small town.

Almost as soon as we stopped, we were surrounded by a crowd of students from various grades, schools, and universities. We always had a great welcome, and all went to the tea house, which we were reliably informed was the best. We had a strong suspicion that the choice depended more on the relationship of the tea shop owner to members of the crowd than on the quality of the wares. The students talked nonstop and wanted to know what we were doing and why. Some of them felt we were on a wild goose chase and had no compunction to tell us we were stupid. Others were much more interested in what our plans were. They also told us a lot about England, or more accurately, about their image of England. We were frequently told that we did not speak English well and had an appalling accent by many young people who themselves spoke with such thick accents and poor grammar that we barely understood them. Despite all this, we had a very good time at each stop and felt glad to have met the people we encountered.

Our next big stop was in Delhi. Our accommodation there had been arranged by a friend I met at the India Society in Cambridge. Chandra's father was the Minister for Tourism in India. We had a telephone number to ring when we arrived, and we thought we might be put up in some hotel somewhere in the city, but we were wrong. After the call, somebody found us in the suburbs and led us further into the city. Driving through Delhi was quite an achievement. The large roads were busy, but the smaller roads were more like the activity in an ant heap with carts, bicycles, trishaws, cars, lorries, animals, and pedestrians going all directions on all sides of the road. Eventually, we arrived at an arch in an ordinary-looking wall. On entering, we found ourselves in a totally different world. There were well-tended gardens, still lush despite the fierce heat of summer Delhi. Everywhere there was water and the sound of running water. The birds were singing, and one could hear them. We had left the noise outside as we were in a Buddhist temple.

A small man arrived and seemed completely unphased to see eight unshaven men in rather tatty clothes climb out of two battered and dirty Land Rovers. He greeted us gravely and assured us that we were very welcome and then led us to some very simple but clean and light rooms and asked us to make ourselves at home. He told us that at the end of the afternoon, we would eat together, and in the meantime, we should feel free to wander around the temple grounds. The person who had led us here said that she would leave but would come back the next afternoon to show us around Delhi. We were staying here for two nights. After taking showers and making ourselves as presentable as possible, we walked around the grounds. It was an odd feeling. Over the past few weeks, we had been driving, sometimes for 24 hours a day, through remote areas, completely reliant on our vehicles and our own ingenuity. We had traversed mountains, scorching deserts, and places where access to help would have involved a long and uncertain journey if we encountered any trouble. Now here we were, being cared for, fed, and given accommodation with somebody taking complete responsibility for our welfare. Suddenly, we felt tired and spent most of that afternoon sitting by a small lake and dozing. We had an evening meal, slept like tops and then the next morning, somebody turned up and showed us the sights of Delhi, the colonial architecture, Connaught Circus, and the Red Fort, and at the end of the day, we escaped back to our sanctuary in the temple. The next morning, we set off again, and within 50 yards from the gate of the temple, we were back in expedition mode, weaving between the traffic and trying not to run over half a dozen people at once, or even worse, running over a cow!

We gradually made our way down the centre of India, following, at times, the route of the grand trunk road. When we felt we had time, we used to drive off the main road and look for a track to a village. We were never quite sure whether the villagers were happy about us stopping near their village, but they never complained. Perhaps that was because we were 8 young men driving quasi-military vehicles, though we did not set out in any way to give the impression of any threat. Often the children came and peered, and occasionally a young person would come and ask who we were and why we were there. Most times, we set up camp a reasonable distance from the village on land that did not look as though it was in use and prepared our meals, did some washing, and set up our beds.

It was evening. We had parked up on some uncultivated land with the Land Rovers back-to-back as usual, with the tarpaulin between. The lamps had been found, and Tim was doing what he did best, telling other people what they had to do. The engine oil and water had been checked, and supper would be in about an hour. I had to get away, so I walked 500 yards to the village and sat on a log where the villagers could not see me. There was a large area of impacted earth with a large old mango tree in the middle. Just off to the right was the well with many women chatting around the parapet. Some of them had babies on their hips. Others were coming to draw water for the evening meal. Children ran or crawled around, sometimes chasing each other and some finding interesting stones and putting them in their mouths. Others just sat there. Perhaps, these were the malnourished ones. During the evening, the mothers would pour a bucket of water over the children as their daily bath. Goats wandered about, and chickens scratched the loose earth in a desultory way, trying to find the grub countless other chickens had looked for during the day. The men sat under the tree, and there was a murmur of voices as they chatted. The sun was setting as an orange orb out over the fields. The dust hung in the air filling the village with an iridescent haze as the light was refracted through it. The poorer men returned from the fields where they had been working as day labourers, and the animals were brought in and settled down for the night in their shelters made of intertwined branches. The sun finally disappeared, and suddenly it was dark.

Lights were lit in some homes. There were no lights in the poorest homes. They could not afford the kerosene. Undoubtedly, the people in such villages at that time had a very hard life, particularly if they were a widow with children or from the wrong caste. For me, the impression was of a timeless way of life without all the rush and striving to achieve the aims that we perceived ourselves to have. A night bird called raucously, and the sound of voices retreated into the small low houses around the village square. It was time to head back to the Land Rovers, two tin boxes on wheels coming from a different universe from the community of an Indian country village.

It was about this time that the stomach problems I had had since entering Pakistan became more of a problem. I lost my appetite, had abdominal pains, and started having to go to the toilet several times a day. Happily, this problem did not become a crisis until we had made our way to Rajahmundry in the state of Andhra Pradesh and then on to Narsapur, a town near the mouth of the river Godavari. There we found Dr Edward Short, his wife Mary and their children. They ran the Bethesda Leprosy Hospital in Narsapur, providing care for people with leprosy and reconstructive surgery for people deformed by this disease. Their specialty was the Brand hand tendon transplant operation, which restored people's ability to use their hand for grasping.

Edward Short, the brother of the Queen's physician, and his wife had decided to spend their lives serving leprosy patients in this part of India. This was at a stage where the disease was becoming treatable, but the treatment was not yet available in all the poorer areas of the world affected by this scourge. Also, there were still many people who had disabilities from leprosy caught many years before. Leprosy causes anaesthesia of the feet and hands, and thus when these limbs are burned or otherwise damaged, the person is not aware of the problem. This can lead to infections and physical damage, which can eventually result in amputation. The nerve damage also causes a deformity that prevents people from grasping or holding anything securely. One of the main problems for leprosy patients is the exclusion they suffer. They are not allowed to live in villages or anywhere where they might have social contact with their families or other members of society other than those with leprosy. Even when these people had been cured, they were still excluded. It is easy to enforce this exclusion because one of the frequent marks of leprosy is the loss of the eyebrows.

The Narsapur Hospital had several main tasks. It treated people for the disease so that the patients were no longer a risk to others. They taught these people to care for their feet and hands as the loss of sensation does not recover with treatment, and they surgically cleaned up any infections or injuries. They also transplanted tendons in their hands so that they could hold things again, and so they were able to find work. Finally, they transplanted some of the hair from their scalp into the position of their eyebrows so that they would not be immediately recognisable as having suffered from leprosy.

The hospital had no government or other public funding. The people they were serving were the poorest of the poor and could not afford to cover any of the cost of their treatment. Edward and Mary believed that they were doing God's work and that He was quite capable of funding His work. If people asked them about the hospital, they would gladly share the details, but they never solicited any form of financial assistance. Typically, enough money would come in to support the hospital and the community of individuals with leprosy under their care. However, there were occasions when finances were tight, and during such times, Edward and Mary would reduce their own living expenses, even below their already modest standard.

Once, just before we arrived, there was no money at all; the whole enterprise ran out of funds. Edward and Mary prayed earnestly for many hours, and nothing arrived. On Monday morning, Edward went to the hospital with an extremely heavy heart to tell all the patients that the hospital could no longer care for them and that all the planned operations were cancelled. Halfway to the hospital, Edward found that he had left some papers he needed at home and went back to fetch them. The post had just arrived, and there was a money order for exactly the sum needed to keep the hospital running for one week. The money order had come from a person in America whom Edward had never heard of and from an area where he knew nobody. The letter said that God had told this man that he had to send this precise amount of money immediately to this address. It is tempting to dismiss such occurrences as mere exaggeration or believe that they do not happen at all. However, it becomes increasingly challenging to maintain this perspective when you find yourself as the director of a hospital on the verge of closure due to insufficient funds, only to be holding a money order in your hands. This instance was the most striking example of God's provision of funds for their service, but it was certainly not the only one.

The hospital was a simple concrete building on a side street of a small rural town in an agricultural area of southeast India. We arrived, set up camp in the grounds, and had the luxury of showers and rest from continual travelling. We were made enormously welcome by the whole community and later by the church. The community had some very disabled members, but there was not the low mood and general area of resignation one can find among leprosy communities. There was a real sense of purpose and hope. Our group was taken around the buildings, the facilities, and the compound.

However, by this time, I was feeling very unwell. I had to run to the toilet many times a day, having stomach cramps and passing large amounts of blood. Tests showed that I had amoebic dysentery. Throughout the journey, we had been scrupulous about only drinking boiled water, except the one occasion when I was offered water guaranteed sterile by a doctor in Afghanistan. I was too unwell to continue up into the isolated and primitive mountain communities to carry out the work we had come for. Edward very kindly agreed to look after me, and to my great distress my friends left in the two Land Rovers which had been our home for so long. The only treatment available in Narsapur for this condition at that time was Emetine, which was toxic to the heart. I had several injections which made no difference to my condition at all. I can remember drifting in and out of consciousness. When I was awake the only thing that really took my imagination was the monkeys chasing each other through the rafters of the room I was in. Eventually Edward found some Metronidazole in the market, which in those days was a new and rare drug. I dread to think how much he paid for it! Very slowly, after being treated with this, I recovered, and after about 10 days, I could walk around and take an interest in things. I have no doubt that Edward saved my life. The sad thing was that we later learned that his younger daughter Ruth caught the same disease two years later and died of it. As my health improved gradually, I was able to accompany the medical team out into the backwoods, sometimes by boat on the many canals to villages, where people were examined for leprosy, any treatment was checked, public health teaching was done, and the small Christian community was taught and encouraged. Quite often, people of other religions seeing the dedicated service given by Edward Short and his team, asked about this Jesus whom they were following. Some came to know Jesus both as Saviour and friend.

After approximately three weeks, my friends returned to Narsapur, having successfully completed their work among the mountain communities. By that time, I had fully recovered. Since four members of our group needed to return to England earlier than the rest of us, we made the decision to split up for our journey home. The first Land Rover and the group of four individuals departed almost immediately, while the remaining four of us stayed on for an additional week to gain a deeper understanding of the ongoing ministry of the hospital and church. The experiences we had during that time greatly aided us in raising funds and garnering prayer support for the work once we returned to England.

We decided to take a more direct route back and drove through Pakistan and then through Isfahan in Iran to Baghdad in Iraq. While we were driving through Isfahan, we got well and truly lost and found ourselves driving the wrong way up a one-way street. Everybody was shouting and waving at us. It was quite a narrow road through the old part of town. Then suddenly, to our absolute amazement, our other Land Rover was driving the right way up the same street. For quite some time, we couldn't believe our eyes. I have often wondered what the statistical possibility of that happening by chance was. We stepped out of the vehicle and warmly embraced our brothers, who had evidently encountered engine problems that caused their delay. Of course, this caused an absolute blockage of the street. Everybody came out of the shops and hung over the balconies of the apartments. Eventually, word got around how we had left South India a week apart and met up in the middle of the city.

Everybody pushed and shouted, and people brought us cups of tea and pastries. People were shouting the story to their relatives; others were shouting because they wanted to get by. Eventually, a rather confused-looking policeman arrived, and the whole story was recited to him, it seems, with all sorts of flourishes. He then came and looked at the two Land Rovers parked bonnet to the bonnet and asked how we got into that situation. Eventually, he called for reinforcements, the road was cleared, the Land Rover pointing in the wrong direction was turned round, nearly destroying a tomato stall in the process, and everybody, including the police, waved goodbye to us like long lost friends. We left laden with pastries, sweets, and all sorts of goodies we had been given. When we eventually reached the suburbs, we decided to continue our separate ways home as our colleagues in the other vehicle were now even more pressed for time.

So on to Iraq, the only country we did not like among the many countries we drove through. We were treated with contempt and made to feel a nuisance, and the police were aggressive. We decided to drive throughout the night to get through the country. The roads were awful, and we were glad to pass the border post and find ourselves in Syria. We continued over gravel-graded roads towards Damascus, where I had arranged to meet a Syrian friend. Several hours into the journey, we had a puncture and had to change the tyre. Some hours later, we were driving through the first suburbs of Damascus and found that we had another puncture. We drew into the side of a residential road lined by pleasant villas and stood looking at the deflated tyre. We had not had time to get the other punctured tyre repaired.

How does one get two tyres repaired in the suburbs of a Middle Eastern town? A man emerged from one of the villas and inquired about the problem we were facing. "He then looked at us and said, 'You look exhausted. Come into my house and have a shower and a cup of tea, then we will see how to sort out your problems.'" We went into the house and were greeted by his wife, who was wearing a headscarf but no other head covering and sat down. Our host gave us all dressing gowns, and we used the two bathrooms to have showers and changed into clean clothes. While we were doing this, our hostess washed our clothes. We then sat down, and certainly, we did have a cup of tea, but that came after a full Middle Eastern meal. Our host then said, "Let's go and see what we can do about your Land Rover now." We went outside and found that while we had been showering and having the meal, he got both tyres repaired, and we were ready to get going again. We left with profuse thanks, and our host and hostess declared that we had done them a great favour by coming and spending some time with them. It is episodes like this, repeated several times during my life, which have given me a great love for the Arab people. There was no explanation for their enormous kindness and service to us, a group of young men who could never repay them, other than an innate goodness, kindness and a wonderful Arab family culture of hospitality and caring for people in trouble. I suppose this was the start of a journey that eventually led to us living for several years in several Middle Eastern countries.

We continued our journey into the centre of Damascus, where we were meeting a friend of mine from Cambridge days. Annas was the son of the doctor in the presidential household in Damascus. We parked in a car park, paid the car park keeper to guard the vehicle, and followed the directions to Annas's house. This led us into the ancient heart of Damascus, where we found ourselves walking along narrow roads lined by featureless mud-coloured walls. We became an attraction for the usual street urchins to peer at, though we did not get asked for money. Eventually, we came upon a door with the relevant number and knocked. The door was opened by a retainer, and Annas appeared. We had a great welcome from him and his father. The female members of the household did not appear. We were taken via a beautiful courtyard with a garden and a fountain playing to the formal guest welcome room. All the walls were of a dark wood-looking like Mahogany and inlaid with mother of pearl and ivory. The chairs were around the walls, very plush and very uncomfortable. On the floor were beautiful Persian rugs.

We were served tea; clearly, there was a set format to welcome important guests. We realised that this was a great honour for us and that it was because we were Annas's friends from Cambridge. Following this reception, things became far more informal. The father disappeared, and we were taken to a restaurant in town where the décor was old Syrian, with beautiful furniture and plush, though much more comfortable, chairs. We had an excellent meal, including a dish that Annas insisted we try. It was delicious, and it was only when we had finished the last morsels that our host informed us that it was sheep's testicles. There was much talk about old times; eventually we left and returned to the Land Rover. Only as we prepared to drive off did we realise that the Annas we had met in Damascus was different from the laid back slightly scruffy and chaotic student we knew at

Cambridge. Annas used to claim that one of his major achievements in the UK was that he managed to wear out every pair of shoes he owned about one month before the guarantee ran out. In Damascus, we met a man, scrupulously polite to everybody of whatever social class, but a man of authority who carried himself with assurance and expected to be able to fulfil any task he had to do with ease.

Salim Haddad, one of our expedition's quietest and wisest members, was Arabic and from Lebanon. At this stage of our journey, we had a reasonable amount of time before we had to be back in England, so Salim invited us to Beirut to see his family. Lebanon is a fascinating country about the size of Wales which in 1962 was a haven of peace in the Middle East with Christians and Muslims living together in uneasy harmony. If the president was Muslim, the Prime Minister had to be a Christian, and these two roles alternated for each faith. Lebanon had been a French colony, so in the middle of this chaotic area the country had two main national aims: to be super rich and to eat, drink and be merry. In the middle of all this money grabbing and people living the high life were numerous ordinary families living ordinary lives and doing ordinary jobs. Salim's family, who were Christian Palestinian Arabs, did their ordinary jobs rather well and so were able to send him to Cambridge to study. They found themselves in Lebanon because one day, after the inauguration of the Israeli state, they were living on the olive plantation on the West Bank in Palestine, which their family had owned for generations, and they had a visit by a platoon of the Israeli army. The soldiers said to them, "We respect our Arabic neighbours, and we wish you well, so we thought that we ought to warn you that if you are still here tomorrow, you will be shot." The family fled to Lebanon. The Haddad family lived in a comfortable flat on a block just inland from St George's Beach in Beirut. The day after we arrived turned out to be a memorable one. We spent the morning having a drink at St George's Beach and, in the afternoon, were taken on a hair-raising drive up to the magnificent scenery of Mount Lebanon. I think this was the only time I had felt cold in the last three months. Salim's family looked after us with wonderful Arab hospitality. On our way home, we asked Salim, as a resident of Beirut, what was the main attribute of the city that stood out for him. He said, "The almost total lack of public toilets. How can a country be civilized if it has no public loos?" Such is the difference in the image of a city for a resident and a tourist!

And so, we headed for home. The journey did not start well. We headed to the Lebanese/Syrian border only to be told that we did not have the right papers to take the vehicle out of Lebanon. Salim tried to reason with the border guards, and Phil lost his temper and started shouting. The guards reacted with a threat of arrest and prison, so there was nothing for it but to turn around and drive back to Beirut. After a full day of going around government offices and eventually getting the right papers, we drove back to the border, into Syria, then Turkey, and so across the Bosphorus and into Europe. From then on, we drove 24 hours a day through heavy traffic, lowering skies and rain. This was the weather we had not experienced for three months, and it was not welcome. Having said that, seeing the white cliffs of Dover from the ferry was a good feeling. We had been on the move solidly for many weeks, and it was time to get back to real life.

I dropped the other three people off in London and took the Land Rover home to Rugby. There I had four days to do a rapid turn round before setting off for London to do the clinical part of my training. During this time, I spent a good few hours reflecting on the whole experience of our trip. It certainly changed me radically. I started as a young man, raised in a very limited lifestyle where our social interactions were restricted to a few families associated with our church. We were taught that anything outside this environment was deemed evil and threatening. However, I broke away from this toxic community when I went to Cambridge. Yet, even during my time there, I found myself confined to another insular community. The university, and especially our college, fostered an inward-looking society, firmly convinced of its own superiority and entitlement. It was ingrained that by becoming a member of this esteemed institution, the world owed us a living and a social standing above others. During this trip, we had the opportunity to experience firsthand a multitude of diverse beliefs, environments, and societies. We had met people for whom our priorities were peripheral or unknown. We had passed through deserts and lawless lands and had been totally responsible for our own welfare without any fall-back position. This whole experience produced a dramatic change in my thinking and worldview. It was like crawling out of a dark box and finding a whole new world lit by a bright light. It bred in me a love of travel, respect and love of people who were different from me, particularly if they were willing to engage in discussion about our differences. Perhaps the biggest change was a love of the Muslim world, particularly Arabic people. Their rich culture, hospitality, and the warmth with which they welcomed us left a deep mark on my heart.

London

Before we set off for India, we had arranged with a friend, Hedley, who was also coming up to London for his clinical studies and whose father was on the faculty of the University of London, that they would find accommodation for Hedley, David, my friend from Cambridge and me, for our time in London. During the three months we had been away, this friend had become unwell and could not take up his place for his clinical studies. He and his father had not done anything about arranging accommodation and had not told us. This meant that with only four days before our courses started, my friend David and I had no accommodation, and at the start of an academic year in London, all the student accommodation had been spoken for many weeks before. We thought about rereading George Orwell's 'Down and Out in London and Paris' for some guidance, but eventually decided to try our luck at getting a room in a YMCA hostel. Even finding such accommodation was extremely difficult, but after much searching, we found one room at a very grotty hostel located in the Kings Cross area. There was one small grubby room with a single bed and a contraption consisting of a very narrow wooden chair which collapsed flat and became my bed. There were shared washing facilities and no cooking facilities at all. From this base, we started our life as medical students at the Middlesex Hospital in Mortimer Street.

The first Sunday we were in London, we decided to go to church at St Paul's Church Onslow Square, where to our delight, we found that the curate was an ex-Emmanuel College Cambridge man. We became friends. It seems odd to say it, but at the age of perhaps 30, he was already a confirmed bachelor, though one with a sense of humour. We rapidly learned that he was coming to the end of his curacy and was moving as vicar to St John's Church Downshire Hill in Islington, just bedside Hampstead Heath. We learned that he was to live in a large vicarage alone, which troubled us for some reason. We developed a mission to persuade him that he would be dreadfully lonely living alone, and having come to an agreement on that proposition, we further advised him that he might care to look for a couple of ex-Emmanuel College men to live with. Having further agreed on that matter, in passing, we reminded him that we had both been at Emmanuel. So, we moved from an extremely grotty room at a Kings Cross YMCA to a spacious vicarage in Downshire Hill, with Hampstead Heath at the end of the road and Michael Foot, leader of the Labour Party, as our neighbour. Well, even in the best scenarios, there's always one thorn in the flesh. Over the course of two years, we set ourselves the task of getting him to respond when we wished him 'Good Morning.' It wasn't for lack of persistence on our part, but it seemed he was equally determined. Throughout our stay as his neighbours, he studiously ignored us, never acknowledging our greetings.

Every morning we climbed on the number 24 bus at South End Green Hampstead and got off at Goodge Street for the Middlesex Hospital. "The Middlesex", as it was affectionately known, was a building of six storeys and was founded in 1745. It moved to its present site in 1757 and was rebuilt in 1928. It had wards on each floor, which were arranged around a central staircase. The ancillary services were mainly in buildings on the same site; the nurses' home was just across one street, and the academic centre was across another street. One of the most important ancillary services, the King and Queen pub, was across yet another street and was the only pub where the hospital bleep call system worked! The hospital cared for the people of Bloomsbury and Fitzrovia but was also a tertiary referral hospital for patients with rare or difficult medical problems from all over the country. Within this cluster of buildings was a close community based around caring and medical problem solving, but also with the education, personal development, and support of many groups of people.

One thing that marked out our years of clinical studies from the purely academic work in Cambridge was that there were no long holidays. Our lives moved according to the patterns of the hospital community. We would typically take a two-week holiday, usually twice a year.

From the beginning, we found ourselves in a completely new world. In Cambridge, we learned a great deal about dysfunctions of the liver and other organs. Here we got to lay a hand on the stomach of people with liver disease. The biggest change from a rarefied academic environment was not so much feeling in real life what a diseased liver felt like when one palpated a stomach, but finding that this diseased liver was part of a real living person, not that different from us. If one gave this appendage of the diseased liver a chance, they would tell you what it felt like to have this illness, what effect it had on their lives and what their hopes and fears were.

Another thing that revolutionised our view of our calling was listening to the trust these ordinary people had in their doctors. We met people of all ages and with all sorts of conditions, from grave to trivial. Throughout the months, we accompanied these individuals on their journeys, witnessing their diagnoses and treatments, which led either to resolution and recovery or to the onset of chronic illness and, in some cases, death. In the latter group, we increasingly met and talked with the family members and saw hope slowly dying as the patient worsened. We learned many life skills during this time. How to rejoice with those who had been ill and now were better. We saw people change from autonomous individuals to the more passive role of patient and gradually taking back control from their doctors who were "doing things to them" and returning to individuals who were in charge of their own lives. We learned the normality of death, something that happens to everybody, must be fought against, but eventually, if one holds the hand of people while they come to terms with their own death, it can be accepted with peace and dignity. None of this was taught to us. We either developed the skills and philosophy of walking with people through these experiences or some of our colleagues closed off their relation skills and became unfeeling and brusque. Being a Christian and knowing a loving God helped some of us in this life change.

We also found ourselves in a new community, one with a very distinct hierarchy and rules, and one divided into a multitude of sub-communities according to the task carried out by the members. These sub-communities were all part of the hierarchy; for instance, the nursing community was higher up the ladder than the microbiology technicians and lower than the surgeons. Having said that, there were oddities. One of the lowest sub-groups in the hierarchy was the porters. However, within this group were the front hall porters. They were in every way the gatekeepers of the hospital. Nobody got in unless the porters decided that they were suitable people. The general hospital porters were the people who took people by wheelchair from ward to investigation and by bed from ward to ward. They also took patients on their final journey to the mortuary. During many of these journeys, it was the porters who accompanied anxious patients, transitioning them from one environment to another. It was often the porters who played a crucial role in calming these individuals down and providing reassurance.

There was one porter who had been a brilliant undergraduate at Oxford University. He developed severe multiple sclerosis in his early years as an undergraduate and was left very disabled. He decided he did not want to sit at home doing nothing, so he took on the role of lift attendant at the manned lift in the hospital. He was a warm and cultured man, renowned for being a wonderful listener, and universally known as Phil the Lift. At times the manned lift did not seem to be available. If one looked at the indicator lights, it seemed that the lift was going up and down the lift shaft without ever stopping or opening its doors. That usually meant that Phil was comforting a widow who had just lost her husband or had a nurse with him who was in floods of tears because she had just broken up with her medical student boyfriend. When equanimity had been re-established, the lift would stop, the doors would open, and somebody smiling through their tears would emerge. He was invited to many marriages between people who met at the hospital, including ours. There was one surgeon who had been an undergraduate at the same Oxford college as Phil and in the same year. He studiously ignored this great man as he was so far down the hospital hierarchy from him.

As the medical students were overwhelmingly young men and the nursing community was overwhelmingly made up of young women, it was unsurprising that this was the hospital community we had the most to do with. Many of the nurses at that time were girls from very comfortable or even wealthy families who were sent to be nurses or chose this career either to have a career recognised as doing good, or to acquire skills useful for married life, or to some degree to find a nice young doctor to get married to. There was an element of the life of the convent about the nursing community, but with the added advantage that one could become a member without the expectation that one had to become an old maid. Having said that, the only ward sister in the whole hospital allowed to be married was the sister on the gynaecology wards. If a nurse did something wrong or showed herself incompetent, this was treated as a moral failure which was unbecoming in somebody in a calling such as nursing. On looking back, it seems extremely old-fashioned and even misogynistic. However, as the hospital was such an enclosed, inward-looking community, there was plenty of opportunity to develop romantic relationships, and there were many medical students who trained at the Middlesex Hospital who landed up married to a Middlesex nurse, including me!

However, the most esteemed members of the medical community were the consultants, with the surgeons considered the crème de la crème. A self-respecting consultant was expected to have consulting rooms in Harley Street and at least a smattering of titled or well-known people on his patient list. Winston Churchill had been treated in our hospital, and Hugh Gaitskell died in the Middlesex Hospital while I was there from undiagnosed lupus. Many consultants were deservedly famous doctors and greatly respected in their profession. However, there were some colourful characters too. One surgeon clarified from the first meeting that his main interest was his pig farm, and his medicine was to fund this enterprise.

The cardiology consultants were an interesting bunch. One of them was always attired in the most exquisitely cut suits and always wore a fresh red carnation in his buttonhole. One week when sitting in this doctor's clinics, all five of his medical students decided to wear a fresh red carnation in their buttonholes. The consultant did not show by a word he said, or even his attitude, that he had noticed anything unusual, and the medical student put this down as a rather expensive flop. The next week the students turned up to the clinic as normal, but just before starting the clinic, the consultant paused, reached under the desk, pulled out a box of red carnations, and handed them around. When every student had put one in their buttonhole, our consultant said, "Now we are properly dressed, gentlemen, we can continue." It was a brilliant putdown!

The other consultant cardiologist was exceedingly proud of his racing green Alvis sports car and always parked it directly outside the front of the hospital. One morning after work, he went to get into his car to go home and found another Alvis of the same model and year and painted bright red parked directly next to his. He returned to the hospital and asked the porters who the car belonged to. He was told that it belonged to an Iranian princess, a medical student in our year, bought for her by her father. The racing green Alvis never appeared at the hospital again, though 4 weeks later, a racing green AC sports car could be found parked in the same place. There was also one consultant who, if there were road works going on below the ward when he was doing a grand round, would send his house officer down to speak to the workmen to tell them that they were making too much noise and the consultant could not hear himself think. They were told to stop work immediately, and they could restart after one and a half hours. The workmen usually gladly complied and sloped off into the King and Queen pub.

The medical students received a mixture of academic and clinical teaching. Much of this clinical teaching was done by the students being attached to a consultant's firm in each specialty. The clinical firm was, at that stage, a key institution of clinical care. A senior consultant would have a team of doctors who worked with and for him. This would consist of a senior registrar, who would be fully qualified and have had training in all aspects of his chosen specialty. He or occasionally she would have taken and passed the exam leading to specialist status, the MRCP in medicine and the FRCS in surgery. He would be a consultant in waiting, often applying for jobs and, sometimes, deputising for the firm's consultant. Below him would be a registrar who would have passed all his exams but could well be doing a research programme leading to the degree of MD (as opposed to the basic MB). This was the medical equivalent of a PhD. Below him would be one or two senior house officers who would be in training and working towards passing the specialist exams. And below them would be the pre-registration house officers who were doctors just out of medical school and very wet behind the ears. These doctors had to work under strict supervision in at least two specialties before they were allowed to take much personal responsibility.

On the grand rounds, the consultant would sweep into the hospital ward with these 6 people in tow, together with the ward sister and perhaps another senior nurse, so a crowd of about 9 people. They would pass from bed to bed with the consultant reigning with absolute power and being treated as a minor deity. A good consultant would personally greet the patient upon their arrival at the bedside. Then, after a discussion involving the whole firm, explain to them what had been decided and why. The bad consultant would barely acknowledge the patient, and everybody would talk over their heads. It was at these rounds and in the clinics that a great deal of the teaching took place, and it was fascinating to see that patients who had had an illness for some years seemed to know a great deal more about their illness than many of the house officers, let alone the medical students. The whole thing was very much like an apprenticeship.

As a student, one changed firms and often medical specialties about once every two to three months and could absorb all sorts of patterns of care as well as the basics of the care of people with all sorts of illnesses. There were some problems with this system, not all related to delusions of grandeur by the consultants. Not all consultants adhered strictly to evidence-based medicine. Some had idiosyncrasies in their treatment approaches or favoured methods with limited supporting evidence, which would then be passed on to other members of the medical team. However, the firm system instilled a strong sense of loyalty among the medical team members, often leading them to work well beyond their designated clinical session or duty period. While consultants played a significant role in teaching medical students, a substantial portion of their education was also provided by senior registrars and even house officers. A large and very valuable part and an unacknowledged part of their education was carried out by the ward sisters. Much of the caring side of medicine, thinking what this illness meant to individual people and how it had and would change their lives, was done by these formidable bastions of good care, and woe betide you if you did not show care and compassion to their patients.

As a medical student, I continued to work with the Intervarsity fellowship, a fellowship of Christian Unions from universities all over the country. In London, we were members of LIFCU (London Interfaculty Christian Union). One of the great advantages of this membership was that one met with students from all sorts of disciplines rather than only existing in an intense medical bubble. There were Bible studies, prayer meetings and other happenings in relation to our faith. I became joint Missionary Secretary of LIFCU, and so continued my international interests.

As well as attending Christian and social meetings, my friend Phillip and I got involved in the community through the Christian Union. We connected with individuals with unmet needs whom we had encountered in the hospital. One person we got to know was Derrick, who had been afflicted with juvenile rheumatoid arthritis since childhood. At the age of 25, he was left physically deformed and entirely reliant on others for his care. He was also very isolated, apart from a carer who came in to do a certain amount for him every day. His great dream was to be able to lie down in a hot bath. So, Phil and

I used to go to his home once a week, carry Derrick upstairs, and put him in a hot bath. The first time we did this, his face was an absolute picture of delight; week after week, he was over the moon about his bath. After the bath, we carried him downstairs again, dried him off and dressed him. The stairs were steep, and there was a right-angled bend halfway down. One week when carrying him past this bend, I experienced a sudden and unbearable pain in my back and down both legs. I have no idea how we got him downstairs, but had we dropped him, he would have broken into bits! Little did I know that injury was to follow me throughout my life and lead to a laminectomy 13 years later.

Our home church at the Middlesex Hospital was All Souls, Langham Place, where Rev John Stott was the rector. This was a Royal Chapel and the BBC church. John Stott had a brilliant mind, and before becoming a Christian, he was destined for a career in the Foreign Office as a young man. He was a scholar and had the gift of taking a difficult theological subject and not only making it seem simple but applying the principles to the lives of his hearers. He also had a gift for meeting young people, discerning their gifts and, through friendship, teaching, and mentoring, developing them to be useful in their Christian lives. He quickly recognised my interest in international affairs and extended an invitation for me to join the Philadelphia Society at All Souls. This group aimed to nurture individuals who felt called to work in Christian missions outside of the UK. The group involved Bible study, looking at mission theology and practice and mentoring about how to seek God's will for one's life. This was a key time for my spiritual development.

Every evening after our work in the hospital, we used to climb on the number twenty-four bus and wend our way back to the greenery of Hampstead Heath. Very often, we found our paths crossing those of Michael Foot when we, with great delight, wished him a cheery good evening, receiving as ever a scowl in reply. Much of our social life was involved with happenings the commercial and social centre of South End Green. Although we went to church on Sunday at All

Souls Langham Place in central London during the week, we often attended mid-week meetings, Bible studies and social gatherings of our host's church St. Johns Downshire Hill. We thoroughly enjoyed these meetings as the people who turned up were an eclectic group from all areas of the local community. There were people involved in films, publishers, and artists as well as postmen, an academic, engineers, and a person who had never had a job and was housed by the local council. The most stimulating aspect of these meetings was the opportunity to be part of a diverse group of individuals, many of whom would never have crossed paths if it weren't for this church group. We gathered, listened to one another, and discovered a sense of community centred around the Christian faith. Among the participants, there were Christians and non-Christians alike. Some held reservations or even regarded the faith as noxious, yet they were curious to understand what drove Christians and what made their beliefs significant.

For our last year, we were given accommodation in the hospital buildings. This was largely because we were gradually being given more responsibility and were expected to be around during the night and weekend duty call periods. So, David and I deserted our host, the vicar of Hampstead. Within one year, he had applied to become a missionary with the Church Missionary Society, and after training, he was posted to Rwanda. I sometimes wondered whether his reasoning was that if he could cope with Dave and me living with him, he could cope with anything. When we moved into our accommodation, David and I found ourselves lodged in different parts of the hospital site.

Just to the right of the academic block, on Cleveland Street, just across the road from the hospital, was a door. It was not in any way a door that stood out, just a standard health service door. The standard brown paint was a bit chipped, but as doors go, it was functional and was opened by a standard round health service key. Inside, one found oneself in a corridor, which clearly doubled as a junk depository. There were old chairs, tables and filing cabinets, in fact almost anything old that needed to be thrown out of rooms in the academic centre by people who hadn't had the time or motivation to ask permission to throw them away. And there was dust. One did not have the impression that one had entered a major Middlesex Hospital thoroughfare. At the end of the corridor was a flight of stairs and then another flight and yet another.

Peering through the doors on the various landings, one found other corridors with no obvious signs that they were going anywhere. Or perhaps one should say, no obvious evidence that anybody ever went anywhere using them. Finally, one found another door. This door was much like the one leading from Cleveland Street, brown, chipped, and functional and opened with a round key. Inside was a room, not a big room, but one with a bed, a table, and a wardrobe and out of the window was a remarkable roofscape of all the buildings on the Middlesex academic site. And there was a huge radiator far too big for the room, and it was mine! The radiator was a key element of my accommodation. I had no control over when it was on, which was very often, or when it was off. Whatever the season, I found that the window had to be wide open to remain comfortable when the radiator had one of its "on" periods. I have many happy memories of entertaining my friends in my room during the winter, sitting on either side of the window with either rain or snow drifting between us and immediately evaporating or melting on entry to the room. The room was secluded and quiet, with an adequate bathroom located down yet another corridor, which seemed to be exclusively for my use. Moreover, I was just a 2-minute walk away from the bustling hospital and all my friends.

Two episodes stand out from this year. The first was the efforts of my friend, who was unable to progress from his years at Cambridge to his clinical studies because of illness. When he was better, he tried to enrol in clinical studies all over the country and in Scotland, where his family originally came from. Despite performing well in his degree exams at Cambridge and being fully recovered, he faced a series of refusals, one after another. Almost certainly, this was because he had suffered from a psychiatric illness. Eventually, he got fed up with this charade and turned up unannounced at the office of the Dean of the medical school at University College London.

When the Dean's secretary asked him what she could do for him, he said he had come for his interview with the Dean about starting his clinical studies at the beginning of the next semester. The secretary looked at the Dean's diary and said that she was sorry she had no record of an appointment for my friend. My friend said he was sorry about that, but he could not be responsible for the administrative problems of her department. He then asked her to tell the Dean that he was there. The secretary duly told the Dean, who called my friend in and apologised for the mix-up over his appointment. At this point, my friend told him that he had no appointment, but posing as having one was the only way to get in and talk to him. He then told the Dean about his illness and the consequences for his medical studies and asked him if he would accept him for the next semester. The Dean immediately accepted him on the grounds that anybody who had brazened his way into his office deserved to be given a chance to complete his medical studies. In due course, my friend graduated as a doctor.

The second episode concerned our teaching at a satellite teaching hospital in Park Royal in a deprived area in East London, the Central Middlesex Hospital. We were told that we were to receive our endocrinology teaching there. The only way to get to this hospital from the Middlesex Hospital was via the Overground railway system. The journey took a long time and thus involved a very early start and cost a lot of money. We were not happy!

On the second day, for a reason I cannot remember, we were in the main hall of the hospital. This was a little used single-storey hall used for some health education activities and on high days and holidays for hospital parties. The hall had a wash basin and toilet block, which was not locked, where I noticed that there was a hatch in the ceiling giving access to the loft space. David and I piled a chair on top of a table and a stool on top of the chair and pulled ourselves up into the loft space. We found a large, very dusty area with strong ceiling beams for a floor and the tiles above. A germ of an idea formed in our minds. That night we packed enough clothes, toilet accessories etc., for two weeks in a couple of cases, plus a sleeping bag each and two collapsible camp beds and took them to the hospital. It must have seemed odd to see two medical students arrive at the hospital as though they were going on a camping trip, but we were not challenged, and we left our baggage under a table in the hall. The day's work proceeded normally, and we ate our meals in the hospital canteen at night, we built our little tower of tables, chairs and stools and took our cases and beds into the loft space. Since it was springtime and the weather wasn't too cold, we found the two weeks spent in the loft to be a very comfortable lodging. The one thing that amazed us was that although the corridor outside the hall was in constant use day and night, nobody thought it worth investigating why, every day, there was a tower of a table, a chair and a stool standing on top of each other throughout the night.

This last year the burden of work became much greater, and the hours worked much longer. Also, I saw much more of my friends, organised a missionary conference for LIFCU, and became more involved in the life of All Souls Church. The summer arrived, as did the final examinations. Although I was studying in London, I was taking a Cambridge University medical degree, so we had to go through the pantomime that I had to decamp to Cambridge for my exams, as did most of the people examining me. One very agreeable side effect of this charade was that during the exam week, I found myself residing in the same courtyard of Emmanuel College where I had lived as a student. Happily, I passed the final exams, as did David, my best friend, and Annas, a Syrian student who had become a dear friend by this time. I can remember the feeling of relief the week after the exams, getting up late every day, having a long late breakfast and then wandering down Oxford Street. It was also later revealed that David and I had won the hospital scholarships for the best two students. David just pipped me to the post, getting the first scholarship, with me being awarded the second. As the senior scholar,

David was required to give a talk at the very grand dinner at the Savoy Hotel arranged by the Middlesex Hospital for all the big donors every year. Both David and I, by this time, had decided that we wanted to become family doctors, a group of doctors regarded as being very second-class in the medical hierarchy at that time. The hospital president told David that if he said that we both wanted to become family doctors, he would never speak to either of us again and would not give us a reference. David declared loud and clear that we both wanted to be family doctors and that this was a logical decision for the best doctors. True to his word, the president did not speak to either of us again or give us a reference, and it made not one iota of difference to us. We both got much sought-after house jobs at the Middlesex Hospital given to us by consultants who admired David for his courage, and we never again needed to ask the president for a reference.

Early Professional Life and Romance

David and I both landed six months jobs in our teaching hospital, which avoided the hassle of finding pre-registration house jobs elsewhere in London or the country. For the first year of our professional life, we were not allowed to take final responsibility, and we had to refer everything to one of the registrars in our firm. We both worked on surgical wards, David with a general surgeon, and I was with Professor Leslie Le Quesne, a very colourful, amusing and highly intelligent bachelor who was professor of surgery at University College London. His specialty was how best to maintain the fluids in the body during an operation and what were the ideal constituents of these fluids. He was a world expert on this and frequently disappeared for lecturing. He also had a very large clientele at his rooms on Harley Street. To offset the drama and showmanship, the second surgical consultant in this firm was Mr Adrian Marston. He was an exceptionally quiet and considerate man, and observing his surgery was beautiful to watch. He also was much sought after but for different reasons. If a patient came to see him in his clinic, while the patient was with him, he gave the impression that nobody else in the world mattered to him. He had an amazing ability to solve problems and rapidly make an accurate diagnosis and action plan. He would then explain what was wrong and what he proposed to do about it, in simple everyday language, to the patient and make sure that they understood. If they had questions, he would answer these meticulously. He was much loved, and I suppose that I have modelled much of my professional life on him.

Our days started with a ward round of the patients done with the registrar of the firm, unless it was an operating day, in which case, we made a somewhat cursory visit to the ward and then spent the rest of the day in the operating theatre. On other days during our early rounds, we would review any overnight changes and ensure that all the necessary test results, such as ECGs, were available for the consultant round later. When the consultant arrived, a comprehensive round was conducted, with the consultant accompanied by a team of doctors, nurses, physiotherapists, ward clerks, and medical students, moving from patient to patient. The consultant was the king of the castle and decided almost everything himself. I am sure that if a reporter from the Daily Mirror had dressed himself up in a white coat and tagged on to the retinue, they would not have been noticed if they said "yes sir" to the consultant at the right time. One could argue that this was all necessary to make decisions about patients, but things would have been different if the consultant was Mr Marston. In this case, the patient was considered by the whole team, but an important member of that team was always the patient themselves who had their say. They were listened to, and their viewpoints were always considered carefully and politely.

We were on call, that is, taking emergencies for one day and night in three, but even when we were not on an emergency call, we were not allowed to leave the hospital but had to be available to manage the patients of our consultant 24 hours a day, seven days a week. This was normal for pre-registration housemen in those days. During these six months, my father, who lived on the Isle of Wight, became very ill, and I was allowed to go and see him. The hospital administration worked out that if I caught the 5:00 am train to Portsmouth, then a ferry to the island, then another train, I could spend several hours with my father and be able to catch trains that would bring me back to London, arriving at 11:30 pm at night. The only other time we were allowed out of the hospital was to go to communion at All Souls Langham Place church, which was the parish church of the hospital. This was only allowed if we were not on an emergency call that Sunday.

In a sense, this was our final initiation into the life of a working man. We had to make the whole of our social life in the hospital community. Having said that, we found ourselves in very close proximity to a group of young women who had also made the break from home, who had a taxing and all-absorbing job and were looking for something agreeable to fill their time. The nurses either lived in the nurses' home, or several of them rented accommodation in the surrounding area of London in a flat together. The ones who lived in the nurses' home were very much on our doorstep. However, the nurse's home was always guarded by a most fearsome "Home Sister" who sat at a desk seeming to be in every way a normal person until she caught a glimpse of a young male, whereupon she became a fire-breathing monster. The nurse was either not at home (we did wonder how she knew that without contacting them), or they were indisposed (whatever that might mean), or they would welcome anybody to see them, but certainly not us (and that was the first time they had seen us). Ingenuity was required!

After extensive research, we found that there was a laundry lift which went from the basement up to the first floor of the nurses' home without stopping at the ground floor, where one might be accosted by the dragon. The lift was small, but one could fold oneself into it, and there was a control inside the lift. There was some discussion about where this lift was to be found, so Annas, my Syrian friend and I decided to do a reconnaissance. We descended to the basement of the hospital and looked for a connection to the basement of the nurses' home, which must certainly have a connecting tunnel under the road. We decided what direction to head in and started walking. It seemed that we walked for miles down dimly lit tunnels, all of them with dusty pipes and cables near the roof and with a dank, musty smell. Eventually, we got completely lost. Then suddenly, we turned a corner, and there was a young woman in a uniform we did not recognise. We politely asked her to indicate the way to the basement of the nurses' home. She smiled and replied, 'I'm sorry, I don't speak English.' Annas turned to me and exclaimed, 'Bloody hell, Eddie, we must have walked under the Channel!' Happily, we soon found another young woman who could speak English who, with a quizzical look, directed us to the basement of the nurses' home, where we found the lift.

Several of the nurses I briefly went out with seemed to be decidedly dull. Perhaps that was because at Cambridge, one of the things I most appreciated was to form an opinion and expect to have that view challenged by friends and foes alike. I would be expected to defend my views, and if my debating partners could convince me that my views were illogical, unethical, or just plain stupid, I would be expected to be flexible. I found that many of the nurses I went out with held views that seemed to lack a logical basis, often leaning towards the right-wing spectrum. What bothered me even more was their reluctance to defend these views. They seemed resistant to challenging the limitations of their upbringing, and it frustrated me how readily they agreed with everything I said. Of course, there were exceptions to this pattern. The Iranian princess we had previously encountered possessed a wild spirit, and a few nurses displayed lateral thinking abilities and extensive knowledge through their wide reading habits. A few were also pretty. However, there were certain benefits of going out with nurses. If the seats for the shows at West End theatres were not selling well, rather than having numerous empty seats in their theatres, the management used to send free tickets to the Matron's office at the Middlesex Hospital. If one knew a nurse, at times, one could persuade them to apply for two tickets and have a free night out. Then suddenly and somewhat unexpectedly, everything changed.

It was Christmas Eve. Every year all the clinical staff of the hospital were expected to turn up on the wards on Christmas Day. The inpatients were a mixture of people who were too ill to go home or those or were not discharged because the hospital knew they would be alone at Christmas. If there were still free beds, they would be occupied for three days by people who were poor, chronically ill, and living alone. Many of the large stores in Oxford Street and Bond Street, along with a few more seedy joints in Soho (stores for which the Middlesex was their hospital), would send in decorations for the wards and small gifts for the patients. The consultants were expected to visit their respective wards, accompanied by their families, including children, and carve the turkey for the Christmas dinner. So, there was a sense of expectation about the hospital. It seemed as though the dramas, the successes, the sadness and bereavement, the hard work and sleepless nights had just for a day been put on hold. It was almost magic! I decided to wander around the hospital to see what was going on, as there was no real work to do. I climbed the main staircase in the centre of the hospital, which led to most of the wards and for some reason, decided to stop at the fourth-floor landing. The door opened to the landing, and before me was a scene straight out of a Mills and Boon novel. The most beautiful nurse I had ever seen was standing still and quite alone in the middle of the landing, directly under a light from which was hanging a sprig of mistletoe. Naturally, I decided this could not have happened by chance, and I had to rise to the occasion. I went up to her and gave her a kiss. She looked a bit startled, turned towards me and gave me a hearty slap on the cheek, informing me that she was waiting for the ward dinner trolley and that if she were to choose somebody to kiss her, it would certainly not be me. I decided, almost on the spot, that this was the girl for me. She was not only beautiful but had her own mind and was quite capable of making her views known.

Christmas came and went. The sad, the lonely, and the chronically ill people disappeared back to their draughty attic somewhere in Bloomsbury for another year, and the rush and bustle, the arrogance and sadness, the life and death decisions started all over again. However, I decided that some research was needed to find out who this apparition that I had tumbled upon was and where she fitted into the hospital community. I did not have to look far. Her name was Peta Catton, and she was going out with a person whom I knew quite well called Ian. I made it my business to became better acquainted with Ian and found that he was a houseman one year senior to me, was a member of LIFCU and went to the same church as I did. Almost from the beginning of my friendship with Ian, he confided in me that his friendship with Peta was going nowhere. My heart sang! Despite my seemingly disinterested advice that it was morally incorrect to lead a girl on in the manner he was doing, and that the right and honest course of action was to end the relationship, Ian took no action. This situation persisted for several weeks. Eventually, he confided in me about his love for opera and his plan to embark on a train tour of the main opera venues in Italy during the gap between his house jobs. However, he expressed his disappointment that he had no one to accompany him. I jumped at the chance and found myself travelling by train in third-class carriages all over Italy for ten days, going to one opera after another. I had always hated opera. During those ten days, I grew to love opera and finally persuaded Ian to give up Peta as his girlfriend. We arrived back on Saturday; he gave up Peta on Sunday, and I took her out the following Wednesday to a performance of the opera La Bohème at the Royal Opera House Covent Garden. It was only after going out with Peta for a year that she admitted to me that she had already been to a performance of this opera at the Royal Opera House on the Monday of the week that I took her there. She came with me because she wanted to develop our relationship.

Peta was and is a beautiful woman but was not a pretty little airhead like some of her colleagues. She was born in a small town in the delta of Egypt where her father was serving as a colonel in the British army. Her mother oversaw an internment camp for the wives of civilians of nationals from the Axis countries who found themselves in Egypt at the start of the war. However, there didn't seem to be much internment regarding their living conditions.

At the age of 2, Peta moved to Mersin in Turkey, where her father had become British consul for south Turkey and where her Syrian grandmother lived. She chatted to her nanny in Arabic, and her first words to her parents were in French, the language of the educated population of that part of the Middle East. She came to England when she was five for her education and was enrolled in a school called Tolmers. Here she was taught alongside the daughters of Greek shipping magnates and other girls from wealthy families. As far as I could find, she was not taught anything there which could have been of any remote use in her later life apart from, perhaps, how to address a Greek Archduke if you happened to light upon him on the deck of a warship. At the age of 13, she enrolled as a boarder at Bedford High School, where she received a comprehensive education that proved invaluable throughout her life. Following her time at Bedford, she proceeded to train as a nurse at Middlesex Hospital.

In London, she knew exactly where all the best bistros were and what they served. She also loved a vegetarian restaurant, Cranks, where all the food seemed to be coloured brown and tasted of earth. It is a mark of my love for her that I ate there frequently and without complaining. She knew where the best shows were all over London and had an uncanny ability to get seats for these shows for free. She seemed to be very highly regarded in the London young adult society, and I seem to spend a large part of my life fighting off suitors from the past who were chancing their hand again and made it quite clear that they did not approve of me at all, that is if they even deigned to notice me. I was a bit confused myself as to why Peta, with a field like this to choose from, chose me. Peta had recently become a Christian and was over the moon about this. It did not seem to change her outgoing personality; it just seemed to give her an added reason to make more friends and have a great time.

She lived in a basement flat with four friends just round the corner from Harley Street and later moved to rent a house in Islington. This was at a time when Islington had not yet been gentrified, so many of the people on the road were old-style Cockney. The Duke of York pub just round the corner was an old spit and sawdust pub serving only beer. The pub community (largely male) adopted this group of four young Middlesex nurses as their talisman. It always gave them an enormous welcome as long as they gave the assembled company some gossip about what was happening in the hospital. If nothing had happened of interest recently, their creative instincts came into play to produce an often-unlikely story which was immediately swallowed whole by the audience of regular drinkers. I was reluctantly accepted in this environment as a necessary evil. Sometime after our marriage, when we lived in Paris at a language school before working in

Djibouti, we had a Myers Briggs personality assessment. One of the things they do at the end of the assessment was to encapsule their findings in one statement which represented the person they had been working with. For Peta the statement to describe her was "let's have a party!"

Life as a houseman was undeniably demanding, but there were occasional opportunities to take a break and attend a show or dine at a restaurant. However, after only a few months, Peta received distressing news: her grandmother in Turkey had suffered a hip fracture from a fall. Unfortunately, due to the limited medical resources in the relatively underdeveloped setting of Mersin, her grandmother's poor health prevented her from undergoing surgery. As a result, she became bedridden and increasingly reliant on others for her care. Olga, Peta's mother, had servants, but Peta decided to take six weeks off between two postings as a staff nurse at the hospital to return home to Turkey and to nurse her. This left me a bit bereft, to say the least. However, at the end of this period, we arranged to meet up in the lounge at the Berners Hotel, just down the road from the hospital, not really my natural habitat! I arrived at the arranged hour and was confronted by what seemed to be a mass of slim, bronzed women who had stepped out of a celebrity show. I wandered around feeling rather out of my depth until I was tapped on my arm by one of the more beautiful slim, bronzed celebrities, who turned out to be Peta. She had lost weight, gained a tan, and also gained a certain air usually found in young ladies lounging by yachts in St Tropez. Many of the family friends in Mersin are Lebanese Arabs with a distinct French culture. It seemed to me that I would have to get to know this slim-tanned beauty with a French culture all over again, though this seemed a very attractive task on reflection.

And so, the round of junior hospital tasks ground on. From the Middlesex Hospital, I progressed to the Central Middlesex Hospital in Park Royal. It seemed that the only notable factors about Park Royal were the North Circular Road and a huge Guinness factory. Other than that, the area seemed full of small, sometimes terraced houses on depressing-looking roads. On learning that we were moving, John Stott, the vicar of our church, All Souls Langham Place, arranged with one of his friends who lived in the slightly more salubrious areas of this suburb to take us under his wing. Mr Hannam, who turned out to be Chief Inspector Hannam of the Scotland Yard murder squad, had been all over the pages of the Daily Mirror about this time due to his work with a particularly gruesome murder. However, we found him to be a warm fatherly figure with a quiet wife who would probably have been happier if her husband had stayed as a village bobby. They were both committed Christians who took us under their wings during our time there and had us round for meals several times.

I was working on a medical ward and had an ineffectual consultant who rarely made up his mind about anything. I later found that he had been depressed, and soon after I finished my 6-month job at the hospital, he committed suicide. Peta and I found it more and more difficult to be separated at this time, so I bought a VW Beetle. I found a recent second-hand model with very few miles on the clock, and for a good price, the only problem was that it was light green, and I knew that Peta hated green cars. I phoned her up to tell her the glad news that I would be able to get to see her more easily, and her immediate question was, 'What colour is it?' I sensed trouble brewing, but knowing Peta's fondness for pistachio nuts, I confidently replied, 'It's pistachio green.' She seemed satisfied with the answer.

It was in this car that I eventually took Peta to see my parents on the Isle of Wight. We had both been on duty the previous night, and I found considerable difficulty in staying awake during the journey. Peta snoozed in the passenger seat. We did not have enough money to take the car over to the Island on the ferry, so we parked it, arranged for my father to pick us up on the other side and went as foot passengers. It was a cold day, and the boat was relatively empty. We went down to the lounge on the lower deck, where it was warm and found ourselves to be the only people there. We nodded off. After a while, we were awoken by some banging and crashing and thought that we must have arrived. We climbed up to the car deck to find that we were, in fact, at sea. Also, all the cars were facing in the opposite direction from when we had gone to the lounge. I approached one of the crew members and asked, "Excuse me, but where is this boat headed?" The crew member stopped and replied, "What do you mean, mate? This boat only travels from Lymington to Freshwater and back." I persisted, asking, "Yes, but in which direction is it currently heading?" It turns out we had slept through the boat docking, the unloading and reloading of passengers, and now we were unknowingly on our way back to the mainland. We told our friend, the crew member, that we were medics who had been on duty all night. He smiled and advised us to go back downstairs and go to sleep again. In due course, he woke us up when the boat was in Freshwater. We found my father totally unfazed that we were not on the boat he was meeting and had decided we had been too late to catch the boat. With no concern, he waited for the next boat. My parents thought that the girl I had brought home was pretty and pleasant, if a bit scatty.

As well as being a medical houseman at Central Middlesex Hospital, I worked for Dr Jack Dominion as houseman to the psychiatric department. He was an inspirational man, and working with him changed my interest in medicine. He was unorthodox in the extreme, a dedicated Catholic man whose whole emphasis was on the patient. What did it feel like to be ill, what did the patient want from the doctor, and how could we help the patient to fulfil their aims and to be well again? He had very clear views on what caused people to be ill. I remember a ward round with him when I was asked to present the case of a young adult woman with totally disabling anxiety. I worked this case up, presenting the problem, the background, the history, a possible full diagnosis, and varying management plans. I presented the case, and Dr Dominion listened carefully and, in the end, congratulated me on the presentation. He then said, "But what is really wrong with this lady? What has gone wrong?" I was a bit flummoxed about this and thought that I had dealt with this matter in detail. Seeing that I was floundering, Dr Dominion stepped in and said, "What evidence have you that anybody has ever treated this girl with unconditional love? What is her self-image? Does she feel loveable? Does she feel empowered to lead an autonomous life? What she needs is a hug from somebody who loves her and whom she knows will always love her whatever happens". He then went on to describe a possible social treatment plan which would enable this woman to integrate into a safe and loving group. There was also some medication, but this was the least important and most temporary of the treatments. The outcome for this man's patients was excellent and working for him changed how I saw and related to sick people.

My next job was in medicine at Chase Farm Hospital Enfield. This was a completely different kettle of fish from Central Middlesex Hospital. It wasn't that much was going on in Enfield; instead, it was rather an upmarket, dull suburb, much like Park Royal but wealthier. Perhaps it was a bustling community with numerous activities happening, and I simply didn't notice due to being in love, but I doubt it. What truly set it apart were the people we worked with. Dr Birch, my consultant, was as different from my previous boss as could be. He was a brilliant clinician who had also wandered the world and done all sorts of weird and wonderful jobs. He had worked in the third world and had been a doctor on both a large cargo ship and also on a top-drawer cruise liner. He said that the people he was looking after on the cargo ship were immeasurably nicer than the snooty passengers, full of entitlement and their own importance on the cruise liner. If you wanted to know how to treat a person with appendicitis when you had no surgical facilities on the horizon for at least 3 days, or you wanted to embalm a dead body, he was your man. He also believed in giving his junior staff responsibilities while always being on call if one got into a mess. Additionally, I had an Indian registrar who was competent and had a great sense of humour. He played the game of pretending not to understand the British sense of humour and getting people to explain it to him. Have you ever tried to explain a sense of humour? He would string people along and get themselves into a real mess and then, by some offhand remark, show that he had understood what was going on from the beginning. While in Chase

Farm Hospital, I published my first clinical paper in a medical journal with my registrar. It was a report of four very unusual cases of Pyrexia of Undetermined Origin, which had been presented to the medical ward over a matter of two weeks.

In this job, I had dual responsibilities as a houseman in both the paediatric department and the medical department. Specifically, in the paediatric department, I was the only houseman, directly reporting to the consultant without a registrar to provide guidance. My paediatric consultant only worked in Chase Farm Hospital for two and a half days a week, and the rest of the time, she was a consultant in Rochester, two-hour drive away. This meant that just over a year after graduating from being a medical student, I was left for half the week in sole charge of the medical care of any children who came to our hospital, often via the accident department and however ill they were. This came to a head when an extremely ill baby with gross anaemia was admitted to my ward one afternoon.

I made a phone call to my consultant while she was conducting a clinic in Rochester, expressing that I felt overwhelmed by the situation. Unfortunately, she informed me that it was not possible for her to come to Enfield and that I would just have to cope until the next day. I spoke with the medical registrar of my other firm, who, gave me some general advice although he had no responsibility for the paediatric department. When I saw my consultant the next day, I told her that this situation was dangerous, and that some child would die unnecessarily. Her response was that that was the way that things were, and I had better get on with the job. I contacted the hospital administration and received the same response. Happily, we had a good resident's committee of all the junior staff in the hospital whom I approached next. They then went to the management committee and received the same response. This was clearly unsatisfactory and dangerous, so we wrote a letter to the Daily Telegraph, the Times and the Guardian explaining the situation and how dangerous it was to be admitted to Chase Farm Hospital if you were a child. We sent this letter to the management committee and asked them to check the facts we had recorded before we sent it off, as we did not wish to make unfounded allegations. Very rapidly, the management staff contacted us and told us that if the junior doctors sent this letter off, none of the doctors involved would get any references for any future jobs, and they would warn any future employers not to employ us. They put this in writing. We wrote back to them and thanked them very much for informing us of what they would do and that we would send their letter with ours to the three papers so that the readers would know how they responded to our concerns. There was an immediate telephone call from the management committee asking us not to send the letters off and asking us to discuss the problem with them. After the discussion, a paediatric registrar was appointed to cover the consultant's absence, and none of the junior doctors was sanctioned.

My final house job was at Kettering General Hospital in Obstetrics and Gynaecology. This was a provincial hospital with consultants who were highly involved in all aspects of their department. They spent a lot of time teaching junior staff, gave them considerable responsibility and were always on the end of a telephone line and willing to turn out if any of the staff were in trouble. By this time, Peta and I were reasonably certain that we would be spending at least part of our careers in the third world and due to that, the senior consultant, Mr Mitford-Barberton, took me under his wing. He had worked for a long period in Uganda. He told me that in a situation like that, I was sure to find myself sometimes as the only person in the area with any surgical training, and I would have to perform operations I was not fully trained for. He told me that I had to be capable of doing a Caesarean Section, a hysterectomy and an ovariectomy, so he trained me to do this. First, I assisted him in these operations with him, as he explained each step as he went along, then he put me in the position of surgeon, and he assisted me. I gained skills that were later immensely beneficial to me and my patients. For this and many other reasons, I thoroughly enjoyed this job.

At this stage, Peta and her friends lived in a rented house in Islington. This was accessible, had a comfortable lounge and was a good place to see Peta. However, unsurprisingly with a bevy of rather beautiful girls such as this, there were a group of young men who seemed to fancy their chances with one, or another, or all of the group. Quite a number of these had been very keen on Peta before I met her and continued to come around and visit. It was very difficult to ask these men not to come as if challenged, and they would say that they were not actually coming to visit Peta, but one of her housemates. There was a notable occasion when Hedley and I went to a party thrown by all the residents at the house. Several of the young men at the party would fit into the category of "interested in Peta". Hedley and I were made to feel very unwelcome by these people, and we decided that the whole party had been set up by the "get rid of Eddie" set.

Peta seemed totally unaware of what was going on and floated around talking to everybody. After a while, Hedley and I got fed up and decided to leave. We collected our belongings, left the house, and entered my VW beetle. We sat in the cul-de-sac. Winston, the small Caribbean boy from next door, closely watched us. He seemed to spend a lot of his time trying to understand these odd white girls and bemoaning faithless women. We had just started moving when there was a flurry of activity from the house. First, Peta came careering out, looking for us. She tapped on the window and quickly jumped into the back seat. She was rapidly followed by a posse of men, who stood in the centre of the road, arms akimbo, preventing us from leaving. Hedley turned to me and said, "Wow! Eddie, this is just like a scene from a Mills and Boon novel." I locked the car doors and waited. The posse of men informed me that if we wanted to leave, we had to let Peta out. Winston sat on the steps outside his house, scratching his head and thinking, "It's more difficult than I thought to grow up to be a suave man in this society." He wiped his nose on the back of his hand and wandered off toward the pub. After a while, realising that Peta was not going to get out of the car, the men wandered off to the pub, seeking a stiff drink to regain their equanimity as dominant males.

Realising that I had some considerable competition, I decided to ask Peta to marry me, and she accepted. I would love to say that I took her to some romantic spot, got down on one knee and popped the question, but it didn't happen quite likc that. Instead, I looked in Time Out and found a Hungarian restaurant which was given a very good write-up and invited Peta out. I turned up wearing a carnation in my buttonhole, and we arrived at the restaurant. It was clear from the beginning that either the person who wrote the review of the restaurant had never been there or maybe he was a relative of the owner and had been told to give it a good review. The whole place was lit with strip fluorescent lights, with neon lights over the bar. There was a smell of a mixture of overcooked cabbage and rancid oil, and there was a large notice that read, "Dogs not allowed". The waiter came up, wiping his nose on his apron and asked what we wanted, which seemed like an odd question. Most people who turn up at a restaurant want a meal. When I told him that I had reserved a table, he looked surprised. That was clearly not the normal behaviour of the clientele. We were handed a menu by the waiter, who was still wiping his nose, and sat at a table with a grubby tablecloth. Perhaps the waiter had a cold, or maybe it was his habit to wipe his nose the whole time. The average dish seemed to be a burger with peas or a burger with peas and mash or to ring the changes, a burger in a bun. The only drink I could see was Carlsberg's Export in cans. After contemplating the scene and realizing that this was an important part of our education—to realize that places classified as restaurants could be quite so grubby and smelly, and the waiters quite so unprofessional, yet still get a good write-up in Time Out—we left, pleading that Hungarian food didn't really seem to hit the spot that evening. I went home with Peta, and she made an excellent omelette. I surreptitiously popped the carnation into a vase and left it in Peta's house, and the question did not get asked.

Three days later, I finally mustered the courage to address the matter at hand, even if it felt like grasping a nettle (if that is indeed the right word for a marriage proposal). I was sitting with Peta, casually sipping tea. I remember being in my socks, with my feet propped up on the coffee table. I said to Peta, "I have been wondering whether you would agree to marry me." Clearly, the bard within me was struggling to get out. Peta, in a moment of excitement, abruptly halted whatever she was doing, possibly taking a sip from her teacup. She let out several squeaks, jumped up and down, and managed to spill her tea. She leaned in and gave a passionate kiss, expressing her provisional acceptance of my proposal. But, she said, "It is customary where I come from for a man to ask the father first if he wants to marry his daughter before she says yes." This posed a bit of a predicament since Peta's father had passed away. We concluded that we needed to contact Olga, Peta's mother, who resided in Turkey. Now, one might think that making an international phone call was as simple as dialling a number and speaking to the person on the other end. But, alas, it was not the case back then. One had to go through the international operator, which we did. At that time, things were even more complicated because there was a major crisis in the Eastern Mediterranean, with Greece and Turkey being almost at war with each other. I was told by the operator that it would be very difficult to find a line to Turkey, and even if they could find one, it might take at least 2 days to get through. At that point, Peta grabbed the telephone and said, "Look here, young man, this is an emergency. My boyfriend has just asked me to marry him, and he needs to ask the permission of my family before I say yes." The operator turned up the trumps and replied, "Leave it to me, madame. I will do my best." After 45 minutes, the phone rang, and Billy, Peta's cousin in Turkey, was on the other end of the line. Peta's mother had been out playing cards in her club, and Billy was the only man around. He was totally unfazed and said, "I am the senior man in the family around, and I give you my permission." I thanked him politely while Peta jumped up and down, squeaked a bit more, and said yes. It turned out that the operator had classified the call as a major emergency, and a line had been found passing via Athens to Turkey, the country that Greece was threatening to bomb. Even now, occasionally, one can find people who will step out of the box and make things happen. Our engagement photos were done free for us by the magazine Country Life on the understanding that they could use Peta's photo and our wedding announcement as the front inside page of the magazine where there was always such an announcement. Our only lasting regret about our engagement was that it was announced in the Times and Telegraph by chance on the day of the Aberfan disaster, a time of great sadness. Probably due to this reason, Peta's photo was never published.

As we were now engaged, we spent most weekends together. I had a two-bedroom flat, which suited us very well. It was located on the ground floor, and unfortunately, everything seemed to be brown. The front door, the carpets, the skirting boards, the kitchen decor, and even the towels provided were all brown. It felt like fate that wherever I moved within the health service accommodation, I would end up in places with a brown colour scheme. I once assumed there was a central regulation dictating that all flats in the health sector should be brown, but then I discovered that some of my colleagues had flats painted in cream or blue. One colleague even took it upon themselves to redecorate their entire flat with rainbow colours because they weren't pleased with the original scheme. Yet, it appeared that I was destined to always end up in brown flats. As well as the overwhelming brownness of the flat, I found that I had followed an Indian family there. I have spent a long time in India, and I love curry, and I love many of the Indian people I have met, but to open one's front door and be immediately hit by the smell of stale curry did not fill me with joy.

Despite this, having Peta, there changed everything. She cooked wonderful meals for me when I was on duty, and when I was off, we went out together. At times, she used to arrive at Kettering quite late in the evening and after a hard day's work, so I asked the catering staff if Peta could eat in the staff dining room and I would pay for her meals under these circumstances. They agreed. At the end of the first month, I duly arrived at the hospital's finance office with my chequebook to pay for Peta's meals, only to be told that there was no facility to receive money for this sort of payment and there was no billing system. I asked what to do and was told that the easiest way to deal with this matter was for Peta to eat the meals, and the hospital would not demand payment. This news brought me great delight. However, my joy was short-lived when I received an official letter from the hospital's matron halfway through my job. In the letter, the matron complained that almost every weekend, I was living with my girlfriend (whom I was not married to) in a hospital flat and that this sort of immorality was a bad example to her nurses and was quite unacceptable. Moreover, I was not only living with my girlfriend, to whom I was not married, but I was brazenly bringing her to the staff dining room for meals I had not paid for. She demanded that I change this unacceptable behaviour forthwith. This attack somewhat took me aback. I wrote back and told the matron that part of Peta and my shared faith was that we should not sleep together before we were married, and this was easy in a two-bedroomed flat. Also, I had tried to pay for our meals, but my offer had been refused. I added that I would be delighted to explain the situation in more detail to her, but only in the environment of a courtroom and in the context of a case of libel against her for writing such scurrilous accusations against us. There was an immediate and absolute change in behaviour from the matron, with her coming in person to the flat and apologising. We had a reasonable relationship for the rest of our time at Kettering.

Marriage and Off Abroad

Towards the end of our time at Kettering, we started planning major changes in our lives. Firstly, we decided to get married, then we also decided that hospital medicine was interesting and challenging, but neither of us truly enjoyed the intermittent short-term contact with our patients. So, we decided that our professional lives would be working in the community, me as a GP and Peta as a health visitor. Finally, we both admitted that we did not want to settle quite yet in the UK. Peta had been brought up partly in the Middle East, and my trip to India had changed me forever. We did not know at that time how that might work out, but we decided that at least part of our lives would likely be spent abroad.

Getting married was at the top of our agenda. However, as Peta was the only member of her core family in the UK, and my parents were living in the Isle of Wight and not in any way proactive people, the organising of the whole thing rested on us. Well, to be precise, it fell on Peta. By this time, she was working for a baby food firm giving advice to worried mothers all over the world. She assured me that this was in no way a sales pitch and that the advice she gave was valuable and clinically correct. I was somewhat sceptical as she often brought home tales of bizarre requests for help, such as a request from a mother about what to call her new twins, a boy, and a girl. Writing under her official name of Dorothy Cameron, she suggested they should be called Peta and Edwin. The mother thanked her profusely but informed her that their father had demanded they be called Omo and Daz. Over the course of several weeks, we made arrangements for the wedding to take place at the daughter church of All Souls Langham Place, St Peter's Church Vere Street, located behind Oxford Street in the west end of London. We booked Hanover Lodge in Regents Park for our reception. We were interested to see recently that this is now part of the Regents Park Mosque. We scheduled the wedding date shortly after I began my next job.

We thought long and hard about what to do over our careers. Eventually, Peta enrolled in a course to become a health visitor at the North London Polytechnic, which has now become part of the London Metropolitan University. Meanwhile, I began searching for a General Practice to join. It seemed illogical to join a practice at a time when this usually meant that you stayed in the job you were appointed to for life when we were turning over in our mind working abroad. Eventually, I came across a relatively new scheme where young doctors became trainee General Practitioners to an established practice. According to the blurb, this meant that you had a designated trainer who would introduce you to the discipline of family practice and give you regular training sessions. The significant advantage for young doctors appeared to be the opportunity to make early mistakes and gain experience under someone else's guidance before eventually establishing their own practice.

It was finally decided that we would get married one month after I started my training at the practice. Suddenly, life became extremely busy as we sent out invitations, arranged the details of the service, and made preparations for Peta's family to come over from Turkey. Peta took charge of most of these arrangements. As the wedding date approached, presents began arriving and were stored at Peta's flat. Since we were getting married, my best friend David decided that he and his fiancée would have their wedding two weeks before ours, and we would each serve as best men at each other's weddings. Olga, Peta's mother, arrived about three weeks before the wedding causing quite a splash. She was a short lady with a huge personality. Her voice had a raspy quality, a result of her heavy smoking, and she had a remarkable ability to command attention whenever she entered a room, almost like royalty. She had very certain views of the way in which her daughter should live as a married lady and made these quite clear. We took her to see my parents on the Isle of Wight, and my mother suggested a brisk walk up on the downs. Olga's worst dreams were of going for a walk on any hill. Instead, she made it quite clear that what she wanted to do was to sit and talk and smoke nonstop, which was a scenario from my mother's worst dreams.

We passed an interesting afternoon, and with gratitude, we boarded the train to return to London. Confronted with Olga's strong-willed personality and her apparent desire for me to purchase a manor house and establish Peta as a country lady, I reached a breaking point. In the midst of this turmoil, I called Peta at 3:00 am to inform her that I was calling off the wedding. With great aplomb, Peta listened to me and suggested that we meet the next day and discuss it. The next day, she simply asked me whether I was proposing to marry her mother or her. Her question struck a chord, and in that moment, she embraced me, and everything suddenly felt right again. One further problem turned up with the music which Peta had wanted to have during our wedding service. She had chosen the drinking song from the Opera La Traviata to play at the start of the service and Ave Maria to play while we signed the register. The organist gently pointed out to her that she had chosen the drinking song from an Opera called The Prostitute at the start of the service and an anthem of praise to Mary, a process which is not biblical, in the middle of the service. The music we had chosen to walk out to, the Grand March from the opera Aida, was apparently acceptable. After some grumbling, different music for the first two periods was eventually selected.

The much-awaited day had finally arrived. The night before the wedding, I stayed with my best man, who then drove me to the ceremony in his somewhat beaten-up Mini car. As we reached Vere Street, where the church was located just behind Oxford Street, it suddenly dawned on us that that we had not arranged where to park the car. While we sat in the car, parked on the double yellow lines outside the church, wondering what to do, a police car drew up to see what we were doing. Both of us, dressed in our morning suits, stepped out of the Mini and approached the police officers to inquire about nearby parking options. Upon seeing us, the officers asked, "Who is getting married?" Somewhat sheepishly, I admitted that I was. The driver of the police car then proposed an idea, saying, "Here's a proposition for you. If you'd like a getaway car, we can provide one with blue lights, sirens, and all the bells and whistles. You could be free of all this and on your way in no time." I genuinely considered the offer and expressed my sincere gratitude but ultimately decided to proceed with the wedding. The driver of the police car turned to his companion and remarked, "There are some people you just can't help." He then addressed me, saying, "Leave the car here; I can guarantee you won't get a ticket." With a playful wink in my direction, he drove away. In those days, it was customary for the bride's family to cover the expenses of the wedding, while the groom's family took care of the bridal car. I was thrilled to learn that Peta's guardian, Uncle Bill, who happened to drive a Rolls Royce, was willing to serve as her chauffeur. He even bought a chauffeur's hat to play the part more realistically. The only problem remaining was that Peta was extremely fond of Uncle Bill and adamantly refused to travel in the back of the car. So, this wedding was probably the only one in the world ever where the bride arrived at the church in a rather splendid Rolls Royce, sitting in the front seat alongside the chauffeur waving to all the American tourists as she drove down Oxford Street.

The wedding service, though somewhat of a blur in my memory, was a wonderful occasion. The moments leading up to Peta and me standing at the altar rail and receiving the blessing as husband and wife seemed to pass in a haze. I distinctly recall looking at Peta and thinking, "I'm not quite sure how I managed to convince the most beautiful woman in the world to marry me." And then, with her first words as my wife, Peta asked, “Please can I borrow your hanky?” As we exited the church, the triumphant notes of "The Triumphal March" from Aida filled the air. I somehow found myself on the wrong side of my bride, though I must admit I wasn't entirely clear which side I should have been on. Nevertheless, we walked out together, with the Rolls Royce awaiting us to whisk us away to Hanover Lodge in the picturesque beauty of Regent's Park. This time, both of us sat in the back of the car, savouring the moments of joy and celebration as we embarked on this new chapter of our lives. As Peta continued to wave to the American tourists, it seemed that all the women were nudging their husbands and saying, "Gee, Albert, there's a bride!" I suppose it meant that they were taking in their surroundings rather than just ticking off "cultural happening" on their tour checklist. We had champagne and canapés, I gave a speech, and we cut the cake, and then we were off for our first night at a rural pub before flying out to Minorca. Those were civilised days when one could say hello to all the guests, at times struggling to remember names of ancient long-lost relatives resurrected for the occasion, making sure that everybody had a third glass of champagne and then making ourselves scarce. After all, though I loved my friends and family, the person I most wanted to be with alone was my new wife. Along the way to the pub, I had a minor row with a driver who cut in on us on the road. I caught Peta looking at me with a reflective expression, perhaps pondering who this man was that she had just married.

That was a time of great austerity, and one was only allowed to take a small amount of sterling abroad. The allowance was, for some reason, called the V form. So, for this reason, and because we had been warned not to think that a completely secluded cottage as an ideal honeymoon venue, we decided to book our honeymoon through a villa party. The company was a rather zany setup called Murrison Small, which rented out groups of villas in out-of-the-way places and put in a couple of girls in their early twenties who were looking for something to do in the summer to cook and look after their guests. These were known as the Murribirds. By arranging our honeymoon in this manner, we paid most of the holiday cost in England, allowing us to have more of the precious V form money to spend as we pleased while on vacation. The next morning, we turned up to Gatwick Airport to catch our plane, which turned out to be a rather superannuated DC3 of Second World War vintage. It rattled a bit if the pilots got a bit enthusiastic with the throttle, and it needed to stop off for a rest and to pick up fuel at Perpignan before it could make it to Minorca, but finally, we arrived safely.

Upon arriving at the airport, we were greeted and transported to Callan Porter, which, at that time, was one of the few villa developments in an island with limited tourist infrastructure. We found ourselves amidst a cluster of three comfortable villas, surrounded by a vibrant group of twelve young people around our age who were part of the same villa party. Our Murribirds were a pleasant couple, two girls of about our age. They seemed to have a fixation on mashed potatoes and peas, which we got served with various accompaniments for two weeks. We were given a room right in the middle of everything going on and looking out onto the balcony where the party ate, drank, and spent long hours during the evening telling tall stories and generally putting the world right. We certainly were not spending our honeymoon in an isolated environment. Our room only had one window opening directly out onto this veranda, and nobody in Minorca at that time seemed to have air-conditioning. So, we had two options. Firstly, we could leave the shutters open and give our fellow villa party members a real-life demonstration of how a couple just married and who had not previously lived together got to know each other, or we could close the shutters and bake. We had previously decided not to tell people that we were on honeymoon, but I sloped off and sheepishly told one of our Murribirds that we were just married. As a result, we were promptly moved from our room in the midst of all the activity to a more secluded and spacious room. This change suited us perfectly, especially since the new room offered more comfort and privacy.

Included in the holiday price was a hire car, one Fiat Topolino 500 cc, which accommodated two adults and two small children in a pinch, for a group of 12 people. For some unknown reason, I seemed to be designated as the driver, perhaps because I was one of the few people to remember to bring my driving licence. We managed to transport nine people at a time with people sitting inside, people standing with heads out of the sunshine roof, people sitting on the open boot and at one time, one person sitting on the front mudguard. Minorca's hilly terrain presented occasional challenges during our explorations.

Despite this, we managed to visit various parts of the island, which seemed to be served by two main roads—one roughly north to south and the other east to west. In the middle of the island, there was an intersection where a police officer was stationed for traffic control. However, since there were very few cars, the officer spent most of his time sitting at a conveniently located café near the junction. When he heard a car approaching, he would quickly stand in the middle of the road and signal the car to continue. Whenever we encountered him, he would have a drink in his hand, and as the afternoon wore on, he would be waving cars on from the comfort of his café seat.

We discovered a nightclub nestled within local caves where we joyously danced away the hours well into the night. Many of the island's beautiful coves were inaccessible by road, so we often rented a boat among ourselves and spent our days sunbathing and swimming in these secluded spots. These coves typically featured small bars, run by well-built, sun-kissed young men with pitch-black moustaches—seemingly all named André. These bars managed to serve local wine, rum and coke, as well as delicious red mullet and chips. Interestingly, during our time on the island, Peta developed a newfound appreciation for rum and coke, despite not having liked either of them before. Perhaps it was a fondness for pitch-black moustaches or a liking for the name André that played a role. Whatever we had been doing during the day, we seemed to land up at about 5.00 pm at a restaurant on the quay at Mahon, the capital of the island, for a large freshly caught seafood meal, purely to fortify us to deal with the mashed potato and peas that we knew were being prepared for the evening meal by our Murribirds.

It all went in a whirl, and before we wanted it, our wheezing rattling old DC3 had come to take us home. One interesting postscript to the honeymoon was that a couple who met on this holiday later got married. When they were getting quotes for the invitations and service sheets, the bride's mother picked up one and said to her daughter, "Even gay weddings get proper invitations and service sheets these days. This wedding was for Edwin and Peter!" Her daughter said, "Let me have a look! They were on holiday with us and on their honeymoon, and they are an ordinary couple. Peter is Peter-Mary" (that was before Peta changed the spelling of her name). It turned out that this other couple had chosen the same music for their wedding as we did, and we were extended an invitation to attend their wedding. The only difference was that the groom, in this case, was a major in the army, and the music was performed by the full regimental band. This was wonderful, except the wedding was held in a small and exceedingly old church, and the band had to play outside of the church in case the sound caused some structural damage to the church, especially when playing the Grand March from Aida.

And so, back to reality. Our new home was the upper story of a very small, terraced workman's cottage in a village. The lower story was a branch surgery for the practice in a nearby town where I was a training registrar in General Practice. The surgery consisted of the front room, which was a waiting room. The back room, which served as the consulting room and off this room was a toilet, the only toilet in the building which was in a lean-to building. Off the waiting room was a door leading directly onto a steep staircase. At the top of the staircase was a tiny landing with a door to the right leading to a small bedroom and a door to the left leading into a room with a table, four chairs and two armchairs. There was a gas fire. If we entertained friends to a meal, we had to turn the gas fire off, and one of the guests had to sit on a chair in the hearth. Through this room was a door leading into the roof area of the lean-to building which had been fitted out with a kitchen sink and a gas stove. There was also a bath with a hinged shelf over it. When this was lowered onto the bath, it was the only working surface in the kitchen. There was no shower. If we were entertaining and I was late back from doing surgery, I could find myself sitting in the bath holding two saucepans for Peta as she was cooking the meal and had nowhere else to put them. While we were entertaining guests, if one needed to go to the toilet, there was often a surgery going on downstairs. So, the hapless guest would have to go downstairs into the waiting room, nod to the waiting patients, go into the consulting room, often interrupting a consultation, sometimes with a partly undressed patient, and go to the toilet. When they had finished, they had to run the gauntlet again in reverse.

I was attached to a wealthy practice with 15,000 NHS patients and about 1,500 private patients, on which the five partners spent much of their time. When I arrived, I spent two weeks with various partners during their consultations and visits. I was introduced to the local hospital, and then I was on my own with my own consultation sessions and my own list of visits. I was told that if there was anything I did not understand, I was very welcome to make an appointment with one of the partners, and they would explain the subject to me.

I was the trainee of the senior partner. There was no scheduled training on the structure of general practice, the specific discipline of the specialty, community medicine skills, professional relationships with hospitals and consultants, or the proper utilisation of investigations. Initially, I found everything to be quite exciting, and as someone who relishes challenges, I was content with my circumstances. However, it gradually dawned on me that this lack of structured training was less than ideal, particularly when I attended a conference organised by the Christian Medical Fellowship (CMF), of which I was a member. At the conference, I discovered that my fellow trainee GPs, who were also CMF members, were receiving organised teaching sessions and benefiting from a comprehensive programme that covered the discipline of family medicine. On return to the practice, I brought up the matter of teaching with my trainer and the offer was again made to explain any difficulty I had, nothing more.

In addition to these challenges, there was an incident one evening when I fell ill with flu on the day I was scheduled to conduct a surgery. I was bedridden with a high temperature of 40 degrees Celsius, feeling extremely unwell. Peta took it upon herself to call the senior partner of the practice I was working with to inform him and apologise for the fact that I would be unable to perform the surgery... His response was, "Oh dear, that is a real nuisance. Well, you can do the surgery. You can take the prescriptions upstairs for him to sign, and if you are not sure what to do, you can go upstairs and ask his advice." Peta told him in no uncertain terms that she was not a doctor, it would be totally unethical to do that, and he could do the surgery himself. It was this that prompted me to speak to a senior General Practitioner whom I had met at the CMF conference about what was going on in my so-called training practice. He contacted the organisation tasked with the supervision of the GP training system. They contacted my practice, and instead of improving their training, I was called up before an assembled group of partners and well and truly slated. They informed me that they would take me to court on a charge of slander and that I would not get a reference at the end of my job. I informed them that I was quite happy for them to go ahead with all that they had suggested, and I would await the summons to court from their solicitors and then enjoy telling the court exactly what had happened. The summons never came, but communication between me and the rest of the practice was very sparse for the rest of my time there.

Despite all the challenges, we managed to find happiness for most of our first year together. We were newly married and deeply in love. Each morning, Peta would commute into London via the Underground for her Health Visiting course. In the evenings, we often entertained friends, some of whom we had known from our time in the hospital, inviting them over for meals or visiting their homes. The surrounding countryside where we lived was stunning, and we had many favourite walks. Every two weeks, we went to London and satisfied our cravings for opera and ballet. We found a church in the next village which preached the gospel of the grace of God through Jesus Christ and of freedom. The vicar was a somewhat serious man, but his wife was a unique character. While she held a strong faith, she had zero tolerance for all the pomp and ceremony of the Church of England and made this clear to all and sundry. We were invited to their house for a meal and found that it was decorated in a very unusual way. It seemed that if any surface looked a bit bare, it was immediately covered in hessian. One of the churchwardens was the CEO of one of the large British investment banks, and the other was the local rat catcher.

One Wednesday afternoon, at about 6.30 pm, it was raining and completely dark. Peta was completing a piece of work for her course, and I was reading a novel. It was quiet; the lorry traffic on the Southend Road had died down. There was suddenly a loud scratching noise downstairs in the front room. We were feeling lazy, having had a pre-dinner drink, so we ignored it. Then it happened again. Visions of drug addicts trying to break into the surgery went through our minds. I decided to go and investigate. I left the light off and slid down the stairs as silently as possible. I gingerly opened the door to the front room. There was nothing. I was just about to return upstairs to eat a hot curry being made for me by Peta when the scratching noise happened again. It was just under the front window. I got down on the floor and crept across the room on my stomach. Slowly I raised myself to look over the windowsill to find myself nose to nose with our venerable ratcatcher churchwarden. He had been checking the property for infestation when he had heard a noise inside and had got down on his stomach to look inside over the windowsill, though goodness knows why he had decided to do this in the dark and when it was raining. We greeted each other warmly, then decided that it would be more comfortable, and he would be drier if we both stood up and he came into the house I escorted him upstairs, and he joined us for our meal. It turned out that he had never tasted curry before in his life. Despite being warned that this particular curry was spicy, he decided to give it a try. He was quite an actor, and we spent much of the evening convulsed with laughter as he demanded Peta mop his brow with a damp cloth, and he drank a large proportion of our milk stock to reduce the heat of the food. We also had a bottle of wine and finished the evening as good friends. For the rest of our time in our village, whenever we went to church, the churchwarden used to advise all and sundry never to accept an invitation to a meal with us unless they wanted holes burned in their stomachs.

We also had our share of difficult times. There were moments when I grew frustrated with being sent to Coventry by the partners in the practice I was in, and as Peta came up to her assessments, the pressure on her increased. Also, there was the matter of where we were going to be working during the next year. A wet, cold winter did not improve matters. We had two cars, a second-hand VW Beetle, which started to give trouble, and an extremely old Austin A40 van painted bright blue.

One Saturday afternoon, it was dark and drizzly; the VW was off the road again and was in the garage, and we had one of Peta's nursing friends over for lunch. She had just returned from working in St Lucia for a year and was full of the experience, the sea and mountains, the warmth of the climate and people and the bright colours. Lunch was over, and we took her back home in the van. It was raining, and the windscreen, which we knew leaked, dribbled water continually onto my trousers. We said goodbye to Peta's enthusiastic friend and drove home, cold, wet and deflated. We sat down in our little box of a flat and thought, "There must be more to life than this!" A friend of ours had just landed a job with the Department of Overseas Development, and after a very little discussion, we sat down and wrote a letter to the same department saying, in essence, "Please send us to an island in the sun." After a remarkably short time, a letter came back saying, "Would you like to work for three years in Barbados, The Bahamas or Fiji?" We thought for a little while, but not long. It was really a no-brainer, we could probably afford to go to the Bahamas or Barbados, but Fiji was a long way away, and we might not make it there unless somebody else paid. We sent a letter saying, "Fiji, please," and again, after a few days, we were offered an interview. We spruced ourselves up to impress a bunch of civil servants, and then Peta spoiled it all by falling over a kerb stone and turning up to the interview with holed stockings and a bloodied knee. In the event, this was not a bad thing as all the secretaries to the stiff civil servants formed a tight little huddle around her, clucking loudly and insisting on dressing her knee and giving us a cup of tea each. Eventually, we found the time to be interviewed by four men with blank faces. I remember very little of the interview other than one of them saying, “You do know I hope that the job will not be all about pretty girls dancing in grass skirts under a palm tree.” I thought at the time what an extraordinary thing that was to say in an interview and replied that I was very relieved to hear that we would not be plagued by girls in grass skirts and left it at that. I believe our academic achievements, such as my first-class honours degree from Cambridge and the Hospital Medal from the Middlesex Hospital, played a significant role in the Civil Service's decision to offer us the job. In fact, we were requested to leave almost immediately. I had to put the date back as I had to work a full year in a training practice to count as a fully trained GP. This was agreed, though we were told that our late departure would leave a gap in the medical care in Fiji.

Fiji

My job at my training practice was finished, and we left with little warmth in the goodbyes. We packed up a few odds and bobs which we had accumulated during our year of married life, and these were collected by the Crown Agents, who dealt with all matters of travel with our remaining colonies and taken to Liverpool to be shipped to Fiji. All our family goodbyes were done and dusted, including a visit to Turkey to bid Peta's mother au revoir. This was associated with times of weeping and wailing, though no gnashing of teeth, as Peta's mother did not have any of her own. The problem, it appeared, was that Olga had found her Syrian mother's atlas of great antiquity and looked up Fiji. She found an accurate map of the many islands and an extensive account of the cannibalistic habits of the natives and was thus expecting us to become a part of the diet of the people we would be serving. Our reassurance that things were different now was accepted with some remaining doubts, but happily, it was enough to arrest the weeping and wailing. Finally, we were off.

When we were organising our journey to Fiji, it struck us that we had friends in the USA who were on the way and as somebody else was paying for the ticket, we decided to go and see them. So, we devised our travel itinerary to include a stop in New York, where one of Peta's former nursing friends resided and worked. Our plan was to continue from there to Los Angeles and then take an Air New Zealand flight to Fiji. Curls, Peta's friend, had somehow managed to marry the lead actor in the London stage play West Side Story, an American who was now working in New York. Curls was working in the New York University Hospital, and one of her best friends was employed in the security of JFK airport in the city. This was a huge advantage for us, as when we landed, we were met off the plane by Curls's friend, escorted into the terminal and then taken through a hidden door in one of the passageways. She stamped our passports, and before we knew it, we were meeting Curls on the other side of security. This meant that we were spared the usual long wait and the crass aggressive rudeness, which is a standard experience when one encounters American airport security. Curls took us out of the city to her house in the middle of a wooded plot of about 5 acres. There we had all sorts of new experiences, such as the huge hospitality of Americans and the enormous meals they serve. Then there was the fact that to watch a film, one must endure advertisements every 15 minutes, which last nearly as long as the episode of the film that one has just watched. There were gadgets for everything, which made one wonder whether the arms of Americans would rapidly disappear through disuse atrophy. The bathrooms were enormous, and one wondered what one did with all that space. Perhaps they had bathroom parties! After 3 days, we were off to Los Angeles and Suva in Fiji.

Our plane arrived in Fiji at about 1.00 am. We were met and taken to the airport medical centre where the nurse was expecting us. She informed us that Dr. Bookless, the Deputy Director of Pacific Medical Services, would soon come to meet us. In the meantime, we were instructed to settle in at the medical centre and make ourselves comfortable. The medical centre consisted of a single room equipped with the basic necessities one would expect in a branch of a general practice in the UK. There were three wooden chairs, a table, a kettle, and two examination couches. After a long and tiring flight, we were utterly exhausted and desperate for some semblance of a bed. We engaged in conversation with the nurse on duty, who was friendly but rather shy and lacking in conversational skills. Eventually, Peta and I decided to lie down on the examination couches and tried to sleep. We rapidly discovered that it is not easy to sleep on a very hard examination couch that had seen better days, especially with the harsh glare of fluorescent lights directly shining into our eyes. And to make matters worse, the medical centre was in the heart of the airport, subjected to the intermittent arrival and departure noises. For some unknown reason, these seemed always to happen at night in Fiji. The hours dragged on, but eventually, morning arrived, and promptly at 9:00 am, Dr. Bookless appeared impeccably dressed to meet a couple of slightly dishevelled and sleep-deprived Brits. He expressed his apologies for the poor welcome, explaining that the Colonial Office had only informed him of our arrival the previous afternoon while they had expected us to arrive two months later. So much for the pressure put on us earlier to bring our departure from the UK forward and the story that our absence caused a gap in the Fijian health service. We later learned that this sort of episode was typical when dealing with colonies or ex-colonies at this time. The British government had decided that colonies were a "bad thing" and had reacted to this view by huge incompetence and sloppiness in anything that had to be done for these territories and seemingly forgetting that the people employed there were UK government employees. One consequence of this attitude was that no specific job had been assigned to us. There were no plans in place for our accommodation, and the idea of us having a family home, as stipulated in our contract, had not even been considered.

We were told that for the next two days, we would be staying in the Grand Pacific Hotel in Suva, the capital and then would be flown to Lautoka, the second city of Fiji, which is on the opposite side of the main island where we would be living and working. The Grand Pacific Hotel had been a magnificent landmark in Suva since Victorian times, and many notable people, including Somerset Maughan, had stayed there. Those days were well and truly over, and the hotel was tatty and not too clean. We arrived at the hotel at 10.00 am and were given a room without an outside window. We put all our cases in a corner and decided to lie down for a few hours before lunch. Because our internal clocks were 12 hours behind Fiji time, we woke up at 10.00 pm, all ready to go out and start a new day's experience. We left the room to find that the hotel restaurant had closed at nine pm, and there was nothing edible to be had anywhere in the hotel. Finally, a kindly porter took pity on us and gave us a sandwich and a cup of tea. We took a brief stroll around the hotel and surrounding streets, although it turned out to be a very short one. Suva did not seem to have invested much money in street lighting, and the pavements, such as they were, were full of holes. Fatigued from our journey, we returned to our room around midnight and went back to sleep until about 6.00 am the next morning.

The next day we flew off to Nadi (pronounced Nandi) and then were taken to Lautoka, which would become our home. We were taken from the airport and installed in the Lautoka Hotel as there was no accommodation ready for us. This was quite a plush hotel with air-conditioning, a well-stocked bar and a dining room with live piano music. The only downside was that the pianist only knew about five tunes which he played endlessly. This was fine if you were an American tourist and you were staying at the hotel for two days, and then you left, but we stayed for a month and by the end of that time, we felt like putting in earplugs or just killing the pianist whenever we went to eat. Just across the road from the hotel was the Lautoka Club, a very upper crust place that had always been a club for the colonialists, with the only locals being the people working there. Now it was a club for locals who dressed and talked like colonialists and treated the servants even worse than in the days when they were all white. There were tennis courts, croquet lawns, squash courts, rugby pitches, a traditional English-type bar and, of course, the regulation picture of the Queen above a fireplace where one could never conceive of a fire being needed. At first, it was like being on holiday. Our accommodation and food were all free, there was no work to do and gradually, as word got around, the people with whom we would be working dropped in to say hello.

If we ventured outside the hotel and made our way downhill, we soon arrived at the town. It felt as though we had stepped onto the set of a Wild West movie. The shops, made of wood with verandas, displayed their wares in a vibrant but seemingly unorganised way onto the pavement. Everybody seemed to be standing around talking to everybody else, with nobody in a hurry or seeming to have any time pressure. The population of the town was divided approximately equally between ethnic Fijians and Indians, and it was evident that Fijians conversed with fellow Fijians while Indians socialised with other Indians. The Indians also seemed to have far more drive to get somewhere and do something than the Fijians. The traffic was both noisy and chaotic. A little further on was the market, a colourful noisy place where people, largely women, were sitting in front of stalls and shouting. The noise in the market was so overwhelming that it drowned out any discernible words being shouted. However, the amalgamation of noise, heat, and piles of mangos, pineapples, pawpaws, and vegetables, along with the colourful attire of the women, created a scene reminiscent of a living tableau from a Gauguin painting. We continued our journey to the harbour and the quay, where we had heard about a restaurant called Raymond's, run by a Chinese Fijian. It was lunchtime, and we took a seat at an outdoor table. I enjoyed a Fiji beer while Peta savoured a mango juice as we waited for our meal. Life felt good in that moment. We were served a seafood meal on oversized plates with the peculiar caption "Home for the incurables" encircling the rim. It seemed likely that these plates were purchased in bulk from an auction sale, but we sincerely hoped that it didn't reflect the fate of those who dined at the restaurant. After our meal, we made a stop at one of the two supermarkets in the area, Morris Headstrom. The supermarket had an atmosphere reminiscent of an outback town in Australia, with items such as tin trunks, rope, cane knives, and camping gear available for purchase. In addition to these unique offerings, the supermarket also provided a decent range of food, including meat, vegetables, and exotic fruits.

After around 10 days, we had recovered from our journey and the initial excitement of staying in a nice hotel at someone else's expense had faded away. We found ourselves feeling bored and restless. Eager for some activity, we decided to visit the hospital where we would be working. The hospital was situated on a small hill, with a winding driveway leading up to it. It was an old wooden building with a tin roof that had been painted green many years ago. Each ward was housed in a separate building, connected by covered walkways. In fact, it looked and felt very much like the mission hospital I had spent several weeks working in, in India.

The staff was about three-quarters Fijians or Indians and a quarter English. There seemed to be a total lack of the rigid hierarchy we had grown accustomed to in England. Everybody seemed on good terms with and chatted with everybody else. The only hierarchy was that of Fijian culture, so if a hospital porter was part of a chiefly family, he would rank above a surgeon who was not. The treatment rooms and operating theatres were reasonably equipped, but anything complicated was evacuated to the Colonial War Memorial Hospital in the capital Suva. The mortuary was a separate building on the hospital grounds and was overshadowed by a huge flame tree. I have never seen a larger flame tree on any of my travels; when it was in flower, it was one of the sights of Lautoka.

In due course, the Public Works Department, which was in charge of the accommodation, woke up to the fact that we had arrived and were moved into the first floor of a new block of flats. Peta was delighted because I had warned her about cockroaches as big as dinner plates, flying foxes and other troublesome creatures which lived in the tropics. She was convinced that there would be no such things in a new flat. She was wrong! Our neighbours were a New Zealand couple and a Fijian family. The New Zealand couple called Perfect were very busy people. They seemed to have a lifelong mission of discovering everything about everybody around them, embellishing what they had heard and then making sure they told everybody else about it. They gave us our first project in Fiji. We used to feed them the wildest and most unlikely tales about what was going on and then wait until we heard through the grapevine how they had dressed up what we had told them. They never seemed to tumble to the fact that we were doing this. The Fijian family living just under us was delightful. They had their cassava, yam and sweetcorn patch beside their downstairs flat, and there were undetermined numbers of chickens and children running about all over the place. They loved Jim Reeves and had two of his records which they played over and over again. This induced a sort of PTSD in me, and weeks later, when we had moved away into a house, I would awake sweating in the middle of the night with the sounds of "Distant Drums" or "I Love You Because You Understand, Dear" playing repeatedly in my mind and ringing in my ears. While we were in the flat, we bought a second-hand VW Beetle and started to find our way around the town and get used to the slightly odd traffic rules. For instance, one could get away with all sorts of infractions of the traffic laws, but if one parked beside the curb but not facing in the right direction for the flow of traffic on that side of the road, one was given a hefty fine. We also had seatbelts fitted. It took some time for the garage to locate any, and when they were fitted, people regarded them as some new-fangled and relatively useless bit of equipment.

The day finally arrived for us to move into our permanent house. It was a traditional wooden house with wide eaves, a balcony, and wooden shutters but no glass in the windows. These were covered in insect netting. There were no ceilings, and we looked right up into the roof. When it rained, it poured in Fiji, and the noise of it beating on the tin roof made it impossible to carry on a conversation. The house was on stilts about a metre from the ground and left a cavity under the house. The circulation through this made the house cooler, and the gap provided a convenient place for the rats to live. There was even a garage for the car. Behind the garage there was a small house for our house servant called our house girl in that part of the world. There was also a large lawn cut by a small Indian man who appeared every week during the wet season and only when he was short of money in the dry season. The front fence was falling down, and we had this mended with wooden stakes with wire stretched between them. To our surprise, within a month, the stakes had sprouted, and the fence transformed into a hedge. The house was relatively near the centre of the town on a hill and in a leafy suburb. From the house, we had a grandstand view of what was going on in the town community. Many of the houses were lived in by British, New Zealand or Australian families, many of whom worked for the government and all of whom became our friends. About 50% of the houses were lived in by middle-class Fijian or Indian families, and many of those also became our friends.

One of the things we most enjoyed seeing was what happened if, in the rainy season, it poured rain when the children were going to or coming from school. If this happened, everybody stopped, completely undressed down to their pants, tied all their clothes into a very tight ball and put it on their head. Then they walked on, and when they got to school, they took the clothes off their head, undid the knot and put them back on. The clothes might have been somewhat crumpled, but they were completely dry because they had been tied so tightly.

Our house was old, slightly decrepit, but it was spacious, had two bedrooms and a large room that served as the sitting room, the dining room and the kitchen. Off the kitchen was quite a large larder. To begin with, we stocked all our stores for the house in this larder, but before long, it became evident that it had an altogether different role in the grand purposes of things. It was a magnificent breeding ground for cockroaches. Peta had been partly brought up in the less civilised regions of Turkey, and so she was used to creepy crawlies. However, she hated cockroaches with a deep and permanent loathing. So, we went off to the local Indian drug store and bought some cockroach killer which the person who sold it to us guaranteed to "kill all cockroaches within ten minutes of using it, if not earlier".

We removed all the food and other supplies and carefully and thoroughly sprayed the whole interior of the larder. We went in after about 30 minutes, and just as promised, there were no cockroaches. We were happy, and we solved the problem. However, it turned out that the cockroaches had just found their way outside through the cracks and they rapidly returned. Determined to address the issue, we sprayed the exterior of the larder as well. For a brief period, there were no visible cockroaches. However, to our disappointment, the next morning revealed that the number of cockroaches remained unchanged, both inside and outside the larder. It appears that as we were annoying them on both the inside and the outside of the larder, they crawled through the cracks in the floor and waited for us to go away. We tried two other products, both guaranteed to get rid of cockroaches within ten minutes, and then we gave up. The larder was just made of two wooden partitions fitted into a corner. We destroyed them, took them down to the end of the garden and burned them. About three months later, a group of friendly individuals from the Public Works Department visited our house to assess any necessary maintenance work. After their inspection, they returned to us with a perplexed expression. They mentioned that the house was in good condition, but they couldn't locate the larder as indicated in the plans. We sympathised with them and agreed that this sort of thing was very annoying. We suggested they thoroughly inspect the entire perimeter of the house, hoping they might stumble upon the elusive larder. However, their search yielded no results. We then proposed they explore underneath the house in hopes of finding the missing larder, but to their dismay, they only encountered a few rats. Eventually, they left, still shaking their heads, and we never heard from them again.

Peta had been brought up with servants, but my family never had a cleaning lady. However, in Fiji, we were told that we were required to have a house servant because, with us, they would have a home in the garden and an income. We put around among all our friends that we were looking for a house girl, and one day, Ateca (pronounced Atetha) turned up and presented herself. She was a girl with a very interesting history. She had been a very well-known prostitute in town when one of her friends took her to a Seventh-Day Adventist church meeting. There she found that they treated her with love and respect, so she listened to what they were saying. She heard talk about Jesus, who loved and cared about people like her. He was God, who came to find His lost children and took the penalty for all the bad things that had happened in their lives by dying on the cross. She came to know this person and became one of his followers, and her life was absolutely transformed in a short space of time. This sort of change in a notable and notorious prostitute made a big impact on the town. Her new lifestyle was very attractive, and she became the house girl of the District Commissioner. When he retired back to England, she became our house girl. She was a real find—a tough woman who could look after herself very well. She was a hard worker and a woman full of grace. Knowing how she had been saved from her sins and her destructive lifestyle, she lived a life of thankfulness and wisdom, often accompanied by extremely apposite and funny jokes and comments about the life around her. As a servant, she had one other advantage: she had two great loves, her church and shrimp fishing. However, the food restrictions of the Seventh Day Adventists meant that she was not allowed to eat shellfish. We loved shellfish, so, of course, we helped her with this dilemma by eating all the shrimps she caught. We decided to go to the Methodist Church in Lautoka, which was conveniently down the bottom of our road.

Finally, after several weeks the authorities had got themselves organised enough to get me registered as a doctor in Fiji and had defined a task for me. The hospital served a large proportion of all the residents in the west side country. There was a much better-equipped and staffed hospital in the capital, and each of the outlying towns and islands, all 360 of them, had access to a local hospital with one or two doctors in residence. These local hospitals could handle minor problems, but for patients in the outlying islands, it could take four or more days to transport them to a proper hospital. In Lautoka, the hospital we worked in was a medium sized institution with some specialist care and about 50 doctors. The departments I worked in for any length of time were the Obstetrics and Gynaecology department and the General Medicine department. The latter was very much equivalent to British general practice but had immediate access to specialist medical wards if needed. Two doctors arrived in the morning to find a hall full of about 200 people. If one wanted to see the doctor, one just turned up and took one's turn. Medical care was not free, but it was very highly subsidised. One had to pay the equivalent of 50p, which bought one a consultation, medication, and referral if needed to a specialist. The local doctors worked alone, whereas the expatriate doctors worked with interpreters, if there were interpreters to be had. The supply was very sporadic. This led to the expats rapidly learning at least medical Fijian and Hindi, which were the two languages used other than English in the hospital.

I spent most of my time in Lautoka in the Obstetrics and Gynaecology department. The director of the department was an Indian Obstetrics and Gynaecology specialist trained in Australia. Apart from him there was a locally trained doctor Dr Sewana Tabua, George, a British friend of ours, and me. There was a medical school in Fiji, but the training was only for four years, and the graduates were classed as assistant doctors. However, the more experienced ones were easily as good in this situation as an expatriate. The director of our department was also the director of the hospital, which meant that we saw very little of him. Sewa, however, was excellent, and we felt very happy working under him. There was also a posse of locally trained midwives. We had a 16-bed Obstetric ward and an average birth rate of 38 babies per day. This meant that women used to turn up in labour and spent the first few hours squatting under a tree. Later as the labour became more established if there was a bed free, they were moved into it, and if not, we had some long wide benches meant for seating. They were almost never used for this purpose; instead, a blanket was laid over them, and women in labour lay on them. When they were approaching delivery, an attempt was made to move the women into beds if one was free. We had a delivery room, but as the unit was so overwhelmed, this was divided into two with a blanket hanging from the ceiling, and women were delivered on a bed either side of this, which led to very cramped conditions. Women needing a Caesarean section were moved to the hospital operating theatre and then returned to the Obstetric unit, taking up a valuable bed for about 1 to 2 days. The delivery room and the operating theatre were air-conditioned. There were only two locally trained anaesthetists for the whole hospital, including the surgical and Obstetrics and Gynaecology departments, meaning they were grossly overworked.

People were always delighted when they had babies and celebrated in true Fijian style, which meant that people on the next road, but one could hear a little of the happiness. The best thing for a Fijian man was having twin boys. One particular man, whose wife had twin boys, put his head around the door to ask if he had a baby yet.

When he was told that he had twin boys, he went off noisily celebrating but still came back and poked his head around the door two more times to ask, 'Did you say one baby or two?' Then, he returned and asked, 'Did you say two boy babies?' Each time, the celebrations went up a few decibels. The work was both continuous and hard, but the team was close-knit and supportive. The patients, particularly the Fijians, were enormously grateful and had a great sense of humour.

It was not all hard work. We often went out for meals with both our expat and local friends, but there was a big difference between these two occasions. When we either invited our local friends or were invited by them, the first question was, “Was the time of the dinner English time or Fijian time?” Fijian time was at least one and a half hours after the time originally agreed on. If one arrived at the time one was invited, one would likely find the hostess in the shower if she was at home at all. She might still be in the market buying the ingredients of the meal. Our Fijian friends thought it was too rigid and odd to behave in any other way.

I became friends with a group of men in the hospital, and we went fishing together every Friday night all night. The group consisted of Ali, a porter who owned the boat we used, which had an old skylark outboard motor. Then there was a Chinese man from the laboratory, a Fijian man, a Tongan man from supplies, and me. We used to set out at about 6.00 pm with a powerful paraffin lantern which we hung over the side of the boat to attract the fish. Meanwhile, Ateca moved into our house from her home in the garden to protect Peta. If anybody came to the door, even the police wanting to know about a person injured in an accident, Ateca told them that the Touraga (master) was away and she was guarding the Marama (lady of the house), so they could push off and come back tomorrow. One did not argue with Ateca!

When fishing, we left the quay and moved out into the lagoon on the landward side of the reef, where the water was shallow. We then fished on a short line rolled around a plastic disc and relatively rapidly caught several fish about 30 to 40 cms long. Most of these were kept acting as bait for the larger fish later in the night. However, Ali also doubled up as the cook and produced a delicious fish curry from the rest of the fish on a galley consisting of a rickety primus stove on the bottom of the boat. We ate this with chapatis which Ali had also brought with him. We refrained from having any beer, partly because we were alone and would later be in quite rough seas, but also out of respect for Ali's Muslim beliefs, as we did not want to upset him. When we were all full, we moved off and shot the reef, that is, went over it when a wave produced enough sea depth that we didn't scrape the bottom of the boat. We then fished on the seaward side of the reef at a depth of about 5 metres using a stronger fishing line on a large plastic disc. We never used rods.

The key thing to remember was that the line must never be around any finger, and one must never catch a finger between the line and the disc. The tug from a very large fish could easily amputate a finger caught in the line. The small fish we had caught earlier were impaled on a hook, and the line with a sinker was thrown over the gunwale of the boat. Then one waited with the lantern gently hissing over the side to attract the fish. The lantern light made it impossible to see the brilliant stars in the night sky. Occasionally, a night bird would come and fly around us to investigate who was disturbing their peace. There was the soft repetitive sound of the waves breaking on the reef. During the earlier part of the night, everybody talked about what had happened in the last week and various jokes were cracked, which after a few weeks became entirely predictable. However, I never heard anybody finishing somebody else's joke. It amazed me that in a group of 5 men, all from widely different cultures that humour was so easily shared between us. Then there would be a bite. The bite of a big fish is very powerful, and the fishing line would unravel at a rate of knots. The boat heeled over, and everybody peered over the side. Usually, after about 20 minutes of fighting, the fish would be brought to the side, impaled with a large hook, and then landed in the boat, causing a great deal of flapping about. One had to be careful to prevent the fish from jumping out of the boat.

Occasionally, we would catch a Barracuda. In that case, when it was landed, everybody had to jump up and stand on the gunwales, as this fish would attack everybody around and could cause wounds down to the bone on unwary peoples' ankles. The fish was rapidly dispatched with a hammer, and the barracuda was delicious to eat. Most of the fish we caught were Walu or Pacific Cod, large fish weighing 15-25 pounds. There were various other edible fish. The only fish we threw back were any red-coloured fish as, for some unknown reason, redfish in Fiji were often poisonous. The one thing that we dreaded was to be hauling in a big fish, then suddenly, there would be an almighty tug, and the line would go loose. Reeling the line in, one would only find a fish head on the end. This would mean that a shark had noticed a juicy big fish disabled by being on the end of a line and had taken the fish for itself. The consequence was that the fish would have bled, and sharks could detect blood in the water from almost a mile away, so every shark in the neighbourhood would immediately head for our boat. If we were to carry on fishing, all the fish would be taken before we could land them, so we had the hassle of pulling up our anchor and moving along the reef for about one and a half miles.

Eventually, there would be a lightening in the sky in the east, and the seagulls and other birds started waking up and coming to find who was sharing their fishing grounds without permission. It was time to pull up the anchor and make for home. Usually, by the end of the night, we had caught enough large fish for each of us to take one home, and there still be enough for Ali to sell off to people on the wharf to pay for the maintenance of the boat and the petrol for the outboard motor aa well as making a reasonable profit. I would proudly bring my fish back home to Peta and leave it in the sink for her to find. Apart from barracudas which we had to kill immediately for our safety, most other fish would still be alive. Quite often, the fish would have one final large flap about and land on the floor. Although this often happened, Peta never got used to it very often produced a scream from her. I then headed for bed, and Peta cut the fish up into enough to provide meals for Ateca and us for at least two days.

On weekends off, we sometimes went to a beautiful beach called Sawana Beach, a beach of golden soft sand in a bay ringed with palm trees and with us as the only people to be seen. Usually, we arranged to go with our best friends, a New Zealand couple whose husband was a teacher at the Lautoka secondary school and had a son about one year old. This is a friendship that has lasted until today. To get to the beach, we drove partly on tarmacked roads and partly on tracks through typical Fijian lowland scenery. Most of the fields were full of sugar cane, as this was the dominant crop of this part of the country. Interspersed with the sugar cane would be fields of yams, melons, cassava, and plantations of coconut palms which produced copra.

The drive was relatively easy, apart from one problem. All the sugar cane harvested in the fields was taken to the sugar factory by a series of narrow-gauge railways. There was a considerable network of these trains pulled by diesel engines that used to travel at about 40 mph. There were frequent and unsupervised level crossings that the trains used to hurtle over with only a premonitory short hoot on the horn. One could not see the trains coming as often they were hidden by the sugar cane. The inevitable result was numerous accidents, which people really didn't seem to talk or worry about much. On the way to Sawana Beach, the part of the journey which I always did with my heart in my mouth was crossing a river, where the railway and the road shared a common rickety bridge. One could not see far enough down the track to see if a train was coming. Even though one had to drive across this bridge, keeping the tyres of the car on two relatively narrow planks, a tricky manoeuvre, I always crossed it at speed. Still, when one got to the beach and looked at the clear blue sky reflected in a calm blue sea, the palm trees lining the beach, the rustle of the waves on the beach and the cry of the odd Mynah bird who was trying to steal your food, it all seemed worth it.

One laid out the blanket and the picnic and poured oneself a glass of Australian sherry. The problem was that I was driving so I could not pour a second glass to lessen the disgusting taste. Another downside of this trip was that hundreds of thousands of frogs migrated for about two weeks of the year. I have no idea where they migrated from and where they were going, but what I do know is that they covered all the roads near us on their journey. This meant that driving to the beach then was accompanied by a continual squishing noise as one drove over the frogs. Occasionally, instead of going to the beach, we used to go up Mount Victoria to the government guest house on a rough unmaintained track. This scenery was very different from that of the plain, and the track was in a much worse state. The countryside was heavily wooded, and we drove through several Fijian villages with their homes called bures made of palm stems and leaves. Children, sheep, pigs, chickens, and dogs seemed to mix and frequently run into the road with gay abandon. Much of the cooking was done on fires and sometimes in holes in the ground called lovus. The inhabitants were always very welcoming and waved and came to chat if we stopped. Once on the way, we killed a chicken that flew out in front of us. I went to find the owner to pay for the chicken we had killed. They simply laughed and said, "We were planning to have a chicken for supper tonight. You have just chosen which one."

When we arrived, we found a large house that had been quite luxurious in its time, which was high enough up the mountain that was sometimes cool enough for a fire in the evening. There was even a log pile for this eventuality. The fireplace had its own specific zoological habitat, with each animal having its own territory. On the right of the fireplace lived the largest cockroach that we had ever seen in our life. On the left of the fireplace lived a small and shy mouse, and on the mantlepiece lived a large and aggressive spider. We called the mouse and cockroach Nixon and Bulganin because if one of them appeared, the other one took off in a huff. We called the spider Pompidou because he always took a higher position than anybody else and was aggressive and dismissive of anything outside his spider world.

Living in Fiji was a new life for our family in more ways than one. Almost immediately after we arrived in the country, Peta found that she was pregnant. This was a blessing for us in many ways as everybody talked to a pregnant mum. Peta had all her antenatal care in Lautoka Hospital in the department where I was working. It's an odd feeling when you are part of a team looking after your own pregnant wife. At the antenatal clinics, Peta made friends with locals and members of the largish Australian community who worked at the local sugar processing factory, processing the sugar cane grown in the nearby fields. Those were the days when few people talked about or even knew of the dangers of consuming alcohol during pregnancy. So, several times a week, I would have a Fiji beer, and Peta would have a glass of Australian sherry, which I found distinctively unpleasant. We might both have a glass of Australian "Hospital Brandy" on special days, which was even more disgusting! Still, it did not seem to have done too much damage as later, our baby son attended Cambridge University, became a competent musician, and later became a successful lawyer.

The months rapidly passed, and eventually, Peta went into labour. She was delivered in the same overcrowded delivery suite as everybody else. After being in labour for some time, it was evident that she would have trouble delivering her baby, so a forceps delivery was planned. At that time, another patient also needed a forceps delivery, which I had to perform. So, we ended up in the delivery room, divided into two by a curtain. I was doing a delivery on one side of the curtain while Sewa, my much-loved colleague, was delivering our baby on the other side. The mother I was attending to was slightly hysterical, and I could hear her before she lay down on the bed. Throughout the early part of the delivery, which was done under local anaesthetic, she kept shouting, "I'm going to die, I'm going to die," although she denied having any pain. Eventually, I asked her not to shout as my baby was being delivered on the other side of the curtain. Immediately, she stopped shouting. Both Sewa and I resumed our tasks on either side of the curtain, now in silence. As I was sewing up my patient, a hand emerged around the end of the curtain, holding a baby upside down, and Sewa's voice said, "Your new son, Edwin." The hand disappeared. We finished attending to our respective patients, and then I was able to give Peta a congratulatory hug and meet Simon Benedict (named after my favourite whisky liqueur) Martin. I also told Sewa that I had liked him before, but now he had become a member of our family.

Sadly, Peta was not able to breastfeed Simon, which was not surprising considering she was now living in a very hot and humid climate, and she was likely to be permanently slightly dehydrated. Also, she was in a completely different community with no family around her. In some ways, it was great fun being in an overwhelmingly young community with an average age of about 32, but in other ways, we really missed the company and advice of older people. Peta longed for somebody to talk to when she was worried about Simon, who would be able to say, "Don't worry, all babies go through these sorts of times. Nothing important is wrong." However, this meant that we had to feed Simon on formula feed. On the spur of the moment, I wrote to Glaxo Australasia and said, "I have a new baby whom my wife is unable to breastfeed. Would you be willing to give us a supply of baby food for our young son please?" As a matter of fact, Peta had previously worked with Corn Products, which was a member of the Glaxo family. The company supplied us with a very generous amount of Golden Glaxo baby food and continued doing this later when we moved to the outer islands. The only thing that they asked was that a picture of Simon, who was a very bonnie baby, appeared on all the Golden Glaxo advertisements all over Australasia and Southeast Asia. So, Simon became probably the best-known baby in about one-third of the world!

As time passed, we gained more insight into the inner world of Fijian and Indian community life. A lot of this rested on one disastrous action by the British. About the turn of the 20th century, the British government was trying to reduce the cost of running its colonies and to increase the efficiency of their economies. However, in Fiji, the inhabitants' attitude was that they would work until they had the money for what they needed, and then they would stop working. There is a famous story of an agricultural worker who, upon coming across a man sleeping under a tree, asked him why he didn't wake up and start working. The man asked him why he should do that. The advisor told him that if he worked, he could earn more money. The man asked him, "Why would I want to do that?" The advisor said that he could then buy more things for himself and his family. The man replied, "Why would I want to do that? We have what we need." The advisor continued, "Well then, you could save up and buy your own fields and banana plantation." The man responded, "Why would I want to do that?" The advisor said, "Then you could earn lots of money and live a life of ease without working." The man said, "That's exactly what I am doing now."

So, the British government decided that the land in Fiji was ideal for sugar farming and brought in indentured labour. 62,500 Indians were brought in, and with this labour group, the sugar industry started up and became very successful. The farmers came to the end of their contract and decided they were much better off in Fiji than in India, so they stayed on and brought their families across. They were not allowed to buy any land but only to lease the land and continue farming. They worked hard, had large families and became very successful businesspeople. However long they stayed and worked a plot of land, they were never allowed to buy it. That was a part of the agreement between Queen Victoria and the Fijian chiefs when they originally formally asked her and the British Government to take over the running of the country in 1874. The land would belong in perpetuity to the Fijian people. Not surprisingly, the Indians were upset that in a country where they had been citizens for many generations, they were not allowed to buy land. However, the Fijians, seeing how successful the Indians had become, were not in any way willing to cede what they conceived as their solemn control of all the land. Even Fijians were only allowed temporary control of their land, which finally belonged to the entire Fijian community represented by the chiefs.

So, one was left with a community of two races: one was an easy-going race, not really seeking great wealth, but with a strong central identity; and another race that was much more individualistic and acquisitive, perceiving themselves as earning the great majority of the national wealth but unable to invest in any of the national land mass. Things were made worse by the fact that, by now, there were an almost equal number of Indians and Fijians in the country. Fiji was a democracy, and the Fijians feared that they would land up being governed by an Indian majority government that would change the land laws. This whole problem was largely managed in everyday life by not talking about it, and true friendships or intermarriage between the two races were very rare. We were entertained warmly by people from both communities. The Fijians were immediately friendly and open, with people always going in and out of each other's homes. The Indians were much more reserved, but when one was invited to their homes, the whole family would turn up, but nobody else would be there but the family. On one occasion, we were invited to an Indian family's home and given a sumptuous meal. The father of the host was not mobile enough to turn up, so after the meal, we were taken to the home of the father, which involved driving across a recently harvested field with no road or track. When we arrived, we found that the father and his wife had made us another full meal, starting with an aperitif of a tumbler full of gin. We ploughed our way through it all and made our way back across the field feeling full indeed.

As well as the racial problem, there was a deep belief in and fear of the spirit world. Many Fijian houses had a picture of the Queen on one wall, a cross on another, and on the third wall would be the emblems of the spirit they hoped to appease. The fourth wall consisted of the door. People did not talk about this, even when questioned, but clearly, a lot of fear was involved. The following true story demonstrates the sort of influence that this had on their lives. Between Lautoka and Nadi, there was a small river crossed by a narrow bridge.

The road descended rapidly to the bridge and climbed rapidly again after the bridge. This caused no difficulty during the day; however, the locals were convinced that the spirits of people who had done evil in their lives dwelled around the valley of the river, particularly under the bridge. These spirits slept during the day but came out at night and roamed around the valley. If they caught you, they could damage you or even kill you. The consequence was that there was very little traffic between Lautoka and Nadi when night fell. There were, however, certain times when it was necessary to make this journey at night. If a patient became very ill at the Nadi hospital at night, they had to be transferred to the Lautoka hospital, and all the ambulance drivers were local employees. So, if they had to transport a patient between the two hospitals at night, they drove quite sedately, as befits people with such an important job. However, when they reached the river bridge, they then drove hell for leather down the slope, crossing the bridge with a sickening lurch as they hit the level road, and finally accelerating fiercely up the slope on the other side. The ambulance and ambulance drivers arrived at the hospital all cool, calm, and collected, having avoided being caught by the spirits, whereas the patients if they were not sicker than when they set off, were considerably more shaken. We were to meet this problem head-on later in our stay in Fiji.

As well as the demise of the "paradise" myth of life in the South Pacific, which we had lived through when we first arrived, we realised that though our life in Lautoka was extremely enjoyable, there were supermarkets and all sorts of shops selling most things we bought in England. There was a competent hospital, and the roads were tarmacked. This was not really the adventure we had been seeking. George, the other expat in the Obstetrics and Gynaecology department working with Sewa and me, had come to the same conclusion, so we both decided to ask the authorities to send us somewhere more remote. The Fiji health service was part of an overriding organisation that managed health services in all the British dependencies in the South Pacific. So, I applied for a post in the Gilbert and Ellice Islands, and George applied for a job in the Cook Islands. In the event, we were both posted to the Lau Islands. These were a whole range of about 40 volcanic Fijian islands way out to the east of the main islands and the most remote division of the Fijian nation. The island chain was about 300 kilometres from the nearest main harbour on the main island. Most of the islands were inhabited by subsistence farmers and people who farmed copra. Peta, Simon, and I were sent to the northern half of the island group, and George, Dianne and their little son were posted to the southern half of the chain.

The Lau Islands

So, we started telling people that we were moving and why. Most people thought that we were mad. Life was comfortable in Lautoka, and there was everything that one needed. There was a good hospital, good roads, an airport nearby and lots of people from England and the Antipodes. As gently as we could, we told our friends that this was precisely why we wanted to move. We sadly told Ateca, our house girl, that we would be moving and that we would no longer be able to employ her. She momentarily thought, then said to Peta, "Have you thought about what you are doing? You will be going to a place where there have been no white people for the past 40 years. The only contact with the outside world will be when the copra boat comes in every 6 weeks, if you are lucky . The children will follow you around because you are different and will stand and stare at Simon. The touranga (me) will have to be away for a long time travelling to the different islands, and you (Peta) will be alone. You will not survive alone, so I am coming with you." We were absolutely delighted that she was coming with us as we knew and loved her, and she was part of our family.

We did not immediately understand the enormous sacrifice she would be making. The Fijians in the Lau had a very different culture from the town Fijians and spoke a different dialect. As well as that, as the Lau Islands were between the main islands of Fiji and the Tongan Islands, many of the people living there were Tongans who were very different from Fijians. They were Polynesians, whereas Fijians were Melanesians. However, when Ateca had made up her mind, there was no moving her. We had many parties and packed up our goods, which took up two large packing cases. Ateca's belongings consisted of what looked like a rather fat rolled-up rug.

We made our final goodbyes, and I sold the VW Beetle, which had so valiantly taken us all over the main islands, along unmade-up roads, tracks and across cultivated fields, and we all had fitted into one grossly overloaded taxi to take us to Suva the capital. There, we were going to wait for a copra boat to take us to the outer islands. It appeared that the copra boats set sailed when the captain felt like moving rather than there being a set timetable. We were once again put up in the Grand Pacific Hotel, where the rooms were air-conditioned, a great luxury for us. The air conditioner did not work in the first room we were put in, nor in the second, but we were determined to have our bit of luxury, so we changed rooms twice. Ateca stayed with her relatives in Suva to say goodbye to them before leaving with us.

Our time in Suva coincided with the first visit to Fiji of the Queen and Prince Phillip for a couple of decades. The Queen was much loved and revered in Fiji, so this was a great occasion. All the streetlamps, buildings, and pavement curbs were painted, and the many bulbs in the streetlights that nobody had got around to changing were finally changed. It so happened that the master of the queen's household at that time was Brigadier Hardy Roberts, who had been president of the Middlesex Hospital Trust when we were both at the hospital, and we knew him. He would oversee all the arrangements during the Queen's visit. Peta had written to him as soon as she realised that our posting to the outer islands would coincide with the Royal visit. The Brigadier wrote back to say that he would be delighted to meet an ex-Middlesex Hospital couple and invited us to meet him on board the royal yacht when the Queen was involved in her official duties on land, and he would give us a tour of the yacht. We were to meet on the second day of the visit. We were delighted. Unfortunately, the captain of the Copra boat decided to leave on the second day of the royal visit, and we never met the Brigadier or had our tour of the royal yacht. However, we could see the Britannia sail into Suva harbour accompanied by a whole flotilla of boats, from government ships to outrigger canoes. We were also able to be present when the Queen drove all around Suva to greet her people. The way Fijians show great respect is to remain silent, so we stood with a very large crowd in the main street of the capital city, and as the Queen drove by, you could hear a pin drop, not a wave, not a cheer. For people like us, this seemed odd in the extreme with such exuberant people as the Fijians, but we were assured that this was the correct way to greet your sovereign and leader.

Eventually, we picked up our bits and bobs and made our way to the port, where our transport to the islands was tied to a quay. The Uluilakemba was just over 100 ft long, made in Japan, and owned by the Fiji copra company to collect the copra from the Lau islands. It went in two loops: one around the Northern Lau, where we were going and one around the Southern Lau, where George would be working. Each trip took about two and a half weeks, allowing for unloading and rest time; this meant that the boat called at any island about every six weeks. There were all sorts of things that could disturb this. If there was very bad weather, or the islands had not collected enough copra, the boat did not come. This boat was the only scheduled contact with the outside world for those living on the islands. Copra, the dried flesh inside the coconut, was the mainstay of the whole economy of the islands, and the government services, such as they were, were provided by these boats. There had been another boat called the Tui Lau (The King of the Lau). This boat had sunk a few years ago with the loss of all hands, the passengers, and the cargo. This was confidently put down to the fact that in calling the boat The King of the Lau, the owners had usurped the authority of the high chiefs, and thus it was cursed.

In fact, the Uluilakemba also sank with the loss of 84 lives just two years after we left. The sinking of these boats had far more to do with the fact that, while travelling to the islands, one was susceptible to all the weather of the open Pacific. As well as this, it was well known that the charts were very unreliable, and there were frequent, dangerous, and unmarked reefs scattered liberally over the area. Most of the crews of the boats had known where these reefs were since childhood, but just one mistake by an inexperienced crew member could sink a ship. For each island, there was a reef passage to get through to the safety of the lagoon. To make this passage through the reef, the tide must be exactly right, the sea must not be too rough, and the captain must be sober. Not all these things always happened together, and so there were delays.

We embarked on the boat, were escorted to our cabin, and were made to feel very welcome. The cabin was tiny with two tiny steel bunks, possibly because the boat had been made in Japan, covered by rugs that looked as though they had last been washed about the time that the ship was built. How heavily built Fijians fitted on the bunks, we had no idea. Maybe they slept on the floor as Simon did. The cabin also had an ancient fan, which moved the air detectably but also made a noise that rivalled that of the engines. We spent a day and a night on the boat, and thankfully the sea was calm. Eventually, we arrived at the island, which would be our home for over a year, Vanua Balavu, pronounced Vanuambalavu. We had to wait for a time before the tide was right for the reef passage, then made our way across a lagoon 22 miles in diameter to drop anchor just off Lomaloma, the chief village of this island. Peta, Simon, Ateca and I were taken ashore in one of the lifeboats, and a whole army of tall fit men from the island waded out up to their shoulders in water to manoeuvre the crates of our belongings onto the beach. I was convinced that they would be dropped in the sea, but all the crates were safely landed. We were formally welcomed to the island, but we were also firmly informed that our proper welcome by the chiefs would take place the next day in the church and would be performed by the chief and pastor.

We were taken to our house, which was a standard colonial concrete block walled, tin-roofed three-bedroom house. There were a few such houses in the village, but most of the houses, including that of our neighbour Isikeli and his wife, who later became very good friends, were made of coconut branches and leaves, and called bures. Our house had everything we needed, a kitchen with sinks, a gas cooker and a gas bottle, a sitting room, a toilet, a bathroom and beds and mattresses in the bedrooms. There was also one very odd feature. All the wardrobes had an electric light fitting placed low down near the floor. Apparently, this was to keep your clothes and shoes from going mouldy in the humidity. We had brought with us a kerosene fridge and freezer. There were a few problems, however. There was no tubing to attach the gas bottle to the cooker, no electricity anywhere on the island, no organised running water, and no septic tank or other sanitary arrangements. All these problems were relatively easily resolved. The gas bottle was attached to the cooker with an enema tube, water was brought to the house by pipes from a partially dammed reliable stream behind the house, and a long drop toilet was fixed up in the back garden.

An unusual feature we noted in the back garden between the house and the toilet was that there were numerous holes in the ground. It turned out that these were land crab holes. These creatures slept during the day, but during the night, our back garden was a menagerie of these creatures having a great time together, walking around and waving their claws at all and sundry. Peta's dislike of creepy crawly animals posed a problem if she wanted to go to the toilet at night. Before crossing to the toilet, she would always stand on the house veranda and shout "shoo" at the top of her voice to frighten them away. This had two effects. Firstly, it meant that everybody in the household woke up every time Peta needed the toilet during the night. We learned later that it also caused a further problem. This problem was related to the fact that I decided to disinfect the disgusting mass at the bottom of the long drop hole by putting paper and other combustible matter down the toilet once a week. I added paraffin to this heap and lit it. The locals witnessed the new white woman shouting imprecations before using the toilet at night. Sometimes, they saw a flickering light from the fire in the toilet during the nighttime. Consequently, they believed that the devil lived in our toilet and that all this activity was related to keeping him in check.

Ateca, our house girl, had come with us to support Peta in this very isolated posting. Still, there was no separate accommodation for her, such as the small house in our garden, which she had lived in Lautoka, so she decided to live in our third bedroom. She did much the same work as she did in Lautoka, but here she ate and lived alongside us and became a companion and friend to Peta and Simon. She was later a great support when I had to go off to work on other islands, sometimes for 2 or more weeks. She was also an enormous help as a link for us with the inhabitants of Lomaloma, who were completely unused to having Europeans living alongside them. Frequently Ateca took Simon off into the village, sometimes for hours at a time, and Simon always felt absolutely at home in a large group of Fijian and Tongan babies.

Once all our goods had been safely placed in our house and before really unpacking, we decided to go and look round the village which would now be our home. We found that Lomaloma was two separate villages, one inhabited by the Tongan residents and one by the Fijian residents. Each had its own tracks and slightly different designs of houses, and each had its own church, worshipping in its own language. The grass was soft and very green and cut short around the houses with cane knives. Lilies, hibiscus, passion fruit bushes, and climbers with huge flowers of several colours were everywhere and always seemed to be in flower. We were greeted with great warmth wherever we went, and they made a great fuss of Simon.

Down near the landing ground, there was a large green, surrounded by the primary and secondary schools and the ruined foundations of a number of what had clearly been houses in the past. It turned out that this was where all the white colonialists had their large houses until the last of them left 40-50 years ago. It was an arrangement much like the maidan greens built into every Indian town in colonial times. Further back from the green was the village shop run by Bhagwan. He was believed to be the only Indian man in the Northern Lau group of Islands. Indians were not welcome in this area, but as he was a quiet, hardworking, useful, and kind man with a small quiet, hardworking, useful, and kind family, he was accepted pretty much as an honorary Fijian. This was no ordinary shop; it was up on stilts with wooden steps and a wooden platform leading into the shop, which was also their home. The steps, the platform, the floor of the shop and the counter were all pretty much rotten or eaten by white ants, and one was likely to put a foot through the floor or find the stair rail collapsed every time one ventured into the shop. Each time, a temporary repair was made. These temporary repairs had been going on for at least the last ten years and gave the building a rather attractive hippy look, which couldn't have been more inappropriate for the residents. Bhagwan sold very few lines. Soap, firefighters, fizzy drinks, flour, when it was available, hard ship's biscuits for when it wasn't and tinned fish. The latter struck us as very odd in a village sitting on the beach of a lagoon full of fish waiting to be caught, but apparently, pilchards were a real delicacy in this community. The other unusual feature of the village was a consequence of no motor vehicles on the whole island, so there was no need to build bridges over the creeks, which were full of water in the rainy season. Instead, all of them were bridged with logs which one walked over. The pushchair we had brought for Simon immediately became redundant, and he went everywhere on my shoulders.

The next day, we were to be welcomed by the church and the overall chief Ratu Kenni with his council. Before we left the main island of Fiji, Viti Levu, we were told that the chiefs on the outer islands had very considerable powers and that despite my being posted to Lomaloma as the government doctor, we would have to ask the chief's permission to live and work in his islands. If he did not like us, he was quite within his powers to say, "No, go away," and we would have had to have obeyed that. We were also told that we would have to bring traditional gifts such as rope tobacco for the chief and his council, yangona root to be used for the welcoming ceremony of any notable including us, and a whole range of useful tools and knickknacks. British people were particularly respected in Fiji at that time, as in 1871. The chiefs had asked Queen Victoria to take control of the territories to stop the debilitating wars and disagreements which were currently causing death and chaos. They attributed the peace that they had experienced since then to this governance. Interestingly Fiji was not the only territory to make this request to Queen Victoria to take control of their territory for this same reason. Much the same thing happened in the Gilbert and Ellis Islands, the modern independent Tuvalu.

I was told that I would be expected to speak in the church and at the chief's welcoming ceremony. I found this daunting and asked how long I was expected to talk for. I was told 3 hours would be about right, which I found even more daunting. Brits at that time were known as Vailangi, which translated means men from heaven, as opposed to Kaiviti, which means sons of Fiji. Very happily for me, the Vailangi were counted as so important that they could not possibly be asked to speak themselves, so I was given a matanivanua, or mouthpiece. This person was hugely important as they were expected to speak for senior chiefs, senior members of the government or visiting representatives of the governments of other countries. I did not need to tell the matanivanua what I wanted to say as it was part of his enormous skill to discern without asking what the person concerned wanted to say. This is a brilliant way of communication as the people that the matanivanua were representing were nearly always somebody from outside who had no idea of the culture that it was so important for him to respect, or it could be a rival chief. Using this method of representing the visitor made sure that whether they wanted it or not, the speech would be absolutely in line with the wishes of the local chief and express an undertaking that the visitor would do their very best to comply with all the desires of the chief. Of course, since the matanivanua was the personal representative of the visitor, all the thoughts and undertakings expressed were the personal thoughts and undertakings of the visitor, and he would have to respect what had been undertaken by his matanivanua as long as he was in the territory. What a brilliant system! If it could be introduced into the Western world, it would immediately solve almost all the diplomatic problems between countries.

The big day arrived, and we turned up to church with Simon. A lady took him from Peta, disappeared into the village, and did not reappear until the service was over. Peta, I, and our matanivanua were seated at the front, looking at the congregation. The church was bursting at the seams, with the pastor at the front leading with great energy and considerable dignity. The singing was marvellous. Clearly, the hymns were all based on old Methodist hymns from the days just after the commencement of colonial rule, when under the guidance of the Methodist church, the local chiefs all announced that the religion of Fiji would henceforth be Christianity, and cannibalism and slavery would cease. The Fijian people have a great gift of music, their singing of traditional hymns or popular songs was wonderful. As they sang, the whole church moved with the music. Despite all this, the service was not stiff and formal. The children, pets and even adults wandered in and out of the service. The service went on for about three hours, and then Simon reappeared, and we moved on to the welcome ceremony.

This was a very grand occasion. We found the chief and his council sitting on the village green on woven mats. Behind them were the burres of the inhabitants of the village and the ruins of the colonial village. To the chief's right was the beach and the lagoon (which really was blue) with small waves breaking on the shore. A bit further away was Bhagwan's shop with its patchwork of repairs. On his left were the low buildings of the primary school. In front of the chief was a powerful Fijian man, naked to the waist and a large wooden bowl containing water. The large Fijian was busy immersing the shredded roots of the Yangona plant in water in the bowl and wringing them out time after time.

We were told to sit cross-legged on mats facing the chief about three paces away from him. Sitting cross-legged for a long time was quite a challenge for two stiff-jointed English people, but it was a skill we needed to acquire. Behind us and all around us were all the inhabitants of the village with people who had come to the big occasion from villages further up the coast. Children wandered everywhere. As soon as we were seated, Simon was taken from Peta's arms again and reappeared at the end of the ceremony. A hush descended over the whole gathering, and all eyes were fixed on Ratu Kennie. With great solemnity, he filled a half coconut shell with the liquid from the bowl. The fluid resembled rather dirty washing-up water, but there was no mistaking that this was a very solemn occasion. He handed this to the man who had prepared the drink, who clapped three times and, once relieved of the cup, Ratu Kennie also clapped. The man then slowly walked across the empty circle and, on his knees, offered it to me. I did as I had been instructed and clapped three times. The bowl was put in my hands, and I had to drain the contents in one go. It tasted rather peppery and made my tongue go numb. Yangona has very mild narcotic qualities and can produce a feeling of peace if taken over an evening. It is not addictive and not in any way regulated. As I emptied the bowl, everybody in the gathering also clapped, and I clapped three times as I handed the bowl back. This whole procedure was repeated once more for me and twice for Peta. Various other members of the group were also offered the bowl.

It was then time for the speeches. Ratu Kenie made a long speech via his matanivanua, warmly welcoming us to the islands, granting us permission to live there, and requesting our assistance in providing medical care for the community. Following that, my matanivanua delivered another lengthy speech, the content of which I did not understand at all. However, judging from all the nodding and grunts, it was evidently aligned with the desires of the local community. Afterwards, I presented my gifts, which were exactly what the local senior officers in the capital had suggested. The part of the gift which caused the most excitement was the rope tobacco. Bits of varying lengths were cut off from the rope, the length of the pieces being governed by the position of the recipients in the pecking order. Another gift that was much appreciated was a 20-yard net that was used for fishing from the beach. The other things we had brought also seemed to gain the approval of the gathered community.

We then rose from the mats and went to where the welcome meal was being served. Again, the placement of the guests followed a well-established pattern. At the head of the table was Ratu Kennie. To his right was the pastor, then the school's headmaster and then me and on my right, Peta. The logic of this arrangement was that first came the

Ratu, as he was the God-given ruler of the community. After him, the pastor followed as he taught people about why we were here and what our responsibilities were to God and the community. Then, the headmaster came next because he was the one who imparted the necessary skills to young people, enabling them to live a good, godly, and productive life. Lastly, there was the doctor, whose task was to keep people here alive and in reasonable health, a role that carried with it a lower standing. We were again sitting cross-legged on woven mats with the meal served on mats in front of us, on banana leaves instead of plates, so no arguing about who did the washing up! The meal was enormous, sumptuous, and delicious. There was suckling pig, beef, chicken, many sorts of fish, crabs, and other shellfish, together with bread, fruit, yams and cassava. Everybody joined in with gusto, but the chief sent us some of the most special foods down the table.

The conversation slowly became quieter as people became fuller and sleepier. The Tilly lights were lit, and the hissing of these lights is one of the most soporific sounds I know. Slowly people walked off towards their homes. Simon reappeared from the village, very full and happy, but slightly peeved to find he was back with his boring old parents again instead of with his newfound friends. He was spotlessly clean, though we did not recognise all the clothes he was in. Eventually, we were told it would be polite if we left. We returned to our new home and put Simon to bed. He slept like a log, and we collapsed into our beds.

Another notable event on this memorable day was that Simon was given a Fijian name. This means that he was accepted as a Kaiviti or a true son of Fiji. A Fijian name was given to every Fijian baby on their first birthday. The philosophy behind this was that they probably would live to a ripe old age if they had survived for a year. The name had to say something about the child. So, Simon became Simonesucumailautokalesikilomaloma, which means Simon who was born in Lautoka and came to Lomaloma. This name would never give him the right to a Fijian passport, but any Fijian would recognise that he was a Kaiviti. Twenty-six years later, he took his new bride back to Fiji and signed into his hotel with his Fijian name. Following that, he and his wife were given Fijian rates for everything throughout their stay, meaning they paid only 50% of the tourist rate. The next morning, we were awoken by scrabbling noises and loud clucking. Still half-asleep, we climbed out of bed and went to the back door where we found a whole stem of bananas, three chickens with their feet trussed up, breadfruit, a watermelon, and some taro (the Fijian name for yams). We wondered whether this was the Christmas season in Fiji and were mystified to find all this generosity on our doorstep. Ateca appeared from where she had been in the village since getting up earlier, and we asked her what was going on. Apparently, having agreed that we could live on the islands and care for his subjects, it was the duty of the chief to feed us and meet all our needs for the next month. We were somewhat overcome and made a point of thanking the chief very sincerely. However, the abundance of gifts continued to arrive on our back-doorstep day after day. This was far more than we could eat or to preserve, and we became embarrassed about what to do with all the food. Again, Ateca came to our rescue. She found out the right thing to do was to give away what we were not going to use, which was simple enough. The Fijian culture, particularly in the outback, such as where we lived, involved a close community life. If anybody had excess, it was expected that they would give this to people who did not have enough food, kerosene, soap, or whatever. This community living even extended to such things as radios, tools etc, and if one had, say, two radios, it was common for one to disappear. One eventually found out that somebody who did not have a radio had come and taken the second radio for themselves. This was quite acceptable behaviour and was known as Kerikeri.

We let it be known that we would like to find a dog as a pet and in no time, we were presented with a puppy with some spaniel DNA mixed with that of 101 other mongrels from all over the island. This request for a dog was interpreted as us liking animals, so in no time, we found ourselves also the proud owners of two kittens, a turtle and a pig. We called the puppy Smuts, the kittens were called Pompidou and Nixon as they were always fighting, the turtle was Puccini, as Peta says it made her heart sing. The pig became known as Chairman Mao as he was a thoughtful pig. Smuts took a day or two to settle in, but after that, he became very happy as he found a bosom friend with whom he played all day long, a piglet owned by Isikelli next door. They ran after each other and tumbled all over each other in mock fights, Smuts growling and the piglet, who had no name, squealing. Our pig was a much more sedate than our neighbour's piglet and was taken to the medical services vegetable patch. This patch was planted with taro, casava and watermelon plants and pineapple and pawpaw for fruit. Happily, it was the job of Sovakelli, the delightful and totally illiterate medical caretaker, to look after this.

Glaxo kept sending Golden Glaxo baby food for Simon in what seemed ever-increasing amounts. We tried to contact them and say they were sending far too much and that we would not need any very soon. However, contacting anybody from Lomaloma was a major challenge and trying to contact a faceless company in New Zealand did not work at all. So, we were left wondering what to do with all this excess food. There were very many babies on our islands, but they were all breastfed. There was no malnutrition, the islands were extremely fertile, and the mothers were not in any way interested in baby food, an attitude we supported, so we fed the milk to our animals. The consequence of this was that our dogs and cats had wonderful shiny coats and lots and lots of energy. The turtle had no idea what milk was and showed no inclination to find out. As for Chairman Mao, he thought long and hard about it, then decided that milk was no food for a self-respecting pig and trampled in the container in which we offered it to him. People came from around the village to look at our wonderful pets and marvel at their wonderful coats. We never revealed why!

After a couple of days of settling in, we went to see the medical setup we would be working with. We found that the medical centre was like a large garden shed. Inside were a table and two chairs and shelves on every wall full of either bottles with indecipherable labels or very small quantities of drugs we did recognise, like antibiotics and various other drugs in general use, among which was a supply of local anaesthetic. The obstetric forceps were almost rusted through, and such instruments as specula or forceps were either in very poor condition or absent. One thing that shocked us was that the only oral antibiotic was Chloramphenicol, a drug that can, in rare cases, cause agranulocytosis; that is, it can destroy the white blood cells that fight infection and kill you. There was a small amount of penicillin, but only in injectable forms. Penicillin injections are painful. Oral penicillin was not available from the central medical authorities. All the syringes were old and made of glass, with only three rather blunt needles. This shocked me as part of our task was to immunise the children of the islands with the triple vaccine and against tuberculosis. On asking the nurses how they managed, they said that they drew up the vaccine and injected it into children one after the other with the same needle without sterilisation! There was no electric light in the medical centre, and there was no electricity on the island when we arrived. When we first came to Lomaloma, there was a local doctor resident who left a little time after we arrived. We realised that this doctor had given some sort of medical care before we came, and it was up to us to do as much as we could after he left. Very definitely, the buck stopped with us. If a person needed to be referred to a hospital, it would take about 4 days before the patient reached the hospital. The main contact with the outside world was a somewhat unreliable single sideband radio and the boat, which normally, but not always, turned up every 6 weeks. Apart from this, there was no telephone, mail service or other means of getting help or advice. We could just about pick up Radio Fiji on most days. The other thing that struck me was that if I got ill, there was nobody within several days' travel who had the training to treat me.

The other medical facility was a thirty-nine-foot boat with an unreliable diesel engine. The boat had a rear cabin with two bunks and a forward cabin where the captain and his assistant piloted the boat.

These two men were extremely friendly, and the captain had a set routine every morning. He got up, read the Bible, prayed, carried on with maintenance of the boat, then he took the boat out. He was not always reliably sober at this stage, particularly if we had to go out on an unexpected call. This was not a happy situation as getting to the beach of some of the islands involved passing through difficult and dangerous passages through the reef into the lagoon.

On the other hand, this man had been born and bred on this group of islands, and he knew every reef, every reef passage, every point where one could shelter from a sudden storm and the effect of every phase of the tide. With this boat, we had to travel to the other islands. There were about 20 islands in the northern Lau group, of which 8 were inhabited with 11,000 inhabitants in all. The other islands did not have inhabitants, but in some cases, they had plantations or other agricultural enterprises. The area of the ocean over which these islands were scattered from Walangilala in the north to Cicia in the South was about 180 sea miles from north to south and about 60 sea miles from west to east.

My first week working at the medical centre was quite dramatic. On the second day, a teenager about 16 years old was brought to the centre. He had been fishing with a spear just off the reef when a shark had attacked him. The shark had badly injured his left arm and was very lucky to have got away. As always, such an occurrence attracted a large crowd, so the first thing to be done was to shoo everybody away. Sovakelli was delighted to be given this job and marched around the clearing outside our hut with a large stick, yelling at anybody who came near and waving the stick aggressively. So, everybody retreated behind the row of trees and peered around the trunks. The boy had considerable flesh wounds but, fortunately, no injury to major blood vessels or nerves. As I prepared to sew his injuries up, the boy became more and more anxious, and I was uncertain how much cooperation I would get from him during the procedure, which clearly would take some time. I also was very worried because my supply of local anaesthetic was very limited to deal with such a large wound. Eventually, I decided to give him a brachial plexus nerve block. With this procedure, I could give the boy a small injection above his collarbone to block off all the nerves going to his arm. The young man was relieved to see me coming to him with a small syringe, and there was no problem with the injection. We then waited for about 20 minutes, and then I was able to repair all the injuries to his arm causing no pain at all. This took about 2 hours, and the boy was allowed to go home. This somewhat dramatic procedure and the total lack of pain felt by the boy was important factor in building up some faith in my competence among the people of Lomaloma.

This was lucky for me as I faced a far more difficult situation four days later. One of the women in the village went into labour with her first baby. After some time of trying to push the baby out, it became clear that the labour was not progressing properly. The baby's heart also slowed, indicating that it was getting short of oxygen, so I decided to do a forceps delivery and asked for the obstetric forceps to be brought. They were dirty, heavily rusted and had clearly not been used for years. Peta turned up trumps, first clearing the rust from the forceps with wire wool. When they were at least smooth, she scrubbed them and then boiled them in the largest saucepan we had. By this time, it was dark, and the island had no electricity. To add to that, there was no delivery bed or any other way of supporting the woman's legs during delivery. The medical hut was old, dirty and dusty. Eventually, a 6-foot steel table was found and put in the middle of the village green, which seemed to be the only place around where any procedure could be done in reasonable cleanliness, let alone sterility. Two women were delegated to support the legs of the woman in labour, and two other women were placed beside me with a tilly lamp each to give me some light. The chief turned up and announced that everybody must go home and stay at home until the whole procedure had been finished. Everybody shuffled off to their burres. I proceeded in absolute silence, apart from the sounds of the night animals, to give the lady a local anaesthetic and then deliver the baby with the forceps.

As the baby came to rest on its mother's chest, it gave its first cry, and there was a ragged cheer from behind the trees on all sides of the village green. Clearly, not everybody had obeyed the chief and gone home!

After a somewhat dramatic start to my practice, life settled back into a routine. We woke up with the dawn most mornings as we always have done during our life in postings where there was no electricity, had breakfast, and I set off to consult under a palm tree outside the hut, which was the medical centre. Most of what I saw was much the same as I saw in British practice. There were a lot of minor injuries from farming or fishing or just falling out of trees. Then there were sore throats, bronchitis, infected skin wounds, etc. One of the main things I gained from the consultations I had with the people both from my village and from villages up and down the island was an insight into normal life around us. We learned of how people behaved in families, how teenagers grew up, how teenage rebellion looked in a traditional hierarchical society like this, how people spent their time and socialised, etc.

Occasionally there were more dramatic happenings to deal with. One of the nurses became pregnant. She was not married, and so this was difficult in this society. She was from the chiefly family and came to me and asked me to carry out an abortion, which I was not happy to do. Another nurse, this time not from a chiefly family, similarly got pregnant and came to me in the middle of a miscarriage. I carried out a D&C operation to clean out her womb, but just wondered whether this was an abortion commenced by a local practitioner.

One day a tremendous wind blew with heavy breakers crashing onto the reef, which was just on the horizon. Suddenly an outrigger canoe, which had clearly been made locally from locally available wood, shot over the reef, and a tall Fijian man stepped off the boat. Seeing pallor in a person with dark skin is more difficult, but this man looked almost white. It turned out that he had been eating a swordfish on an island about 60 sea miles away, and a bone had got caught in his throat. He had attempted to pull the bone out of his throat, but this had caused very heavy bleeding, so he had decided to get out of his canoe and come to see the Vuniwai (the Fijian term for doctor) on the main island. He sailed from his island to Lomaloma through huge seas, shot the reef on a large breaker and presented himself to me. I have no idea how he made that journey or why he came alone. He had a very high pulse rate and, when standing, was dizzy. He had clearly lost a very great deal of blood. I managed to remove the bone very carefully without much more blood loss, which was a relief as I had no transfusion equipment of any sort and found him a place with one of his distant relatives with strict instructions that he was to remain in bed at least until I saw him the next morning. The next morning was Sunday, and I popped in to see him before going to church. He was not there! I found somebody in the next bure and asked where he was. I was told that he was in the choir in his church on the island he lived in, and he had gone to choir practice before the service at the local church and was to sing during the service. I saw him later that day, and he seemed none the worse, so I arranged to see him again in two days. The next day both he and his boat had gone. Even though there was still a strong wind and a very high swell in the open sea, he had clearly taken off to return to his island.

As well as clinical medicine responsibilities, I was responsible for a campaign to wipe out filariasis in the islands. This disease is caused by a mosquito-borne parasite that causes elephantiasis, a very disabling condition. Happily, there was no malaria in the country. To eliminate filariasis, everybody on the islands was expected to take tablets every day to kill the parasite. So, there would be none for the insects to carry. The chiefs and village heads had the job of making sure that all the inhabitants in their care took a tablet a week, and this was all recorded in a closely guarded official-looking book, which became a bit like a badge of office. The chiefs were meticulous in this task of tablet giving, so much so that when a young man returned to the village after spending six months doing an apprenticeship on the main island, the chief gave him 26 tablets, all the tablets he had missed by being away, and required him to take them all at the same time. The medication was not toxic to humans even in that dosage, though the man looked a bit under the weather for the next week. The chiefs had also realised that because of the island population's high birth rate, they were running out of land and were supporting a family planning programme. The only family planning available to our service was the pill, but the nurses were trained in managing people who wanted this protection.

My main problem with giving medical care in this setting was the lack of facilities and drugs. Happily, when we were on the main island, we became friends with the Fiji representative of the New Zealand branch of the large drug company Allen and Hanburys. We remained friends with John while working in the Lau islands, and this friendship has lasted to the present day. He has been to see us in the UK and remains a frequent letter writer despite now being 95 years old. When John learned of our dilemma, he contacted his head office, and they agreed to supply us with drugs that were just out of date. My contact in the head office of this company assured me that they were confident that drugs retained their efficacy for at least 6 months after their use-by date and probably much longer than that. This was a total godsend for us. We became probably the best-supplied medical centre in the whole of the country. All I had to do was to let them know what I needed, and if it was available, it arrived after a delay of about two months.

As well as looking after the inhabitants of Lomaloma and those of the other villages in Vanua Balavu, our large island, I was also responsible for the inhabitants of the other eight inhabited islands. Two of the larger islands had resident nurses, who were experienced colleagues, but who also had very few drugs or equipment. My main responsibility in the islands was visiting each island with a team of two or three nurses every two months. During this visit, the children would be brought up to date with their immunisations, I would deal with any clinical problems that the local nurses could not deal with, and I would discuss with the leaders of the local community any concerns that they had. This sounds quite straightforward, but there was a catch. Four of the eight islands had owners who were characters straight out of a boy's storybook with some such title as "Brave Sons of the Empire" (I own a book inherited from my grandfather called just that!).

Munia is an island that is part of the huge reef with a diameter of 22 miles surrounding Vanua Balavu. This was owned and run as a copra plantation by a half Fijian and half German woman. She had the warmth and hospitality of a Fijian and the efficiency of her German upbringing. She seemed to be very content with living and working with the small community of her work team. She had a comfortable home though no electricity. She had a can-do method of identifying problems and sorting them out. For instance, she had continual problems with dogs on her island, finding and eating chickens' eggs before the mother hen could hatch them. So, she had a routine that when a dog was born on the island, after several weeks, she gave each of them a chicken's egg injected with hot chili. The dog would eat the egg, be extremely ill and never touch an egg again.

Mango was a large island that was run by a British gentleman called Jim. He had once been married, but his wife realised she could not cope with this utter isolation and left. He ran a copra plantation which was organised with military precision. The housing was in small but weatherproof huts, all in a line painted green with tin roofs. There was a school where all the school children wore immaculate uniforms, a medical centre, a church, and all painted green with tin roofs. The grass all-round the buildings was cut to produce a finish like a cricket pitch. He lived in a much larger house which was relatively sparsely furnished. A jetty built of wood was in perfect condition for landing cargo just down from the village. There was no doubt at all who was the chief of this island. If one turned up unannounced at the jetty, Jim would arrive with a rifle and tell you to go away, or he would shoot you, and it was no idle threat. You were informed that if you had business on the island, you should explain it over his private radio, which actually worked(!) and make an appointment to come and see him. He used to radio me when it was about time for my visit and invite me to come, but only on the understanding that I brought deworming tablets for all his dogs: no tablets, no visit! When we arrived, everybody who needed care or immunisations was lined up, ready to be seen and then marched off again. He was always very friendly as long as we kept his rules. If we were working late, he invited our boat crew and us to stay the night, and his staff prepared excellent meals for us in Fijian earth ovens called lovus.

The whole atmosphere in Kanacia was completely different. This island was owned by Carpenters, an Australian supermarket and investment firm. It was run by a very quiet and hard-working New Zealand manager and his wife, together with a team of local Fijians. This couple was a delight. There was no side to them at all, and they reminded me of some of the Scottish farmers I had met when I had been hitchhiking around Scotland as a student. Whenever we met his wife, she was dressed in a house coat and pinafore and was busy working in the kitchen of their rather old and decrepit house. Her husband carried out his work with very old-looking tools. The only transport we saw was an old Ford Thames lorry dating back to the fifties. This machine was rusted because much of the island could only be reached by driving around the island at low tide on the beach, spraying salt water everywhere, including all over the chassis and frame of the lorry. He had a team of loyal workers and seemed happy with his utterly isolated life. Sadly, he died from a heart attack on the island shortly after we left Fiji, far from any competent care and days away from any hospital.

Naitauba Island was different again. It was owned and lived in for about three months of every year by Raymond Burr and his friend Robert Benevides. Raymond was a film star and starred in "A Man Called Ironside", "Perry Mason", and many other films, whereas Robert was his director in many of his films and series. Raymond had had a very sad life, having lost two wives in tragic circumstances. They had a beautiful large, and comfortable house with a terrace, lawn and gardens. The house was air-conditioned, and there was a constant electricity supply from a generator. Raymond and Robert raised magnificent cattle and pigs and had a wonderful collection of orchids. Most of the island was taken up with a well-run copra plantation. One day when we were staying, Raymond saw out of a window one of his cattle eating one of his orchids and commented that the orchid was worth many times more than the cow which was eating it. Liveried servants served the guests at the house; there was silver cutlery, the food was wonderful, and there was proper French wine to drink with the meals. They had an extensive record collection, out of which they gave us several to play on our battery record player back at Lomaloma.

Raymond and Robert were also excellent employers. About 2 months before our first visit to the island, his pig keeper's youngest daughter, a person very low down on the hierarchy of importance in a Fijian community, had developed serious pneumonia. They had chartered a ship with comfortable accommodation to take her to the main island, Viti Levu, where she could be treated in a hospital. This would have cost a very large sum of money, and it was acts like this that led to an enormous loyalty towards them by the local Fijians. One odd thing that we noticed the first time we arrived was that the knife was always laid on the left and the fork on the right at the table at mealtimes. The first thing the guests did at each meal was pick up the knife with their right hand and the fork with their left hand, thus crossing their hands. The next time we visited, we asked Robert what the significance of this was. He told us that soon after they had bought the island and were training the house staff how to lay the table, one of the staff had asked him where the knives and forks went. For some odd reason, probably as a joke, he said you put the knife on the left and the fork on the right. This had been done from that time on, and he had not told the servants that it had been a silly joke as that would have diminished them in the eyes of the others. Apparently, now there was the rumour going around the island that Europeans and Americans have this strange ritual at each meal of swapping their knife and fork around before they ate, bringing good luck. Of course, all guests had to be warned about this idiosyncrasy before they were served a meal.

When we came to Naituba, we often brought Simon with us, and usually, saw little of him as he was whisked off into the village. However, once we were all sitting on the lawn on a rug, having a drink with Simon beside us, when one of the lorries from the estate drove by on the other side of the lawn. Simon looked fascinated at this weird apparition, then he laughed so much that he fell off the rug. He was 16 months old at the time and had never seen a motorised vehicle in his whole life. Staying for a few days in this beautiful estate was like entering paradise for us, a wonderful relaxation and relief from basic living, even though we were at home with that. Of course, whenever we arrived, I had work to do, which was a pleasure because I knew the people were well cared for and that whatever they needed would be provided.

The other four island communities I looked after were all traditional Fijian communities with a chief and chief's committee in charge. They were serious, hardworking, hospitable and close communities where people looked after each other and where if there were health needs, they were brought to my notice. I always enjoyed visiting and working with these communities, and if there was a crisis that, I was informed about by radio or by a man appearing on an outrigger canoe, I was glad to make an immediate visit. However, I always took my own food as the communities were relatively poor, much less affluent than the foreign-owned islands and also less prosperous than the main island where we lived. I usually spent two days at the island communities, sleeping overnight on the boat. However, if the weather became dangerously stormy, which could happen very rapidly, I could get trapped on an island for up to two weeks. For these reasons and because the reef opening for Kanacia was a dog-legged passage and thus dangerous, I rarely took Peta and Simon with me.

I once decided to take them with me on a visit to this island because it was very beautiful and volcanic, and the weather forecast was good for the next few days. We had a wonderful first day, with Peta and Simon being very welcome. The wind and the sea increased a bit on our second day, but my crew was quite happy to make the journey back to Lomaloma. About 30 minutes out from Kanacia, the wind suddenly increased to cyclone strength. The boat I was supplied with was 39-foot-long, and the waves were considerably higher than the length of our boat. Peta and I were lying on the two bunks at the back of the boat, where I was hanging on to Simon on my stomach to stop him from being thrown all-round the cabin. There were no available life vests or life rafts.

Peta became extremely distressed and begged me to go and ask the crew to turn back. There was no direct communication between the rear cabin and the controls where the two crew members were fighting to keep the boat afloat, so the only way I could communicate with them was by going across the roof of the rear cabin. There were two very small rails across this roof. I prayed, and I launched myself into a roaring hell. I have relatively weak arms and I hung on to these rails for dear life. The boat was being thrown violently in all directions, and I honestly do not know why, apart from the grace of God, I was not thrown off that boat. I was convinced that I was going to die. Eventually, I made my way to the front cabin and asked the crew to turn back, but they said that if they turned even slightly out of the wind, the boat would immediately be flipped over. I then had to make my way back to the rear cabin and Peta and Simon. I entered the cabin, burst into tears and took Simon back onto my stomach. He seemed to know something very bad was happening and was completely silent. Eventually, the captain found his way toward the leeward side of a small uninhabited island, where we rode the storm out. I still have PTSD from this experience and awake with my heart racing and sweating heavily. I find myself back on the roof of that boat with an inferno of huge waves, huge winds and driven spume all around me. Some hours later, the wind dropped a bit, and we found our way back home. I have never been so happy to see the beach at Lomaloma, and since that day, I have had a deep fear and hatred of the sea.

As in all the places in the world which we have called home, we quite quickly developed a routine in our island hideout. In the morning, I did about 3 hours of consulting and then had lunch with Peta, Ateca and Simon, then Simon slept. The village we lived in was half Fijian and half Tongan, and the village was divided into the Fijian village, Lomaloma and the Tongan village, Sawana. Sawana was a much tidier village and much better kept. The houses were in a better state of repair, and the plots were full of flowers and the lawns well cut. There was continuous rivalry between the two villages. One never heard Fijian spoken in Sawana or Tongan spoken in Lomaloma. Each village had its own church. Not infrequently, I had discontents coming to see me from Lomaloma complaining that the people of Sawana were throwing their weight around and they did not seem to realise that this was not their country and discontents from Sawana complaining that they had no say in the running of the divided village and were being pushed around. This was difficult for me as I was the senior government officer in the whole of Northern Lau at the age of 29 yrs.

Peta was recruited into the fishing team to use the 20-yard-long beach net which we brought as a gift to the village when we arrived. Imagine a group of about twenty women meeting on a sandy beach lined with palm trees and leading to the relatively calm blue waters of the lagoon. They are dressed in the local colourful Bula cloth wraps. Some have babies on their backs, and other older children chase each other through their parents' legs and up and down the beach. There is no worry about the children; all the children and all the parents have known each other since birth. This is one huge community, really a large family. One of the teenagers is designated to look after the children, and immediately starts a great big sulk as this means that she cannot participate in the fishing. One of the women takes charge, and everybody strips off the outer layer of clothing. The net is brought out.

It is quite bulky equipment as it is about 20 yards long and is tightly pleated up at the start of the fishing manoeuvre. One woman stands as the anchor on the beach, and the others enter the water. Gradually, the net is unfolded with a woman every couple of yards or so. The top of the net is at the level of the water, and the base reaches the sand below. Gradually, the women go further and further into the water as the net unfolds. They move slowly, and there is total silence so as not to frighten the fish. When the lead woman is up to her neck in water, the group unfurls the net sidewards, making a wide arc back to the beach. All the women now gradually draw the net in on each side until, the edge of the net approaches the beach, the water boils with movement as the fish trapped in the net try and escape. The catch is landed, and the fish are shared between the fisherwomen. The teenager is relieved of her role as child guardian and thus feels she can also give up her sulk. The fish go into the various families' baskets, the outer clothes are put on again, and the women wander off to their homes, still chatting away. This evening there will be a smell of cooking fresh fish all over the village. We were always given 10 % of the catch whether Peta was in the fishing group or not, as we had given the net, which was what happened by their customs.

Peta was also recruited into the dance group, which performed at all weddings and whenever anybody could think of some reason to have a party. When watching the dance, it seemed to go like clockwork and was very beautiful. However, the arm and hand movements were very complicated and needed to be done in a very fluid fashion. One realised that the local women had been trained to do this since they were very young girls, but it was very difficult for Peta to acquire this skill as a grown woman. She was still expected to turn up whenever the women danced, but then she tried to fade into the background gently.

During the morning, when I was doing my consultations, most of the cases I saw were much the same as anywhere else in the world. I usually consulted sitting outside my hut, but if anything required me to examine a patient or where something embarrassing or confidential needed to be discussed, we went inside the hut, where there were two chairs and a metal table used as an examination couch.

During the afternoon, after Simon's sleep, we often wandered around the village, always with Simon on my shoulders. Sometimes we dropped into Bhagwan's store to buy some soap or some very hard ship's biscuit if the whole country had run out of flour, which happened with a degree of regularity. In the evening, I would check up on people who were poorly at home or had turned up in canoes. Every month I would join the chief's council to discuss any health problems and listen to their worries. This could take a whole afternoon. About once every 3 weeks, I went off in the boat to see people on the outer islands to do clinics and to check up on programmes such as the filariasis programme. I was accompanied by a nurse. Peta and Simon usually did not come along with me unless we were going to immunise the children. If Peta was not there to supervise the process, all the children would be immunised with the same needle. When Peta was there, the three needles, of which we were proud owners, were sterilised and then used. Subsequently, the same three needles were resterilised in boiling water, and the next three were immunised. This process slowed things down enormously and caused a lot of muttering about foreign people coming in and changing traditional habits that had worked well for decades before.

The most difficult task I had while working in the islands by far was deciding which of two emergencies presenting at the same time I should deal with. One day, the wife of the schoolmaster went into labour with her second child. The baby was a breach, meaning it would be delivered feet first. This is far more difficult to deal with than a normal delivery. However, I was confident I could manage this without too much trouble. About halfway through the morning, a call came through from the head office of the islands health service to say that there was a boat with quite a number of people on board, which had been seen to be on fire by a passing plane. I was instructed to go and rescue the people in the medical boat and treat any injured people on board. So, I had a dilemma, which people should I treat? I talked at length with the most senior of my nurses about her experience of delivering babies presenting as a breach. She certainly knew the way to do this and claimed to have carried this procedure out. Eventually, I decided that a boat full of people which was on fire, possibly sinking, and with the possibility of badly burned people to treat should take priority. We set off in the Vuicake, our medical boat.

We searched high and low for the boat in the area indicated to us without finding it. Late in the afternoon, we were told that the boat had had engine trouble and had produced a great deal of exhaust smoke but had never been on fire. We could not return to Lomaloma that night and stayed overnight in Naitauba. On returning the next day, I found that the baby had been born the day before, but because of inexpert management at birth, had had brain damage and died soon after I got back. Neither the schoolmaster nor his wife ever spoke to me again. I have had a great sense of failure and sadness about this situation ever since, though if I had the time again, I don't know whether I would have made any different decision with the information I had. This is just one of the costs of practicing in extremely isolated situations where the buck stops with you. There are many wonderful things about practicing in such situations to weigh against this.

As well as the clinical work, I had to fill out the health statistics forms and request money to buy cleaning supplies and pay Sovakelli and other public servants. This work was largely done by Peta as well as her paid job. As the administrator of the nursing staff in the Northern Lau islands, she was responsible for this. If nurses' houses were in a poor state of repair or they found it difficult to buy food, it was up to Peta, using our very poor communication system, to sort the problem out. Similarly, if a nurse was taking maternity leave or could not work for any other reason, Peta moved nurses around among the island nursing and medical centres. This often involved moving nurses from an island in the Southern Lau islands, which was in a different subdivision, to islands in the Northern Lau. An added problem was that this involved them travelling by copra boats, and the Southern and Northern Lau boats ran to a different schedule. So, if the nurse was not to spend a long time stranded in the capital, Suva, waiting for the copra boat of her new area to set off for the islands, this involved careful planning of the trips. Even then, the captains could easily decide to change their sailing schedule on the spur of the moment. To say that the system worked like clockwork would not only be wrong, but it would be a direct contradiction of real life.

During the time I was working in Lomaloma, we had a typhoid epidemic. It was a great help to live in a hierarchical communal system as the chief could decree that people should isolate themselves and their families and it would be done. When the chief said everybody should wash their hands frequently, that was also done. The main problem with managing this epidemic was that I did not have anything like adequate quantities of Chloramphenicol tablets or any intravenous infusions. Happily, the government agreed to airdrop these to us. I think it is a credit to the fitness of the island people and their ability to pull together under their chief that nobody died.

During our time in the Lau, we had quite a number of visitors on the copra boats, and these fell into various categories. Among these were people who just wanted to look at some of the world's most remote areas. In this category, we had three sets of visitors.

One day, the Copra boat arrived, and we went down to the beach hoping to find the shopping we had ordered on the last boat six weeks ago. All the relevant cargo, among which was our shopping, was unloaded and brought to shore on the shoulders of the islanders. Then a boat arrived, and two young women in their early twenties climbed into the boat and landed on the beach. It appeared that they were South Africans who had been trying to journey where white people had not been. Perhaps, they were disappointed to see us! The ship stayed in Lomaloma overnight, so we invited them to our home for the night. As soon as they appeared, Simon took one look at them and wailed loudly. They asked why our baby was crying, and we told them not to worry. There was no real problem, and it was just because they were white. Everybody else that he knew was black apart from us, and we were just part of the furniture. Ateca picked Simon up, took him into the village to be looked after by a dependable family, and returned to prepare the meal with Peta. The light faded; the Tilley lamps were lit, providing a soft light in the room with a gentle hissing noise. It was a rather beautiful time of day, and the soft and hissing lights helped bring the day to a relaxed, gentle end. The meal was cooked, the table was laid, and we all sat down to eat Peta and I, Ateca and our guests. These two South African girls had come from apartheid rule in their home country, and they found it very odd that a black employee should sit down and eat a meal she helped cook with her employers and their guests. We told them not to worry; Ateca was much like a sister to us, which they also found very strange. About halfway through the meal, they asked us where Simon was. We said, "Somewhere in the village, he is OK. He will turn up in the morning." They were absolutely staggered by this and said, "You mean to say that your baby is somewhere in the village, but you don't know where and that you are quite happy for him to spend the night with a black family?" We said that we were perfectly happy. When they left the next morning, our guests thanked us very much for our hospitality, but when they returned to the boat, they were still shaking their heads.

Our next visitors were perhaps the strangest people we had met in the Lau Islands. One day, we woke up to see a rather beautiful yacht coming over the lagoon towards us. We were intrigued to discover who these people were, where they were from and what they were doing here. However, they anchored just out from the beach, and nothing happened. People came to us and asked who these people were, but we had to tell them that we hadn't a clue. Eventually, a man got into the yacht dingy after a few hours and came ashore. We met him when he came to the beach and sat and listened to a truly unbelievable tale. Apparently, there were two couples aboard who both lived in Los Angeles. They had been friends and decided to sail to the South Pacific They did not articulate where they were heading.

By the time they reached our island, they had fallen out, and currently, they were not talking to each other.

Additionally, the man with whom we were talking was not talking to his wife. We asked them what experience they had with sailing, and apparently, before setting out for the 'South Pacific,' their only experience was sailing in the harbour of Los Angeles. We asked them what marine charts they had and how they were navigating. They told us they only had a commercially produced Atlas of this area, which they bought in a bookshop. This story was so unlikely that we were very suspicious and told the chief he should be involved. We wondered whether they were running guns or smuggling something, though on the face of things, coming to the beach of the chief seat of the government (such as it was) of a national subdivision would have been an extremely stupid idea. The chief investigated what was going on, and it appeared that the unlikely story given to us was correct. We have no idea how they had found their way to any inhabited land and how they had avoided being wrecked on the extremely dangerous and unmarked reefs all over the Koro Sea. They did not really engage with the island community or us, apart from buying some food (including buying some pilchards from Mr Bhagwan) and loading up with fresh water. They then asked which way the main island was. I was only able to help them by saying, "Over thereabouts," but my captain gave them a compass bearing with which they could probably avoid the reefs on the way to the main island. They took off, and we never saw or heard of them again.

The third lot of strange visitors were two young American men. They arrived one day on a copra boat and introduced themselves as being Peace Corps workers who the American government had sent to promote peace, skills, and well-being on these backward islands. We offered some help but were told they needed no help at all as they had had a six-month training course in Hawaii, were fully conversant with island communities, and spoke Melanesian fluently. They disappeared into the village, rented a village house for an enormous sum of money, and didn't socialise with us at all. The man from whom they rented the house was walking around the village for a long time with a smile as wide as a Cheshire cat. We heard nothing directly from them for about a month apart from people telling us they did not know why they were here and asking us whether we had anything to do with their coming. We told our neighbours we had nothing to do with their arrival.

After about a month, we heard that they had had a flaming row, and now one of them was living in Lomaloma, and the other one had rented a house in the next village up the coast, and they were not talking to each other. We thought that this was a strange way to promote peace. We never learned what skills they were trying to impart, but after about three months, they told us they had formulated a project. It was to liberate the young people of the island from the suffocating hierarchy of island life and teach them how to be free as American teenagers were. The chiefs of our subdivision had decided that alcohol was a destructive agent in the context of island life and had banned the import of any alcoholic drinks. These two young men had decided that despite this, they would import four crates of beer and arrange a dance with a bar for the young people. As the senior government servant on the islands, the chief learned of this and came to see me asking me to ban the dance. I told him that, according to the laws of Fiji, what they were doing was not illegal, just highly dishonouring to him and damaging to island life. I suggested that he should contact the overall chief, who was also the Prime Minister and the leader of the entire island group. I strongly advised the American couple not to go ahead, but they ignored me and proceeded anyway. The chief clearly expressed his views on this matter, and I supported him. Shortly after, the two promoters of peace(!) disappeared. However, a few weeks before their disappearance, another young American man appeared on the scene. He had more to do with us and informed us that he was a follower of the Bahai religion and had come to enlighten the island inhabitants. When I asked him to explain the Bahai religion and to tell me why he thought that the islanders needed enlightenment, he was unable to do either. He also disappeared on the next Copra boat.

A different form of visit took place annually when the judge made an appearance. This rather esteemed individual established trials for individuals who had been accused of breaking the law during the past year. These were the minor infractions. The people who had seriously blotted their copy books had to go to the main island for a proper trial. The judge sat and heard the cases, and some were fined. Others who had misbehaved themselves more seriously were given jail sentences. I had assumed these people would be unceremoniously loaded on to the judge's boat and hauled off to Suva. To my surprise, this was not the case; there was a waiting list to get into the jail. So, life continued unchanged for the miscreants. After a month or two, I would be informed that Waga (Fijian for ship) number nine would be calling at the island in 10 days. Could I please gather the convicts, as they were called, and make sure they got on the boat to go to prison? I had imagined scenarios involving scouring the islands or even engaging in boat pursuits reminiscent of a 007 film in order to apprehend these criminals. However, this was far from the truth. On the contrary, they were all ready and waiting at the designated time, chatting animatedly to all their mates. Apparently, nobody minded going to prison at all because one was given three substantial meals a day, and any work that one had to do was minimal compared with what one had to do on the island. When they arrived in Suva, they were taken to the prison, which was stone-built with high walls at the front and the two sides. Yet, this facade concealed the truth – at the rear, there were merely two lines of barbed wire to prevent escape. Even if anybody tried to escape, everybody knew who everybody else was in Fiji, where they were and their family history. It was impossible to just disappear as one can do in Europe.

Finally, the government set up events on the islands every year or two to remind people that there was a world beyond the palm trees and reefs of the island and that they belonged to a country called Fiji. When we were there, the Fiji police department band and marching group arrived to spend two days on our island and to put on a full band concert and marching demonstration. They came on a special government boat, and seeing all the drums, trumpets, horns, tubas, and very dramatic uniforms was quite a sight. They would not let the locals touch anything but unloaded it all themselves. Heading this ensemble was a British individual who had previously held a high-ranking position in the Coldstream Guards' band. He knew what he was doing and got on very well with his men. Because of this, they were enthused and very professional. This largely meant that they did not get drunk until after the concert and marching were over, and the following reception was finished.

We all sat on either side of the village green as the performance was prepared. Once everything was ready, the chief and his council arrived and sat on one side on chairs under a makeshift canopy. Everybody else sat on mats, and children were running everywhere. The band leader arrived with his men, the children were cleared from the marching ground, and the band struck up. The music was superb, as was the discipline of the men. We had been quite worried about Simon for some months before they came because, at 14 months, he was still not walking; he just shuffled along on his bottom. However, even at this stage, he was very musical and very excited by the band. We were holding him standing up, and as the marchers passed by where we were sitting, Simon just took off and walked after them with no difficulty at all. After this, he had no problem with walking. He has always been a person with his own mind and clearly, at this stage, decided that on balance it was a good idea to walk and then, having started doing this, saw no reason to change.

When all the music, marching, and reception were over, we invited the band leader to our house for supper. However, we warned him that since the country was currently out of flour and there was no meat or fish available at the moment, all we could offer him was an omelette and some taro (yam). He was delighted. He told us that as the band travelled from island-to-island night after night, they were given huge meals of suckling pig, enormous chunks of beef, and rich food of every description cooked in the traditional Fijian way using ovens dug into the soil. The idea of having something simple delighted him. And so, they loaded their boat and took off again, leaving behind lots of gossip and tales about what had happened during their visit. These tales grew more and more unlikely as time passed.

Once Raymond Burr and Robert Benevides from Naitauba came to visit us in Lomaloma, they expressed horror that we were expected to live in such primitive conditions and decided to do something about it. We told them we were quite satisfied with our lot and had asked for a remote posting while working on the main island. The one thing that particularly struck them was how scraggy the chickens were in our chicken run. When they returned, they sent us a magnificent cockerel and three beautiful chickens. We put them in the chicken run with our other chickens, but they did not thrive at all. They looked very sorry for themselves and developed sores on their combs. I asked Ateca to find out from the locals what was wrong with them, and she came back saying that it was chicken pox, a different chicken pox from the one we knew. Nobody seemed to know how to treat them. So, determined we would not lose our wonderful chickens, I decided to give the cockerel an injection of penicillin. Word got out in the village that the Vuniwai would inject his cockerel with penicillin, and half the village turned up to watch. I duly gave the injection and then stood back to look. The cockerel shook himself, walked around his pen and then dropped dead. My clinic was very quiet for a few days after that, and absolutely everybody offered injections refused them. Both my brothers-in-law were vets, so I wrote to them to ask what might have caused the sudden death of the cockerel. A letter came back 6 weeks later on the boat, saying, "What penicillin did you use?" I wrote back, "Procaine penicillin." Again, a letter came back on the next boat which simply said, "Procaine is lethal to birds." Well, I suppose one lives and learns, but it was a pity to lose our wonderful cockerel.

On another occasion, Raymond and Robert arranged a big party in Suva, to which Ratu Mara, the prime minister and half the government were invited and invited us. We thanked them and said that we couldn't possibly come as we had no leave due and had no transport to get back to the main island. Raymond arranged for us to be given leave. He chartered the Queen of Tonga's boat, the Heavafua (locally known as the 'heave and spewer' because it rolled so badly), which just happened to be in Fiji at the time. We had a wonderful few days on the main island, rubbed shoulders with the elite and ate and drank food we had not tasted since we left Europe. Afterward, we needed to return to our island community. At that time, an exceedingly old flying boat made occasional trips to some of the islands, and we were booked on a flight that took off from Suva airport and landed on the lagoon just off Lomaloma. This plane was flown by a rather bizarre Australian who used to frighten his passengers by getting on the plane in civilian clothes. Then, about ten minutes after the flight should have taken off, he moved to the pilot's seat and said to one of the passengers, "If nobody else is coming to fly this plane, I will. Will you please come and hold the book open so I can see what I must do?" All went well on the flight until we were coming into land. Instead of asking everybody to fasten their seat belts, we were all told to sit in the central aisle of the cabin. As we landed, it became evident why. The plane was so old that all the windows leaked water as we landed, and the seats were soaked. We were quite glad to have made it back in one piece.

One day, out of the blue, we received a message saying that a generator was on its way. Naturally, we were delighted, but we thought long and hard about what had triggered this outbreak of generosity on the part of the government. It was only later that we discovered that the government had -advanced plans to build a small eight-bed hospital at Lomaloma to care for my small flock of about 11,000 souls. In due course, the boat arrived, and a very heavy crate was manoeuvred onto the store. This was installed in a shed in a wooded area just behind our house, happily far enough away that we did not hear it when it ran. As there was no indication of when the new hospital would be built, we decided that we would be able to run the generator from 6.30 pm to 10.00 pm each day with the fuel ration we had been allocated. The main difference we found from having this new piece of machinery was that as the light faded, we could turn a light on with a touch of a switch. For months, we had survived using Tilley lamps. These lamps produced a warm, rather romantic light, but there were big disadvantages. Firstly, they required a mantle to produce any light, and these kept collapsing. Secondly, they produced light about equivalent to a 60-watt bulb, and thirdly, they produced a very soporific hissing noise, which sent us both off to sleep. We found that we went to bed later with electric lights and got much more done in a day.

To his huge delight, we put our friend Sovakelli, the caretaker, in charge of starting and stopping the generator each day and keeping it full of diesel. Sovakelli could not tell the time, so we asked him to turn the generator off when Radio Fiji closed in the evening, which was at 10.00 pm. All went well for the first week until Saturday. The generator was running merrily at 9.50 pm but still running smoothly at 10.10 pm. We thought that Sovakelli must have gone to sleep, so we sent somebody to wake him up and turn the generator off. The person we sent found Sovakelli awake and chatting with his friends. Moreover, they discovered them listening to Radio Fiji. It turned out that the radio programme finished at 10.30 pm on Saturdays, and we had to apologise to our faithful caretaker for doubting his dedication to his job.

In due course, the government started building the hospital. There had been no consultation about what was needed in a remote environment such as this, and it appeared that the mandarins of the Colonial Office and the Overseas Development Office had decided that they would use a hospital design that had been produced for use in Uganda in an area where there was mains electricity. So, when it was built in Lomaloma, we found that they had included a full radiology department and laboratory even though we only had a small generator fit to provide energy for lighting and perhaps a refrigerator. Other than that, it was a great improvement on the hut from which I had worked until now. There was a proper outpatient department with a waiting room, a theatre for minor operations and eight beds in an easy-to-clean building. The hospital was also built very close to our house, and when I was consulting, Simon used to shuffle across on his bottom until he learned to walk and come into my consulting room to say hello to me and the patients. This hospital was built between our house and the sea, almost on the beach. Although I have not been able to find out exactly what has happened to it with climate change and rising sea levels, it must be at risk of flooding. The Fiji government has already had to move 40 villages inland away from the beach because of inundation by the sea.

1970 was a very important year for the Fijian nation, the year they gained independence from Britain. Even here, miles in the outback, there was a lot of discussion. People huddled under the mango trees and the breadfruit trees and talked for ages. Eventually, towards the beginning of August, a special meeting of the council of chiefs in the islands was convened, and I was summoned to appear. I was shown into the room where the chiefs were meeting, and a yagona ceremony was performed, which was unusual; usually, when I met the chiefs, I sat down, greeted people, and we got on with the business. After the ceremony, the overall chief told the story of how Fiji had become a colony at the request of the chiefs and how the British had ended the interminable fighting, killing and cannibalism. He recounted how missionaries had introduced the Christian religion, how the Fijian people turned to Christ as a group and how it had changed them and the nation. They recounted how schools had been introduced, how agriculture improved over the years and how grateful they were. They now turned to me and talked about the upcoming independence from the British crown and how they thought that this was a terrible mistake. They had made their voices heard in Suva to the Fijian government, and nobody had listened to them. They then said that as I was the senior civil servant living in Northern Lau, I was the representative of the Queen. They informed me that they were making a formal request to me to leave immediately and to go to England and to tell the Queen that this whole plan of independence was acknowledged by her loyal subjects as a very big catastrophe and please would she refuse to accept the request for independence. This rather dumbfounded me, and I had to think very rapidly on my feet, or more accurately, on my backside as I was sitting cross-legged on a mat. I replied to them that I was indeed the local representative of the Queen. However, the recognised representative for their country was the governor of Fiji, who was in Suva, so it would be going totally against the authority structure set up by the Queen to bypass the governor. So, if I went to see the Queen in London, she would quite rightly refuse to see me if I had not come to her through her recognised representative.

Moreover, this independence had been requested by the Fijian government led by the Prime Minister, Ratu Mara, who, as well as being prime minister was the overall chief of the Southern Lau islands and a chief who held precedence over our local chiefs in the Northern Lau islands. The chiefly council went into a huddle and talked among themselves for a while. They then thanked me for my attendance and my work and said they would not detain me further.

In the few days before 10th October 1970, there were great preparations. The green was decorated, and a stand was built for the visiting dignitaries. Raymond Burr from Natauba was invited to be the guest of honour, and there would be speeches by all and sundry. A great feast was planned, and everybody would be fed, and the great day dawned. And we drew back the curtain, only to see that a force 8 to 9 gale was blowing with the palm trees all bent over by the wind. There was some damage to the stand where the dignitaries were supposed to be seated. It would have been far too dangerous for Raymond Burr to have travelled from his island; the boat would probably have sunk. The Fijian people are very resilient people, and they all carried on despite the setback. Raymond Burr was to have lowered the English flag, and I was invited to do that, but as only a few weeks ago I had been asked to halt the whole process, I decided that this would be unwise, so I offered to raise their flag instead. My offer, not surprisingly, was declined. The national anthem was played, and everybody cheered and saluted the flag. Then came singing, and there was lots of it. It was singing as only the Fijians know how to do—in close harmony, with actions; the sort that you could listen to all night.

The most difficult role that I had to take over from Raymond was judging the beauty competition, which followed the general jollification. The Fijian maidens were all big girls, and they had all been liberally smothered with cooking oil, making them very greasy. I had no idea at all what the Fijians found attractive in their women. As always happened, Ateca came to my rescue. "Just choose the fattest one," was her advice, and when I gave my judgement, it was clear that Ateca was spot on. There was much nodding and approving grunts. I then found that I had to also choose the second best, which was easy, the second fattest. There were many more nods and approving grunts. The time for the feast came, but before that, there was a solemn yagona celebration. Each member of the guest party was individually offered a bowl of yagona with due ceremony. However, I found myself put first on this occasion. Not only was I presented with the bowl of yagona, but I, as representative of the Queen, was also presented, with much solemnity and ritual, with a Tabua. This was a tooth of a Sperm Whale, and a presentation of this symbol was normally reserved for visiting heads of states, diplomats and national heroes. This was a tremendous honour and an expression of gratitude for my medical services and my position as a senior civil servant. The feast was magnificent. Despite the doubts about independence on the part of the chiefs, the day passed well and with great community spirit and joy. Simon had the time of his life, wandering from person to person and eating far more than was good for him. Peta, as usual, was chatting away the whole time with her Fijian friends. As for Smuts, our dog, he just lurked in the background, and when he saw an unguarded tasty morsel, he grabbed it, made off and ate it and then came back for more.

It was an ordinary start to a week. We had been to the Fijian church this week; last week, it had been the Tongan church. We did not fully understand either of them, but the singing was wonderful, something to die for. Simon had been playing with Tevita, Isikelli's son from next door. Smuts had been playing with his friend the piglet, who was now becoming more of an adult pig. We still relished turning the electric lights on when it became dark and going off when the generator was closed at 10.00 pm.

Early the next morning, Isikelli came across and tapped on our window to say that Tevita was very poorly. I went across to see him and found him bloated, a bit like a Michelin man with reddened swollen skin and a very high temperature. He had severe generalised erysipelas and was very poorly. This very much surprised me as he had been full of energy the night before and had seemed very well. I gave him an injection of penicillin and another one later in the day. The next day, he was perfectly well and playing with Simon. It was difficult to believe that he had been so unwell just yesterday. The day after that, Isikelli again came across to see me, very worried again about Tevita. I went to see him, and he was clearly very unwell again. He was grey with a sunken face and appeared dehydrated. I tested his urine and found that it was loaded with sugar. Diabetes was rare in this population, which made me curious about what was going on. I gave him the standard emergency treatment for childhood diabetes. The next day dawned with brilliant sunshine to find Tevita completely well again. He had no sign of illness at all, and tests of his urine showed no sugar at all. Again, he was happily playing with Simon. The next day, Tevita was very unwell again. He had extremely severe asthma. His chest was almost silent, and he looked grey and very ill. I gave him the standard treatment for asthma as was available in the outer isles. Asthma was rare in the island community, and again it was inexplicable why Tevita was so ill. The next day again, our little neighbour was entirely well. I had no idea at all what could have been causing all this.

I visited Isikelli and his wife, and while Tevita was happily playing on the floor of their bure, I explained to them that I was completely out of my depth. I had no clue what was going on. Isikelli then said to me, “I know exactly what is happening with Tevita. I have offended the witch in Sawana, and she has placed a curse on Tevita. He is going to die. It's a common occurrence in these islands.” I was taken aback by this revelation. Although I had heard stories of such occurrences, I had never faced the prospect of it happening to one of my patients. I said I would sort the matter out and left to talk with Peta. We decided that I should write to the witch in Sawana and demand that she takes this curse off Tevita forthwith. If she refused, I said that she would be removed from the islands, her land would be confiscated, and she would never come back. This was something that I felt I could do because of my position in the civil service. I did not receive a reply.

Two days later, at the end of the day, I had a shower with Simon. This was always good fun, and we larked about splashing each other. I then handed him to Peta to dry off and soaped myself down. Suddenly, there was a scream from the bedroom. Peta had been drying Simon normally when he went limp and grey. I examined him and found that his heart had stopped. Peta and I resuscitated him and eventually put him to bed. Neither of us had much sleep that night, and we were continually checking up on Simon. The next day, at first, Simon seemed fine, but then he suddenly had a fit out of the blue. He didn't have a fever. After the fit, we discovered that he was paralysed down the right side of his body. Remarkably, Simon himself didn't seem overly concerned; when he wanted to move his right arm, he lifted it using his left arm. Around this time, Isikelli came to visit us, and we informed him about the events of the past 24 hours. He said that, in his view, the witch had now extended her curse to Simon as well and that if our two sons were not off the island within a week, they would both be dead. Sitting in a comfortable chair in middle-class Britain, one thinks how ridiculous this all sounds, but it does not feel like that at all when one is sitting in one of the most isolated places on earth with one’s sick, threatened child on one’s lap wondering what to do. Isikelli, Peta and I decided that the only thing we could do was go, but that was easier to say than do.

We were able to contact headquarters by radio and explained the situation. There was a ship in our area, but it was too large to navigate through the reef passage, we had to approach it in the Vuicaki, my medical boat. We arranged a meeting point with the larger ship, but there was a substantial swell in the sea. The Vuicaki was bouncing like a cork on the waves, while the larger ship was rolling heavily, with its deck positioned 6 feet higher than our boat's deck. The large ship lowered a rope ladder, but it was clear that no one would be able to climb it while carrying Simon. Panic momentarily set in. However, one of the sailors on the larger ship assessed the situation and said, 'Throw the little boy to me. I play rugby for the Fiji national side. I can catch anything!' And that's precisely what I did. If that sailor hadn't caught Simon, he would have fallen between the two boats, likely resulting in tragedy. Fortunately, the sailor caught Simon, and then he caught Tevita. From that day on, I always cheer for the Fiji rugby team when I see them playing, even if they're up against England.

After a couple of days on the boat, we arrived at the harbour in Suva. As we were coming in, a VW Beetle was driving along the quay. Neither Tevita nor Simon had seen any cars in their short lives, so Tevita jumped up and down shouting “Vonu, vonu” (turtle, turtle), and Tevita shouted for Isikelli to go and catch it. On the quay, we said goodbye to Isikelli and Tevita and made our way to the Colonial War Memorial Hospital, where we saw the paediatrician. Happily, there was a New Zealand paediatric neurologist coming to the hospital during the next week, and Simon was booked in to see him. I had to return to Lomaloma as soon as possible as I had left them with no medical care. I was still in Suva to see the neurologist with Peta and Simon, as there was no boat before that time. After taking a history and examining Simon, the neurologist told us that the most likely diagnosis was that Simon had a rapidly growing cerebral tumour. However, the equipment to confirm or reject this diagnosis was not available in Fiji. He advised that Simon should be transferred as a matter of urgency to a competent hospital either in New Zealand or the UK. I phoned up my old chief in my teaching hospital, Dr Hart, a Paediatrician in the Middlesex Hospital in London, and a bed was reserved for him in the hospital. We also phoned Simon's godfather, a doctor in another London hospital, and then booked a flight for Peta and Simon to fly home two days later. We informed British Airways that they would be flying a sick child that day. The day of the flight was New Year's Day, and because of the time changes, this flight would be travelling on two New Year's Days as they would be crossing the international date line on their way. The flight was serving all passengers a free glass of champagne, but poor Peta could not partake of the bubbly as she was looking after a sick child.

I had to make my way back to Lomaloma, feeling very sad as now this was a place of menace instead of a place of fulfilling work and friendly people. The people of the islands were a wonderful support as I packed up and shipped our belongings to go home. Ateca was a tower of strength, a true gift of God. Many of our possessions would be useless in the UK, so all of these went to Ateca, and we also gave her a sum of money to relaunch herself on the main island. The time for departure arrived, and the islanders said goodbye with a yagona ceremony and the presentation of another Tabua. In Suva, I said my goodbyes to Ateca, and she left in absolute silence, which was a sign of great respect in Fiji. I caught my plane and embarked on a long and boring trip back to England.

During my flight, I had time to reflect on our time in Fiji. We arrived as a young couple in their twenties, married for less than a year. During the first year, Peta had our first baby, and I found myself working with far more responsibility than I would have had in England and doing Caesarean sections and hysterectomies with, at times, very little supervision. We were in a very multicultural and very young community where we came into close contact with people with considerably different backgrounds and priorities from us. When we went to the Lau islands, Peta and I found ourselves in an utterly remote environment where we had tenuous and intermittent contact with the outside world. In that situation, we had very wide and important responsibilities for the care of our patients and more general responsibilities for the administration of the community, with very little backup at all. The buck really did stop with us. We were the only people from the Western world who had lived on our island for forty years, so Peta and I were thrown very much together. This experience was the cause of a very close cementing of our relationship. It also taught us the skill of assessing a situation where we were relatively inexperienced in the action needed but where there was nobody else with any skills and experience, then of getting on and doing our best. This was the training ground of a life lived working with people around the edge of society and in several isolated and threatening environments.

Practice, Prison and Smack

The return flight took Peta and Simon 44 hours. They had two stops: one in Los Angeles and one in New York. In New York, they were delayed by 5 hours because of a blizzard, a nasty shock after the warmth of Fiji. When the plane eventually landed at Heathrow Airport, to her surprise, Peta found an ambulance waiting for Simon on the tarmac. Hedley, Simon's godfather, had got the wrong end of the stick when I telephoned him from Fiji and thought that Simon was unconscious. Peta and Simon disembarked before the other passengers, and Hedley came to the plane's door. As Simon was being carried down the steps, he pointed at the skies and said, "Moon, stars."

Hedley said, "Please shut that child up. He is supposed to be unconscious." Simon was taken straight to the paediatric department of the Middlesex Hospital. The staff looked at Peta and Hedley, who had also come to the hospital and said, "You two look exhausted," assuming Hedley was Simon's father. This caused some confusion later when I turned up and presented myself as Simon's father. In those days, mothers could not stay with their babies in the hospital, so Peta went back to Hedley and Jean's flat, leaving Simon in the ward. The next day when Peta went to see Simon, he saw her across the ward and came crawling across the floor to see her. By this time, Simon had been walking well, and Peta's heart dropped a beat, thinking he had had another fit and had become disabled again. In fact, the staff had put him in shoes, and as he had never worn them before, he had no idea how to walk in them. In Fiji, like all the other small children, he had always gone barefoot.

Eventually, I was able to join Peta in Hedley and Jean's small flat, causing some congestion but being made extremely welcome. The first thing that happened was that I developed an awful stomach upset and spent days vomiting and suffering from diarrhoea. I always tell people that the British bugs are the worst in the world. Simon had undergone extensive examinations, scans, and tests, and I was not at all surprised to find that all the tests were reported as normal. We were told that in situations like this, where such severe problems had happened to children and where the problems had been observed and verified by third parties finding no cause at all was rare. However, I was convinced that the cause of Simon's problems was a curse on him carried out by a servant of the devil. Almost anybody who has worked in very remote places has stories of such happenings, often leading to the death of the people who had been attacked. Simon was discharged and, apart from some mild fever fits, remained well.

Our next task was to find somewhere to live and a general practice to join. This was difficult as we had come home with no preparation about a year before we had planned to. Before we left England, I had agreed to join David, my best friend at Cambridge and our best man at our wedding in his practice in Clay Cross in Derbyshire. Shortly before we had to come home, Rolls Royce, the major employer in this area, had gone bankrupt, and people had started to move away to other jobs, so we were quite reasonably told that the offer of a partnership was no longer available. To add to this problem, we found that the country was in the middle of a long and bitter Post Office strike. This meant that there was no postal service at all, and the telephone service, which was operated by the post office at that time, was badly affected. While we had been in Fiji, we had decided to live on our local salary, which was the same as any Fijian doctor and not to touch the British salary supplement paid by the British Government. This meant that we had money for a deposit for a mortgage, but there was no point in finding a house without finding a job first. Meanwhile, we needed somewhere to live. There were plenty of flats to let, but universally when the letting agencies learned that we had a 20-month-old child, they refused to let us rent their property.

One of Peta's relatives offered to put us up while we were job-seeking. There were no medical journals advertising jobs available due to the postal strike, I could not send letters to friends who might be able to help, there were no lists of jobs available from the BMA and we panicked. There was even talk of a national general strike. It was tempting to turn around and head straight back to Fiji. Eventually, I managed to get through on the telephone to the Christian Medical Fellowship, who were extremely friendly and efficient. They arranged two appointments with practices that were seeking partners. We arranged an appointment to go and see a practice in Cambridge, which I was delighted about as taking this job would mean that we were living back on my old stomping ground. We were going to stay overnight and look around the practice over two days. Right from the beginning, though, it became clear that the practice was unusual, if not odd.

It was a bitterly cold two days. The senior partner welcomed us, appearing incredibly fit and exuding tremendous enthusiasm about everything. You got the sense that if you mentioned going to the toilet, he'd declare it to be a fantastic idea and ask if he could come along too. The doctor led us to his house, and we entered through the front door. A long passageway stretched before us, with rooms on either side. One of the rooms was his consulting room. The entire passageway was adorned with bottles, mostly whisky, all wrapped in Christmas paper. We wondered if this was his emergency supply. After a particularly taxing consultation, did he step out of his consulting room, nod to anyone present, and sneak a gulp from one of those bottles? The reality was slightly different but no less peculiar than our speculation. It turned out that he received several bottles of whisky as Christmas gifts every year. Despite being a teetotaller, he had apparently never got around to informing his patients of this fact. Each bottle was gratefully accepted and put with all the other bottles down against the wall in the passage. They just seemed to add up over the years, and nobody thought of clearing them up. So, there was a long line of about thirty bottles when we arrived. It did just cross my mind that I could offer to solve the problem for him and put them all in my car, but at that time, we had not yet decided that this practice was too bizarre even for us. I let the opportunity slip.

We were shown into our room with an open window and a one-bar electric fire if things got too nippy. Not a friendly environment when one has just got back from Fiji! Our host was a sailor who loved the "great outdoors" and the wind in what hair he had left. Later that day and the next day, we learned that this was quite a large practice with many students and faculty members on their books. We were introduced to the secretary, a "dear lady" who could not type and the practice nurse who, among other things, could not do cervical smears. We started to wonder whether you got a job in this practice according to the tasks that you couldn't do. At the end of the second day, Peta had developed bronchitis, Simon had a cold, and I wondered whether we were in some reconstruction of Alice Through the Looking Glass. We thanked them kindly and said how much we had enjoyed visiting. We doubted whether many practices had so many unusual and outstanding characteristics, but it was not for us.

We had also made an appointment to see a practice in Bedford. The partners of this practice had written to us when we were in Fiji inviting us to come and see the practice and perhaps work with them, but as we had expected to stay another year, we had told them that we were not at that time ready to choose a practice. Another factor in not investigating this practice was that Peta had boarded at Bedford High School as a teenager, and although she had enjoyed the school, she had no wish at all to return to the town. We went straight on to see this practice. There was an enormous difference straight away in the way we were welcomed. The partners were interested in us and what we had done and were considerate of us coming back to such a cold climate with a small child that had been very ill. The senior partner was going off to become a lecturer at the Southampton University Medical School, and I would be his replacement. It was a three-partner practice working in the centre of town on the ground floor of a listed building. There was another practice on the first floor. The two remaining partners were a serious man with a mild stutter and a rather anxious man just a little older than me. What impressed us was that they were evidently interested in their patients and had the ethic of doing the best medicine and giving the best care possible in any situation.

The older of the two remaining partners was a man with a "get up and sort it out" attitude. If something didn't work, he would find out why and quite likely to be able to put it right. I was offered the post, and we accepted it immediately. It was a good job that we did, since as soon as we got back to Solihull, where we were staying with a somewhat distant relative, we were told that we needed to get out. Apparently, the room we had been living in was not tidy enough, and we had made too much noise. I am not sure how one arranges to have a tidy and quiet room when one is living with a twenty-month-old baby who has just suffered a severe illness and has had a total disruption of his everyday life. So, we became homeless. Peta's mother was in Turkey, and my family was in the Isle of Wight, not the best place from which to find a practice in the middle of a communications strike. We phoned the middle partner, who was about to become the senior partner of the practice we were joining and told him that this situation could delay the time we could arrive in Bedford to start work. The immediate response was, "Come and stay with us until you find a house for yourself and your family. We have four children, and a few more people around won't make much difference to anything". With very grateful hearts, we did just that and Martin and Ruth Colebrook had us as guests for nearly three months until we moved into the house in which we still live, and we will be eternally grateful to them for their kindness.

The practice was a three-partner group practice that looked after about 7500 patients. We did all our own weekend and night calls. The practice office was manned from 8.00 am-12.00 pm and 1.30 – 7.00 pm. Our wives were the receptionists over the lunch period and throughout weekends on duty. There were no mobile phones or other call mechanisms when we started, so when the partners were not in the practice building, unless the receptionists or wives knew exactly where we were and this place had a telephone, we were uncontactable. They were left (sometimes literally) holding the baby. We did two or three surgeries per day except for a half day once a week. On an average day, we did about eight home calls. If one was on night call over the weekend, one had to work Friday and Friday night, Saturday and Saturday night, Sunday and Sunday night and Monday. By Monday evening, the doctor was exhausted and, in retrospect, probably dangerous because of tiredness.

At that stage, we had a small group of receptionists whose main job was taking messages, booking appointments, and finding the notes for the patients having consultations on the day. They also did some typing of letters to the hospital and the health service administrators. The working week for the partners was about 70 hours a week. A district nurse was attached to the practice but was not employed as part of the practice team, and her office was not on the practice premises. I was in a middle-class practice with patients living in a very wide area. We had patients in many villages within about 5 miles of the town centre where the practice building was. Overall, the patients were considerate and thought many times before they called us out, particularly at night. All babies, apart from the first babies or where the mother had had risk factors identified, were delivered at home with the help of district midwives. The simplest births were carried out by the midwives alone. The doctor could be caring alone for a patient in labour on an isolated farm about 4 miles from the town with the nearest telephone half a mile away. There might be a midwife there also if she was not managing another birth. Things could get very difficult if the baby or the mother ran into trouble in these cases. We always carried obstetric forceps with us. As well as seeing patients on the practice premises, we looked after a retirement home and three local boarding schools, Bedford School, Bedford High School, and Dame Alice Harpur School.

I found that a good number of my older patients had been in the Indian Army, probably because there had been a strong link between the Indian Army and Bedford School. I tried to book these patients in at the end of surgery as if one had time to listen, they had a huge store of fascinating and funny stories about their career. They also all seemed still to love shooting, and I had an endless source of pheasants, rabbits, pigeons, partridges, and anything else that moved in the countryside. They all needed plucking, skinning, and cleaning. This was something that Peta wisely refused to have anything to do with, though she did roast them and make them into fantastic casseroles once I had plucked and cleaned them. Maybe that was why we hardly ever went through a week without one or two groups of friends coming for meals.

I soon found that I fitted into the rhythm of consultations, visits and on-duty periods. I overlapped with the departing partner by about two months, and gradually his patients moved across to me. It took me nearly a year to fit into the definition of health and what one went to the doctor for in England. In Fiji, people lived in close, secure and hierarchical communities. Most personal and family problems were sorted out in this environment, meaning that most of what I saw was injuries and physical illness. I had to learn the concept that I had to be a life skills advisor, marriage guidance counsellor, career guide, managing the usual colic and crying fits of small babies and at times spiritual advisor as well. People who consulted me were far less physically ill than those who consulted me in Fiji. It became evident that here in England, one was dealing with many people with few roots or support systems in the communities. Another very big change I had to adjust to was that the buck did not always stop with me. In some ways, that was pleasing, but it became clear that people in my new medical environment did not seem so committed to seeing a patient right through a medical problem and not giving up responsibility until they were back in the normal rhythm of their lives. Also, although the medical programme was punishing in my new practice, in Fiji, I was the doctor all day and all night, seven days a week, for the whole population. I found it difficult to give over the care of patients when I was not on duty.

About two months after starting work, we moved into our new house in the village of Biddenham, an ancient village near Bedford in which there was a church with a list of the vicars going right back to

1245. The church and the village are mentioned in the Domesday book. We found the village very hospitable and rapidly became part of the community. One thing we found amusing was that the credit system in the babysitting circle, which we became members of, was glass beads. If one asked for a babysitter, one paid out a bead an hour; if one did a babysitting duty, one received one bead an hour. We had just returned from utter isolation, living at the end of the world where one paid for services with money to find that the currency in our new English village was glass beads! A few months after we moved into our new home Peta had a miscarriage, and both of us were surprised at what a big emotional blow this was for Peta. However, in August of our second year, we celebrated the birth of our second child Dominic. This was a joyful occasion, but not a simple one!

Peta's family had lived in Mersin, Turkey, for three successive generations. They embodied a fusion of Middle Eastern cultural attributes and British identity and citizenship. Peta's father held the position of British consul for Southern Turkey. Her uncle, Enrico, served as the Italian Consul, and Michel, the spouse of her second cousin, held the role of the Swedish Consul. This arrangement might have appeared quite nepotistic to a straightforward English lad like me, but it evidently functioned effectively. The whole family had adopted certain Middle Eastern family and hospitality habits, thus when Peta's cousins' children came to secondary school age and the standard of teaching in the Turkish upper schools was found to be very poor, it was expected that the four children should be sent to England to school, and we would look after them. Also, it was the habit that when a child was born in the family that the family should get together to congratulate the mother and bless the new baby. It so happened that these two imperatives happened together. August was the time when the older two of the four children needed to come and live with us to start school in September This was also the month that Dominic arrived. and it was necessary that the family should come at the same time to welcome our new baby. So, when Peta returned from the hospital after delivering Dominic, and after recovering from a postpartum haemorrhage, she came into a house that was bursting at the seams. There was her mother, Olga, plus her cousin Billy and his wife and a friend of Billy and his wife and two of Billy's children who would be living with us, Claudia and Mark. They stayed for about a week, and then Billy, his wife, his friend, and his wife moved on, leaving Olga, Mark and Claudia, Simon, Peta Dominic, and me. When Peta first came home, the only way Peta could get any privacy was by having a bed in the dining room. I had a bed by the telephone as I had to answer and deal with night calls, and the rest of the merry crowd was liberally scattered around the house where a space and a bed could be found. Peta amazed me by sailing through all this without turning a hair. One particularly heartwarming moment was that on the day of Dominic's birth, I coincidentally happened to be preaching at a local Baptist church. During the service, word spread that we had welcomed a new baby that day. In response, the congregation gathered every flower available in the entire church. This church was known for its generous display of flowers, and they sent me home with the entire collection, accompanied by a lot of love. It was a wonderful gesture, but our house was already overflowing with people, so arranging the flowers all around the house became quite an interesting task.

The circus eventually moved on, and we were alone with Mark, aged 12 and Claudia, aged 10, together with Simon and Dominic. Simon was a little bemused by the sudden deluge of people, a new brother, the house starting to look like a garden centre and at the end of it all finding that he had two new brothers and a new sister counting in Claudia and Mark. From his behaviour it seemed that, on reflection, he thought that this could probably be to his advantage. First, the visitors gave him ridiculous amounts of sweets and chocolates, and even when they disappeared, Claudia and Mark wanted to play and talk to him. Quite naturally, the two children coming from a very different culture into a chaotic house with a new baby and then their parents disappearing found life at first difficult. One of the centres of our life was our church. At this time, we were members of Christ Church, a large and lively Anglican church in central Bedford. The church had excellent and well-attended children and youth work. We became house group leaders for a support and bible study group, which met in our house, and from time to time, I preached on Sunday mornings in church. The Levante family was Catholic, so we found a lively Catholic Church with an active youth work for them.

During her early days with us, Claudia's salvation was that she had a real living doll in the person of Dominic to play with, talk to, bathe and eventually change nappies for him. Things were more difficult for Mark as he was taken off to St Richard School in Somerset after about a week, where he would be boarding. Claudia continued to live with us and went as a day girl to St Andrew's School, where they were very caring and apart from being teased about coming from Turkey (gobble gobble!), she fitted in well and was happy. She was a sweet girl with an easy temperament, a quick mind, and an incredible sense of smell. When she had been with us for a while and met all our friends, she could come in after school and tell us who had been to visit us from the smell in the house of the perfume that the friend had worn. Mark, on the other hand, was a much more mischievous character, and this eventually got him into some trouble. He found that he was not made very welcome in his new school, but he and one of his friends were given the job of looking after the school goat(!). They did not seem to develop much empathy with the goat and decided that goats were not their favourite animals. However, being normal curious boys, they rummaged around in the back of the goat pen and found that there was a door. It was no problem to force the door, and they found that they had entered Ali Baba's cave by the back door. There stacked up in front of them were all sorts of cakes, biscuits, sweets and other delicacies attractive to young boys. Having tasted samples of most of these, they then noticed that there were also many bottles. After trying several of these, they decided that the sweet sherry was most to their taste and finished off the bottle. It seemed that they had landed in the storeroom for the upcoming parents' evening.

Having eaten and drunk to their fill, they returned to the goat's pen, carefully closing the door after them and then to school. Mark was well and truly sick, but after a few hours, he recovered enough to present himself as just rather groggy. However, the other boy went unconscious. He was shipped off to the hospital, and when the school realised that he had been with Mark, he was hauled up and asked what they were doing. Mark was terrified and panicking, saying that he had given his friend a Turkish drug. Blood was taken from the unconscious boy and rushed to the national toxicology laboratory, where extensive tests were carried out for all the drugs that anybody could think of. The result came back strongly positive for a drug that was not specifically a Turkish one, ethyl alcohol. Mark was hauled up again before a furious headmaster and confessed what had happened. He was expelled on the spot. It was a Sunday when the headmaster called us to inform us about the situation. That night, we had been out for dinner with a neighbour who excelled in two areas of expertise. Firstly, he was a professor at Cranfield University and a world-leading expert in Computational Fluid Dynamics. Secondly, he was the only man we've ever met who made pea-pod wine. He was noted in our neighbourhood more for the latter talent than the former. This was not because of the taste or other quality of the product, and it was absolutely disgusting, but for his pride in his product and the strength of the wine. When one was invited to his house, one had, each time, to weigh up whether to go and to enjoy his wife's cooking, which was delicious, or whether to refuse as one knew that one did not get to the food without having passed the hurdle of downing some of the wine. This evening the food was excellent, and two other very good friends were also guests, and the atmosphere was relaxed and convivial. Even the wine did not taste quite so disgusting after the third glass.

We arrived home rather late, and the babysitter informed us that Mark's headmaster had called, requesting that no matter the time we arrived, we should call him immediately. I promptly dialled the headmaster's number, perhaps struggling a bit with slurring my S's, a detail that I'm sure he noticed. He told me at length what a terrible evil boy Mark was, how he was a complete loser, how he would never succeed at anything, and how he should be put straight on a plane and sent back to Turkey. I was expecting him to be out of breath after all that, but this was not the case, and after taking only a small breath, he informed me that we were to meet him in a certain car park in Oxford which was halfway between him and us. He would deliver Mark to us and never wished to see him again. I would love to have met this headmaster again after a few years when Mark had attained a good degree at Keele University and after postgraduate degrees had become European manager for Vodaphone, the international telecommunications firm, and then had gone to the USA where he owned his own satellite communications firm. However, once we had Mark back home again, we learned that the headmaster had phoned up Douai School, where Mark had been due to go from St Richards and warned the headmaster there under no circumstances to take him. Mark's father had previously been to Douai School and had known the present headmaster, Father Peter. Father Peter phoned me up and asked what all the fuss was about. With some trepidation, I told him the whole story, at which he roared with laughter. He commented that if this young man had that investigative ability to find the store and the ability to think on his feet to produce his story, these were just the sort of talents he was looking for. He could come to Douai the next term without passing the common entrance examination.

Two years later, Mark and Claudia's brother and sister, Eddie and Jenny, also came to stay with us. Eddie never really settled in England and returned to Turkey, where he thrived and is now a successful businessman. Jenny was a quieter version of Claudia, intelligent, warm, amusing, and gentle. Like her sister, she was a great blessing in our home, and they were in many ways like the daughters that Peta wished she had had. Claudia and Jenny lived in our home for several years, then they went to Clarendon, a Christian boarding school, and Claudia went on to Bryanston School for her sixth form. We were sad to see them go, though they still came home for holidays and exeats. All the children stayed with us for the Christmas and Easter holidays.

The favourite way to pass these times was to go to Lee Abbey, a Christian community and conference and holiday centre at Lynton in Devon. This is situated in a large house with its own farm in a fold in the hills on the North Coast of Devon and is very beautiful. It is totally interdenominational and is a truly welcoming community, whoever you are. We tried to go there during the sixth form conference week. Most of the guests at that time were much older than our three older children, but the organisers tried to include Mark, Claudia, and Jenny in everything they did. There was one notable occasion when we had been told that there would be a fire alarm test at 11.00 am one morning. We were sitting outside on a rug with Claudia, Mark, Jenny, and Simon, having left Dominic asleep in our second-floor bedroom. At eleven o'clock, the fire alarm went off as we had been told it would, and we took no notice. Then we saw two fire engines coming up the drive with blue lights on. We commented to the people next to us that we were amazed at the lengths that Lee Abbey went to make fire alarm tests realistic, only to be told that there was a fire. I am not a sprinter, but I must have broken several world records running across the lawn and up the stairs to fetch Dominic.

The children went home to Turkey for the Summer holidays, travelling as unaccompanied minors by plane. This was quite a palaver, as it usually happened in the middle of the week. With only three partners in a very busy practice, it wasn't easy to take time off on weekdays other than in holidays booked many months ahead. We dealt with this problem by booking the very earliest flight in the morning, normally about 7.30 am. This meant that we could hand them over to the care of airline staff at 5.00 am. They were all packed into the car at about 3.00 am, taken to the airport, and handed over to the care of the airline, and I could be back in Bedford in time to do my morning surgery. I must admit that I might have nodded off occasionally in the evening surgery that day when an elderly lady would be telling me about the pain in her back for the fourteenth time despite having refused to take any medication for the problem. The three children became, in part, at least our children for ten years.

Claudia then moved to Milan in Italy to study design and appeared on the front page of Vogue magazine, Jenny went back to Turkey, and Mark went to Keele University and then worked in Canada and the USA. We were very sad to see them all go!

Meanwhile, the practice grew and thrived, and I passed my exam to become a member of the Royal College of General Practitioners, the acknowledged specialty qualification for British general practice. However, when we tried to find new partners, we found a problem in finding self-motivated and lateral thinking candidates. Among many young doctors, the prevailing attitude when encountering problems was to try to avoid or pass the issue to someone else, rather than find ways to resolve it themselves. In response, we began to seek individuals who had worked abroad or taken unconventional paths in life. Using this criterion, we discovered Marguerite von Bergen, who had served as a missionary in Uganda, and Andrew Grey, who had worked in district hospitals in South Africa and Somalia. Finally, we came across Dan Fenske, who, after a successful academic career in biochemistry, decided he wanted more direct interaction with people. He chose to retrain as a doctor but encountered a challenge as he had received only one financial grant for a degree and no further support. Undeterred, he decided to fund his own education. He would rise early, starting a milk delivery route at 5:00 AM and finishing just in time to change and attend medical school classes.

With partners who could think laterally and were accustomed to hard work and self-reliance, the practise underwent gradual transformation. Ethical considerations, as well as a desire for a more engaging practice, prompted us to gradually become part-time medical officers at Bedford prison. We also became open to serving individuals transitioning out of the prison system as patients within our practice. Our interests expanded to include providing care for people in the town struggling with opiate addiction and attending to the homeless population. We took charge of the night shelter, the day shelter, the halfway house, and the reintegration programme to support individuals back into the community. Much of this work was carried out in collaboration with a team of trained professionals from the Kings Arms church in Bedford. These endeavours led to an immensely interesting and diverse professional life, although they did have the unintended consequence of significantly reducing the practise's income.

Our work in the prison involved us going there every day in the morning. We were working with the prison staff running the prison hospital, and we took a history from and examined the prisoners who had just arrived from the courts or other prisons. After that, we did a daily sick parade. It did not take long to realise that the population we were caring for was in every way sicker than the patients in our practice. About thirty percent of the people we consulted with had some sort of mental disability or sickness. Many of the prisoners also had chronic diseases such as pulmonary disease, cardiovascular disease, diabetes, or hypertension. Many came from very troubled backgrounds, and a considerable number had had disturbed childhoods or dysfunctional families. From the outset, it was abundantly clear that since we weren't directly employed by the prison service, we were considered second-class doctors in this context. The administration of the prison hospital comprised well-intentioned individuals with some training, although lacking medical, paramedical, or nursing qualifications. Medication prescriptions and procedures adhered to a very outdated approach. The primary sedative employed was bromide, and there was significant resistance to any form of change. Individuals thought to be at a high risk of suicide were placed in padded cells and sometimes secured in a body belt, effectively strapping them to a mattress. When I met the director of prison medical services, I asked what postgraduate medical training there was for medical officers and whether I could attend some of the courses. I was told that all the staff working in prison were fully trained professionals and thus had no need for further training. I decided to look at the literature on the daily work of prison medical officers. I searched the medical literature for such papers without success, so I decided to record what I did in the prison, the range of problems encountered and the actions that were possible to carry out and what was carried out. This was published in the British Medical Journal. I was supposed to be supervised by a prison doctor who worked directly for the prison service, but I never received a supervisory visit.

The duties at the prison were spread out over the male partners in the practice. During the IRA problems, as I was working in the prison system, I was recommended to have an alarm monitored by the police at our home, given the number of IRA prisoners in Bedford Prison. If the alarm went on, the police always turned up very rapidly. Every morning I was recommended to look under my car in case a bomb had been planted there, and my wife had to be present every time I started the car in the morning.

There were other problems, too, stemming from looking after prisoners, both in prison and signing them onto our practice list when they were released. One morning I was quietly working my way through the coughs and colds, bad hips, and worsening angina of a normal surgery when I called a new patient into my room. The door opened, and I found myself face to face with a man who had caused all sorts of problems when he was in prison. He had clearly had quite a lot to drink. He sat down in the patient's chair and spent some time telling me what a bastard I was and how I had made his life in prison even worse than it otherwise could have been. He was referring to my having refused to prescribe a very high dose of a powerful tranquilliser that he had requested for long-term treatment. He then told me that he was going to teach me a lesson. He also told me to sit precisely where I was; otherwise, he would kill me. Our surgery was in a listed building with very heavy doors and thick walls, so nobody outside my room would have heard if I had shouted for help. I reached for the telephone, but the man yelled at me and smashed the instrument. He then went around the room and systematically smashed the furniture, the pictures, and the drug cupboards and upended the plants on the floor. As a final gesture, he took my stethoscope from around my neck and threw it out of the window. He then left, leaving me sitting on a chair in the middle of a scene of destruction. I have no idea why he did not attack me as well. I was very shaken and alerted the receptionists, who called the police. After that episode, we installed attack buttons in the knee wells of the desks of all the consulting rooms.

Over time, I grew increasingly concerned about the inadequacy of the medical service provided to prisoners. Since my attempts to address this issue with the director of the service were unsuccessful, I reached out to the House of Commons committee responsible for overseeing prison medical care. I suggested they visit Bedford to assess the situation firsthand. Rene Short MP, along with members of her committee, arrived and spent several hours in the prison. They later joined us for lunch at our home. Following this visit and a highly critical report about the state of prison medical services, I was invited to serve on a government committee focused on improving the delivery of this service. The committee was chaired by Sir Raymond Hoffenberg, who also served as the chairman of the Royal College of Physicians. Our meetings took place at the college premises in Regents Park. Sir Raymond, an excellent chairman, happened to be a South African who had been expelled from his homeland for his anti-apartheid efforts. He had a steadfast rule that committee meetings should not exceed two hours and a determined commitment to staying on point. Despite his firm demeanour, he was a warm and affable person, making our interactions a delight. Our collective efforts eventually led to the integration of the prison medical service into the NHS, significantly enhancing standards. Among the committee members was Richard Smith, the editor of the British Medical Journal. He was known for navigating London on a decrepit bicycle, dressed in a tweed jacket and scarf, regardless of the weather. In the future, he proved to be an invaluable ally when I found myself in a difficult situation.

Even after these changes were made, I still found myself working in a profoundly dysfunctional service. However, there were individual acts of devotion and kindness shown by the staff of the prison hospital.

Quite a few of our inmates were basically inadequate people who had never found a stable way of earning their living or relating to other people. They would sometimes resort to violence or petty larceny. These people turned up in prison with monotonous regularity, and I never worked out what prison was supposed to do to them or for them. A number of these people were homeless when they were not in prison. These men became well known to the hospital staff, and they tried to give them small jobs when they were inmates. About Christmas time, some of these people would throw a brick through a shop window and steal something they really did not want to make sure that at this time, they would be back in prison, warm and well-fed. If these 'special clients' didn't appear in prison around Christmas, the hospital staff would search for them under the bridges of the river and other sites where homeless people congregated, ensuring their well-being and preventing death due to exposure. If they found them in distressing conditions, they would take them to the Salvation Army, where they were treated with kindness and care.

Eventually, things came to a head with my concerns about the care of the prisoners. A prisoner came in claiming that what had happened in his trial and commitment to prison had been totally unjust, so he went on a hunger strike and refused to drink. I spent a long time talking to him over several days as he became increasingly sick. Eventually, he agreed to accept medical help. I phoned a Bedford Hospital medical consultant and discussed his case with him. He decided the prisoner needed to come into the hospital immediately and be rehydrated intravenously. He arranged a bed, I informed the discipline branch of the prison, arranged an ambulance to take him to the hospital and went home. The next morning, I went into the prison for my normal morning session and found my patient still in the prison hospital. On enquiring about what had happened, I found that the prison governor had found that he did not have the staff to guard the prisoner in the hospital, so he cancelled the bed and the ambulance. Instead, he had contacted a doctor at Grendon Underwood prison, a prison usually concerned with managing prisoners with psychiatric problems. The doctor, who had not practised any clinical medicine other than psychiatry for 10 years, had advised the governor that the prisoner did not need to go to the hospital. I contacted the medical consultant whom I had spoken to the previous night. I agreed with him that this was outrageous, so I went to see the governor and asked for an undertaking that would never happen again. The governor refused to give this assurance and said that it was essential that all prisoners were properly always guarded and that this must take priority. I asked who I could take this to and who was more senior and was told that there was nobody I could talk to. I then decided that I would take this to the media as this contradicted all my ethical standards for the medical care of my patients. I went directly to the studios of the Three Counties Radio station and did an interview with one of their journalists, which was transmitted that night, and the next day, I did another interview with BBC Look East. This caused much fluttering in the dove cotes. I was summoned to the governor's office and told that I had infringed Part 2 of the Official Secrets Act, which was true, and that I would have to bear the consequences. I was also phoned up by the new Director of prison medical services, Dr Kilgour, a doctor who had already had a notable career, including spending time with the World Health Organisation. He was not a career prison doctor. He informed me that he did not in any way condone what I had done but that he understood why I had done it. I still had hanging over me the threat of conviction for infringing the Official Secrets Act and the possibility of even a prison sentence. I phoned Richard Smith, the British Medical Journal editor with whom I had worked on the Hoffenberg committee and explained what had happened. That week he largely devoted the news pages of the British Medical Journal, which was read at that time in 51 countries, to the ethical dilemmas of prison doctors. The Times newspaper also asked me to write an editorial on this subject. Following these articles, I had a civilised and professional discussion with Dr Kilgour, and there were no further consequences. As I thought that it would be impossible for me to continue to work at the prison in these circumstances, I handed over my responsibility at the prison to my partner Andrew Grey, in whom

I had great confidence and who approached ethics in medicine in a way very close to mine.

My work with the homeless and drug-abusing population of Bedford was largely done alongside and in support of the programmes run with these people by the Kings Arms Church in Bedford. Many of the gaps in social service provision at that time, and still today, are filled by this church. I did a weekly session for the homeless population at the BECHAR day centre. This was a day centre set up and, for many years, run by a group of local churches and run by a mixture of paid professional staff and volunteers. This centre provided a very highly subsidised lunch every weekday. It also provided access to social service support, clothing, various courses, counselling, and friendship, not only for the rough sleepers but also for the people surfing their friends' sofas. Many of these people had undiagnosed chronic diseases, unaddressed mental health problems, as well as problems with alcohol, heavy smoking and, at times, drug use. I was also on permanent call for the night centre and the halfway house, both run by the Kings Arms Church. This church also ran a support service for rough sleepers who could not cope with using the day and night centres. Each identified rough sleeper was allocated a worker from the church who got to know this person and made sure that they had warm clothes and enough to eat.

There was also a large group of people in the town who were illegal drug users. Our practice only engaged with opiate users, not those taking other addictive substances. Many of these people had been on drugs for many years and were in their 40s and 50s. Over 10 years, I looked after 200 drug users. The official way of dealing with these people was to replace opiate use with a prescribed drug, methadone, which was done in NHS drug clinics. An assessment was made of the level of their use, and a suitable dose of oral methadone would replace this. A contract would be made with each person involved, and part of that contract would be that the dose of replacement drugs would be decreased gradually over a relatively short time. There were some difficulties with this management.

Firstly, many of these people would be injecting the drugs they bought on the streets and transitioning to oral drugs, particularly a drug like methadone which did not give you a high, was not easy. Secondly, the reduction schedule for the dose of the drugs was set by the clinic. It was their agenda, not that of the person concerned. Thirdly, it was easy to accept the drugs and then sell them, using the money to buy the drugs they normally used. This problem could be overcome by getting the drug user to take the methadone in the place where they pick this up and under supervision. However, this was very disruptive for the people who still had jobs and could lead to the loss of their job. Very few people managed to become and stay drug-free on this regime.

We implemented a distinct treatment approach in our practice. For individuals who were engaging in injecting drugs and could provide evidence of this to us, we prescribed injectable methadone, alongside the necessary syringes and needles. After achieving stabilisation on a specific dose of the drug, we didn't enforce the requirement of gradually reducing their dosage in line with the standard drug schedule. Instead, we continued prescribing at that established level. This approach provided many of these individuals with their first opportunity in years to stabilise their lives. They no longer needed to resort to theft or shoplifting to fund their addiction. The funds they had could be redirected towards securing accommodation and sustenance.

We supplied a week's worth of methadone at a time and took precautions to ensure the drug wasn't being sold. Periodically, we asked them to administer their dose in our presence. If they had been selling a part of their dose, their opiate tolerance would have decreased, leading to a reaction when they administered the entire dose in front of us. To counteract the opiate overdose, we always had a recovery drug available in such instances.

Gradually over the weeks and months, very many of our patients used to come to us and say that having experienced a more stable life, they were fed up with being junkies, and wanted to get off the drugs. We never produced a programme for them to do this, but we told them they had to produce it. Very often, they came back with a very rapid drug reduction programme, and we advised them to think again. Eventually, we asked them why they thought that they would be able to come off when so many people failed. Often, they became quite angry and told us not to tell them what they could and could not do. At this stage, we agreed to prescribe them whatever dosage they wanted as long it was not an increase in the dosage. We also pointed out to them that this was their programme, not ours and the only person they were proving anything to was themselves. It was their agenda nor ours. Many times, these people found that they could not manage the programme, and we told them to go away and rewrite their programme.

A surprising number of these people did, in fact, manage to reduce and stop their drug use. Between a third and a half of all our patients became drug-free. Many of these patients received considerable help from the Kings Arms Church, and some of them for whom the change in life was too great after leaving the drug scene were able to live in the church halfway house for a time. One of my major sources of support during this time was the drug officer of Bedford Police, a man called Griffiths. He bought into my philosophy of drug treatment, giving the drug users themselves the right to decide how they would manage their condition, and of course, he gained some kudos from the increased number of people who became drug-free. He and I frequently presented jointly at meetings about drug problems at schools around the town. He was unwell with multiple sclerosis and had severe pain for much of the time. He gained considerable street cred by admitting that taking cannabis helped the pain enormously, and he frequently went to Amsterdam to take this, but he would never take it in the UK because it was illegal. He told the schoolchildren that if they thought that cannabis for medical or other conditions should be legalised, they lived in a democracy, so they should convince their fellow citizens of their point of view. Until such time, they should not take any illegal drugs.

Life settled into a routine primarily revolving around children and the practice. In the subsequent 10 years, the practice expanded, leading to the appointment of additional partners. There was a movement of a multitude of procedures and the treatments, especially of chronic illnesses, from hospitals to general practise settings. We brought in specialist nurses to manage patient follow-ups for conditions such as asthma, diabetes, hypertension, and gynaecological issues. As we looked after two girls' schools and developed our care for obstetric and gynaecological problems, we started looking for women partners. We also became a training practice for general practice registrars studying for their accreditation. The registrars joined us for one year; they had one day a week in classroom teaching, and for the rest of the week, we gave them on-the-job teaching. In many ways, it was like an apprenticeship.

Czechoslovakia

About seven years after I started in the practice, I was asked to visit Czechoslovakia to manage some details of the mutual health agreement with this country arranged through the British Council. Before I left, I received a briefing from the Foreign Office about how I should behave as a representative of the British government in a communist country. One of the key points they highlighted was how to express gratitude and give gifts and tips. It turned out that I needed to bring stockings and packets of cigarettes, both of which were in very short supply, and distribute them in various circumstances.

I spent a week in Czechoslovakia and held a blue diplomatic visa during my stay. I was fortunate to have my own interpreter, a delightful member of the English faculty at Charles University in Prague. I resided in an overseas student hostel where a curfew of 11:30 pm was imposed, requiring me to be back in my room. To my surprise, I discovered that my interpreter's husband was a refusenik, an artist and jazz musician, even though jazz was prohibited in the country. During the evenings, my interpreter, Zdena, and her husband, Mirek, would often take me out to various interesting parts of the city, where it was apparent that most people were not supportive of the communist government. On two occasions, following the guidance from my briefing, I left cigarettes and a pack of tights on the table when leaving a restaurant. Zdena was curious about this and asked if such gestures were customary in England. So, I shared with her the details of the briefing I had received from the Foreign Office regarding tipping and giving gifts. Her reaction, along with Mirek's, was a burst of incredulous laughter. Evidently, about 20 years prior, there had been a period of stocking and cigarette shortages, but those times were long past, and the idea of distributing such items to everyone was considered quite peculiar. This experience left both them and me wondering whether the British Embassy in Prague truly understood the current cultural landscape of the country they were operating in.

One evening, my two hosts picked me up and we ventured downtown. The bitter November cold had set in, and Mirek, sporting a weathered trilby hat, was with us. As darkness crept in, we found ourselves strolling across Old Town Square, the only souls present. It was snowing hard, and the flakes were swirling around a single lamp in the middle of the square. The film *Amadeus* had recently been shot in this part of the city, and all the buildings had been renovated. On top of all the churches, the government had replaced the crosses with gold-coloured stars. We dived off down a small side street lined by ancient houses and eerily quiet. Suddenly Mirek stopped and knocked a code on a nondescript door. The door opened on a chain, and somebody asked who Mirek was through the partially opened door. Once verified, the door swung ajar, revealing a spacious room adorned with round steel tables, their spindly legs giving them a delicate appearance. Seated on iron chairs around these tables were clusters of men, many donning trilbies and engaged in lively discussions alongside somewhat disinterested women. We settled at a table in the company of Mirek's acquaintances, and he initiated conversations. Zdena deftly translated for me. The focal point of discussion was none other than jazz. As I surveyed my surroundings, I couldn't help but draw parallels to the stylised sets of Hollywood spy thrillers.

Another evening, I was invited to Zdena and Mirek's flat and met their children and some of their friends. The friends were extremely friendly. They chatted about their own situations under communist rule, and then they started to ask about all the propaganda they had been fed by their government, particularly regarding gross poverty in British towns and police brutality. I decided not to try in any way to present a rosy picture of our society, so I talked about the difference between the rich and the poor in the West and some of the cases where the police had indeed not behaved well. However, I also discussed government programmes to rectify these situations, to reduce poverty and to train the police better in handling difficult situations. The people in the room were astounded that any government would admit to such problems and even more amazed that anybody could point these problems out in the press and demand that action be taken without landing in prison.

On another occasion, I was alone for the evening and went to a different part of the town by the metro. This was a challenge as nobody seemed to speak English, and the script was Cyrillic. I randomly disembarked at a station and stumbled upon a basement restaurant. There, I enjoyed an excellent meal and was introduced to an essential aspect of Czech culture: 'Delicate Dumplings.' However, no matter how hard I tried, I could not fully embrace this cultural element. The menu prominently featured beer. As soon as I took my seat, a litre of authentic Czech pilsner, brewed in the town of Pilsen in Bohemia – not the pale imitation brewed by Americans and called Pilsner – was placed before me.

After consuming about two-thirds of the litre, another foaming glass appeared, ready to replace the first. The meal was both exceptionally affordable and of high quality. After leaving the restaurant, feeling pleasantly full, I purchased a ticket and boarded the train back to my hostel. Upon disembarking, I was approached by a middle-aged woman dressed casually, who rapidly spoke to me in Czech. I explained that I had no idea what she was saying, so she repeated herself in Russian. Once again, I indicated my lack of understanding, and I attempted to pass by her. However, she was insistent, physically preventing me from leaving. I soon realised I was being apprehended, which I thought would make for an interesting story at a future dinner party back home. Reluctantly, I followed her to an office where I was required to empty my pockets. Among my belongings was the ticket I had purchased. The entire atmosphere suddenly shifted. It turned out that the woman was an undercover metro ticket inspector, and she had detained me for not showing my ticket. We exchanged handshakes, and I left the station no worse for wear, aside from a slightly sore arm from her grip. The next day, Zdena, Mirek, and I shared a good laugh about the incident.

During my visit, I met another very interesting young Czech man, Jiri Horacek. He was a bright young doctor who had recently graduated from the excellent medical school of Charles University in Prague. He accompanied me to several sessions during the week, and I got to know him well. He had an interesting history. As a young student, he had been befriended by an Oxford graduate who had been teaching English in Prague at the time of the commencement of the communist regime and who had stayed on. She taught Jiri almost perfect English and gave him a broad outlook on the world. When she died, she left her house to Jiri. After my visit to his country, the British Council arranged a professional visit to Northwick Park Hospital for Jiri, and he came and stayed at our home for a few nights. Since that time, we have met each other either in the Czech Republic or in England every year for 34 years. Jiri is now a Professor of Medicine at Charles University Hospital. He has a son and daughter-in-law, a daughter, and a grandson, all of whom we know and who have stayed with us at our homes in England and France.

On my return to the UK, I was required to produce a report of what had happened during my visit and, in passing, I mentioned that I had seen a lot of a refusenik group, one of the leaders of which was the husband of my interpreter. A few days later, I was phoned up by the Foreign Office security branch, which turned out to be MI6. I was informed that an officer would be coming to talk with me, and I should keep a certain morning free. I cancelled all my patients for that day, and at about 10.00 am, there was a knock on my door. Outside stood a middle-aged man. He had grey hair, pasty skin, a charcoal grey suit, a grey tie and a standard-issue civil service briefcase which was the only thing that was not grey. He was quietly spoken and did not relate on a human level at all, keeping a distance from me physically and emotionally. He was a beautiful example of a cardboard cut-out man. In any film, anybody would have designated him a spy, though as he had been sent to interview an ordinary non-descript Home Counties GP, one would deduce that he must have been a bit of a failure as a real spy. He sat down in our sitting room and refused a cup of tea or coffee. He then interviewed me in detail, wanting to know exactly whom I had met where and what they had said. He wanted to know the names and addresses of all the people who expressed any disagreement with the Czech government. At one stage, he asked if he could use our downstairs toilet. When I said yes, he packed up all his papers, put them into his briefcase and locked it. Afterwards, he headed to the toilet, bringing his briefcase along. I responded to all his questions as accurately as possible, but I steadfastly refused to disclose the names or addresses of any individuals he was enquiring about. I believed that complying could place my new acquaintances in significant jeopardy with their government. Finally, after approximately two hours, he concluded the questioning and departed, and I never received any further communication.

After I had been working in the practice for about 12 years, we started developing itchy feet again. At this time, our list of patients had grown to such a degree that it was difficult to manage the work with the partners we had, but if we had employed a new partner at that stage, the income of the original partners would have fallen considerably. During this period, a young doctor emerged who seemed to be an excellent potential partner. It was decided that the young doctor would be hired, and I would be granted a 15-month leave of absence. While the leave would be unpaid, I would still continue to make pension payments. I was already interested in a post being offered in the medical division of the Saudi Military through an agent of the British Government called Allied Medical. I would be a consultant in family practice. The long-term aim was to develop a Medical Boards in Military Settings course and examination for the Saudi Military with the help of the British Royal College of General Practitioners. This would be the exam leading to recognition as a specialist in this field. A contract was signed with the Bedford practice that they would take me back as a partner at the end of the programme. We let our house in Biddenham, the boys became boarders at Bedford School, and we set off towards the east.

Saudi Arabia

In the early 1980s, the Saudi government asked the British Government for help with improving the quality of the medical services of the Saudi Military. This organisation also provided medical care to the Saudi Royal Family. The British government gave the contract for this task to the company Allied Medical who in turn asked for the help of the medical royal colleges to find and recruit the personnel with the right qualifications for this task. The task involved the provision of medical services together with a comprehensive programme of education and postgraduate development of local doctors. The base unit for this project was the Riyadh-Al Kharj Medical Programme, and this consisted of a large multi-specialty hospital in the capital, Riyadh, with a satellite hospital in a desert town about 30 miles outside the capital. When we were considering applying for posts in this programme, we decided that I should do a short posting of 6 weeks at the satellite hospital at Al Kharj to see if it would be possible for us as a family to cope with living and working in what was a very different culture from the one we were used to. This posting went well with interesting work, comfortable living accommodation, and good recreation facilities, so I applied for a job in the main programme.

I was interviewed by Dr Alistair Donald, a senior member of the Royal College of General Practitioners with whom I was to work very closely later. I was already a member of the College by examination. I was accepted and offered a post. However, we heard many reports about how restrictive life was for women in Saudi Arabia. It was the policy of this programme only to offer posts to one member of a married couple, almost always the man. Once the agreement had been drawn up for me to sign, I went to London to sign the agreement. Before I signed the document, I raised the point that if we were to work in Riyadh, it would be necessary for Peta to also be offered a job. They informed me that their policy did not support such arrangements. I expressed my gratitude for their time and promptly informed them that under those circumstances, I would decline the position. I then departed. The following morning, a senior representative from Allied Medical contacted our home by phone. They conveyed that, in our case, they were willing to make an exception to their policy of not employing spouses. While they agreed to hire Peta, they did not commit to employing her as a nurse. We found this arrangement acceptable and proceeded to sign the contract. We enjoyed Christmas as a family, established the two boys in their boarding houses at Bedford School, let our house, and flew off to Saudi Arabia early in January. We were delighted to find that, as I was a consultant, we were eligible for first-class travel. However, we encountered a less pleasant surprise when we discovered that our travel arrangements were with Saudia Airlines, a completely dry airline. In the context of Saudia, 'First Class' merely meant priority boarding and disembarkation, larger seats, improved cuisine, and a continuous supply of stuffed figs throughout the flight.

We landed in the early hours of a January morning. On leaving the plane, we were directed to the immigration and customs area of the airport. At customs, our cases were placed on a table, and one by one, they were completely emptied. Everything was minutely examined. They were looking for any alcohol, which would have been confiscated at once and poured away, or anything that could be counted as a salacious nature of showing any part of the female body. Peta had a paper-backed book with a picture of an older man comforting a younger woman on the cover; this was taken and thrown away. If the customs officer happened to be in a sour mood, they could seize any personal Bibles, tossing them onto the floor and even spitting on them. After enduring this disheartening process – an unwelcoming experience for newcomers to the country that was to become our home – we proceeded to the arrivals section of the airport, where we expected to meet the director of the family medicine department. He greeted us, adorned in a heavy Harris tweed jacket, despite the temperature being a chilly 13 degrees Celsius. We were dressed lightly, having anticipated moving to one of the hottest countries on earth. However, we found ourselves shivering, unexpectedly confronting the reality of living in a desert environment within a city at a considerable elevation. The director led us to the hospital compound and a temporary flat, our initial residence, until more permanent accommodation could be arranged. To our relief, the flat was warm. Even in Saudi Arabia, it seemed that central heating was available in the form of air-conditioning set to heating mode. We settled into the flat, unpacked our belongings, and braced ourselves for the journey into our new life.

Riyadh was chosen as the capital of the Kingdom of Saudi Arabia for its position in the middle of a vast desert and high on a plateau which tempers the heat to a degree. The wealth of the kingdom at that time was written all over the town. Lining the universally dual carriageway main roads were huge towers of glass and steel often built by fashion houses, digital enterprises, or hotel chains. In the small streets behind the main roads, there were still the original concrete block buildings housing the small local enterprises, the small shops, the hairdressers, and the car mechanics. However, a percentage of these were run by expatriates, often Arabs from other countries. Everywhere there was building, and everywhere the builders were Bangladeshis, Filipinos or, in the case of road building, Yemenis. These immigrant workers living away from their families were treated badly, living in crowded buildings, poorly paid and often working in unsafe conditions. A law in the kingdom stated that all outside manual labour must stop when the temperature reached 50 degrees Celsius. The consequence was that the official temperature during the summer climbed through the 30s and the 40s until it reached 49 degrees, and it stayed at that level for days or weeks, so the work did not have to stop. Although this was a desert town, it was also a green town. Millions of dollars were spent planting and caring for trees, flowers, and gardens. It only rains in Riyadh about 5 days a year, and when it rains, it pours. The town planners, in their wisdom, did not think it was worth putting in any water drainage system, so when it rained, everywhere was flooded. The streets were often under at least a foot of water, so everybody coming to work in Riyadh was advised to bring Wellington boots. The hospital was near the middle of the town and under the flight path to the nearby airport.

One of the cultural differences that was most evident to Westerners in Saudi Arabia was the place of women in society there. It was rare to see an unmarried woman and a man could marry up to three wives if he were able to treat all of them equally in all ways. From the age of puberty, all women had to be completely veiled. This included covering their faces and often their hands as well. The external covering had to reach down to the ground. A woman could not be in any public place without her husband, brother, or designated guardian. She was not allowed to drive in any circumstances and could not make any legal transactions without one of her guardians being with her. If she had any children, those children were her husband's property. In a traditional house, there would be two front doors and two sitting rooms, one for men and one for women. A woman could not be in a car with anybody other than her husband, and the police had the right to stop a car and demand the woman's marriage certificate. If she were not married to a man in the same car, the man and the woman would be arrested for sexual indecency. This cultural norm has been modified to a degree since we were in Saudi Arabia, but women still lead very restricted lives there. This attitude to women had a very large effect on the way that medicine could be practised.

The first two days of our hospital stay were taken up with an orientation. The person leading this process was the senior security officer who dealt with cultural and climatic matters and how to fit into our work in the hospital, all of which could be a challenge to new arrivals. He started by telling us that in the desert, one can find hoarfrost on the bonnet of a car in the very early morning and fry an egg on the same bonnet by midday. We were living in a climate of extremes. We were also told several other things of note. Firstly, the Saudis employed people from various corners of the world, yet they officially recognised only three religions: Islam, Judaism, and

Christianity. Anyone of Hindu, Sikh, or Buddhist faith was required to register as either Muslim, Jewish, or Christian. Regardless of the registration, if your faith wasn't Islam, you had no freedom to practise your religion openly.

Furthermore, if someone identified as Jewish, they risked deportation. Surprisingly, there were numerous registered Christians in Saudi Arabia who had little understanding of Christian beliefs. We were also informed that authorities were well aware of the widespread winemaking happening within hospital compounds. In fact, if a fire broke out in a hospital, the resulting blaze could last for a week due to the fermenting of wine. Engaging in such activities, however, carried significant risks. Those caught might face severe lashings and, more likely, immediate deportation. Lastly, to survive in Saudi Arabia, we were advised to grasp a crucial protocol: If a member of the royal family made a request, we must halt whatever we were doing and promptly comply. This applied regardless of the task's urgency. Failure to comply could result in deportation. Notably, there were around 40,000 members within the Al Saud royal family.We were then taken to the family medicine department and given a tour of the facilities. It was a spacious, well-designed area where the doctors were organised into teams, each having its own dedicated space. These teams consisted of six doctors, two of whom were local Saudi Arabs, and the other four were primarily British doctors, along with a few Japanese, Antipodean, and Korean colleagues. For the first two days, I consulted with the department's director, working through a Lebanese interpreter. I was put under some pressure to prescribe antibiotics for potential infections, as 'this was what was expected of us.' After this introduction, I was allowed to consult on my own. There were certain aspects that made life much easier than in England. For instance, I could order an X-ray or a blood test, and they would be performed immediately, with results typically returned within an hour. Patients were provided with a test or X-ray form and instructed to proceed to the relevant department. Afterwards, they were asked to return to the team waiting area, where we would notify them once we obtained the results. While this process may sound simple, it had its challenges. Each woman who visited us was dressed in a black burqa, completely covered in a black lacy cloth. This presented a dilemma: how to discern which direction the lady was facing, given that she appeared the same from both the front and the back. To solve this, we quickly learnt to observe the shoes, which provided a clue about the side of the burqa to address. Furthermore, identifying one's assigned patient in the waiting room was another puzzle. With twenty identically dressed patients, their faces obscured, the solution lay in remembering the handbag carried by your patient and using it as a distinguishing marker. Whenever any of my patients required a specialist consultation, it was nearly always possible to arrange for it on the following day or within a maximum of two to three days. I had a team of three Lebanese interpreters working alongside me: two were Muslim, and one was Christian. They were educated individuals, exuding warmth, mischief, and a great sense of humour. Whenever any issue arose, they could almost always find a way to resolve it. Despite some of their solutions seeming unconventional, they never disappointed. The population we were serving was the army and the royal family. Among the people from the army, there were all sorts of soldiers and their wives and children. People from all ranks turned up and were treated in the same way, from Bedouins, who were happier when they were out in the desert with their sheep and camels, to the senior ranks, who were of a completely different culture, often very rich and whose whole life was lived in the bustle and hyper-consumption of Saudi town life. There was one exception to this rule, and that was if your name was Al Saud. This meant that you were dealing with a member of the royal family, and the royal family didn't do waiting. One of my colleagues faced a serious emergency situation when a princess requested him to retrieve her X-ray. He responded, 'Could you please wait for a couple of minutes while I arrange treatment for this critically ill patient?' The following day, he was on a plane back home. You don't make a princess wait even for a minute.

Much of our work was like general practice in England, but one thing that shocked me was the level of alcoholism. This was even though consuming alcohol was strictly forbidden and could be punished with 50 lashes. One day a senior city council member came in to see me and told me that he had a problem, and on further enquiry, it became clear that he had an alcohol problem. I proceeded as I always have done firstly, by asking him how much he drank, and then by enquiring about his intentions. He told me that he was currently consuming two bottles of whisky per day and that he didn't want to quit alcohol entirely but rather reduce it to a more moderate level. When I asked what he considered 'normal,' he explained that he aimed to cut down to one bottle a day, like most of his friends. During this time, all sorts of alcohol were readily available, and many wealthier individuals indulged, often excessively. It was transported discreetly over the desert under the cover of night using large Mercedes lorries. The supply system operated smoothly, with the authorities conveniently turning a blind eye to the practise. However, a turning point occurred when disaster struck: the Saudi Air Force purchased three AWAC detection planes from the Americans, along with American pilots, to operate the electronics and fly the planes. The first intruders they detected were the whisky-carrying lorries. Since these had been spotted by a foreign military agent, they couldn't be ignored like a friendly Saudi soldier could dismiss them in exchange for a crate of whisky bottles. As a result, the whisky's importation landscape shifted. It now had to be brought in by the princes using their private planes, causing the cost to triple overnight.

As well as working in the family medicine department, we were also expected to do some shifts in the Accident and Emergency departments. This was good fun as during these sessions, we met people working all over the hospital and could get a feel for how the hospital worked. The department was busy and -equipped, and the other doctors who worked there were well-trained and motivated overall. There were two situations when there were almost no patients at all in the department. The department was empty on the very few days when it rained, or when there was a major football match on the television. Who could be ill in the middle of a football match or if it meant getting wet on the way to the hospital?

The hospital had rest areas with comfortable seating and restaurants where people could relax during break periods. One of the restaurants was managed by a South Indian family known for producing the best biryani I have ever tasted in my life. Peta and I often met up in this restaurant for lunch together. There was also a recreation block that featured air-conditioned areas for playing tennis or squash. Additionally, there were three identical swimming pools: one for women, one for men, and one for families. This separation ensured that situations where a woman in a skimpy swimming costume was in the same pool as a man in swimming trunks were avoided. At the beginning of our time in Riyadh, the authorities didn't seem to realise that such situations were occurring in the family swimming pool, where, in one family, perhaps the mother was taking the children swimming while another family was accompanied by the father.

We swam in the family pool occasionally, but most of the exercise we had was from walking the one-and-a-half miles to and from the hospital. This could be a challenge in the middle of the summer due to the heat, but a much greater threat was the behaviour of the Saudi drivers. There were perfectly good pavements along the roads, but nobody at all walked anywhere in Riyadh; they went by car, even for a journey of 100 yards. Peta always dressed very discretely, but on the advice of the British Embassy, she did not wear a head covering. Seeing a Western woman walking alongside a man without a head covering seemed to enrage Saudi men, and three times drivers tried to run her down, even mounting the pavement to try and do this. Overall, the sort of people who did this were very bad drivers, and it was easy to get out of the way. One advantage of walking home instead of coming on the hospital bus was that we could drop into the small shops and buy beautiful Lebanese or Syrian food, such as manakeesh to eat for our evening meal.

Soon after we arrived, Peta, a qualified secretary, nurse, and health visitor, was given a job in the typing pool. This was not a good experience, and she found herself in a group of particularly bitchy women among whom the director was the worst. She quickly applied for a transfer and was relocated as a secretary to the officers' clinic situated in an encampment some distance into the desert. Since women in Saudi Arabia were not allowed to drive, she had her own driver to take her to and from the clinic. Here, she found a very pleasant team of doctors, nurses, physiotherapists, and secretaries. Her dress code mandated wearing a suit with a jacket featuring long sleeves and a skirt that reached down to the ground. The desert heat would have been unbearable were it not for the air conditioning.

We moved into our flat about three weeks after arriving. It was in a large block of flats outside the hospital compound and on the other side of the town. It was spacious, with three bedrooms and ornate furnishings and chandeliers in both the sitting room and the dining room. The whole flat was air-conditioned except for one room, which was the kitchen. This was eminently logical in Saudi society as it would be the domain of the women and, specifically in most families, the maid, so there was no need for air-conditioning. We had a balcony where one could hang washing, but it was absolutely forbidden to hang any sort of lady's underwear where it could be seen by other inhabitants. So, we were provided with a large and powerful tumble dryer. On the roof of the block of flats was a large and well-maintained swimming pool, much used by the children when they flew out from England during the holidays. There was also a minibus service which started at the hospital, visited all the blocks of accommodation for hospital staff around the town and dropped people off and picked them up at the three best supermarkets before returning to the hospital. There were two routes which were the same except that the buses did the round in opposite directions so once dropped off at a supermarket one did not have to go all the way round to get home.

Almost everybody in our block was an expatriate, largely because we lived very differently from Saudi families. Two guards on the door checked you in and out, and we supposed were the ears and eyes of the authorities. In our block, we noticed that the guards often read books covered in black leather that looked exactly like Bibles. One day I asked one of the guards if they were Bibles, and he said yes. I then asked him if he was not frightened of doing this as any expression of any religion, including reading a Bible in public, was severely repressed. He said that he was not in the least bit scared because the Bibles were in his language, Korean and that the script in this language was very complicated and could be read by very few people. He also informed us that all three of the guards were actually pastors of churches, and they were in the process of saving up to establish a dog farm intended for producing meat to be served in restaurants. The profits from this venture would be channelled to support their respective churches. We found it quite amusing that the Saudis were unintentionally employing Christian pastors to fund three churches by engaging in a business that was considered completely repugnant to the local culture—namely, dog consumption.

Our neighbours were friendly and worked in widely differing areas of the Saudi military medical machine. As with all other residents, we fermented our own wine. This was a very simple procedure. We went to the supermarket and bought 10 litres of grape juice, a lot of sugar and enough yeast for the wine we were producing. At the beginning, we also bought a 15-litre container, much like a reserve petrol can. The supermarkets were very helpful in all this. They offered two types of yeast for sale: 'baking yeast' and simply 'yeast,' the latter actually being wine yeast. Interestingly, everyone at the supermarket seemed to know exactly what your intended use was for these three ingredients. On one occasion, we discovered that we already had enough yeast for the fermentation batch we were about to start. Thus, we only needed to purchase grape juice and sugar from the supermarket. However, as we approached the checkout, the cashier suddenly remarked, "Excuse me, sir, I believe you've forgotten your yeast."

Despite everybody making wine and the upper levels of society being awash with alcohol in the Alice in Wonderland world we were living in, the civil police periodically did raids to check for alcohol. Happily, as we were a military unit, the civil police had to give two days' notice before they raided our block of flats. When the Saudi security officer for the expatriates learned that we would be raided, he came and parked his Jaguar across the entrance of our flats and warned us to pour all the wine down the drain and wash out the receptacles we had used. As the security officer was a prince, Prince Faisal, the civil police could not pass his Jaguar until he gave permission. When the prince was certain that everything had been poured down the sink, he allowed the police to come into a building reeking of alcohol and where the sewer rats were reeling about totally drunk. They always made a careful search and found nothing.

One of the biggest aids for us during our time off was the departmental cars which one could book free of charge. Even the petrol was a few pence a gallon. The great pastime in Saudi was shopping, which was true for all ages and races. The supermarkets were excellent, well-stocked with very high-quality food. Almost anything could be purchased except for alcoholic drinks. If one desired Middle Eastern cuisine, Chicken Street was the destination, where the ambiance closely resembled that of Syria or Lebanon. The scene featured noise, dust, and stray cats chased by scraggy Saluki hounds—wild creatures likely infected with various diseases. People were shouting, arguing, making deals, breaking deals, or simply exchanging greetings with individuals across the road. In a society where men couldn't hold hands with women, they were often seen holding hands with other men as an alternative. This bustling street was the haven for shawarmas—flatbreads sliced open and generously filled with a variety of meats, predominantly chicken, accompanied by parsley, a hint of rice, and an array of spices.

The concoction was then pressed down by hands that had just stifled a sneeze. The taste was divine, so much better than any of the ingredients alone. It was probably the germs from the hands of the man who served you that gave them the *je ne sais quoi*. Then after the visit to Chicken Street and having put the loot in the car, perhaps a walk down to the gold souk seemed a good idea. Here there was small shop after small shop with huge quantities of gold, precious stones, necklaces, bangles, rings, watches, and ingots. If you want it, they can get it. Generally, regardless of the intricacies involved in crafting the jewelry, pieces were sold based on the weight of the gold. One couldn't help but feel overwhelmed by the abundance of 22-carat gold present all around. What struck us the most was the apparent absence of any security measures. It was quite common to come across shops where the owner had temporarily stepped out to pray or enjoy a cup of tea, leaving the shop unattended and unlocked. In this society, the threat of having one's hand severed as punishment for theft seemed to serve as a potent deterrent.

On the way home, we might drop back into one of the big supermarkets to stock up on the larder. However, if one did that, it was good to check the time. As prayer time approached, the muezzins' calls resonated from all the minarets. Unfortunately, they would chant the calls in varying keys in the town, creating a cacophonous effect. This signalled the supermarkets to close their doors and guide everyone out of the shops. If you happened to be halfway through your shopping with a partly filled cart, you'd have to abandon it and step outside—sometimes sitting on a wall—for around 20 minutes, even during the scorching 45-degree summer temperatures. Afterwards, you were allowed to reenter and continue your shopping. However, this routine differed for the local Saudis. As soon as the muezzin called, we noticed that all the local men and women headed at speed for the toilets, and we wondered what it was about prayer time that had such a diuretic effect. The reason behind this practise soon became evident: as soon as the call to prayer echoed, the mutaween—known as the religious police—made their appearance. Armed with long poles, they were ready to enforce their mandate. Charging towards any group, they would shout, "Salah, Salah!" (prayer, prayer!), demanding everyone to hurry to the mosque or risk being struck on the legs with their poles. A curious exception existed: the mutaween wouldn't pursue individuals into restrooms, hence the sudden increase in the urge to visit the toilet during prayer times. Beyond prayer times, the mutaween filled their hours by patrolling the town, occasionally striking women's legs if they deemed their clothing inappropriate. Peta, who never wore a head covering, proudly bears a few honourable scars on her legs as a testament to these encounters. She had been advised by the British consul not to cover her head. Some years prior, the French residents of Riyadh had been encouraged by their embassy to adopt head coverings, but this led to the Saudi authorities also demanding that they wear the long black robes worn by Saudi women. The British stance was to avoid setting out on that path and instead endure a few blows from overzealous mutaween.

As is usually the case where there is a large expatriate community, there were many parties that one could go to. Often groups of people from other compounds, such as those of BAE or one of the pharmaceutical companies, were invited too. More frequently, one just had dinner with people who worked in the hospital that one had become friendly with. Just occasionally, there was a themed party. This was not always in our residential block, so attending one of these get-togethers could present challenges. We were invited to a punk party and a wild west party at various times, and we had to go by car and park the car, then walk to the compound. We did rather wonder what the morality police would make of it if they found us walking the streets of Riyadh dressed totally in black dustbin liners pierced with large safety pins or wearing an exceeding large stetson and riding a hobby horse.

At other times we headed off into the desert. One of our favourite places was the camel trail. This was a place where there was a sharp escarpment from the high plateau on which Riyadh was built down to the base level of the desert. Here there was an ancient twisting track that used to be climbed by the camels making their way with produce for Riyadh. The views over miles upon miles of the desert were magnificent. The view was even better if it had recently rained. If it rains, the desert suddenly springs into life. Plants emerge within 36 hours and blossom within another 24 hours, blanketing the entire desert as far as the eye can see in shades of red, blue, yellow, and a myriad of other colours—about 100 in total. The sight is truly breathtaking. However, after roughly a week, the vibrant display vanishes, and the desert landscape returns. On different occasions, we would visit the Golden Sands—a vast sand dune composed of exquisite golden, fine sand. The challenge was to ascend to the dune's summit. Regrettably, I never succeeded! The soft sand continually shifted beneath me as I attempted to make my way up.

By far, the most enjoyable pastime was going off into the desert overnight. We didn't have access to a four-wheel drive desert vehicle, so we used to go with friends who were related to some friends of ours in Biddenham, back home. We travelled in two vehicles with eight passengers. First, we were required to inform the hospital's security office about our whereabouts in case we got lost. Afterwards, we packed tents, overnight gear, and plenty of water and food. We set off first on the main road, then onto minor roads, and finally onto a track that led us into the desert. The people we were with were experienced desert travellers. We drove down barely distinguishable tracks that seemed to be going nowhere. The desert was rocky, and we had to dodge boulders all the time to protect the suspension. The track ascended and, rounding the side of a hill, we came across a solitary acacia tree. There was no water, no other trees, just a whole self-contained ecosystem. A bird was perched in the tree, and nearby, there was a patch of grass with a diameter of about 40 yards before it faded into the desert. A small rodent scuttled away, and the insects it had been hunting looked around. Seeing that the coast was clear, they basked in the dappled sunlight. It was a complete ecosystem reliant on a single tree and a small perpetual spring not too far below the surface. We moved off, driving deeper into the desert, and towards evening, we set up camp under the lee of a rocky outcrop to shield us if the wind got up at night. We ate and settled down for the evening. Maybe it was the silence. One felt almost drunk—not that any of us had had anything to drink. Not a distant car or plane. No glow from any lights. Just the stars and an occasional sigh as the wind moved the branches of some desert scrub. Eight people sat around on an old tarpaulin. By starlight, the patches looked like one of the better modern paintings. Looming in the background, the humps of the two vehicles seemed to guard the campsite. They were vaguely reassuring. Our connection with the world of noise, dust, and fumes we called home. Here, the massive pattern of the stars made the place seem unearthly, as a part of the world that nobody had yet moulded and tamed. It was wild, and we were intruders. Eight people sat silently, experiencing one of those moments when words were not necessary.

Somebody got up. There was a glare as the jeep door opened. The radio crackled, and a plum voice announced the latest details about a fight in a nearby, more troubled desert. The programme crackled on, there was a burst of music, and the radio snapped off. Irrelevance. The beds were distributed and taken to the periphery of the camp. A snake—a sidewinder shuffled off into the bushes, and the camp settled for the night. All that bumping over desert tracks causes backache. It's good to stretch out and look up at the stars, the same ones seen by Abraham and Moses. Silence again, not even a snore, or maybe the desert has muffled them. Tomorrow there's the bumpy ride back.

Suddenly, it's morning, and a cool breeze sweeps through. The wadi is etched in perfect detail in the early light. Humps in weird shapes lie around the camp, slowly moving as the light disturbs their sleep. Camels lingered near last night, though concealed from view; perhaps that was for the better. The sun ascends in a hue of orange. Someone needs to dust it off before it has any heat. A lizard looks out and decides that it is still too cool. The camp below stirs. People open one eye, then another, scratch, then close both eyes.

Someone must have brushed the sun clean, for it now blazes with heat. A cricket begins to serenade, its song growing too bold, leading to its swift capture by the lizard—an unintended breakfast. Breakfast time for the lizard, too. The sun climbs higher, coercing the mere humans with all their paraphernalia into their air-conditioned tin box jeeps. The camels appear relieved as the invasion of their territory retreats. Much more comfortable for us to return to the dust, odours, and cacophony that constitute our daily lives. The desert remains, basking in its formidable heat and solitary existence. As we depart, the lizard ventures out again, content from its meal, and retreats to slumber beneath a bush. And so, we journey back home.

One of our favourite couples in Riyadh was Richard Northern and his wife. Richard was the British consul in Riyadh and had been brought up by his farming parents in a village just outside our hometown of Bedford. He had attended Bedford School, the same school that our sons were at. He was at the start of his diplomatic career and in his late twenties or perhaps his early thirties. It was bizarre that the British Embassy in Saudi Arabia was in Jeddah and not Riyadh; the capital was only served by a consulate. There were historical reasons for this: Jeddah was a far more cosmopolitan city than Riyadh, and its people were less narrow-minded. Until about a decade before our time in Saudi Arabia, the heart of the Arabian Peninsula was considered threatening and untamed. Nonetheless, in Riyadh, if, as a Brit, you encountered trouble, it was Richard's responsibility to resolve the situation. On a couple of occasions, we went for lunch at his home, and it was interesting to see how his accommodation and its furniture were so like that endured by us when we were working in Fiji. There must be a factory somewhere, perhaps at Basingstoke or somewhere else genteel, where extremely basic and very uncomfortable furniture is made for overseas government servants working in the back of beyond to sit on and worry about the impossibilities of their jobs and to dream of home. One good thing about the consulate was that there was a plentiful supply of alcoholic drinks. Even with this, there was a sting in the tail. If you were invited for a meal by Richard and his wife accompanied by the most delectable wines and then were picked up by the Saudi police when driving home and arrested for having imbibed alcohol, you were punished just as severely as if you had imbibed a beautiful wine in the British consulate as if you had been caught after drinking some vaguely disgusting home-made brew in the home of a friend who lived in the BAE compound.

However, there was something very special about Richard. About a year before we arrived in Riyadh, a plane crash occurred at Riyadh airport. The plane had caught fire when approaching the airport, probably because somebody had been brewing up a kettle of water on a primus stove in the aircraft gangway, and the primus stove had tipped over. Realising they were in deep trouble, the pilot had asked for immediate landing permission from the airport and explained his problem. Permission was not granted as the king's aircraft was coming into land, and the plane was told to circle the airport despite it being on fire. Eventually, the pilot was allowed to land the plane which he did safely, but by this time, the aircraft was a blazing inferno, and nobody survived. On investigation, it was found that this was a plane containing pilgrims who had been to Mecca to perform the Haj. There was no passenger list or indication of who might have been on the plane. The Saudis had decided that nobody would be able to find out who the passengers had been, and just to clear up the mess. However, there was a report that some British nationals could have been on the plane, and Richard was asked to investigate. He spent three days and three nights at the airport going through the plane's debris, any documents, letters etc., contacting the airport from which the plane took off and to which it was flying. Eventually, he was able to identify who most of the passengers on the plane were. He made sure that the relative was contacted. He did this for all the passengers, not just the Brits. The Saudi authorities had been staggered that anybody would take such trouble and work so sacrificially for many poor people, many of whom were not even Richard's responsibility. The Saudi King contacted our queen and asked if she would be agreeable to giving Richard a British honour. In due course, he was awarded an MBE, an honour given by Her Majesty herself at

Buckingham Palace. This was a richly deserved honour and one that was of no small value to Richard in his future career.

A large part of the task we were given in our contract was to improve the skills and the ability of the doctors in the family medicine department to practice evidence-based medicine, leading up to an assessment under the auspices of the Arabic Boards programme. The easiest way to start a programme was to start a regular weekly case discussion meeting. Every doctor encounters patients with puzzling diagnoses or complex treatment requirements, and they appreciate the opportunity to engage in discussions about such cases. The challenge with these exchanges lies in their potential to transform into something quite different. One doctor might offer their perspective on the issue, and another could contribute their opinion—neither rooted in anything more substantial than fragmented recollections of advice received during their student years or even insights gleaned from newspaper articles they've come across. The skill is to guide the discussion into reviewing the evidence on a matter as published in peer-reviewed medical journals, which will record the latest research evidence. It rapidly became evident that none of our colleagues in the department was reading any sound medical journal with any degree of regularity. It was just a short step from this to decide as a group to convert two of the case review meetings per month into journal club meetings. In these meetings, problems discussed in the case review meetings and where the problems were not resolved from adequate, evidence-based sources were given to one of the group members. Over the next week, this doctor would go to the hospital library and find out what had been written in the medical literature about the problem and report this back to the group in the meeting the next week. The pattern of alternating case review and journal club meetings seemed to go well, and the meetings were well attended.

While instituting this programme, we were also preparing a programme based on one developed by the British Royal College of General Practitioners for training family doctors. We had now established the need to base clinical decisions on research evidence, and we presented to the group the need to base the whole of our practice on research evidence. Firstly, we decided that we should decide upon the subjects we needed to consider as a priority, and having decided this, we presented the participants with a course. This involved regularly reading relevant medical journals, case review meetings, joint consultations, and a project for each person to research and present. We promised them an assessment at the end, which would lead to a qualification, marking them out as fully trained family doctors. This would lead to future recognition and promotion. A sizeable group continued to meet and work together. For the projects, each member of the group was supervised by one of the tutors. One of the students I supervised was a girl named Al Saud, meaning she was a member of the Royal Family. When we first met, she refused to shake my hand, which I completely understood as some very pious women will never touch any man. However, when we discussed her project, there were some things that she had not thought through. When I tried to suggest different ways of approaching the subject, she rejected my advice with little grace. I accepted what she said and happily never saw her again. She did not do well in the exam, though most women doctors did. In fact, the whole matter of women working harder than men and gaining better results than men caused a major problem for the teaching group, given the misogyny of society.

At the end of the course, the exam was built using the criteria we had used in the UK; the candidates sat the exam, and the papers were marked. We presented the results in rank order of their marks and presented the report to General Dr Alamari, the head of the Saudi military medical services. His reply left us utterly dumbfounded. In the list of candidates' results, the top 6 candidates in the ranking were women. General Alamari wrote to us that it was quite unacceptable in Saudi culture that women should be placed above men like this, and please could we remark the papers to put the men first? We asked for an appointment with the General. We explained to him that what he was asking for would be counted as corruption in the UK. Anybody who did this would never be allowed to function in any academic capacity again, and we would agree with that sanction. He returned saying that we were not in the UK now and had to conform to Saudi norms. We went home and sat with our heads in our hands until Rob Walker devised a solution worthy of the mighty King Solomon. We would produce two lists, one for the men and one for the women. Each would be rank-ordered, and the marks would be recorded for each candidate. There would be no comparative document comparing the men and women, but it would be evident to anybody having both lists who had done best. We sent the male form off to the General one day and the female form two days later. We received no complaint, and General Alamari's office published both forms.

As Christian believers for whom faith was an integral part of daily life, living in Saudi Arabia presented significant challenges. The Saudi authorities strictly prohibited any practice or discussion of religions other than Islam within the entire country. Upon entry into the country, during the customs process at the airport, even if one carried a personal Bible, it could be confiscated by certain customs officials, with instances of bibles being thrown on the floor and even spat upon. However, as relationships developed with colleagues and friendships were formed, it became evident that there were individuals who held steadfast Christian beliefs. Among them was a colleague in a senior management position at the hospital. Taking the initiative, I approached this colleague and proposed the idea of meeting in my flat for Bible study and prayer sessions. He was a member of a large evangelical church in England, but he said that we could not meet under any circumstances and that this was totally forbidden. We thought about this and prayed about it. It felt unjust to us that our Queen had allocated land in Regent's Park for the Muslim community in the UK to have a place of worship built. However, in the very heart of the Muslim world, Christians were denied the simple privilege of gathering in a flat for Bible readings and prayer. This incongruity prompted us to organise meetings in our flat. Our friends, who were guards on the block of flats and had aspirations to fund their church through a dog farm, offered advice. They suggested that attendees to the meetings conceal their Bibles in plastic bags while on hospital property.

About 7 of us came together and prayed and studied the Bible, and in due course, we invited others. This was quite a challenge as almost everywhere where we were meeting people (apart from at parties), we were mixed in with our Muslim colleagues, so we used to come up behind colleagues who had expressed a wish to have some sort of Christian life and whisper in their ears "would you like to come to a Bible study?". It was a bit like selling dirty postcards in the 1920s, not that I have ever indulged in this practice. An increasing number of people started to come along. Some of the people we invited were working in Saudi alone and not living on the compound and were very lonely, which might well have been one of the reasons that they were so keen to attend. Quite a number of these people developed a faith of their own.

Eventually, we developed a conscience about meeting like this and hiding what we were doing from the authorities, so after praying about this, I decided to go and have a word with the security authorities about this. I made an appointment to meet Bill Mocambo, the deputy security officer for the military compound. The day arrived, and I tapped on the office door, was told to go in and found myself in front of Prince Faisal, the director of security for the whole military unit. Having prayed before I went in, I took courage and told Prince Faisal that we would like to have a cultural discussion group in our flat every week and please could we have his permission. The prince looked at me and said, "I know exactly what you mean, Dr Martin. That will be fine, but don't sing too loudly." I was quite staggered about this, but I suppose that I had prayed about it, which was an answer to prayer. It was also very useful to have a Prince's permission. Sometime later, following the passing of the King and amid disagreements within the Royal family regarding succession, a ban was imposed on all gatherings of more than three people across Riyadh, including the hospital. Meetings such as those of the hospital management committee, the anaesthetic department committee, the surgical committee, and various others were cancelled. However, our Bible Study meeting, though strictly illegal, was permitted to continue. This exception was granted because we had received permission from a Prince to hold our meetings. It turned out later that our benefactor Prince was a man who believed very little about any religion, avoided Ramadan every year by going to Hawaii and was very liberal in what he allowed people around him to do.

As our time in the country extended, and as people became more acquainted with us and grew to trust us, it gradually became apparent that there were indeed several underground churches convening throughout Riyadh. Those gathering within diplomatic compounds enjoyed a degree of privilege since the Saudi authorities were unable to intervene there. However, among the approximately fifteen churches, only about four met under these protected circumstances. The remainder held their meetings in the homes of individuals who possessed spacious villas. Nearly all the residential compounds in the city were enclosed by towering walls, and their entrances were guarded by imposing steel gates. These features significantly contributed to the confidentiality of the gatherings. Participating in one of these Christian meetings was an unlawful action, which carried a certain level of risk. The meetings took place on Friday, which was the day of rest. Each Thursday, we would receive a photocopied page of a small sector of the road network in an area of the city and up at the top right-hand corner would be a small picture of a fish. The emblem of a fish has been a Christian mark among persecuted communities dating right back to Roman times. The services were at 11.00 am. So about 10.30, one would get into the car and drive up and down the streets included in the photocopied bit of the town network. Once we spotted this marker, we would park our car around the corner, out of sight from the house, and then return to the designated gate. There, we would lightly tap on the gate's surface. When the porter opened a small hatch in the gate, we would inform them that we had come for 'the fish.' Upon verification, the gate would swing open, granting us entry. Inside, we would be met with a warm and hearty welcome from a diverse group of around 30 to 40 individuals representing roughly six different nationalities. Here, a simple yet profound service encompassing worship, communion, and teaching would unfold. The leaders of these gatherings were often trained pastors employed as staff support workers by some of the larger corporations. There were very few Arabic Christians at these services, though there were many of these working in the city. This was because the Saudis were much stricter with Arab people found taking part in Christian worship or teaching. According to the Saudis, the Arabic nations were deemed to be the chosen people of the Muslim God, and any divergence into Christian practices was seen as a more significant transgression for them. These fellow believers held their own gatherings, operating under heightened security measures. The people for who Christian activities were a huge risk were the Arabic Muslim people who had become Christians. If these people were found, they were executed.

On Easter morning, a gathering was arranged in the desert for Christians from all over the city, nationalities, and races. In the very early morning of Easter Sunday, there was a stirring around the suburbs. Small groups of four-wheel drive vehicles could be seen driving towards the desert from the four quarters of the city. They tried to ensure they did not congregate in large groups to draw attention to themselves. They entered the desert, headed towards an area about 40 miles from the city, and parked up. There were Chinese, Filipinos, French, Indonesians, South Americans, people from the USA, Europeans, and British people, among others. They parked their vehicles quietly and came together in a group of about 2000 people. It was very cold. People blew on their hands and looked to the East. There was a sense of expectancy. Imperceptibly at first, there was a suggestion of a lightening on the Eastern horizon. Then the sky went pink. Suddenly the sun burst up over the horizon. Hands lifted, voices united, we sang an Easter hymn, rejoicing in the resurrection of Jesus and the triumph over sin that his sacrifice had achieved. Tears welled in many eyes, and a profound sense of participating in something ancient and profoundly significant enveloped us. Amidst the crowd of around two thousand, arms were raised, and praises resonated in 20 to 30 languages, an awe-inspiring symphony of worship to the God of ages. We found ourselves treading the path of countless Christians who, throughout history, had endured oppression and persecution. After the worship concluded, long tables were set up, and a collective breakfast was shared—a diverse feast representing nearly every corner of the world. Following this communal meal, we acted swiftly, avoiding the attention of passing aircraft. One by one, using different routes, we embarked on our journeys back to the cities, ensuring our presence remained inconspicuous.

During the summer, our family found ourselves in Cyprus for a vacation. While there, we decided to visit St. Barnabas Church in Larnaca, which served as the Middle East headquarters for the organisation 'Open Doors.' This group was dedicated to supporting Christians in countries facing persecution and limited religious freedom. Among their initiatives, they sent Bibles and Christian literature to countries where these resources were scarce or prohibited. 'Open Doors' also advised the British Government on matters related to this topic. As we shared our experiences of working, worshipping, and sharing our faith in Riyadh, they attentively listened. We discussed the challenges we encountered and the issues we navigated. Subsequently, they joined us in prayer, interceding for the difficulties we faced. After our conversation, they requested a brief pause to confer among themselves. Approximately twenty minutes later, the three gentlemen with whom we had spoken returned, expressing that they believed it was God's prompting to ask us for assistance. They produced a wadge of books and booklets, which were passages of Scripture and tracts all in Arabic and asked us if we would be willing to take them with us when we returned to Riyadh. We were somewhat dumbfounded. Bringing Bibles or Christian literature in Arabic into Saudi Arabia was strictly prohibited. Violation carried severe penalties such as long imprisonment or immediate expulsion from the country. When we were approached with this request, we made sure those asking understood the potential consequences. We enquired about the logistics of bringing the books and what to do with them once inside the country. Their response was rooted in faith. They believed that if God intended these books to be in Riyadh, He would ensure their safety. They also expressed that they saw this challenge as a test of God's power to protect His mission. As for the question of what to do with the books upon arrival, they were confident that the guidance would become clear as we embarked on this endeavour.

Peta and I took the books back to our holiday flat and prayed about what to do. We had a clear impression that it was God's will that we take them into the country. Every time we had travelled in and out of Saudi Arabia, our cases had been opened and emptied, then all the items had been examined before we were allowed to enter the country. We decided that if God was going to protect us and these books, we did not need to help Him by trying to hide them, so we put the books right on top of all our clothes. If the case were opened, they would be right there in full view. We sent the boys back to England and booked our flight back to Riyadh via Al Khobar, an oil town on the East side of the country. We arrived at the airport and went through to the customs hall. We had three cases, and the books were in the second case. We put our cases up on the customs table. The first case was opened, emptied, the contents examined and then repacked. A chalk mark was put on it, and it was pushed across. The second case containing the Arabic Christian books was pulled before the customs officer, the chalk mark was put on it and pushed across. The third case was pulled before the customs officer, emptied, the contents examined, a chalk mark put on it, and we loaded all the cases on our trolley to go through to the domestic terminal for the flight to Riyadh. We left the customs building, and both collapsed onto a bench. We looked at each other and said, “What on earth happened there?” After our hearts had stopped pounding, we realised that God had indeed protected us and the books as He was capable of doing, and we thanked Him for His grace.

We found ourselves with many Bibles and books about Jesus, all in comic form, with no idea of what to do with them. We asked our Christian friends and various people who had lived in the country for a long time, and we prayed. Eventually, we decided to distribute them generally in the city. Clearly, we could not stand in the street and give them out as various groups of both Christians and Muslims do in England. However, one well-documented characteristic of Saudi people was that having been brought up in an extremely controlled environment, they were incurably curious. So, we decided to visit the 4 major supermarkets in town and leave several of these books on the shelves on top of the tinned goods and see what happened. We travelled by hospital bus and used a shopping trolley with the books in our shopping bag. At some point, when we were the only shoppers in an aisle, we put a few books on top of the baked beans or whatever was on sale and walked on. We then walked all round the stores and did some shopping and then returned to where we had left the books. They had gone, so we left some more, and these disappeared too. We then left the store, moved on to the next supermarket, and did the same thing. By the time we did this in all four stores, we had used up all our books. We then prayed that God would direct the books into the right hands for Him to speak to people through them.

We deliberated on the ethical implications of this action. However, commercial companies and Muslim groups in England employed similar general distribution methods to engage people's interest in their offerings. Furthermore, we were engaged with an organization led by a Lebanese individual named Fawzi, situated in the British Midlands. Having once been a Muslim himself, he converted to Christianity after encountering the Bible. He requested us to collect as many telephone directories from various places in Saudi Arabia as possible during our return. These directories held significance for his work, and we found ourselves grappling with the responsibility of fulfilling this task. The Saudi telephone directories had the full address details of everybody listed. The organisation Fawzi ran would use the directories to mail into this country a simple invitation to the recipient for them to ask for a Bible and a very simple guide on how to read this book. Many people responded to this invitation and sent a letter asking for a Bible. This was sent off with a further invitation to receive a Bible study course to explain the faith with the opportunity to correspond with an Arabic Bible teacher in England. Many people replied, and a considerable number became Christian believers, even a number in Mecca. When we were leaving the country, the Saudi authorities tumbled to the fact that this was happening. They published a full-page article on the front page of a national newspaper showing a picture of the sheet and inviting people to respond. The article instructed recipients to promptly dispose of these letters. However, their attempt backfired when the image was clear enough for people to discern the address designated for replies. As a result, there was an overwhelming surge of individuals writing in, expressing their interest in receiving a Bible and seeking an explanation of the faith. Fawzi, the Lebanese individual who led our organisation, was elated by the unexpected aid provided by the Saudis, which greatly furthered his mission.

Being a Christian and practicing one's faith in Saudi Arabia is not without risks, even for a Westerner. For a local Saudi and especially for a Christian who had previously been a Muslim, it could result in execution, often by public beheading. This happened in the central square in front of the main mosque for various crimes about once a month to six weeks. As I have already described, there were meetings of Christians all over Riyadh every Friday, and Saudi security must have known about this. However, at Christmas time, a group of Christians, mainly from the USA, decided to run a private carol service at the American International School on private property and with attendance by invitation only. This went ahead, and immediately after it had happened, the Saudi authorities arrested the six people who had organised the service. They were put in prison and interrogated each day for three weeks. They were allowed to go and sleep at home at night between about 10 pm and 8 am. They and their families were expelled and deported at the end of the three weeks. Among these six people were several CEOs of the Saudi subsidiaries of large international companies. Despite the importance to the Saudi economy of these companies, this did not prevent their CEOs from being deported.

Our time in Saudi Arabia was coming to an end. Looking back, there were certain things that stood out as memorable from our fifteen months stay. Perhaps the most precious memories are of our fellowship with believing Christians from all over the world and the number of people who found faith in Jesus while working in a country which tried hard to ban all expressions of our faith.

Another bizarre happening that caught our fancy was road safety week. The number of people killed on the roads in and around Riyadh was truly appalling. Part of the reason for this was that the rules of the road were almost totally ignored. Many people climbed into a car without training and just drove. Also, children from the age of fourteen were sent to pick their siblings up from school or from shopping in the family car, which in many cases was a top-of-the-range and powerful model. Once a year, large tripods were erected at numerous crossroads as part of a road safety initiative. As a prominent example, law enforcement officers would suspend on these structures the most severe examples of mangled cars recovered from accidents over the past year. The intention was to use these displays as a cautionary measure, urging drivers to exercise greater care on the roads. Curiously, this programme faced an unintended issue: during this specific week, road accidents and fatalities experienced a significant increase. Daily, people would drive around, fixated on the wreckage and engaged in discussions about it. This distraction often led to them rear-ending the vehicle in front or, in some cases, even colliding with pedestrians due to their diverted attention. Although this outcome was widely acknowledged, the practise persisted year after year.

Each holiday Simon and Dominic were flown out from England to join us; these were great fun and enjoyable times. We had no problems looking after them when we were working because the Saudis employed two people and set up a Recreation Centre to look after the expatriate children flying back for the holidays. The children were taken swimming or on trips to the shops, and water polo matches were arranged, as were craft sessions. A lasting memory etched deeply into Simon and Dominic's minds was a desert excursion they experienced at the ages of 10 and 13. During this trip, they were taught how to drive a Toyota Landcruiser in the desert, followed by camping under the vast expanse of stars. The military hospital's exceptional care for young individuals left a significant impression. Towards the conclusion of one holiday, the two boys were scheduled to board a flight back to England at 3:00 am. We escorted them to the airport, ensuring they were in the care of stewards, and then proceeded to do some shopping at a nearby supermarket. Part of my responsibilities included periodic shifts for the airport's emergency on-call medical care team. I had verified that all arrangements were in order for that evening and that I was equipped with the necessary call system before dropping off the kids. Having left the children at the airport, we decided to do some shopping at our preferred supermarkets. Eventually, we returned to our flat and retired for the night. Fortunately, my next day was off-duty, thanks to my shift with the airport team. We were fast asleep when my bleep sounded, and I was summoned to the airport. There was a plane in trouble due to an engine failure which was going to land at the airport. The emergency care programme was activated, and we all stood by. The plane landed safely, and we returned to the flat and to bed. The following morning, we received a phone call from the boys' guardian in England, who wanted to reassure us about the children's well-being. We hadn't a clue what they were talking about, but it transpired that the plane that the emergency medical team had been activated for was the plane on which Simon and Dominic had been travelling. I am extremely glad I did not know that when we were on standby as the plane landed.

In Riyadh, there was no doubt about the highlight of the annual social calendar: the camel race. It stood as an Arabic version of Ascot, with the king, government officials, the diplomatic corps, and a multitude of attendees from around the world, including us, coming together. The event held such prominence that a bus was even arranged from the hospital compounds to transport those interested. Being from the military, we were allowed to park near the racecourse, and there was a special section in the grandstand for us. After a while, it became obvious why the chairs seemed so uncomfortable to sit on. They were for standing on. Everybody was doing it-that is, those who didn't fall off. They were folding chairs. It would seem more logical for everybody to sit down, but everybody else was standing on the chairs, so why not join them? Over to the left was a black veiled figure who looked like the lady Peta had just taken tea with. It was impossible to be sure, as Arab ladies, veiled from head to foot, look so similar. They had been very kind to Peta as we went by. She was beckoned to sit down on a rug between two trucks with five ladies and eight children, one of whom rapidly made themselves comfortable on her lap. The ladies and Peta drank hot sweet tea, and the older children drank Pepsi.

They are off - the camels, that is! The annual camel race has commenced. Dignitaries maintain their dignity, Arabs donning their distinctive red head dresses, while local Europeans wield cameras as long as their arms, bouncing with enthusiasm. Except, the camels are heading in the wrong direction. Chaos ensues. The effort to round them up and restart begins, accompanied by jeeps with flashing lights zipping around and a helicopter soaring overhead. An ambulance even joins the merry chase. How does one corral 4,000 camels veering off course? It takes an hour, an hour spent perched on a folding chair. Finally, they're back on track, moving in the right direction. Camels with riders trot around the five-mile course thrice, except for one who sat down and opted for a nap instead. Meanwhile, the king navigates the course in his opulent coach. It's hard to tell if the coach is attempting to keep pace with the camels or if the camels are deliberately refraining from surpassing the king. Each time the king passes the enthralled crowd in the enclosure, applause drowns out the camels' thundering hooves, even causing a few people to tumble off their chairs. The favourite is quite clear. At last, they reach the finish line. Police cars patrol the area while spectators jump in excitement, eagerly anticipating the outcome. Finally, the winner emerges victorious. The event is a delightful mixture of fun and fellowship, a sense of unity palpable in the air. As the day comes to a close, we all pile into the big yellow hospital bus for the journey back home. A poignant scene unfolds as a father and his son stand beside their car, facing Mecca, and offer their prayers in the Islamic tradition—a lasting image of devotion. The fact that the bus driver, fed up with the traffic, steers onto the central reservation of the motorway becomes a minor concern. Even his colourful curses and comments on the family histories of fellow drivers seem to blend seamlessly with the overall scene of dust, vibrant colours, camaraderie, and devotion.

And so, to the final week. There was the regulation party to say goodbye to us given by our department. Speeches were made, and gifts were given across cultural divides, which meant that we were left with things we didn't really need and which, in any case, we had no room for in our boxes. There were even things that we had no idea what they were for. We wrote a spoof about the disgrace of having books by male authors and female authors lying side by side on shelves in the library. This incident ignited a major disagreement, greatly offending the Saudi sense of propriety. The security services were summoned, conducting a thorough examination of all typewriters to identify the source of the offending letter. Fortunately, their investigation remained inconclusive, safeguarding our bonus from potential repercussions. Amidst the changing circumstances, there was a palpable sense of melancholy as we bid farewell to dear friends who had become an integral part of our lives. Life moved on, and priorities shifted, not only for us but also for our friends back in Riyadh. We eventually reunited with our sons for a final holiday, graciously funded by the Saudis. Our journey took us up the western side of the USA, commencing at the residence of friends in Los Angeles. We ventured on to explore the wonders of the Grand

Canyon, the beauty of Yosemite National Park, and the allure of San Francisco. And so back to Bedford to pick up from where we had left off. Our boys were sad to see the end of our time in Saudi Arabia. They asked us to extend our contract because they had enormously enjoyed their holidays and the activities arranged by the recreation department, but it was time to come home. There was one postscript to our time in Riyadh. On our return, Rob Walker, with whom we had worked very closely, wrote a leading article in the British Medical Journal likening the treatment of women in Saudi Arabia to the Apartheid regime in South Africa. On reading the editorial edition, the Saudis collected every copy of the British Medical Journal in the kingdom and ceremonially burned them. Rob was informed that he was banned from ever entering Saudi Arabia again for the whole of his life.

Return to Bedford

We returned to our house in Biddenham to a great welcome from our neighbours and to the pleasure of living again with our two sons. The practice had changed somewhat during the sixteen months we had been away. They had bought the building in the centre of Bedford from which we practiced. This was later going to pose a problem as the building was grade two listed, which meant that it was very difficult to change anything without going through endless committees and jumping through numerous hoops. We had a new partner, an original, lateral-thinking man with whom I had been friendly before he became a partner. Another practice initially working from the first and second floors of the building, had relocated. This relocation provided ample space, allowing us to establish multiple treatment rooms. It also facilitated the allocation of offices for practice nurses, specialist nurses, and health visitors. The transformation extended to the practise office as well, resulting in improved filing of patient notes and the provision of a dedicated workspace for the practise secretary. Shortly after our return, a significant development occurred—the practise began computerising parts of the clinical notes. This initial step laid the foundation for subsequent progress, ultimately leading to the comprehensive computerisation of our operations over the years.

Following my work in Saudi Arabia in the development of courses and assessments for young doctors and having published two papers in peer-reviewed journals, I joined the local faculty organisation of the Royal College of General Practitioners, and after about a couple of years, I was elected to the council of the national organisation. This involved 2-day meetings every two months in London. Council members were not paid, but their travel costs and accommodation in London were paid for. As I was always given a double room in any hotel I booked into, this meant that every two months Peta could come with me to London at no extra cost to the college to go to a museum, a concert or go shopping.

After doing my afternoon surgery on a Friday, Peta and I would catch the train to London St Pancras, where I would make my way on the Piccadilly line to Knightsbridge. From there, I would walk along Knightsbridge to Princes Gate, where the college was housed in an elegant house that had been the childhood home of President John F Kennedy when his father had been American Ambassador. There I would check in and have perhaps a few meetings before the main council meeting while Peta went and checked in at whatever hotel we would stay in that weekend. The hotel was always chosen by Peta, within the price range allowed by the College. Peta is a creative lady and has very clear ideas about what she wants to do and what she enjoys. At various times we stayed in a hotel off Sloane Square run by an old British couple. It was extremely cheap, conveniently placed and exciting to stay in. Most of the rooms were satisfactory, adorned in a style reminiscent of a working-class home from around 1934. Occasionally, one might find oneself in a room lacking curtains. However, that was easily explained—they were simply being washed. The breakfast was always excellent, well cooked, copious, and very traditional. The owner always served at the table and was always up for a chat, sometimes leading to me being late for the council meeting and the next customer having a somewhat cold breakfast which had been liberally waved around as our host was gesticulating as he made some point.

I then left to go to work, and Peta left to do what a woman does in London when off the leash of the troublesome restraints of children and husbands. In the evening, I returned to the hotel, and Peta had always found some restaurant to eat in that night. The restaurants were varied, not mainstream, and not infrequently led to interesting experiences, such as when we found ourselves in a Russian restaurant that did not have an alcohol licence. Peta had astutely observed this situation and thoughtfully provided us with a fine bottle of Rhone wine to accompany our meal. One thing could always be counted on:

Peta's tendency to initiate conversations with fellow diners at nearby tables. On this particular occasion, our table neighbour happened to be an American who hadn't realised the restaurant lacked a licence for serving alcohol. Naturally, he was welcomed to our table and invited to share our wine, resulting in a delightful and enjoyable evening together. As conversations flowed, we discovered he held a prominent position as a senior official in the New York City Council's ecological department. Our discourse revolved around ecological matters throughout the evening. Peta's curiosity, however, remained insatiable—she extended an invitation for him to visit us in Biddenham, despite our never having met him before. To our surprise, when he did arrive at our doorstep, he proved to be a fascinating guest, and we maintained a connection with him for some time. This inclination to invite people, both known and unknown, into our home seemed to be an inherent trait in Peta, perhaps inherited from her mother. My mother-in-law regarded every stranger she met as a friend that she had not yet made. On another occasion, we met a rather angular German man who was a resident of Berlin. He regaled us with the joys of teaching young men of the immigrant community of Berlin who were getting into trouble and the wonderful experiences he had had immersing himself in their culture. He was a cyclist who was cycling all over Europe. Peta, as always, invited him to come and stay if ever he were our way. Sure enough, he turned up, bike and all, about two weeks later in Biddenham. Eventually, the weekend came to an end, and I reflected on the train returning home that I remembered much more about the hotel and the evenings we had spent together than ever I did about the subjects discussed in the council.

From being a council member, I was recruited onto the membership committee of the college, which governed the expected standards of doctors who could be admitted to college membership. This committee set and ran the examination for entry to the college. Being a member of the board of examiners was academically very challenging, but it led to my acquiring both many new skills and an insight into the challenges of how to make standardised reliable assessments that reflected the skills of the candidate rather than the personality of the examiner. The college worked closely with the examination study department at Cambridge University, which gave us enormous help in designing and running reliable examinations. All the examiners met for three days in January each year, usually at a hotel in the Lake District, to build the examinations for that year and to determine the marking programme and schedule for each session. The membership committee also regulated the admission to the fellowship of the college and the designation of FRCGP. There was much discussion about whether this should be an honorary designation, awarded for the outstanding quality of care or services to medicine, or whether it should be awarded after an assessment that measured the quality rewarded. At that time, it was a college rule that anybody who was going to be an examiner had to prove that they were still capable of passing the exam themselves, so in due course, I took the exam again. It was interesting for me to sit doing the exam as a 40+-year-old doctor in a room full of bright young medics in their late twenties, just starting out on their careers as family practitioners. I survived the ordeal of the viva and clinical section of the exam and, to my surprise, landed up with a distinction.

In due course, I was elected by the council members to the General Purposes Committee of the college, which was a handful of members who fulfilled the position of the board of directors ensuring that the work of this academic institution fulfilled its stated aims. There was a meeting of this committee about once every month, which gave Peta extra shopping time in London when she accompanied me. As a member of this committee, I also became the news editor of the British Journal of General Practice, a peer-reviewed journal produced under the auspices of the college. This involved coming to London to college headquarters one day a week to meet with the editorial group and the lay editor who reported to me. On this day of the week, usually Wednesday, this involved me doing a morning surgery, then going to the station and catching a train to London. During the hour-long journey, I would catch up with the paperwork for the meeting and then work with my lay editor over lunch. At about 4.00 pm, I caught a train back to Bedford, did an evening surgery, did my house calls into the evening, and got home from 8.30 to 9.00 pm.

The college was an interesting academic institution. Its oversight of the standard required to be a member was exigent. The exam to measure this standard was well designed, run by a competent exam board and supervised by a third party, a Cambridge University faculty. The college also defined aims and rationale for medical practice in a community setting and instituted studies to test hypotheses. It had an important advisory role in advising the government about the aims, reach and quality of General Practice. Many of the senior members of the college who held influential positions were members of the newish General Practice faculties of various universities. They had access to the resources of those universities. My one big criticism of the college at that time was that there was very little help, direction or mentoring for ordinary General Practitioners who wanted to examine their own practices or answer questions about subjects where the answers were merely assumed. Numerous questions of this nature abounded. For example, within the realm of General Practise, there were four established concepts—shibboleths, if you will—where the prevailing practices were widely recognised and deemed acceptable. These four were:

1. Everybody knew that patients all wanted to see one General Practitioner who was their doctor.
2. It was widely acknowledged that incorporating a counselling service within a practice positively impacted patients' mental well-being, leading to reduced consumption of psychoactive drugs.
3. Everybody knew that making video recordings of patients' consultations for teaching purposes was not intrusive or resented by patients if one asked for permission before the consultation.
4. Everybody knew that a good, experienced GP could listen to and talk with patients so that an agreement could be reached

in consultation and the doctor and patient understood each other.

Despite my efforts, I was unable to locate anyone within or outside the college who could offer guidance on delving into these subjects. With no direction available, Peta and I took it upon ourselves to establish our own approach to investigating these facets of medical practice. Among a group of doctors, we discovered an interesting trend: patients seemed less inclined to revisit doctors who demonstrated passionate dedication to being available for 'their' patients. In our examination of general practise counselling services, we unearthed a surprising revelation. Patients who had undergone a series of counselling appointments were slightly more prone to using psychoactive drugs six months after commencing counselling compared to those with similar conditions who hadn't undergone counselling. In the course of our research, we discovered that patients who completed feedback assessments regarding their willingness to have consultations video-recorded on the doctor's premises indicated that they didn't mind at all. However, when the same forms were sent to patients' homes and completed there, the majority expressed a strong aversion, feeling that such recording was an intrusion upon them. Furthermore, a project aimed at comprehending patient motivations for consulting and the ensuing dynamics highlighted a significant disconnect. In over 50% of consultations, a profound misunderstanding surfaced between the doctor and the patient. Our findings from these studies were shared in peer-reviewed journals, contributing to the broader understanding of these aspects within the medical community.

Malta

One of the most interesting times in my career as a college officer came after a group of family doctors in Malta asked for the RCGP's help designing a family medicine postgraduate course and assessment for all doctors with Maltese as their mother tongue. It turned out that only a minority of these live in Malta. It was arranged that Dr Alistair Donald, who had originally interviewed me for my work in Saudi Arabia and who was now president of the Royal College of General Practitioners, and I would visit Malta and discuss what the doctors in Malta requested. Alistair and I flew out on Air Malta to be greeted on the tarmac at Valletta airport by Dr Denis Soler, who was the main mover in this project, and some of his colleagues, and we were taken into the VIP lounge of Valetta Airport. From there, we were taken to a reception with the President of Malta and then on to meet the committee who would oversee the programme. The aim was to replicate in many ways the functions and structure of the British college at first and then to develop the function of the Maltese college according to the needs in Malta. It became quite clear when we met some of the medical school faculty at Valletta that Family Doctors were regarded as a lower form of life when compared with "real doctors" who were consultants and worked in a hospital. Before gaining independence in 1979, the medical school in the capital, Valletta, functioned much like any British medical school, with many postgraduate doctors spending time in Britain. Unsurprisingly, after gaining independence, the Maltese people expressed a strong desire to chart their own course in medical training, as they did in numerous other fields. My hosts informed me that at that time, Dom Mintoff, who led the country, and his government decided to model the medical school after patterns used in China. This involved medical students spending several months each year engaged in manual work, such as farming, in addition to their medical studies. Many of the teachers hired by the medical school were recruited from Libya, which was located only 60 miles south of the island. As a result, a significant number of students and medical teachers from that period departed the medical school and came to England. The students completed their medical education in England, and numerous teachers secured positions in British medical schools. This departure also included many qualified, practising doctors. Only a small handful of doctors chose to remain and uphold standards. One notable figure among them was our host, Dr. Denis Soler. The medical students who remained, as well as those who joined the school later, received a medical education of notably low quality. A considerable portion of the doctors practising on the island when we arrived, particularly those in family medicine, had undergone their training in this programme. Regrettably, this led to a general decrease in the standard of medical care provided on the island. As a result of this, a primary objective of the emerging college of family doctors was to enhance the overall medical proficiency of practising physicians.

To add to this problem was another structural problem. Family practice was not very profitable in Malta, and in part, to rectify this situation, many doctors worked in rooms at the back of pharmacies. I never saw any actual evidence of this, but I was told that this led to pressure on doctors to prescribe more medication than they otherwise would do. Indeed, a considerable number of doctors also possessed pharmacies within the same premises where they practised. All of this introduced an unintended political bias into what should have been primarily an academic endeavour. To further add to the problem was the resistance to starting a college of family practice from the local branch of the British Medical Association, which I was told had done nothing to improve standards for many years. We flew into this maelstrom of competing historical, political, entrepreneurial, and personal pressures.

I was immediately made to feel at home and valued by Denis and his team, who, with great skill, deflected the efforts of those people who did not want the project to survive. Alistair and I stayed at a hotel on our first visit, but on all other visits, I stayed in the home of Denis and his vivacious Italianate wife and two daughters. For the next four years, I visited Malta for four or five nights twice or three times a year to run courses, talk about progress, and plan the future with the core team, working as the RCGP/Malta fellow. This took up all my annual leave apart from a two-week summer holiday. There was no budget to fund this from the RCGP or anywhere else, so I could not pay for locums at my practice and thus had to use leave time.

After talking to many people in the College development group, the government health services, the medical school, and the local BMA, I decided with my Maltese colleagues that the main task was to achieve two things. Firstly, there was a great need to give doctors already in practice basic foundational medical training, which they did not receive in medical school. Secondly, there was a need to instill in doctors the practice of lifelong learning, emphasising principles rooted in evidence-based education, cultivating an inquisitive mindset, engaging in basic research, and most importantly, fostering the instinct within every doctor to question 'why?'. Whenever feasible, our goal was to organise courses in the UK for our Maltese colleagues, enabling them to interact with international peers and garner motivation to implement changes upon their return. I also set out to arrange for other doctors to come to Malta and take part in the programme. The initial subjects addressed were quite straightforward, encompassing tasks like identifying suitable premises for efficient family practise, maintaining records, establishing disease registers, and implementing patient recall systems for those with chronic illnesses. Furthermore, we introduced an emphasis on recognising and addressing psychological issues as an integral component of routine family medicine. The pattern for the programme was to have teaching conferences, usually twice a year and teaching using local colleagues between the conferences. During this teaching programme, by happy coincidence, the Mediterranean Medical Conference was planned to take place in Malta. Although this meeting was very highly specialist and consultant-orientated, at least local doctors met colleagues from other countries who practiced medicine according to exigent standards. A Malta Medical Journal was produced in a new format, and family doctors were encouraged to publish papers in this magazine.

Malta is an island steeped in history. It is mentioned as a very hospitable place in the Bible, and after spending a considerable amount of time there, I found that my opinion was very much in tune with that of St. Paul in the Book of Acts. It is a rocky outcrop with some agriculture. There are small fields with rows of prickly pears acting as hedges. In the springtime, the whole countryside is full of flowers and a beautiful riot of colour. There are numerous small towns, each with an enormous church, each one of which seems to be based on the plan of a basilica. Mdina, the ancient capital, was largely deserted after the capital moved to Valletta, so it remains almost as a museum, a silent and very beautiful place with buildings consisting of a mixture of Italian and Venetian design. On each of my visits to Malta my colleagues took me round to see the sights and tell me the stories of their country. One of these was a young doctor called Wilfred Galea. We still count Wilfred as a good friend and have grown to love his wife and family. Most years, I paid a visit to Malta in February. It is fearsomely hot during the summer, but all the buildings seemed to be built of somewhat porous stone. It rains in February; the temperature is about 13-14 degrees Celsius, and everywhere is damp. The two countries in which I have been coldest during my travels are Malta and Egypt. They both are hot countries with only short periods during the year when it is cold, so nobody seems to feel that it is worth putting in adequate heating.

The story I was told in Malta that I liked best was of how the large cathedral was built in the small town of Victoria, the capital of Gozo, the small and poorer neighbour to the main island of Malta. Apparently, a new priest was appointed to the main church in Gozo. When he arrived, his flock asked him what he hoped to do during his ministry in the town. He replied that he was going to build the biggest and most magnificent church in the whole of Malta. When his congregation asked how on earth he was going to do that, as they were all very poor, he told them that it was just a matter of having faith in God. Nothing much happened for a couple of years. There were collections for the new church from time to time, but they produced very little money. Then, one day, construction started, and over a year or two, a very large and ornate church rose beside the town. Everybody was astounded, but when they asked their priest where the money came from, he would only say that it was a gift from God. It was only on his death bed that he admitted that he had put all the money that had been collected from his parish on a ticket for a large Italian lottery and had won, which, as he said, was, in fact, a gift from God, though in this case, God had used an unusual channel to send the money.

For many years, Malta was ruled by the Knights of the Order of St John. It had been invaded and ruled over by many different powers, some of them very unfavourable to the islanders' Christian faith. This had particularly been true during the Turkish occupation. One day, I was taken down into some enormous and extensive catacombs. After navigating through winding, lengthy passages, I was led to an altar where daily masses had been conducted for countless centuries, spanning numerous occupations. Remarkably, even when attendance at these masses could have led to fatal consequences, they continued. In that space, there was a palpable sense of God's presence, an aura I have seldom encountered elsewhere. Without a doubt, this spot became my cherished haven in Malta.

After four years, the committee and I jointly concluded that much of what I was engaged in could be effectively managed by local colleagues. By that point, the Malta College of Family Doctors (MCFD) had been officially established, complete with its own dedicated journal. An examination process had also been implemented, leading to membership within the college. There were excellent relations with the British college. The university was developing a Department of Family Medicine and an MSc in this subject, Denis Soler being one of the major movers in this development. Dr Soler was invited to London as the first president of the college and was presented with an honorary membership of the British Royal College of General Practitioners. The RCGP has helped in the inauguration of new colleges in several countries worldwide over the years. There is a standard way of dealing with this procedure, which involves each college giving honorary membership of the colleges to representatives of each academic institution. Oddly, although Dr Soler was awarded his honorary membership of the British college, and despite excellent ongoing relations between the two colleges, the Malta College never offered Dr Donald or any other senior officer of the British college an honorary membership.

Back at the Ranch

Meanwhile, back at the ranch, at the practice in Bedford, the range of services offered by the practice expanded. We had health visitors, an osteopath and a counsellor working in the practice, and we started offering minor surgery to our patients. We also started having review meetings between the partners over lunch once a month. In these meetings, we reviewed patients whom the partners had found puzzling or perhaps the management of patients with a disease or problem that the partners were unsure about. Occasionally, those partners and paramedical colleagues who had faith would meet to pray. We hired a practise manager and organised training and accreditation for our receptionists and secretaries. Additionally, we convened monthly meetings with our team and the practise manager to plan the future and address current challenges. Our guiding principle was to grant the manager full autonomy in overseeing practice operations. She had the authority to request working hours adjustments, or adoption of new procedures from anyone, including the partners, and such requests were expected to be accommodated. However, she would have to answer to the partners at the administrative meeting every month.

With all the changes happening in the practice, the increase in services offered, the development of regular critical reviews of our work, the research, and the necessity to maintain our skills and knowledge, our day-by-day life still had the interest of being involved in the lives of people and families through the highs and lows of life. I consulted from the front room of the first floor of what had been a large, elegant doctor's house in the centre of Bedford. All the bustle of daily life happened right outside my window. My room was spacious, and I constructed a more intimate space in a corner of the room, within which I consulted. I surrounded my desk with tables with plants, toys, and pictures on them. The patient sat at the side of my desk, and I arranged my computer so that when I was looking at it, I was also looking toward the patient. Much of the rest of the room was chairs and a large play area for children. This meant that the patient was almost within a bubble with me during the consultation and a young mum would also have her children playing beside her. My examination room was separate from the consulting room. If a mother came in with her children and needed an examination, she would go into the examination room to undress, and I got to get down on the floor and play with the Tonka toys with the children. At this time, this was acceptable practice. After a suitable period, I would scoop the children up and take them into the examination room where they could sit without seeing what I was doing with their mother. I think that the children enjoyed this process. I certainly did.

The work among the homeless, the prisoners and ex-prisoners and the drug-using population of the town continued. This could have some amusing side effects on one's everyday life in the town. The individuals among the drug users we cared for often comprised a solitary people. Some of them had identifiable psychiatric problems, while others remained entangled in behaviours like shoplifting and theft, displaying a general wariness toward their surroundings. Occasionally, one of them would accompany me during my shopping trips. On one occasion, I went shopping for gloves, and Jack, one of my drug-using patients whom I was fond of, joined me for a walk and followed me into a store where I intended to purchase gloves. I couldn't help but notice that another man seemed to shadow our movements within the shop.

Curious, I enquired of Jack about his identity. He casually replied, 'Oh, that guy? He's the store detective and quite familiar with me. Don't worry about him; he's harmless unless you're attempting any shoplifting, which tends to make him indignant.' I concluded my glove shopping, bid farewell to Jack, and returned home. Regrettably, the gloves proved to be too small, prompting me to return to the store the following day to exchange them for a larger pair. As I perused the store, I noticed the same man once again tailing me. Evidently, my association with Jack had led to my inclusion on the list of suspicious characters in his eyes.

Peta and I carried on with our research programme. Sometimes, Peta was the co-author of papers we produced, and often she was an assistant. There were some disadvantages to this arrangement. If we were stuck and things were not coming together, I had the troubling habit of suddenly having a brainwave about resolving the issue at about 3.00 am and jumping out of bed with a shout of "Eureka!" or something similar. It was clear to me that this was not the way to make a wife who was already caring for many children happy. Despite that, she usually made me a cup of tea and brought it to my study as I was committing my thoughts to paper before the illumination disappeared. By the time we retired, we had published 32 editorials, papers, and letters in peer-reviewed journals such as the British Medical Journal, the British Journal of General Practice, Family Practice, The Lancet, the Medical Journal of Australia, The Saudi Medical Journal, the Maltese Medical Journal and the Journal of the Royal Society of Medicine. Peta also got involved in another study course. She had always loved literature and was widely read. She decided that she would like to take a defined study course in English literature and joined a class of students about twenty years younger than her on an A-level course. She passed the exam with flying colours and thoroughly enjoyed herself. This was as well as helping me in the research programme.

Our boys at this time were both pupils at Bedford School but were growing up in very different ways. Simon, our older son, was turning out to be a very talented musician. His two instruments were the piano and the violin. He became a member of the Bedfordshire youth orchestra. His music master asked us if we would be agreeable for him to put Simon in for an assessment for admission to the King's College Cambridge choir school. We looked at the time commitments of Simon doing this, the fact that he would have to board, and the encroachment on holiday time and, much to his master's disappointment, said no. I taught Simon how to play squash and used to play with him from time to time. After losing five games on the run, I decided that that was the signal for me to move over and take up something a bit less taxing. Simon also excelled in his academic work, and when he had his intelligence tested, to my chagrin, he turned out to have a higher score than me. He did excellently in his A levels and gained a place at Fitzwilliam College Cambridge, where he continued his music and squash while studying to become a lawyer.

On the other hand, Dominic was just as intelligent as Simon, but he had a very different character. He did not easily go with the flow of the school and constantly asked why people did what they were doing and was exploring alternative patterns of life. In school, instead of going into the Cadet Force, he started working with people in the Bromham long-term psychiatric hospital, an interest he continued long after university. He was also a very creative writer and produced, off his own bat, an underground school magazine called "Unreal". In this, he pointed out many of the weird routines of the school, and he lampooned many of the masters acutely and amusingly emphasising the oddities of each victim. One could recognise the person he was writing about immediately. He then photocopied the magazine and passed it out under the tables in the school refectory about every two months. During this period, I served as the school doctor and became aware that the staff were well aware of his activities. I was told that the refectory only experienced a rare moment of quiet during lunchtime when Dominic was distributing his magazine. On a particular day, one of the teachers approached Dominic with enquiries about the magazine, and he was understandably anxious, fearing potential expulsion. To his surprise, the teacher asked who was responsible for photocopying Unreal and who paid its associated expenses. With some apprehension, Dominic confessed that he personally undertook the photocopying, and that that proved rather costly. The master then said that, in his view, that was unacceptable and offered to photocopy it in the school office free of charge. Dominic was dumbfounded, and this situation continued for three more issues, with him still studiously passing the magazine around under the tables. At the end of that time, he was asked by the headmaster to become the editor of the Ousel, the official school magazine. It struck me that this was a brilliant bit of recognising the talent of a boy who was not fitting easily into school life, valuing it and eventually using the talent within a mainstream school activity. Dominic continued to take his own view on life and was often found working in the town library rather than on school premises. However, he gained respectable A levels and a place reading English at Coleraine University in Northern Ireland, the furthest university he could find away from home.

At about this time, we had been to the Sunday service at Christ Church and chatted with a friend of ours before coming home to lunch and the regulation Sunday afternoon walk. At about 5.00 pm, we were phoned up by the friend to whom we had been speaking in the morning. She told us about how she had been sitting next to a girl in the evening service and found that she had nowhere to sleep that night. After talking for a while, our friend told the girl that she was living in a flat with a spare room and if her flatmates agreed, she could come and stay there until she got herself sorted out. Our friend spoke to her flatmates, who said that the girl she had been speaking to certainly could not come and sleep in the empty room as they needed to have somebody living there who could pay rent to make the rent of the other people in the house affordable. So, our friend was phoning around to see if she could find a bed for this girl for the night until matters could be sorted out. We said that this girl would be very welcome to come and stay with us. We found that Esther was a Exeter University student who suffered a major family disturbance and could no longer stay home. She eventually ended up staying on and off with us for 6 years, through the rest of her course at Exeter and through a local PGCE course. We became very fond of her. Again, she was a very creative person who was a non-conformist, refusing to start from the accepted norm and work from there but always wanting to find out why people were doing what they were doing. She was also very disorganised and always late for everything, all of which seemed to add to her charm. She became very successful in her profession and we have remained very good friends over the years.

Uganda

Everybody in our practice was entitled to take unpaid leave of four weeks every ten years or so to go away, recharge the batteries and do something medical or paramedical. One of my partners went off and did a month's service as a medical officer of a demining team working in Afghanistan with HALO, the demining team that Princess Diana famously supported during her project of trying to abolish land mines. Another of our partners spent a month travelling with the American military while working as peacekeepers in Somalia. Andrew would set up impromptu clinics in the villages they passed through during patrols. When it came to my turn, I was going to work in Afghanistan with the same team as my partner. However, the director of the organisation - Mad Mitch, who came to fame during the Aden wars as it happened - had just died, so chaos reigned. Despite having a defined period that I could work with the team; I could not get replies to my letters and eventually gave up trying to organise working with HALO. Instead, I was invited to work with YWAM and agreed to go. This Christian organisation was working in the island communities on the Buvuma group of islands in Lake Victoria, where there were effectively no medical services. The organisation's name was Youth With A Mission, and my sons fell around laughing that I would be working with such a group at my age. During this period, they regularly wrote to me as Dr Edwin Martin WWAM (Wrinklies With A Mission). The aim of the project was to train and equip village health workers to do a defined series of tasks in these remote village communities using algorithms developed by the World Health organisation for use in isolated areas where there are no doctors. I think they invited me because of my experience working in island village communities in utterly remote areas in Fiji.

I arranged to leave for Uganda in April and flew by Sabena Airlines from Heathrow to Brussels, then following a wait of 5 hours, on to Entebbe, the airport that served Kampala as the capital. Sabena had always been my least favourite airline and the only one where I had witnessed an airline stewardess swear at a black passenger who struggled with both English and French when he found difficulty answering a question. I was not surprised when it went bankrupt in 2001. On this occasion, they got me safely to Uganda without swearing at me. I was met by Ralf, a German nurse who was the only white member of the team other than me and who had already spent a year working on Lingira Island in the Buvuma island archipelago on Lake Victoria. The Ugandan islands on Lake Victoria were counted as the wild west of the country. The countries bordering the lake were Burundi, Kenya, Rwanda, Tanzania and Uganda, and there was a great deal of travelling between these islands, with people who had run into trouble in one country taking refuge in the islands belonging to another country. Effectively, the border of Uganda was at the shore of the lake, particularly at Jinja, where there was a strong presence of both the army and the special branch. There were very few government personnel, either medical, security forces or civil government, on the islands, and they were lawless communities. The country had barely recovered from the nightmares of the presidencies of Idi Amin and later the second term of Milton Obote when we were there, and there was another current armed insurrection further north on the mainland called the Lord's Resistance Army. Ralf took me by road from Kampala to Jinja through the lush, fertile countryside. We arrived at Jinja, the second city of Uganda and the YWAM bungalow. I settled temporarily into a tiny box room and was introduced to the rest of the larger YWAM team.

I went for a walk around the town. Just across the road from the bungalow was a large rubbish skip that was supposed to be emptied every month, but there often was not a lorry functional enough to do this, so the individual rubbish items became familiar neighbours to us. The rubbish was picked over by a large bird with an even larger beak every day, which provided a bit of extra space. The town itself looked a bit like a set for a wild west film but for a film that had been shot about five years ago, and the set had not been used since. Many of the shops had been the property of the Indians who had been thrown out at the time of Idi Amin and had not been used or maintained since. A few shops were still open and sold a bizarre range of goods. One got the impression that rather than a shop being a stationer or seller of white goods shop or having a particular range of wares, the owner wandered around and if he found something that somebody might buy, he bought a supply of it and put it in his shop. So, some books would be next to a sack of flour, which was next to the light bulbs, which were next to a pile of shoes. On the other side of town was a large compound surrounded by a high wall with broken glass along the top, and there was a guard at the gate. This was the compound of an American mission, which seemed to have a somewhat different concept of a mission from YWAM. I was told that everybody living inside the compound was from America. When a new missionary arrived, they were given a house furnished with everything an American needs to live: air-conditioning, a car, fridges, freezers, sofas, tables, chairs, internally sprung beds, etc. However, about a quarter of the missionaries who arrived stayed for less than three months and left because they could not bear to live in such a primitive place. When this happened, they sold off everything that they had been furnished with in their house as one could not possibly give a new missionary second-hand house furnishing in such a hardship place as this. This was an enormous blessing to the YWAM base as they were able to buy chairs, fridges, freezers etc., at a knockdown price.

The most colourful place in town was the market, an expanse of small, often homemade, stalls selling everything under the sun. There were all sorts of fruit and vegetables, some of which I did not recognise, plus cloth, stationery, buttons, building supplies, padlocks and keys, cooked meals and a hundred and one other produce and services. There was a tremendous noise, everybody kept shouting at the top of their voices, and apparently nobody was listening. The shouting seemed quite a skilled task, as many of the stall owners, who were overwhelmingly women, seemed to be conversing with the owner of the stall next door in brief pauses between the shouting. As soon as I entered the market, almost in unison, everybody started shouting at me. 'Hey Muzungu' (white man), 'don't go to that stall, they will cheat you. Come here!' 'Hey Muzungu, do you want good Matooke (boiling bananas)? Mine are very good; they will give you a big belly.' 'Hey Muzungu, are you looking for a black wife?' If you purchased something heavy and needed a ride home, there were three types of taxis available in Jinja. The most common one was the bicycle taxi, where you would sit pillion on the luggage carrier at the back of the bike, and the person at the front would pedal you to your destination. Then, there was the motorbike taxi, reserved for those who considered themselves to be middle class. In this case, you would still sit pillion at the back, but the person at the front would drive you around. Lastly, there was the car taxi, of which I only ever saw one. This vehicle only deserved the name of a car as its shape resembled that of a car with 4 wheels. The structure was held together with wire. There were no working instruments or even a dashboard. There was a plastic ice-cream container at the back into which the taxi driver poured a very small amount of petrol before the journey, placed the pipe leading to the engine, and off we went. If the taxi driver had made a bit of a miscalculation and put too little petrol in the ice cream container, the engine spluttered and stopped halfway through the journey. If this happened, the taxi driver pulled the petrol bottle out of his pocket, put a small amount more in the plastic container, and we resumed our journey. Around the town, there were a very large number of men in khaki with guns. Some of them were drunk, and it was rather off-putting to see drunk men waving around powerful guns.

Back at the YWAM bungalow, we had no security at all. The doors were wide open all day. Inside, there was a community of a variable number of people, normally about twelve people. The majority were Ugandan people working with YWAM, but sometimes there was a smattering of Europeans or Americans or sometimes South Americans. The main centre for YWAM for the whole of Uganda was just 20 miles down the road, and people rotated through the bungalow who were working at smaller centres such as the one on the islands we would be working in. They often came to buy supplies from the market and get medical care (of a sort). The permanent people were a man and his wife and baby. They lived in two rooms and were the people responsible for the bungalow community. Then there was Ruth, a young, slim, vivacious girl with a permanent smile on her face. She was always rushing around making meals, singing, cleaning and generally motivating the world - that is, in the interludes between her having to race into the hospital when she had a crisis. She had severe sickle cell anaemia and, from time to time, developed a crisis and became suddenly and severely ill. A few days later, she would appear looking a bit pale and not so energetic, but after a day or two, she went into super drive again. The long-term outlook for her was grim, and she knew that. However, she had an unshakable faith in a loving Father God who looked after her while she was here and was preparing a place for her in heaven when she was promoted there. The purpose of the bungalow and the aim of the whole YWAM setup was to show the love of their Saviour in actions and in words to anybody and everybody. To further this, they talked frequently to their master, so prayer happened a lot, hopeful and confident prayer despite the unstable and chaotic conditions. Also, if the Ugandans were happy, they sang beautifully and in tune. It seemed a place where people were happy to work and where they all had a common cause.

After two days, having bought some goods and food for the island community, Ralf decided it was time to take off for the island. I was advised to leave anything of value in a box in the bungalow, so packing my belongings into a smallish bag, we set off in the four-wheeled taxi held together by wire for the wharf from where the boats left for the islands. As we approached the wharf, the number of people in khaki and holding guns increased, as did the general tension around us. Eventually, we reached the place from where we would be embarking. In fact, it was not a wharf at all, just a very dirty beach with many large boats with very old-looking outboard motors pulled up on the shore. A small market and many men with guns surrounded it. We unloaded our supplies from the taxi, and a policeman approached us asking for our passports. I had not been told I needed to bring mine, so I left it back at the bungalow. Because of this, I was told that I could not board the boat. After a talk with Ralf, the policeman eventually agreed that I could go to the islands. This sorted out the immediate problem but created another worse problem. When I came back from the island in two weeks' time, and I did not have a passport the special branch could arrest me. That would not be good news, and these guys did not have a name for being either polite or gentle. We decided to face that problem when it occurred.

We identified the boat going to Lingira and climbed on board together with mothers and babies, building materials, chickens, a goat and lots of produce from the market. As each new passenger climbed on board, the boat sunk lower in the water. A soldier came up to us and demanded a Coke. We refused as this could be construed as a bribe, and the evidence was that once having given in to this pressure, it became known, and everybody would ask for increasing amounts of goods or money. To vent his anger, the soldier opened all our bags and emptied them, then he went through all our possessions to do a "check". Happily, he didn't note my lack of a passport. When we were all packed up again, the boat took off. It was grossly overloaded, and there was very little freeboard. Happily, the water was not rough, and we did not ship much water. Among the passengers was a soldier who spent most of the journey bullying a young, poor-looking woman with a baby to give him 100 shillings. This was not much by British standards but may well have been most of what this woman-owned at that time.

We passed numerous islands of various sizes and eventually came to the large Island of Buvuma, which gives its name to this wild west province of Uganda. As usual, the wharf at the village of Lingira was a rather grubby beach with lots of children jumping up and down and shouting, liberally interspersed with goats bleating and eating anything in sight. Behind the beach was a shop and then the mud huts in which everybody lived. The boat was so heavily loaded that it could not get in very close to the beach, and everybody disembarking had to jump off into the water up to the upper thighs. Practically the whole village turned out, and there was much hugging, looking for parcels, shouting that the parcels had been left behind, finding the parcels which had been there all the time, but an old lady was sitting on them and was refusing to get off the boat until somebody carried her as she refused to get wet. In other words, it is a normal arrival of a boat from Jinja. Some people from our team turned up, and with their help, Ralf and I offloaded our supplies, took them up the beach, and then back to the base. This turned out to be three mud huts with thatched roofs sitting on the very edge of a deep gully to take rainwater away from the village when it rained, which it did almost every day. Inside was just sleeping accommodation; all living was done outside, sitting on mats and cooking on open fires or in earth ovens. At the side of one of the huts was an area closed off with what looked like rattan with nothing but two large plastic bowls inside it. This was the washing area. Apparently, the routine was that one filled two large bowls with water, then went inside, shut the door and got undressed. This closing of the door bit seemed a bit superfluous when one realised that as soon as a Muzungu went into the bath area, there was a signal that collected all the children from all over the village who stood with their noses poking through platted rattan peering at this odd body being soaped and then rinsed and dried. When I was washing, there must have been at least 20 small faces squinting through the slots at me. However, if I caught the eye of one of them and winked, the little faces disappeared immediately as they were not meant to be there, so they should not be acknowledged. One poured a basin full of water over one's head, soaped oneself, and then used the other basin to wash off the soap by pouring that over one's head. One landed up with a clean body, muddy feet, and a conviction that every peculiarity of one's body was known to everybody under the age of 6 years in Lingira. Just beside the washing area were several forty-litre plastic jerry cans. These were for the water for washing up, cooking and drinking after it had been boiled. There was no running water on the islands and no well at that time in Lingira, so the cans had to be filled from the lake, which was fresh water. The water near the shore was extremely dirty, so the only way to get moderately clean water was to wade out until the water was up to one's shoulders, fill the jerrycans, put them on one's shoulders and carry them back to the huts. The lake was absolutely teeming with bilharzia parasites, which can cause severe problems with the intestines and the kidneys, but that was something that might, and often did, cause problems for tomorrow. For today, the only way to get fresh water was to wade into the lake.

We settled in and were made very welcome by the other members of the team. The inside of our hut was filled with rather battered mattresses on the floor, and being the men's hut, there was a fair covering of clothes on the floor, too. There was a large room and a very small room in which I was told I would be sleeping as I was a lot older than most of the other members of the team. This is a throwback to the Wrinkles With A Mission issue first raised by my sons. However, I was very grateful for my own space. There was just room for my kit bag and bed. All the supplies were unpacked and put away in locked cupboards where it was less likely that they would "disappear". Throughout this whole procedure, each windowsill of the hut had a row of small brown faces peering at these odd people and another row behind them, jumping up and down to get a view. When unpacked, we went outside, sat on the mats with the team, and chatted. It was warm but not hot. The sky was darkening over the lake beyond the next island, and there were distant rumbles of thunder and flashes as a thunderstorm developed. It was slow moving, and a meal of posho and beans was cooked and eaten long before the storm arrived. This was the standard diet in Uganda, with posho being maize flour mixed with water until it had the consistency and taste of thick wallpaper paste and brown beans cooked with certain local spices and a reddish sauce, probably including tomatoes. I asked what the name of the beans was and was told that they were "common beans"; apparently, they did not have another name. At times, the beans were replaced with cooking bananas or, if one struck lucky, with fish. The lake was teeming with fish, mainly Tilapia and Nile Perch, but the fishermen had a ready market for these both on the islands and on the mainland, so they were expensive.

As the light faded the Tilley lamps were lit and the groups huddled nearer to the lights so that people could see what they were doing. The whole time the radios were playing music from a Tanzanian radio station just across the water. The music was a repetitive phrase of music repeated over again, leading to a not unpleasant somnolence. The people all around us were drinking palm toddy which was strongly alcoholic and made in the first branching of a palm tree. Everybody seemed to be imbibing apart from the YWAM group. The Ugandan Christians had a firm belief that if you drank alcohol or smoked you could not be a Christian. I found this difficult though understandable as alcohol abuse is a major problem throughout the country. However, I just wondered how they fitted that with their view that salvation is by faith and grace alone, not by works. The YWAM group sang. In fact, many people sang in many places in Uganda, the difference was that YWAM almost always sang about their faith, their God, and their Saviour. Although there were Muslims on the islands as well as native religions nobody seemed to have any hang up about talking about their faith whatever it was.

And so, to bed. My mattress was reasonably comfortable, as was my pillow made from a rolled-up jumper inside a pillowcase. I had a torch and a key in case I needed to use the YWAM long drop loo on the other side of the village and across two deepish gullies that could be full of water if it had rained. I dropped off, and apart from being awoken occasionally when a cockroach in the thatch lost its footing and fell on my face or a mouse decided to take a shortcut across my chest I slept until about three o'clock in the morning when it rained hard. I found that when it rained outside, it also rained inside here in Lingira, and it seemed that the function of the thatch was to diminish the force of the rain rather than to keep one dry. Mind you, there were certain dry spots around where the thatch was a little thicker than in other parts, and I could hear shuffling all around the hut as people tried to find these dryish spots before somebody else got there first.

Eventually, I sorted this problem out. The next time I went into Jinja, I bought two sheets of plastic, one large enough to cover my body and one to go under my mattress. Every evening when I went to bed, I pulled the plastic sheet up to my chin, opened my umbrella, and arranged it so that the handle was behind my left ear and the top covered my face and neck. With this arrangement, on the whole, I slept well and awoke dry. The only problem was that when the rats ran across my chest during the night, they skidded and could slide into my neck and in any case, there was outraged squeaking from them about these new arrangements concerning which they had not been consulted.

The next morning, we had a meeting of the team to discuss the village health worker project. The idea was that every village should be given the opportunity of having a village health worker (VHW), and the village should elect this person. The village would undertake to look after the fields or fishing by which this person maintained their family for one day a week, during which time the VHW would occupy their time with health matters. Outside this time, if anybody was sick, they could also consult the VHW. These people would do a limited number of health-related tasks and work from algorithms developed by the World Health Organisation for places where people did not have access to doctors or other competent, medically trained workers. The VHWs did not need to read. If they were illiterate, they just learned the algorithms by heart. The five main tasks that these workers would be responsible for were immunisations, which were much the same as in the West, the diagnosis and treatment of respiratory infections, diarrhoea and vomiting; the diagnosis and treatment of malaria; and the diagnosis and treatment of Bilharzia. Severe respiratory illness was diagnosed by increased breathing rate and indrawing of the skin under their ribs with each breath, and they had a small stock of antibiotics to treat this. The VHWs were taught to diagnose dehydration caused by diarrhoea and vomiting and to rehydrate individuals using sachets of powder containing salt and sugar, which were dissolved in water. Blood in the urine was often assumed to be due to Schistosomiasis (Biharzia), as this was a common concern for everyone here. Any fever without an obvious cause was typically assumed to be malaria, and patients were provided with antimalarials. In addition to managing these issues, they were also given bed nets to distribute to children for sleeping under. By the time people reached adulthood, most of them were immune to the malarial parasite. The health workers also gave family planning advice and carried contraceptive pills. By far, the most important skill they were taught was to know when they had come to the end of their competence and to advise the patient to go to the mainland. This could cause problems as this was not really a money economy, and some people could not afford the cost of the boat to the mainland or the cost of being seen at the hospital. After the first training course, the new VHW worked with a more experienced colleague until both she (and it usually was a woman) and her mentor felt that she could work alone. Every few months, the VHW had a brush-up course given by Ralph. To set up this programme it was necessary to sell the idea to the various village communities, and we spent many hours going to the islands, meeting with the village councils and elders, electing the VHW and arranging the courses. In most communities, this process went smoothly. We would talk to the village council, sometimes on two separate occasions. The village would suggest three candidates for the post, and then the villagers would vote for the person whom they wanted to care for them. The election was carried out by the three candidates going to the village green, where they would line up side-by-side, and people would line up behind the candidate they wanted to be the VHW. The person with the most villagers behind her was elected. This was a well-established means of carrying out elections and was also used for the regional councils and parliament political elections. Occasionally, a village did not want to have a village health worker, which was usually because they were unwilling to do the work to release the workers to do their health work. Ralf, who had lived on the islands for over a year, could normally predict which villages would take this path. In this case, we did not immediately broach the subject of having a village health worker when we arrived on the island. Instead, we asked the village chief to take us to the cemetery. Most of the village population tagged along as well. We then asked the chief to tell us who was buried in the graves. Almost always, there were a lot of children's graves and some of the others would be of adults who had died of bilharzia, malaria or "slim," which was AIDS, as well as a few after accidents. We then asked the gathered crowd whether they would be happier if these people had not died. Very often, the relatives of the dead children and adults would be in the crowd, and a great discussion would start as they knew very well that if they said yes, then they would be offered a VHW, and they would have to cover some of her daily work in her fields. Usually, the decision finally was to agree to the election, training, and support of a health worker. Another health project that had been adopted by the team was to get people to build toilets, hopefully eventually water lock toilets, which would cut down the incidence of fly-borne disease. This involved quite a bit of work, some costs and an agreement to undertake regular maintenance, so it was not felt that it was feasible at this time to give this task to the VHWs.

A part of the role of the YWAM team was to take part in the Christian teaching of the community on the islands and to spread the gospel of Jesus Christ to anybody who would listen. There was a church which we attended every Sunday. The Ugandans can do many things well, but the thing they can do best of all is sing. The only singing I ever heard which was of the same fervour, quality and tunefulness was in Fiji on the islands. Maybe this has something to do with living on a small mass of land surrounded by water. One entered the church hut and as soon as a reasonable quorum was there, the singing started. Everybody sang their hearts out; they swayed, shouted Praise the Lord or Hallelujah in several languages, raised their hands, and sometimes wept with joy, which was a bit different from an Anglican service in the UK or even in Uganda. At some time, time was found to give out some notices and time was certainly made for a message, often an extremely long message. However, if you felt that you needed to stretch your legs it was quite OK to go outside and have a little stroll and come back again. On Sunday afternoon sometimes a small Christian group either on the main island or a smaller island would ask us to go and preach a message. Not infrequently I did this. We would set out on foot, and I often went with Catherine a local girl whose favourite phrase seemed to be "You munzungues are very funny people." We would walk through the fields and along the paths passing through forest and along the coast. Every person who we met we would greet, and we would chat for a minute or two. We met a lot of people which meant that we were about one and a half hours late for the meeting. But so was everybody else. An hour and a half late was on time on the islands because everybody else was greeting everyone they met. I can remember one occasion when we were in a fishing village and standing with a small crowd on the beach. Behind us were the huts in among the trees with children and goats wandering around and playing. The beach had the usual tackle from the fishing boats, ropes, baskets, bags for the fish. One boat was lying on its side being repaired. Several the fishing boats were out on the lake too far off to see. The people coming to the meeting were arriving, greeting everybody, and sitting with their friends on the flat rocks used as seats when the village came together. It was a beautiful sunny day and not too warm. There, over the lake though there was a thunderstorm blowing up. The sky was dark out on the horizon, and one could see the flashing of lightning on the lake and hear the grumbling of the thunder. The water can get extremely rough on the lake in a bad storm and the local fishing boats were out of sight. There was a frisson of anxiety underlying the murmur of conversation. I had been asked to preach on Jesus stilling the storm and for the first time in my life that whole story became real to me. One could hear a pin drop as I spoke about the power of God to enter our lives and deal with our storms and give His peace. There, we were with the storm for that village being just the same sort of storm as in the story, but all of them and us had their private inner storms too. The boats arrived safely home that evening and we walked home to Lingira, greeting everybody once again as we went back.

We travelled into the mainland and stayed at the bungalow twice during the time I was in Lingira. The boats were always grossly overloaded. On one occasion travelling out to the island, we were even more crowded than usual, with heaps of merchandise and mothers with babies and goats. It seemed that we had almost no freeboard at all. Halfway through the journey, the wind got up and the lake became extremely choppy. The boat was rapidly shipping water and rolling badly in the swell as the local people were petrified. As the situation became more perilous the Ugandans struck up a weird low-pitched chant, which made the hairs on the back of my neck stand up. I am not quite sure what they were singing about, but everybody joined in and the whole mass of people was moving with the boat rolling with the cadence of the chant also being governed by this. The people looked almost as though they were in a trance, and one had the impression that something very ancient indeed was going on and perhaps something occult. I was very glad when we finally crept into the lee of Buvuma island and limped to the shore at Lingira. Within 5 minutes of arriving, everybody was greeting everybody else, the boat was being unloaded, two people were having an argument in a way that suggested that this was a long running argument, perhaps going on over several years. Nobody alluded in any way to the fact that we had very nearly sunk. Boats in these islands sink every year or two with many people being drowned, but this does not seem to change behaviour.

My time in Uganda was nearly up and it came towards the end of my project. It was time to leave. I packed up and headed to the mainland. To send me on my way there was a special meal and a church service. I found that I was sad to be going but Biddenham and my family called. I arrived for the last time at the non-jetty at Jinja and was asked for a last time for a bribe by the special branch. For the last time I sat in the back of the taxi held together by wire with an open petrol tank just behind where the driver was smoking. And was taken with my luggage to the bungalow. There was the usual crowd of people from various parts of the country and world who all seemed sad to see me go, even the people who had never seen me before. The wife of the deputy director of YWAM for the whole of Uganda, a lovely Swedish girl expecting her second baby, drove me from Jinja to Kampala and dropped me off at the bus station. Here I caught the standard minibus for the journey to Entebbe where the airport and the hotel I was spending the last night in were situated. The bus was the 15-seater Toyota minibus that one sees all over the third world with about 35 people on board. It had been a Toyota minibus, at some stage, but it had been repaired with all sorts of bits and bobs and so it seemed to have become a mongrel that no employee of Toyota would ever agree was anything out of his factory. The one thing that had not been repaired was the dashboard. It was there and there were spaces for all the instruments but no instruments in the holes. The bus only had two speeds, full speed and stop and it was a bit difficult to reach the second speed as the brakes did not really seem to be working. I decided that this was all working to a plan to make sure that everybody leaving the country left in a prayerful mood and conscious of their dependence on the grace of God. We arrived safely though with a slightly rapid pulse at the Lake Victoria Hotel, and I rescued my cases from under several sacks of millet and a chicken and walked towards the door. Suddenly I found myself in a totally different world, a bit like walking through the door at the back of the wardrobe. A very smartly dressed man came and took my case, came with me to reception, made sure that I was checked in and had booked the shuttle for the airport tomorrow and took me to my room He ushered me into a luxurious air-conditioned double room gratefully accepted the tip I gave him and noiselessly disappeared. I unpacked a bit with the odd trickle of rat droppings falling on the floor from my room in Lingira and then rather childishly bounced up and down for a while on the first internally sprung mattress I had seen for 6 weeks. I had a shower then a swim in the swimming pool and then on to my evening meal. The menu was wide ranging, the cuisine excellent and I had the first alcohol since I had arrived in Uganda. After all, I felt if this was a different world, maybe the Ugandan rule that you can't be a Christian if you drink any alcohol or smoke didn't apply here though I didn't try the smoking bit. I found a good bottle of Rioja wine and was about to order it when I noticed that if you bought two half bottles of this wine it was cheaper than if you bought a full bottle, so that is what I did. It was reassuring that even in a smooth hotel small echoes of the quirkiness of Uganda still crept in. The next morning after an excellent breakfast the shuttle came, deposited me at the airport and I climbed on the Sabena flight to Heathrow. The air hostesses remained as impolite as ever, and the food was still as unappetising as it had always been. In a sense, it was reassuring to see that the world hadn't changed during my time in Uganda. Peta was at the airport to greet me and then drove me home. This trip had been an experience during which a project had progressed to make a real difference to a poor community in the back of beyond and I had had the privilege of living and working with a group of joyful but very poor Christian brothers and sisters. I would not have missed it for the world, but my great sadness was that it had not been possible to share it with Peta. I vowed that that would be the last project that I would be involved in without her. As a post-script to my trip, a few weeks after I left somebody came into the bungalow in Jinja and tried to steal Alphonse's computer. Alphonse resisted and was shot dead in front of his wife and children. The YWAM community did not retreat behind a high wall with broken glass on the top. They carried on exactly as they had been doing. They committed themselves to the Lord and carried on showing His love to a sad and broken world despite what that might cost.

Retirement

Back in Bedford, it felt a bit like waking from a dream and it took me a few days to get back into the normal rhythm. General practice was changing in Britain. The GP had always been the advocate for his or her patient, fighting their corner against all comers. Increasingly, practices were given budgets, and it fell to the GP themselves to, in the last instance, ration the patient if they had problems that cost a significant amount of money. To a degree, this changed the doctor-patient relationship. Additionally, one had to engage in a lot of box-ticking for procedures that were not clinically relevant to the patient's condition. We were required to collect reams of statistics, which could have easily been harvested automatically from the computer, as we were now fully computerised.

We were in the post-Thatcher era at that time, and the population had been told that there was no such thing as a community and that if they wanted something, they should demand it and not accept no. The supermarkets were open 24 hours, why not the doctors' surgeries. The out of hours work became unmanageable and so was passed over to doctors outside the practice working for night call companies. Overall, these doctors were perfectly competent, but they did not have any idea of the health or family background of the patient in front of them.

There was considerable investment in hospital medicine at this time, but an eight percent cut was made in the resources available to general practice. The consequence of all this was that the waiting time to see a doctor increased in line with the increasing workload expected of the practices. Much of the work was becoming administrative and financial, so the work satisfaction gradually decreased, few young doctors wanted to come into the specialty and those that did worked as salaried doctors not partners. Salaried doctors did not have to do administrative work, just clinical work. This meant that for the same number of sessions they could do what they were trained for and earn almost as much as the partners, as well as not having to do administrative work or invest their own money into the practice. The experience of patients was that they had to wait longer to see the doctor, he or she did not turn out to see them at night, and when they did see the doctor, they did things to him which were necessary for box ticking but seemed to have no relevance to their problems. They were not happy, neither were the doctors.

I was tired and demoralised. One morning, as I was getting up, over a matter of about a minute, the visual field in my right eye rapidly narrowed down to a pinprick and disappeared. I was totally blind in that eye. I phoned my doctor who spoke to the ophthalmologist at Bedford hospital whom I knew well, and I was seem immediately in the outpatient's department. While I was getting to the hospital my vision returned to near perfect. I had an MRI scan which showed that I had had a mini stroke with three infarcts (areas of dead tissue) in the part of my brain dealing with my vision. I was referred to a neurologist who put me on blood thinning tablets and told me that I should not drive and should refer myself to the DVLA. I was told that I could not drive for at least two months and my driving licence was taken away.

Nobody told me that I should stop work or take any time off work, so I went in to work and did visits as normal, except my means of transport was now a bicycle. I never understood why my partners did not point out to me that I should have had at least a month's rest. My drug-using patients were surprisingly considerate, even more so than the majority of the patients or my partners. One of them once told me, "Doc, it's a shame to see you cycling around on that rundown old bike. If you had let me know about it, I could have arranged a new bike for you within 20 minutes." When I enquired about the source of such a bike, he declined to provide details but mentioned an excellent bicycle that had captured his attention for a while.

After a few weeks, I noticed an increasing difficulty managing my consultations, and one day, I had four pharmacists phoning me up, telling me that I had made potentially dangerous errors in prescriptions. I decided that I needed to go and see my personal GP, who told me that the infarcts in my brain could have affected my cognitive abilities, making me a danger to patients if I continued working. He signed me off work for a month and referred me to the neuropsychology department at Addenbrookes Hospital Cambridge. When I eventually saw them, they diagnosed a severe depressive illness triggered by my stroke and affecting my memory more than my mood. They suggested that I should, at the age of 58, apply for early retirement. This I did, and the NHS, after getting medical reports, gave me retirement on full pension 2 years early. I was also well insured privately, and two of the three insurance companies paid up immediately. General Accident, with whom I had had insurance for many years, suggested that I was making up my problem and refused to pay until I put in process a referral to the ombudsman.

And so, ignominiously, my career in British general practise came to an end. That being said, it was a career filled with excitement and intellectual challenges. I found that my faith was strengthened as I experienced the faithfulness of my Heavenly Father. None of that though was the kernel of my career, that was the close, trusting and caring reciprocal relationship between me and the many patients who had given me the great privilege of sharing part of their life's package of joys and sadness, success and disasters, smiles and tears. I am very grateful to them.

It was a Monday morning, and the alarm had gone off at 7:15 am, which was half an hour later than the past 28 years. Peta was just beginning to wake up. It struck me that I didn't have to rush out of bed, grab a quick breakfast, and try to beat the traffic jams to complete my administration tasks before starting my surgery at 8:30. My only task now was to get Peta off to work, do the dishes, and then I had a whole day with no urgent appointments. For the first few weeks, there were several loose ends to tie up at work, and a few tests were still outstanding to try and uncover the reason behind all of this. As it turned out, all the tests came back normal, except for having lost a small proportion of my brain. My vision returned to normal, as did my memory with the functioning of my antidepressant treatment, yet nobody could determine the cause of this ordeal.

Not long after my retirement, we went on a holiday to our French home, although we could still only stay for two weeks due to Peta's work. On my return to England, I walked, read, tended to the garden, enjoyed music, entertained our numerous friends, and in turn, was entertained by them. I led church Bible study groups, among other activities. One significant skill I developed during this period was the ability to pause — not just to look, but to truly see and reflect. It became a time of healing, contemplation, and listening to God, rather than simply reading the Bible every day, and informing Him of my plans and requests.

Soon, I began to feel the absence of daily contact with the people I had interacted with. It wasn't so much the absence of my partners or the ordinary flow of individuals in and out of my office that I missed, but rather the individuals who lived lives entirely different from my own. I longed for my patients who had battled depression for a decade, those whose lives were entangled in the grip of substance abuse, the homeless individuals I had worked with, and those who hadn't conformed to the middle-class norm of a spouse, two well-behaved children, a comfortable home, a car or two, and a picturesque summer holiday once both children had excelled in their exams — something they never failed to broadcast to everyone they encountered.

I was being entertained by one of my friends one day when a guest shared a story. The tale revolved around a Catholic priest named Abbé Pierre, who ministered in a church located in a poverty-stricken area of Paris just after the conclusion of the First World War. His parishioners were impoverished, yet beyond the church walls, there existed even more destitute individuals who slept in doorways, begged for survival, and frequently endured hunger and freezing temperatures while resting under inadequate coverings. These were the homecoming soldiers, many of whom found that the whole world they had been used to had changed since they left home. They had no jobs, no homes, and often no families; whole families had been wiped out. The government did very little to help them.

Abbé Pierre spent a considerable amount of time sitting on the kerb, or at night in doorways with them. He felt that this was not right and started asking God what He was going to do for them. Very clearly, he felt God pointing out to him that he as a single man had a large comfortable presbytery to live in and plenty to eat. God told him as He so often does that, he could be the answer to his own prayers. Abbé Pierre invited a few of these men into his home to live with him as his companions, but this made hardly a dent in the numbers. He found that a large part of the outbuildings of his church were very rarely used and so he invited more men in as companions. The diocese began to raise questions, and he encountered significant difficulty in persuading them to permit these men to stay. Eventually, he posed a question to them: 'If the essence of God's law is to love God with all my heart and to love my neighbours just as I love myself, then who exactly are my neighbours? And how can I show love to a starving homeless man as I would to myself?' His persistence paid off, and he succeeded in convincing the diocese. Subsequently, he initiated a national campaign that compelled the French president to offer some financial aid, albeit woefully insufficient, for these companions.

It soon became clear that these men required not just shelter and food, but skills so they could regain the dignity of being self-sufficient. From His acquaintances and his parish, the Abbé found people to set up training schemes to reskill his companions. This programme, called Emmaus, grew and grew all over France and into other countries, and until today help is offered to homeless people in more than 30 countries. The pattern of the programme is still the same as when Abbé Pierre started, accommodation and skill training is offered with the aim of allowing the recipients to develop a stable lifestyle, address health issues, acquire new skills and become independent, though no time limit is imposed for this to happen.

I was interested and found that Bedford had a "Emmaus village community" at Carlton, a village just outside of the town. I very much wanted to work in among the village community members. I had spent numerous years working with individuals who had encountered legal issues, experienced homelessness, or struggled with substance abuse. Throughout that time, I was consistently the person they turned to for assistance. This dynamic significantly alters the nature of relationships. I had found that in Fiji, where we lived alongside the community and living in the same circumstances, we had been accepted as full community members whereas in Saudi Arabia and Uganda we had been the people from outside who were delivering a service. I went around the Emmaus community and met several of the companions, was interviewed and was taken on as a white van driver.

In Bedford, as in most other communities, the Emmaus village was given all manner of things that people no longer needed. These were renovated by companions who had received training in the necessary skills and sold in the shop. There was also a café run by the companions. Quite a few of the gifts were brought to the village community, but the Emmaus white van could collect larger items and gifts from older or sick people.

I signed on to work two days a week and turned up to meet my two workmates Pete and Phil. They both told me that they could both drive but had lost their licences after being breathalysed, as had most of the companions. I made my acquaintance with our trusty steed, and we set off for an address in a nearby village. I had always somewhat fancied the notion of being a 'white van man': driving a powerful Mercedes van, wearing my baseball cap backwards, always in a rush, and tailgating the slowpokes ahead of me. However, the reality of our white van was quite different. It turned out to be an extremely slow and ageing Ford Transit van, equipped with a minuscule diesel engine that lacked a turbocharger. This meant that pressing the accelerator pedal to the floor resulted in a waiting period of several minutes before any noticeable increase in speed occurred. Ironically, on several occasions, I found myself peering into my rear-view mirror at a robust

Mercedes white van tailgating me. Behind the wheel was a young man sporting a backwards baseball cap, evidently quite eager to overtake, driven by impatience.

We had an instructive time driving around the countryside of Bedfordshire. Both of them smoked nonstop and strongly disliked having any windows open as it gave them stiff necks. The consequence was that Peta got used to me coming home smelling like a kipper. My workmate Pete had been a merchant seaman for many years. He had briefly been married, but it had not lasted. When he left the sea, he had never settled in a job or any permanent accommodation, so he had spent 15 years sleeping under hedges in the summer and in empty barns and buildings in the winter. Phil had been in the army and similarly had a broken marriage and had been unable to settle outside a disciplined pattern of life. He had been homeless for 7 years. They had a huge repertoire of stories; most of them were true, and some of them were more unlikely than others.

I asked Pete how one became a companion at Emmaus. Apparently, a person can be referred by several agencies, including social workers, police, probation officers, vicars and various other community workers. The next step is an assessment by the Emmaus organisation. The companions play a large part in this. No alcohol or drugs are allowed in the community, which can be a problem for some people. These people are offered help with this before they become companions. If they are accepted, they are given accommodation and told that they will no longer be people dependent on the state for their livelihood; they will be working men and women in the same way as everybody else. They are expected to develop skills; many of them taught by the companions themselves and then to work a defined number of hours in the workshops and the shop. After many years of homelessness, begging and often sleeping rough, they are very proud of their new standing as working members of the population.

The most difficult part of the early induction as a companion is that they have to call social services and cancel all their benefits. This process is always completely managed by the companions themselves. The new members are sat in front of a phone and asked to telephone the social service office and tell them they no longer need the benefits they have depended on for years. Some of the applicants sit trembling before the phone and say that they cannot do this. A couple of companions designated to support them sit down with these new members and tell the stories about their lives, the rootlessness, the fear of others and what becoming a member of Emmaus has done for them. Usually, the benefits are duly cancelled, and from this point on, these men and women start their long journey to become stable, self-supporting members of the wider community. Eventually, most of them move on to living In their own flats.

I dressed in the same way as all the companions when were in our wanderings around the county to collect the offered items. The loading and unloading were dirty jobs and so we dressed appropriately. I was reasonably well known in the town and often meeting people I knew who did not recognise me in this setting. One winter afternoon we had to call in to an address to collect a cooker. I seemed to recognise the address and when we arrived, I realised that it was the home of Dominic's godmother, a good friend of ours who had been to our home many times. Pete, Phil, and I spent some time bringing the cooker through the house and loading it onto the van. Just as we were on the verge of departure, Margaret turned to me and remarked, "You know, your face seems familiar to me." I responded, "Indeed, Margaret, you are my son Dominic's godmother." The poor girl was overwhelmed with confusion – a poignant illustration of how encountering a familiar person in unfamiliar attire and surroundings can result in complete nonrecognition.

I thoroughly enjoyed my time as an honorary member of the Emmaus community. As my health improved, I decided to work another two days a week for the Department of Social Security in assessing people for benefits. These assessments were done in people's homes and seeing the homes of people who were sometimes severely disabled and how they coped was very interesting, however, it was not a pleasant occupation as there seemed always to be a subliminal pressure to produce evidence to refuse the payment of benefit. This impression might have been erroneous, but for me it did not sit well with my life view, and I was happy once I no longer did this work.

Paris

A year passed, during which Peta grew accustomed to having her husband around more often than before, while I regained my health and confidence. We devoted time to prayer, seeking God's guidance for what He had in store for us during the remaining active years of our lives. My youthful journey to India had ignited a deep passion for the Muslim world, the desert landscape, and particularly the Middle East. In contrast, Peta had always been captivated by French culture and ways of life. By a stroke of chance, we became acquainted with John and Audrey Coleman. They had served in a Christian hospital in Shiraz, Iran. However, with Ayatollah Khomeini's arrival in the country, the hospital was closed, the bishop was killed, and John and Audrey were imprisoned separately for nearly a year. Interestingly, John and Audrey happened to be neighbours of our older son in Hackney, London. After extensive prayer, numerous discussions, and extensive reading, we arrived at the conviction that God was directing us to collaborate with the Red Sea Mission. It turned out that John held a senior position on the mission's board. The Red Sea Mission was known for its work in regions where few other missions ventured. Their primary focus included Yemen, Djibouti, and later expanded to Somalia, Pakistan, Mali, and Port Harcourt in Nigeria. Initially, my heart leaned toward Mali, but as we delved deeper into our research about Djibouti, our conviction grew that this was the destination meant for us.

Djibouti, a tiny country the size of Wales, was originally French Somalia and was ruled as a colony under the name of Le Territoire des Afars et des Issas. It was almost totally salt desert and one of the hottest countries in the world. In the summer, inland in semi settled areas lived in by the Afar nomads, it regularly reached 50 degrees Celsius and stayed there for more than six weeks. The official language of the country was French, and it was the overseas headquarters of the French Foreign Legion.

We decided that the first thing we should do was to attend one of the annual meetings of the mission and this we did. We walked into the venue and wondered where on earth we had arrived. The place seemed full of very old couples with the men in tweed jackets and the women in twin sets and with permed hair. To be fair, more than half of the people were young, engaged and tremendously enthusiastic about the work. It was not until we attended a prayer meeting that we understood why all the old people were there. What we encountered during that meeting were individuals who had cultivated a profound relationship with God, often in distant corners of the world, conversing with Him as both a steadfast guide and a dear friend, discussing the needs of this country. This experience left us deeply humbled. These people firstly knew God as their Rock and also knew intimately what was going on in Djibouti and the other countries worked in by the mission and brought its needs and the needs of the people living there to Him in confident prayer.

One other very happy occurrence in our visit was that I met an old friend. I was standing in the toilet doing what men do in toilets when I glanced sidewards at the man standing beside me. He looked familiar. I asked him what his name was, and he said Salim Hadad and at that point we recognised each other. He was the Palestinian member of the team who had driven together to India after our time at Cambridge and whose home we visited on the way back. We had lost contact over the past years. Overflowing with excitement, we quite literally jumped up and down despite our slightly advancing age. The conference attendees bore witness to the sight of two grown men emerging from the toilet, embracing tightly and patting each other on the back in a burst of camaraderie. As word spread about the source of this fervour, the gathering joined in the celebration. Even the elegantly dressed ladies, though refraining from jumping or back-slapping, shared in the joyous spirit.

Having gained some idea about what the mission did, who they were and their vision of service to Jesus we decided to make a formal application to work with them. We were interviewed by a group of three people including John Coleman and accepted. I would have to work in French and although Peta would be working in the local languages of Afar and Somali, all official activities would take place in French, so we would need to have a far greater working knowledge of the language than we currently had.

We received advice to dedicate a year to learning French in France. At that time, there were two Christian language schools in the country. One was situated in Albertville in the Alps, and the other, named Les Cèdres, was located in Massy, a suburb of Paris very close to Orly airport. We opted for Les Cèdres. It brought us great joy to share with people, in response to their enquiries about our plans, that we were undergoing training to become missionaries. When they enquired about our assigned mission field, we proudly answered, "Paris." This often prompted reactions like, "Well, we've always thought the French were lacking in religious devotion. No doubt they can benefit from missionaries like you," or "Fascinating! Could you guide me on becoming a missionary?"

We let our house, lent one of our cars to somebody in the church who could make use of it, said goodbye to our family and decamped to France. At this time Simon and his wife Jo were expecting their first baby and we undertook to come back and look after things while Jo was having the baby. Also, we promised my mother who was 92 and who by that time was a widow that we would come home every month and see her. We set off in our car which was laden down to the gunnels and arrived at the language school which was based in the grounds of a Baptist church.

The school was mainly set up for non-Francophone Christians who were going to be working in the francophone world, though there were about 10 % of students particularly from Switzerland who needed to improve their French for work. There were about 7 different nationalities. The school was run by a British couple working together with a staff of French teachers. David and Jessie Boydell, the director and his wife had worked for some years in the Congo. There were two options for our accommodation, either we could be given rooms in the school building and live alongside the other students which was quite an attractive option, or we could live in a block of flats in the town as the only English household in a totally French environment. After some reflection we chose the latter option in the hope that we could make friends of our French neighbours.

We moved in, and before long, Peta had made friends with the concierge, a man of a rather short temper who came from Le Mans in the north. Peta soon tamed him and had him eating out of her hand. The question then was how could we get to know our neighbours? Our French, certainly at the start of the year, was not good at all, and we were very foreign in our lifestyle. Peta again used techniques she had used in many cultures. Firstly, admire any pets you meet and give treats to the dog of anybody living near us, however ugly, fat, and bad-tempered the dog is. This almost always starts conversations. Then one listens very hard to what the neighbours say and usually one can pick up when special things are happening in their lives. If one can find out their birthday, one sends them a card. If they have a cold, one offers to take the dog out and do the shopping, and then one can invite them for a meal. This never fails in France. They are fascinated to find out whether English people could cook or not. I can still remember when we invited a French family with a three-year-old daughter for a meal. Between the main course and the dessert, the child wandered out to the kitchen where Peta was preparing the dish and said, "You know, that was really quite nice".

Before long, we were firm friends with a couple on the floor above us and a lady on the floor below us. The man of the couple was a retired professor from the Paris Nuclear Institute. The wife was a delightful, way over-the-top character wearing slightly outlandish clothes, almost a cartoon character of a French lady from a children's book. They had a dog, whom we made a fuss of. Whenever we went round to their flat, the man rummaged around in a large chest from under the table and pulled out some aperitif I had never heard of. The lady who lived below us was a sad character who was permanently depressed and was convinced that everybody hated her. To add to that, she had a severe heart problem. Happily, she did have a dog. Later in the year, she posed quite a problem for me when she telephoned me quite late one night just to tell me that she was about to commit suicide! I then had the task of ringing the evening medical emergency service and explaining the problem in my bad French.

The school majored in teaching grammar and vocabulary, which some people did not like. We also had lessons on French culture, and we had to lead prayers or preach in the church. We had lessons on philosophy and French art, and quite a scary teacher taught phonetics. The amusing factor with this man was that he quite frequently spoke English to us with very poor English phonetics. I was very grateful for the teaching method as, although I did not speak fluent French when we finally left the school, I did have a good vocabulary, and I could both write and speak grammatically, something that we found to be very important if one wanted francophone people to listen to you. The fluency came gradually as we lived and worked among French friends and colleagues.

Once a month, we used to pile into our car on a Friday and drive to London to stay with Simon, Jo, then latterly Jonny overnight, then the next day drive to Malvern and spend the day with my mother and back to Hackney in the evening. We would drive back to Massy the next day ready for the new week's teaching.

About 2 months after we arrived in Massy, Jo went into labour back in Hackney. We piled into the car halfway through a weekday and set off for England. Soon after we arrived, Jo advanced in her labour and went into the obstetric department at the Homerton Hospital. The poor girl was 48 hours in labour before delivering our first grandchild, Jonathan (meaning friend, which in due course he turned out to be for many people). Jo did not have an easy time after her birth and developed a grumbling low-grade fever, which the staff found great difficulty diagnosing. We stayed around trying to help for 3 weeks and then returned to Massy to catch up on the time we had lost. It was a great privilege to be able to be part of one of the key happenings in our wider family.

During Christmas time, we celebrated Christmas day in Hackney and then returned to Massy on Boxing Day. While we were back, we heard on the radio about a devastating hurricane causing enormous damage in Northern France. As we arrived in Paris, chaos and debris were widespread. A tree had been blown into a flat close to ours, and the school had suffered extensive damage to its roof. Fortunately, our flat remained intact. We had allowed a student to use our flat during the Christmas period so that her mother could stay with her. The mother and daughter were still in the flat when we arrived as all transport had been stopped all over France. We stayed up chatting late into the night and then set off for our house in the south the next morning.

As we drove down through the central motorways of France, we noticed that the roads were almost totally empty, so much so it was quite spooky. We arrived at our house, turned on the television, and the presenter was urgently saying, "Wherever you are, find cover immediately and do not go outside; otherwise, there's a risk to your life." Then, the electricity went out and didn't come back on for three days. Since we had been engrossed in conversation the previous evening, we hadn't checked the weather forecast. Unbeknownst to us, a red weather warning had been issued for a more powerful hurricane expected to hit the central and southern parts of France, following the one in northern France. In haste, we cooked a meal on our gas cooker and went to bed. As the wind's speed intensified, it produced an eerie, animal-like sound. Soon, we began hearing a steady 'drip, drip, drip' in our roof space. We concluded that there was little we could do except wait, intervening only if the water threatened to soak us. By morning, we discovered a sizable hole in the roof of our barn and a smaller one in the house. Many of the houses around us were in a far worse state than ours, and people had been killed all around us by barn doors falling on them or being killed by flying debris. We phoned up our local handyman and he came and stood looking at the scene of devastation, scratched himself (a common activity in rural French it seemed to us) went and got some tiles and put them back on the roof. The charge was 34 euros.

Back at the school, the director had set up two excellent programmes: 'Aides de Langue' and 'Échanges de Savoirs.' The aim of the first programme was to provide every student with a French conversation partner whom they could meet with weekly to practise speaking French and receive language corrections. These conversation partners were residents of a rather upscale elderly care facility located next door to the school. The service provided by the residents was incredibly valuable to the students, and the companionship of students from all around the world was greatly appreciated by the elderly residents. Peta was paired with a delightful lady named Madame Peltier, who had a quiet and gentle demeanour. In contrast, my conversation partner, Madame Bouquerelle, was neither very gentle nor particularly quiet. She belonged to the Protestant upper class.

There were not too many protestants around in France as the French tended to kill them in periods throughout their history, so they formed a select group. The upper-crust protestants were even more select, and Madame Bouquerelle was an outstanding example of this select group. She was from an extremely wealthy family and had been a rebel since she was a girl. When she was going to get married, her parents gave her a sum of money to cover the cost of buying the necessities for her bottom drawer. However, within a few days of being given the money, she had spent it all on clothes. Once she was married, she found it very restricting to spend all her time with this man who had become her husband, and the husband was not happy with her total inability to cook edible meals. One day, things came to a head, and Madame Bouquerelle said that she would jump out of the window and kill herself. The husband got up, opened the window and said, "Go ahead". Following this, she settled down and had quite a notable career as a politician, becoming an elder in her community.

She was exigent about the way I spoke and completely ruthless in her criticisms. She was the most wonderful character with a life full of stories and a personality full of humour and irony. I grew to respect her enormously, and Peta and I kept in touch with her after we left the school. From time to time, she used to invite us for lunch at the residential home she lived in. One was met at the door by a Maître D', and having chosen a meal from the menu, the next important task was to choose the wine from the home's excellent cellar. As I have got older, I have been trying to find a home like that in England, but currently without success.

The second programme was organised by the Massy town council and was open to all residents of the town. It was named 'Échanges de Savoirs,' which translates to 'exchange of skills' or 'exchange of competences.' The concept behind this initiative was that if you possessed expertise in a certain field but desired to acquire skills in another area, you would be connected with someone who had that particular expertise and was interested in developing your own. We wanted to develop our conversational skills in French, and we were put in touch with Malika, who wanted to develop her skills in English for her job in a Parisian bank. What made this especially good was that Malika and her boyfriend Martial lived in the same development of flats we lived in. Once a week, we went to Malika's flat, or she came to ours, and we spoke for 30 minutes in one language and then the second half hour in the other language, each of us correcting the other's speech. We became very friendly and entertained each other with meals in each other's flats. Malika was a naturalised Algerian girl who came across France when she was a small child. As she said, her parents had to work so hard to earn enough money to live on that they were brought up by the television. They sat in front of the television and then left alone in the flat for many hours.

The evening we spent with Malika and Martial in their flat was memorable. We were invited at 8.00 pm as Malika had to return from her Paris job to do the cooking. When we arrived, she was not yet home, but Martial was there waiting to welcome us. Their kitchen was separated from their dining and sitting area by a low wall, and when we arrived, this wall had a whole line of bottles of North French beer arranged along it. Martial was a proud member of the Ch'ti minority in the Pas de Calais, the most northerly department of France. His firm conviction was that the general perception of French culture by people outside the Ch'ti area was quite wrong. People mistakenly thought that one of the great products of French culture was the wonderful wines produced there. He declared to all who would listen that the best demonstration of the finesse of French food and drink was quite clearly the beer produced in the North of the country, and he was about to prove it to me. He had decided to offer me just a taste of the wonders of the beer from his homeland – 'just a taste,' clearly indicating that I had to sample and comment on each of the beers in an appropriately adulatory tone, all in French. With a total of 15 different beers on display, I quickly resolved to sip very slowly and engage in extended discussions about each one, all in the hope that Malika would return home and rescue me. Martial poured beers for both Peta and me, yet Peta backed out, stating that she didn't enjoy any type of beer. Martial scarcely acknowledged this rather odd perspective and didn't converse with her again until Malika finally returned around 9:00 pm. By that point, my speech was somewhat slurred and speaking slowly was no longer a matter of choice but of necessity.

Eventually Malika breezed in as fresh as a daisy and bustled around, gathering things together and starting to cook while pouring each of us an aperitif. There were four courses, with a different wine served with each, I'm told. Martial didn't comment on any of them, but he drank them nonetheless. We began with an amuse-gueule, a sort of pre-first course dish, followed by a first course, main course, salad, and a cheese course. Malika both cooked and served each dish as we progressed, all the while engaging in lively conversation. After the cheese course, by which time it was 1:30 am, the conversation continued endlessly. Assuming the meal was over, we started to express our gratitude to Malika for the wonderful meal. However, she suddenly stood up and insisted that we couldn't leave just yet; we hadn't had dessert. Eventually, dessert was served with great finesse, followed by coffee and brandy. We finally arrived home at 3:00 am.

Peta informs me that she held very tight to my arm on the stairs home, though she did not reveal whether that was to stop her or me from falling over. Malika had to catch the train at 6:00 am that same morning, and the school chapel service for us was at 8:30 am. Fortunately, I wasn't scheduled to either read or preach that morning. After we left Massy, we entertained Malika and Martial in our home in the south of France, though, on this occasion, I only served Martial two beers, with which he seemed content.

During the year, there were certain things that stood out for us. For instance, the young people in Massy always seemed to walk to the supermarket, and they all pulled granny trolleys with them to bring back their shopping. The supermarket itself was huge, and a large part of the staff got around on roller skates. The trip into Paris on the rapid transport trains only cost the equivalent of £6.00, and the sight of Notre Dame de Paris after surfacing from St Michel Notre Dame Station was breathtaking. Every train that we travelled on in Paris had beggars on them, often people who played a tune with varying skills on a musical instrument and then explained how they had fallen on hard times and now were homeless and hungry. We thought long and hard about how to deal with this and discussed it with our class in the school. Eventually, we decided to carry a tin of Tuna with a ring pull opener and give it to people who were begging. This was never refused; the beggars often thanked us warmly for this gift.

On one occasion, we were on a train with a well-dressed Parisian lady sitting opposite us. A beggar arrived, played his instrument, delivered his spiel, and went around the carriage. We gave him a tin of tuna. He paused and exclaimed in a loud voice, “That is wonderful, thank you! With a baguette and a tomato, it will make a wonderful meal.” As he exited the carriage, the lady across from us remarked, “You should not have done that, monsieur; he was a bad man.” I responded, “That may be so, madame, but even bad men need to eat.”

Just at that moment, the man returned to the carriage, approached us, and asked, "Are you English?" to which we replied, "Yes". He then turned to the rest of the carriage and said loudly: "You see these English people are generous, not like you miserable stingy French people" and left. We wished that the floor would open and swallow us up. The well-dressed woman neither spoke to us nor looked at us for the rest of the journey.

At breakneck speed, it seemed the year had come to an end. We were given a certificate of competence in French, were prayed for in the chapel and sent on our way to service with our mission as had been the case for so many thousands of young people over the years setting out from Les Cedres. We flew to our French home and said a sad au revoir to our friends there as we would not be seeing them for at least a year and then off to our specific training for Djibouti.

This took place in an area of Birmingham, which was almost solidly inhabited by people with roots in Pakistan. Even the locals used to call it "Pakistan B 13". We were staying with a Christian couple on a road off Ladypool Road, where we were the only Anglo-Saxon inhabitants. It was certainly not a standard British environment, but then it wasn't the Somali or Afar environment we would live in Djibouti either. The people we met were universally warm, polite and ready to chat. We stayed in this home for a month while we had instruction in the local mission headquarters on Islam, the Quran and how to comport ourselves in a totally Muslim community. We were also taught how to survive in desert conditions with a great lack of water, temperatures regularly up around 50 degrees Celsius and on a very low income. Finally, we spent a few days with Simon and Jo and our new grandson before being delivered by taxi to Heathrow, with Peta in floods of tears as she was leaving Jonathan, for the Air France flight to Paris and Djibouti.

Djibouti

Our plan was to catch the Air France flight to Charles de Gaulle Airport in Paris and then make our connecting flight to Djibouti. Unfortunately, there was fog at Heathrow on the day of departure. Despite boarding the plane, we found ourselves waiting and waiting. After about an hour and a half, we finally took off. But upon arriving in Paris, we learnt that the Djibouti flight had already departed, and the next available one was scheduled three days later. We headed to the Air France flight desk where they presented us with two options: returning to England and spending the next three days with our son's family before attempting the journey again, or staying at an airport hotel in Paris—although they would only cover the expenses for the first night. Given the emotional toll of saying goodbyes all over again, Peta and I chose to stay in Paris and begin our mission journey with three days of being tourists in the city. We revisited all our favourite sights and enjoyed meals at the special restaurants we had discovered during our time as students at Les Cèdres.

We realised that the RER line taking us into Paris passed directly through Massy, so we decided to stop off and say hello to our friends at the language school. Sneaking into the back of the morning assembly on the third day, we discovered them praying for our initial days in Djibouti. They were somewhat surprised to turn around at the end of the service and find us there. We told them we had decided on one final fling in Paris before going to Djibouti!

Three days later, we made it onto the flight to Djibouti. The Air France plane was in a terrible state of disrepair. My seat would not stay upright, and every time the air hostess passed, she told me off for not having my seat in the upright position. The cabin furniture was stained and grubby. At mealtimes, the food was truly awful. Eventually, I went to see the cabin steward and told him what I thought about the flight and the plane. He asked me to write down what I had said and send it in as a report. Maintaining the flight to Djibouti was a diplomatic necessity as the country was still partly dependent on France, and the headquarters of the Foreign Legion was there. However, the company made a large loss each year on this route. Therefore, they used the oldest and most grubby planes and served the worst food on the flight to reduce their costs. We arrived late at night at the airport in Djibouti town (the capital of Djibouti is also called Djibouti; making it easier to remember). The airport had clearly seen better days. The building was low and not air-conditioned, the floor tiles were cracked, and the passport control and immigration procedures took an age.

As we emerged from the airport, we were greeted by Richard, a hugely wise and warm ex-chemical engineer and teacher who was the local "organiser and fixer" of the mission and teaching in the language school. We were driven through the town along decrepit roads which once had been tarmacked to a block of flats. The large steel gates were opened by Suliman, the guard. He was pure gold! He had a small house just inside the gates. Suliman would lift, mend, fetch things, and guard the entire compound using a medium-sized metal rod as his weapon. I never saw him need to use it. Our assigned accommodation was the first-floor flat on the left. Looking towards the sea directly below our bedroom was a petrol station; it was open day and night and where numerous old wrecks of cars and minibuses in various stages of disrepair rolled up all through the day and night and were refilled by staff. The staff and the drivers were almost always smoking cigarettes. I have no idea why at some stage during our 2- years stay in Djibouti we were not incinerated by the petrol station blowing up.

Richard and his wife Patricia lived in one of the two downstairs flats and the other one was lived in by three single girls working for the mission. The other flat on our landing was inhabited by an exceedingly odd American family. I never actually worked out what exactly they were doing in Djibouti; it seemed to change every second week. The only notable thing about the family was that they owned a small Suzuki jeep. On the one time I drove it, it seemed that the only serious problem with the vehicle was that it seemed not to have any functional brakes. They did not work for our mission. We had a two-bedroom flat with an ensuite bathroom, the first time that we had ever had this luxury. The luxury wore off when we noticed that the bath had a hole below the water line and that the only tap was cold. In fact, the problem was not the cold water but rather that one could not get cold water. It was so hot that all the water all the time was hot. The bedroom had a double bed which measured 2 metres by 2 metres. This was because a huge American pilot and his equally enormous wife had previously lived in the flat. We later heard that the man who had made the bed for the pilot commented when he had finished it that its surface area was larger than the hut he lived in, together with his wife two children and mother-in-law. The bedroom had air-conditioning, but we were only allowed to run this during the time we were in bed and for the afternoon siesta to save money.

Beyond the petrol filling station towards the sea was the national sports stadium, built by the Chinese government. It was a crude structure, but the Djiboutians were duly grateful until part of one of the roofs fell off and killed several people. On either side of the flats was a flat desert area leading to the secondary school on one side while on the other was another flat area that had not yet been bult on. The first time we looked out on this area one morning, we were shocked to see the sight of approximately twenty bodies wrapped in shrouds lying on pieces of cardboard. However, we later realised that these were homeless men; the sheet of cardboard was their bed, and this was probably the only thing they owned apart from the clothes on their back. The shroud was to keep the flies off their faces.

When we first arrived, we found that these men between them owned one rather over-the-top uniform, peaked cap and all, which looked as though it had belonged to a hotel porter at some time in the far distant past. This uniform was passed from man to man to man with each person allowed to wear it for one day. It would have been fascinating to determine what this uniform meant to the men. The front of the flats was the packed earth road, which led to the entrance.

We had electricity, except when we didn't. There was only one very ancient generating station that was not properly maintained for the town and ran on oil. All too often, either the generator would break down, or on some occasions, the electricity authority would run out of oil. During these challenging times, we were fortunate to have a reliable generator for our flats.

Our team was usually about 20 strong and included people from England, the USA, Switzerland, Hungary, Australia, Canada, and South Korea. The main work carried out by the team involved running an English school, teaching English according to CELTA rules, the medical work carried out in the Arhiba Clinic, translating the Bible into the Afar language and running a library in Tadjourah, the second town of Djibouti. Manfred also taught people how to build foot pumps to pump water up from under the desert and how to plant and care for the crops that they could grow because of having the water. To support this work, we had three Toyota Land Cruiser Jeeps, the youngest of which was 20 years old. These vehicles, while rusty and not particularly reliable, were essential for our operations. We convened weekly gatherings that included worship and teaching sessions every Sunday. On Fridays, a day off in the Muslim world, we would watch a DVD. Additionally, we held planning sessions for our services, along with individual meetings focused on the various aspects of our work.

For shopping, we could either go downtown in the minibuses, which usually led to a prayerful attitude throughout the journey as one's life was at risk while travelling on these vehicles, or, if a Landcruiser was available, we could use that instead. Once a week, on Wednesdays, we went to the market. Djibouti is a salt desert with temperatures reaching the high 40s or 50s in the summer, where no agriculture is possible, and nothing can grow. Therefore, all the vegetables were brought in by train from Ethiopia. These were transported in open goods wagons for the 24 hours that the journey took and normally in a temperature in the 30's or 40's so they arrived in a totally wilted condition We would drive into the central area of the town and park the car. Immediately a boy in his middle teens would appear and offer to guard the car. We never worked out what they were guarding it from, but we had a strong suspicion that this was a protection racket and if one did not pay one of the "Guard's mates would put a brick through the windscreen. In fact, the unemployment in Djibouti was over 80% and was 100% among young people and starvation was rife so this was a way of giving a family money while maintaining their dignity. They were being paid for work and not begging.

Many younger kids would turn up and beg as soon as we left the car. They used to rub their stomachs and say they were hungry; they probably were. We never gave money to children who begged as their parents would usually take it, and the fathers would use it to buy Khat, the local drug. Instead, we chose one of the children and said they could help us carry the vegetables back to the car after we finished shopping. When we got back, we gave the children some of the food we had bought and ensured they ate it there and then.

Some supermarkets in town stocked the best luxury food available: foie gras, the best French cheese, baguettes, and croissants. This was because the headquarters of the Foreign Legion was in Djibouti, all the French banks were there, and the government employed several French families. These people got paid three times as much in Djibouti as they did in France, as it was labelled as a hardship post, so they could buy everything they could buy in France but at the double the cost. One could also buy good French wine, but that was from a shop hidden in the suburbs. We did not buy from the supermarkets but from the little "holes in the wall" where the local people bought their food. The team members subsisted on the equivalent of £90.00 per month. We were self-funding, but we felt it right to live at the same level as our other team members.

When we got home, we placed all the vegetables and fruit we had bought in diluted bleach as Cholera was endemic, and all sorts of other bugs were rampant. The vegetables perked up and looked reasonably healthy as soon as they were in water. After about an hour, we took them out of the bleach, washed them and put them in our exceedingly ancient fridge. It was not until toward the end of our time in Djibouti that we realised that we were actually rehydrating the vegetables with moderately concentrated bleach and then eating them. So I suppose that when President Trump of America told the world that the best way to avoid Covid virus infection was to drink bleach, we got there before him, but relating to Cholera, not COVID-19. We must have come home with the whitest, cleanest bowels of anybody in the world.

As well as the food market, there was an area where craft items were sold, known as the blue doors, largely because all the shops had blue doors(!). Here, all sorts of rough carvings made out of nondescript wood, plastic plates with elephant or panthers painted on them and rickety painted tables were sold, all complete tat. I often wondered who bought these things because I cannot imagine the local people having enough money to buy them. The expat community had enough money to buy good nick-nacks because they were paid so much to work there, and there were no tourists.

Historically, the settled townspeople of Djibouti had been largely of Somali origin, and the Afar people, who were nomads, had travelled with their camels all over the Danakil desert, the hottest desert in the world. The Nomads did not acknowledge national boundaries and had moved with their flocks wherever there was pasture, moving between Djibouti, Somalia, and Ethiopia. This was their traditional way of life, and nobody seemed to bother about them wandering over national borders. However, with climate change and the diminution of the rains, pasture had become more and more scarce, the animals had died, and many of the nomads had come to camp around the towns of the country.

As they became a settled people, they demanded more services and power from the government, and this friction caused a civil war. During the war, which the Afars lost, the Somali government shelled the Afar encampments around the towns, resulting in the deaths of many women and children. As a consequence, government servants were unable to enter the Afar areas without risking their lives. Consequently, very few services were provided to this segment of the population—no electricity, water supply, or sewage services were available. It was clearly unwise to have a significant portion of the capital city's population lacking access to healthcare, as this situation could lead to the spread of epidemics, which indeed occurred, primarily in the form of cholera epidemics.

To add to all these problems, within Djibouti, there were tens of thousands of refugees, largely from interracial tension in Ethiopia and from the chaos in Somalia. One wonders why anybody would flee their own country to be a refugee in one of the poorest countries in the world, a salt desert where nothing grows. These people's only options had been to be killed or to flee to Djibouti, hoping to pass through this country to somewhere better. Many of these people landed in the slums around the town.

As a start to trying and sort out all these problems, the government built a health centre in the Afar area and asked the French to provide the staff. Not surprisingly, no French people wanted to work in this area as it was dangerous and a hotbed of Muslim fundamentalism. When we were there, French people and all foreigners were forbidden by their embassies to enter this huge slum called Arhiba. So, the government asked the Red Sea Mission Team to staff the health centre, which they did. We comprised a team of two midwives—an American and a Swiss midwife—along with Peta, a health educator, and me as the health centre director. Additionally, there was a local director who was afflicted with AIDS and possessed limited competencies, apart from his background as an Afar commander during the Civil War. Our team also included three nurses and a lab technician, who had undergone six weeks of training. Our responsibility was to care for an estimated population of around 30,000 in the slum. However, due to the perception that the Arhiba clinic was not operated by Somali staff, all the Afar individuals in the vicinity sought our services. As a result, we ended up catering to a population ranging between 50,000 and 70,000 people.

Djibouti had all sorts of problems. Apart from being a salt desert where nothing grows, the citizens come from two races who hate each other and deal with that by fighting a war, then living alongside each other but not talking or mixing at all. A failed state surrounds it on one side, Somalia, and an area of Ethiopia of considerable civil disturbance and disorder on the other. It is situated on the Bab el Mandeep, which is the narrow channel that controls the entrance of the Red Sea, so nobody will allow such a strategically important state to rule itself without interference. It is a tiny state, which means that its people get ignored, and things happen over their heads. With all these disadvantages, the economy's rulers and directors need wisdom and a clear head. However, nearly every man in the country, and even some women, chew the leaves of the Khat plant. This practice releases a drug that induces a dreamy sensation while preventing sleep.

The Khat is grown in Yemen and flown into the country, and the purchase of this drug uses up almost all of the country's meagre foreign exchange. The Khat plane comes into the airport at 1:00 pm, and there is a mad rush of men in pickups racing to the airport just before that time. It is a very dangerous time to be on the road. After 1:00 pm everything stops, and everybody is under the effects of the drug. All government offices are closed because everyone, including the ministers, is under the influence of Khat. Nearly all the doctors and nurses are similarly affected, so falling ill in the afternoon is not advisable. This circumstance leads the country towards bankruptcy and clouds the judgement of anyone attempting to address these issues, thus exacerbating an already desperate situation.

Soon after we arrived, we made our first trip to the clinic. This was one large building with several outbuildings in a large compound. The compound was bare desert earth, liberally littered with wrecked beds, filing cabinets, chairs, tables and various containers, in places, in large heaps. A path led through this chaos to an entrance that once could have been imposing with a big sign indicating that it was a health centre. On entering the doors, there was a courtyard with an internal circular walkway leading to the rooms with shade produced by an overhanging roof supported on pillars. The whole inside of the building had once been painted white, but now it was grey, light grey at the top and filthy at the bottom, with all shades in between. There had been a pond in the middle at one stage, but now it was a hole containing some indeterminate junk.

The doctor's room was at the opposite end of the entrance and had an air-conditioner which worked when there was electricity, and the machine was in a good mood. There was a consulting room with a desk, chairs, and a lockable steel cabinet. Beyond the consulting area was an examination room with an examination couch, separated from the main room by a low wall. There was also a photocopier which, during the two years we were living and working in Djibouti, was working for only 10 days. After that, it died but never seemed to have a proper burial in the clinic compound with all the other wrecked furniture of the last two decades. The consulting room had two doors, one on each side of the desk.

On the left on entering the building was the paediatric department. This was the domain of Mousa, a large, silent man who always carried a large stick. He and his family had a homemade house out of recuperated corrugated iron in the Clinic compound and in a clearing among the wrecked furniture. The paediatric department consisted of a small room with a desk and two chairs where Mousa consulted with the families, bringing the families in. Then, a very large room again had a table and two chairs, which were Peta's domain.

Just beyond the paediatric rooms was the laboratory, where examinations for tuberculosis and malaria could be conducted, along with blood tests for anaemia. On the right side of the doctor's room, there was another space furnished with a table, chairs, a couch, and a screen. This area belonged to our obstetric colleagues. Beyond that, there was a spacious open area where many malnourished babies gathered each day with their parents. Here, they were provided with a visually unappealing, yet highly nutritious porridge supplied by the World Food Programme. This programme certainly saved many of these children from dying of starvation, but even if they grew up, there was no employment for them, and they would live on the very edge of starvation all their lives. Thirty percent of children died before they were five, and among older children, Tuberculosis, AIDS, Cholera and Malaria killed many of them.

In one corner of the building was the pharmacy. A room with desks, shelves, cabinets, and a counter, it had the potential to be useful but was lacking in one key aspect: drugs. Upon my arrival, the inventory included suppositories for treating the almost universal constipation stemming from water scarcity, aspirin, a single anti-malarial medication, rehydration solutions, and a substantial supply of antitubercular drugs provided by a WHO project dedicated to treating TB. General patients were given prescriptions to take to a local chemist when they required medication. However, a significant number of patients lacked the financial means to purchase anything from a commercial chemist. As a result, many returned home to endure their suffering and, in some cases, quietly succumbed.

In the adjacent outbuildings, flush toilets, linen sluices, basins, and showers were available. Yet, the clinic was lacking in one crucial aspect: running water. All water used had to be manually transported into the clinic in 60-litre jerry cans from a stand tap located at the border of the clinic compound. This stand tap was one of only three in the entire slum. Notably, adjacent to the clinic compound's border stood the main mosque—a notable fundamentalist one. Each Friday, the imam would fervently condemn the foreigners in their midst during his sermon.

Early on, I conversed about security with the chief of Arhiba, the slum we served. He assured me, “I can ensure your safety within Arhiba. Trouble will not arise while you are here, as anyone who harmed you or the clinic would face immediate lynching. However, beyond Arhiba, my authority wanes." Consequently, we existed in a peculiar bubble. We operated in the heart of the most fundamentalist part of the country, where our security was safeguarded by the community. Yet, we would be left vulnerable if any threats emerged in other parts of the town.

About 500 people came to the clinic every day. Some of these were babies coming to the feeding programme, some came to see the TB nurse, and others came to the midwives for antenatal care. The rest were unwell and, in the first instance, came to the triage staff, our local six-week trained nurses. About 10 to 15% of these were judged ill enough to be passed on to Peta or me. I saw about 40 patients a day, and Peta saw about 100. The first thing Peta did every morning was triage the children passed to her a second time. There were always grossly malnourished children weighing just a few kilos at six months, many with the typical orange hair, many of them cachectic and listless. Several of these would clearly die during the next few hours, and they, with their mothers, would be put into a designated part of the large paediatric room and cared for by one of our local colleagues until they died. Then there would be perhaps another 10 children whom it might be possible to save, and these children were taken down to the local hospital where Dr Mahdi, the paediatrician, was the only uncorrupted doctor we met. The remainder of the children were either rehydrated in the clinic, sent home, or referred to me.

Having collected the children who needed treatment in the hospital, Peta would load them and their mothers into one of the mission's Landcruisers and drive them down to the hospital. The first time Peta did this, she drew up at the hospital gate to find a very large man holding a very heavy stick standing in front of a closed metal gate. He demanded the equivalent of £12.50 for everybody in the car before he would open the gate. Two problems arose in this situation. Firstly, the entrance to the hospital compound was meant to be free. Secondly, the majority of the individuals under our care wouldn't earn the equivalent amount in six months. Peta firmly declined, causing the man to repeat his demand in a louder tone. Peta maintained her stance, prompting the man to start waving his stick, raising his voice, and adopting an intimidating demeanour. Unfazed, Peta rolled up the car window and retrieved a book to read. Initially, the man continued his agitated behaviour, but as Peta continued to ignore him, he gradually lost interest and returned to his hut. Peta remained engrossed in her book. After approximately 15 minutes, a lorry arrived and pulled up behind Peta's vehicle. There was insufficient space for the lorry to pass the Landcruiser. The man with the stick reappeared and informed Peta that she needed to move to allow the lorry to enter. Peta responded, 'Of course, just open the gate. I will drive in, and the lorry can follow. Otherwise, I won't move.' The man's shouting resumed, prompting Peta to close the window once more. The lorry began honking, and Peta continued reading. Eventually, after the lorry driver conferred with the guard, the gate was opened. Peta drove in, with the lorry following suit. This manoeuvre allowed the children to be delivered to the paediatric ward.

This charade happened every day for 4 days, then the guard gave up and opened the gate as soon as he saw Peta arrive. I could have told him initially that getting in the way of something Peta was determined to do was not a good idea. Once in the Paediatric ward, Dr Mahdi always rapidly and expertly examined the children, and treatment was prescribed. The hospital had no drugs; in fact, nowhere in Djibouti had any drugs, so Peta then had to take a prescription into town to a pharmacist, buy the medicines and infusions and bring them back to the hospital, and then treatment commenced.

Back at the clinic, I used to consult with a translator, a woman who was the fiancé of an imam and was a sweet girl. If there was a gap in the consultations, I read my Bible, and after watching this for a few days, she brought in her Quran and read it. So, I suppose that our sessions could be classed as interfaith consultations. Every patient had a patient-held book that recorded their medical history. These books were treasured, and there was no trouble in getting patients to bring them in. One big problem was that they tended to get eaten by rats, and sometimes, the damage was so great that they became almost illegible. All our patients lived in very close proximity to rats.

During the morning, the patients who had been told by the triage staff to consult me would drift over to my consulting room. Patients used to enter via the door to the right of the desk and leave by the door on the left. There was a waiting room behind the door on the right, which would have sat 15 patients, but there was always a huge scrum around the door as anything up to 50 patients were waiting to be seen. In Djiboutian culture, men always took precedence for food, medicine, clothes and everything else. As the children tended to be the sickest patients attending and the women the next sickest, I decided to reverse this priority system. So, before I started consulting, I used to go round to the waiting room and ask to see everybody's book. I then put the children at the head of the queue, the women next and the men last. When I started doing this, the men were outraged and shouted, jumping up and down and sometimes threatening me. Looking back, I am not quite sure how I dared to wade into a huge, unruly crowd in the shadow of a fundamentalist mosque and do this in a place where foreigners were not allowed to come because it was so dangerous. It would have been very easy to stab me in the crowd. However, as always happened, they all got used to the idiocies of these weird white unbelievers, as they called us.

Periodically, the director of family medical care for the Djibouti government community care service, a certain Dr Kasim, used to come and see me. He had done his medical training in Bulgaria and had failed his final exam. On his professional card, he had written MD (failed), which struck me as odd; why advertise the fact? One knew he was coming before one saw him. As soon as the car stopped, he started shouting. Absolutely everything was always wrong. He shouted at the guard on the gate, at any of the staff who had not hidden in time, at my interpreter, even at the odd patient who happened to be around. He then dropped his voice before he told me that my consulting room was a disgrace (I had toys for the children without permission). I looked like a tourist because I refused to wear a white coat, which would intimidate patients. I always wondered what a tourist in Djibouti looked like, but I never saw one. I had no drugs; well, that was because there were none in the country. Eventually, he stopped shouting and seemed suddenly to run out of things to complain about. I then escorted him back to his car and thanked him for his visit and courtesy. He never seemed to tag on to the fact that I was being ironic, or perhaps he didn't know the meaning of the word courtesy. We then got on with our jobs until the next time Dr Kasim decided to lift the spirits of all of us at the clinic.

The main problem with consulting in Djibouti was that there were no drugs available that the majority of the inhabitants of the area we looked after could access. The government didn't provide any drugs, and the likelihood of someone not being able to afford prescription medications from a town pharmacy was well over 90%. The Catholic mission offered a limited supply of drugs, but their availability was inconsistent, and most of the drugs addressed only minor symptoms like coughs or mild pain. This situation essentially exposed the fallacy within the entire concept of medical care. Compounding matters, the fact remained that neither the clinic staff nor any public servants in the country had received their pay for the past six months. As a consequence, valuable items within the clinic were frequently stolen and sold in the market to generate enough money to provide for their children's needs. It was a situation that invited understanding more than blame.

Peta and I thought long and hard about this. We eventually decided that we had worked or done professional visits in eight countries around the world, so we wrote to all our friends in all these countries, including the UK of course, explaining the situation we were facing and asking whether they could lay their hands on any drugs we could have and use. We sent them a list of the drugs we needed most and also told them we would be unable to pay them anything for any drugs they sent. Friends from all eight countries turned up trumps, and soon, large boxes full of very valuable medical supplies started arriving at Djibouti airport.

We had an agreement with the Djiboutian government that as we were doing government work at absolutely no cost to them, anything we imported that was specifically for the work we were doing would be free of customs duty or any taxes. However, when all the drugs started arriving, the customs department started asking for huge sums of money as customs duty. They completely disregarded our agreement. Eventually, we had to quietly say to the minister in charge of customs that he knew, and we knew that these were the only drugs available in the whole country. They would be available only in the health centre for the Arhiba health centre, serving the huge slum of a refugee camp. However, we regretted that if we had to pay this sum against our agreement with the government, if his extended family attended this health centre, we would be unable to supply them with any drugs. A couple of days later, he telephoned to say that he had reread the agreement and had previously misunderstood this document and that there would be no customs duty payable. We were sent over £40,000 worth of drugs. This changed the whole complexion of our practice, but it also nearly doubled the number of patients consulting.

As soon as one left the health centre one was in the middle of the Arhiba slum. We often walked around to get to know our patients in their home settings. On this occasion, it had been Eid, the festival after Ramadan. People greeted each other, there was a great deal of noise, children everywhere, and there was a perceptible lightening of the spirits. Nothing much else had changed. Arhiba was the poorest area of one of the poorest countries in the world. The rate of undernutrition in the Somali area of the Horn of Africa was 78% compared with 68% in Afghanistan and 52% in North Korea. In Arhiba, the rate was about 90%. Twenty percent of the children we saw all around us were so severely undernourished that they would die without the special feeding we gave them. In any case, 26% of children died before they were five years old. Children with Kwashiorkor were all over the place, and their parents were walking skeletons.

We had an agreement with the Djiboutian government that as we were doing government work at absolutely no cost to them, anything we imported that was specifically for the work we were doing would be free of customs duty or any taxes. However, when all the drugs started arriving, the customs department started asking for huge sums of money as customs duty. They completely disregarded our agreement. Eventually, we had to quietly say to the minister in charge of customs that he knew, and we knew that these were the only drugs available in the whole country. They would be available only in the health centre for the Arhiba health centre, serving the huge slum of a refugee camp. However, we regretted that if we had to pay this sum against our agreement with the government, if his extended family attended this health centre, we would be unable to supply them with any drugs. A couple of days later, he telephoned to say that he had reread the agreement and had previously misunderstood this document and that there would be no customs duty payable. We were sent over £40,000 worth of drugs. This changed the whole complexion of our practice, but it also nearly doubled the number of patients consulting.

As soon as one left the health centre one was in the middle of the Arhiba slum. We often walked around to get to know our patients in their home settings. On this occasion, it had been Eid, the festival after Ramadan. People greeted each other, there was a great deal of noise, children everywhere, and there was a perceptible lightening of the spirits. Nothing much else had changed. Arhiba was the poorest area of one of the poorest countries in the world. The rate of undernutrition in the Somali area of the Horn of Africa was 78% compared with 68% in Afghanistan and 52% in North Korea. In Arhiba, the rate was about 90%. Twenty percent of the children we saw all around us were so severely undernourished that they would die without the special feeding we gave them. In any case, 26% of children died before they were five years old. Children with Kwashiorkor were all over the place, and their parents were walking skeletons.

The area consisted of huts and tiny houses made of tin, wood offcuts or cardboard, which just dissolved on the rare occasions that it rained. The tracks between the huts were full of large puddles of raw sewage unless it rained; of course, when the sewage flooded into the huts, the whole place became a sea of stinking mud. This was not like the refugee camps one sees on television. There were no orderly rows of huts, overseen and provided by a competent NGO like Save the Children. No staff members were present to organise matters or construct functional latrines. This was because there was no sense of urgency or emergency here. This was simply the way things were—it mirrored the past and would continue to define the future. It was a stable and enduring norm.

The reality was stark: approximately 10% of the population had HIV, and another 10% had tuberculosis. However, even if they sought assistance at the clinic, there was no access to water. This predicament meant that the staff might inadvertently spread disease instead of curing it. Many individuals who became severely ill recognised that if they visited the clinic, they wouldn't be able to afford treatment. Consequently, they would retreat to their cramped huts and succumb quietly and painfully.

Some might argue that this was an insoluble problem. This small country's soil was so arid that a simple tomato plant couldn't yield fruit without intervention. Chickens, which often subsist on scraps and lay eggs, were scarce due to extreme starvation. In this environment, even scraps were scarce, leading to a reality where everything edible was consumed, and plates were licked clean. Those who did have plates, that is. One perplexing aspect was that 20% of Arhiba's population consisted of refugees from Somalia or Ethiopia. If these people had fled to this place, what unimaginable nightmare had they escaped from that could be worse than this?

The country's sole source of income was the port, yet there weren't enough jobs available there to sustain even one in twenty families. Perhaps the task of attempting to make a difference was

We encountered Fatouma once more. She grieved for her sole child—someone who had been gravely ill, showed signs of recovery, and yet succumbed. The grim fact that a quarter of Djibouti's children don't make it to their fifth birthday was both unfamiliar and insignificant to her.

Meanwhile, back at the clinic, there were positive developments. We formed a connection with a group of Dutch soldiers stationed at the airport. The Dutch contingent was overseeing a peacekeeping mission between Eritrea and Ethiopia, who had recently engaged in a bloody conflict leading to Eritrea's separation from Ethiopia. This event marked Eritrea's sole access to the sea, apart from the Djibouti port, a development celebrated by the Djiboutians. The airport contingent served as the base troops, operating a medical clinic for both the Djibouti-based soldiers and those stationed at the Ethiopian-Eritrean border.

We got on very well with the doctor in charge of the clinic, and she asked us to come and talk with the Dutch soldiers. We turned up one Wednesday evening and gave an illustrated talk, using the experience of several of our patients. We thought that there would be about 15 people present. In fact, there were 150. As we always do, Peta and I took turns to talk for consecutive 10-minute sessions. By the end of our talk, several soldiers were in tears and asked if they could come and look around Arhiba and the clinic. We told them that coming to Arhiba was not without risk, but the contingent commander gave his permission. They arrived and started walking around the clinic and finding out how it all worked, and then they came with us into the slum. Several soldiers were again in tears about what they saw, and one dropped out because he could not bear to see the suffering.

After this, the contingent asked us what they could do. We mentioned to them the shortage of drugs, and once again, large cardboard boxes full of drugs started arriving at the airport. At some time during our talk, we must have mentioned that constipation was a major problem because of the lack of water. This led to the odd situation that when all the gifts were totted up, we found that we had been sent several thousand glycerine suppositories, among other drugs. Glycerine suppositories melt in the heat, so these became large squishy balls of goo after a few days. About 6 months later, the time of duty with the Dutch soldiers ended, and their medical centre gave us as a gift all their fridges and refrigerators as well as everything they had left in their pharmacy. Bliss!

We were two of only seven British nationals living in Djibouti. The port of Djibouti was an important refuelling and reprovisioning centre for British naval ships east of Suez. This meant that if any British ships were in port, we always got invited on board. The deck of a frigate does not have much shade and very few places to sit down, and although the receptions were mainly in the early evening, the temperature could well be above 35 degrees. Also, we were routinely offered alcoholic drinks, which we accepted with alacrity. Peta had a disturbing habit of fainting on these occasions, but I did note that she seemed to wait to do this until a very good-looking young naval rating was talking to her.

Our understanding of naval terminology was rather limited. One day, while conversing with a young officer, Peta asked him about his role. She thought she heard him say he was a welfare officer, so she responded, 'How nice. Are you focused on the well-being of the ship's crew or the people you encounter ashore?' The officer corrected her: 'Not a welfare officer, madam. I'm a warfare officer. My duty is to engage in combat.' Peta felt a bit taken aback, though the officer had a noticeable twinkle in his eye.

HMS Nottingham would occasionally dock in the port. On one visit, it transpired the crew of a previous naval ship had indulged in heavy drinking and ended up causing some damage in a couple of local bars. Consequently, the crew of HMS Nottingham were required to perform community service as an apology for the misbehaviour of the previous ship's crew. They had brought supplies like papers and pencils for the schools and participated in a general clean-up of the town centre. The captain, who was fluent in French (a significant advantage in this country), inquired if there was anything he and his crew could do for the clinic. The clinic compound was brimming with all sorts of damaged furniture, and the clinic itself was in a state of disarray. I had repeatedly urged the clinic guards to clean up the compound and paint the building, but they insisted it was a daunting task that would take months to complete. Additionally, they claimed there was no paint available.

We asked the ship crew to do these tasks, and they willingly agreed. When I inquired about the colour they planned to paint the clinic, I was informed that it would be the navy's signature battleship grey. The clearing of the compound took two and a half hours. All the twisted metal and other rubbish disappeared on the back of a naval lorry. I have no idea where it went. The clinic was fully painted inside and out. I landed up as the proud director of the only clinic in Djibouti, perhaps the only clinic in the world painted in battleship grey water-resistant paint. This was a great advantage as it did not show the filth, which rapidly returned, and we could schedule the cleaning of the walls for every week regardless.

After the cleaning and painting were completed, the officer in charge, who happened to be a woman, instructed the men to form a line. She declared that they would take a walk around Arhiba so they could grasp the reality of true poverty and develop gratitude for what they had. The soldiers were profoundly moved by their observations. Two of them approached the officer, expressing their inability to continue after witnessing the conditions in the slum. In response, the officer in charge insisted that they join the formation and continue walking. She emphasized that this experience was an integral part of their education as human beings.

Not long after the visit of the ship's crew, we received a note. The note said that we had no right to live in this Muslim country as unbelievers and Christians, and they would kill us. This threat was made to the whole team, not just the people working in the clinic. I asked the medical department to pass this by the Djiboutian security services and let us know if this was just a malcontent. They informed us that this was a serious threat, and we must be extremely careful.

We knew the British consul in the area (a French man!), who was kept busy by people who lived in Djibouti and had British Overseas Passports, which gave no right to live in Britain but the right of protection. We also knew socially the British Ambassador, who was also the ambassador for Ethiopia and Somalia. On his next visit, we went to see him. His wife was a Christian believer, but he wasn't. We told him that we knew if we were shot, this would cause trouble for him. So, how should we respond to this threat? Did he think it would be wise for us to leave? His response was to ask us if we thought that God had sent us here. We replied with a 'yes.' He then said, "If you have told people that God sent you here, and then you run away when you are threatened, what will that say about your God? Can't He protect you if He wants to?" After saying that, he confirmed that this threat was indeed real, and we should be very careful. We thanked him, as we felt that was God's word to us. Previously, we used to go on a walk every afternoon and walk to work every day. We continued walking to work but changed our route each day. In the evening, instead of walking down by the sea, we walked around our large flat roof 16 times every day. We could see the inhabitants of the neighbouring houses peering at us, convinced that English people were completely mad.

Friday was the weekly holiday. There was the service in the morning, either in the dining room of a large villa or in the French protestant church. At these meetings we would come across people who had the most amazing stories. An American couple had served as teachers at Badere in Somalia for 10 years, somehow managing not to get killed by the precursor of the Al Shabab terrorist group. Another single American girl had done the same thing in Mogadishu. Yet another 2 members of our team moved out into Hargeisa in Somaliland to set up a chicken breeding station to start producing enterprises and reduce poverty. Martyn the husband was shot dead in front of his three-year-old son when out shopping. He had got on the wrong side of somebody. Richard, the person who picked us up from the airport had also worked in Hargeisa for some years and was taken hostage by an ex-employee. He eventually managed to argue his way out of captivity before he was killed. All these people's motivation was to show others Christ's love. The risk to them was in fact not much more than the risk to most other members of the population. Life was cheap!

After church, we would pile into a couple of the Landcruisers and make our way out of town down an extremely rocky track to a beach where we would set up a shade, light a barbecue and snorkel over the beautifully coloured pristine coral. Occasionally, we would go further out of town to a beach at the training base of the French Foreign Legion. To get to this beach, one had to go down a track through a very narrow defile between two high hills. The Legion always made us very welcome. We would occasionally go further inland to Lac Assal, the most saline area of water anywhere on the planet. As one approaches, a vast lake comes into view, fringed by what resembles powdered sugar. This 'icing sugar' is, in fact, salt. There were always several trains of camels either heading to the lake or coming back laden with salt to take to the Nomadic tribes who were still living in the Danakil desert. As one approached, one noticed that the lake had a pink ring to it. Coming closer, one saw that there were hundreds of Flamingos fishing in the shallows. I have no idea what on earth they could find alive in such intensely saline water.

However, the one thing that made life much easier for us related to the hamlet where we had our second home in the Lot department of France. One of our closest friends in the hamlet was Sébastien Jouclas, a gendarme. Another gendarme, Fabrice Castanet, from the gendarmerie at St Gery, the neighbouring village to ours and responsible for our hamlet, had been posted to Djibouti to maintain peace among the diverse set of individuals in the Foreign Legion base. Sébastien put us in contact with each other and Fabrice, his wife

Natalie and their son Romain became firm friends. The detachment consisted of 15 gendarmes and their families, and Peta and I were invited to all their barbecues, meals, and outings. Thus, at their gatherings, one would encounter 15 remarkably fit young gendarmes along with their beautiful wives and children, accompanied by two older grey-haired Brits, us. They truly embraced us as part of their community.

One of the outings we went on with them involved a trip across the desert, with no track to follow to Lac Abbé, a lake right in an elongated corner between Somalia, Ethiopia, and Djibouti. It was an utterly wild and remote spot. It had been used because of this as a location for the first film of Planet of the Apes. An enterprising French company, realising that many French people were looking for trips into utterly remote areas around Djibouti, had set up a camp under canvas here to welcome such people. They were armed. We stayed overnight, and some local people put on a mock intertribal battle for us. We had an excellent barbecue and slept well in a tent, except a rather drunk Frenchman went to the loo in the desert during the night and then tried to go back to bed in our tent.

Fabrice was a great support for us. When he first learned where we were working and under what conditions, he was extremely worried and told us that no Westerners should ever be around Arhiba, let alone working there every day; it was far too dangerous. Not infrequently, we would be working in the middle of a busy morning when somebody would come and tell us that we had a visitor. We arrived at the door of the clinic to find Fabrice there, wearing his kepi (the gendarme cap), with his military jeep and his Legionnaire driver. We invited them in for a cup of tea and then mentioned that we thought French people were not allowed in this area for any reason at all. Fabrice straightened himself up to his full height and explained that they were here on a very important mission: to ensure that no French people were in the area and to arrest them if they were found. Afterwards, they asked us how we were and whether there were any current threats.

The first year of our stay in Djibouti, we went on holiday in August to cool off in our French home. The temperature was only 39 degrees there as opposed to 49 degrees in Djibouti. We stayed through the summer during the second year and worked daily. However, as we lived all the time in these conditions, we had acclimatised to the weather, and the 50-degree heat was not in any way unbearable.

Towards the end of that summer, tensions appeared to be rising in the community. People appeared to be worried and unsettled. Then, one morning, there was an attempted coup d'état by the armed police against the government. The main battle went on at the police encampment about half a mile from us with machine gun fire and a few heavier explosions. The reaction of most of the people who lived around us was to go up to their flat roofs and look to see what was happening. We followed suit, but then when I got bored, I walked across the area of desert beside our flats to the bakery to get some bread for lunch. The baker bent down, picked up something from the floor, and said, "Do you know what that is?". It was a bullet. Then he said, "If you had been there when that arrived, you could have been killed. Go home and stay there!" which I promptly did. The coup was unsuccessful, and about 60 people were killed. The next day, everything went on as though nothing had happened.

During this second year, we went with Manfred, the agriculturalist in our team, out into the Hanle Valley, which was an area in the Danakil desert, to visit a partly settled Nomad tribe. Manfred had been working with them for about 6 years. At one period, the tribesman had run him and his family out of the area at knife point because he would not give them money or equipment. He taught them how to make their own. We went with him on his first visit after this incident, and I took a medical box to do an impromptu clinic.

In this area of the desert, there was water only about 20 feet under the desert in large aquifers. Some of this water was brackish, and the skill was to find fresh water. There had been several attempts to do this. The Saudis had come along and drilled in several places for water where the local people told them to. They only found brackish water. When we asked the tribesmen whether they knew that where the Saudis were drilling would produce brackish water, they told us that they knew full well that they would find useless water, but the Saudis were paying such huge money to the local workers that they did not want them to find fresh water and then go away, so they tried to string then along as long as they could by getting them to drill one well after another all of them producing salt water. Then the Americans came along, found fresh water, put in diesel pumps, and took off again, very pleased with themselves. However, the local people did not know how to maintain diesel pumps properly, and in any case, the nearest place where one could buy diesel was 50 miles away, and they could not afford it. So that programme collapsed as well.

Then along came Manfred. He found fresh water, and then he taught the local people to build a very simple foot pump that provided a good flow of water and could be built from locally available materials. Using the water, the tribesmen produced grass for their camels, which in turn produced milk. This milk was given to the children, resulting in a significant reduction in their mortality rate. With the availability of water, they were also able to cultivate gardens where they grew tomatoes, peppers, cucumbers, and various vegetables, which they sold in a local market to generate income. This initiative did more for the health of the population than any number of clinics could have achieved. Furthermore, it empowered them as self-reliant individuals, leading to a sustainable lifestyle.

To get to this valley, we drove deep into the desert along the lorry road to Ethiopia. The road was busy with huge desert lorries lumbering their way along a road which had been tarmacked but now was little more than a desert track. There had also once been bridges across the wadis so that when it did rain, and the wadis became rivers, this did not stop the traffic. The bridges had long collapsed and become heaps of broken concrete, so the lorries had to make a wide detour into the desert to avoid the rubble. As the port at the Djibouti town docks, and the transport route into Ethiopia were, in effect, the only sources of income for the country, it seemed odd that nobody thought it worthwhile to repair the road.

After a while, we turned right onto a poorly defined track and drove for another two hours. A brisk wind carried a mist of sand with it. Periodically, a few palm trees would appear where the water table was near the surface. Suddenly, out of the murk, emerged a cluster of three huts that looked like spheres cut in half. They stood in the middle of a flat desert area, covered with skins and featuring a door on the side. Some goats were near the door, although I couldn't see anything that the goats might eat. The temperature was about 48 degrees.

We stopped, and Manfred approached the door and called a greeting. He spoke fluent Afar. An extremely thin lady appeared at the door and greeted Manfred with delight. She was a widow who had embraced Christianity by listening to the radio and engaging in conversations with the Red Sea team members, who visited the Hanle valley periodically. She had been cooking inside the hut when we arrived. All the inhabitants had to cook inside their huts even in the height of Summer so that the wind-driven sand did not spoil the food. She gave us a cup of tea. Manfred and she had a lengthy conversation, during which Manfred prayed with her, and then we continued on our way.

Finally, we came upon a much larger encampment of similar huts, again in the middle of a desert plain with wind-driven sand getting into the eyes, the hair and the nose and mouth. There were several temporary-looking enclosures for the camels and the goats here, though again, we could not see how the animals could be fed. As soon as we arrived, the local chief came out and greeted us with cups of coffee. Manfred busied himself with finding out how the foot pumps, the buildings, and the gardens, which were about a mile away and out of sight, were going. These were clearly the source of the animal fodder.

We set up a clinic in an unused hut with Peta acting as my nurse. Although the encampment seemed to be isolated, suddenly, a whole crowd of people of all ages appeared out of nowhere once they heard that a doctor had arrived. We were about ready to get going when the chief appeared again with one of his camels in tow. He told me that before I started treating the patients, I first had to treat his camel, which had a large, infected ulcer on one of its legs. I duly provided an antibiotic salve and was ready again to start the clinic.

Once again, we were interrupted. The sky suddenly went black. The wind increased to gale force, and sand blew everywhere—anything that was not attached or secured in some way took off across the desert. There were flashes of lightning and several claps of thunder and heavy rain. After about 10 minutes, the rain, lightning, and thunder all stopped. The clouds disappeared, the wind dropped, and everybody resumed their activities as though such occurrences were an everyday event. The crowd of people reappeared from where they had been sheltering, the desert rapidly dried off, and we got on with the clinic.

As the light faded, we packed up the clinic and returned to the lean-to shed, which had one side open to the elements and which had been provided for us to settle into. We lit the Tilley lamps, set up the camp beds, and had our meal. While we lay on our beds, chatting before falling asleep, I noticed that Manfred appeared to be worried. When we had initially arrived, following the traditions of desert culture, we had brought gifts for the chief, including a radio. Manfred could hear the programme that the chief was listening to in his hut, and as he spoke Afar, he could understand it. It was a programme from a local small desert town. The Imam was giving directions about which travellers one should immediately kill when they arrived and which ones should be welcomed. It would appear that we fitted the second category as we were alive and well the next morning to tell the tale. The next day, we packed up and headed home. Just as we were leaving, a grateful patient arrived with a goat for us. The goat was tucked into the back of the vehicle and was cooked in Manfred's earth oven the next weekend.

Another highlight of our second year was that the WHO, out of the blue, informed us that they were going to make money available for the upgrading of our clinic. We had grown accustomed to things as they were, but it would have been wonderful to have a proper laboratory, a place to wash our hands and clean soiled linen, and a proper toilet. Of course, all of that relied on one essential factor: a reliable water supply. The necessary paperwork was completed, and the plans were approved. Finally, one day the builders arrived. That was the start of 3 months of noise, dust and confusion as we had to work around the builders. However, as things progressed, the laboratory had a complete facelift, the sluices were given a facelift, and the toilets were rebuilt. Everything was bright and shiny for about a day until the desert wind deposited a thick layer of fine sand on all the surfaces. Even then, if you rubbed hard with a strong cloth, you could find the shiny surface under the grime.

It was almost finished, then one day, the work stopped. Nobody knew why. We asked the secretary of the minister of health, but she didn't know. We asked all our friends in high places. They didn't know. We asked our French friends whether they had heard any rumours, and they laughed. Finally, everything became clear. It appeared that somebody very high in the hierarchy, somebody very, very high, had said that the work could not begin until some of it had been used to retile the whole of the downstairs of his house. So, the work started as planned and proceeded well until, the money ran out just before the very end. Of course, what was supposed to happen at the very end was that the clinic was going to be connected to a water supply. Unfortunately, this didn't happen and still had not occurred up to the time of our departure from Djibouti.

We entered the last six months of our work in Djibouti, and the news was that the Americans had paid the government a large sum of money to lease a base just beside the airport. They would enlarge and modernise the airport and have a dedicated area of the port for themselves. This would be a shake-up as, up until then, the French Foreign Legion had ruled the roost in all security matters. Overall, they had been liked and respected. The big day came, and the Americans arrived.

First, they dug out anybody who spoke English in the country and offered them twice their current salary to leave their present employers and work for the base. This caused enormous damage to the trading community, most of whose work was done in English, and to the banks which also needed Anglophones for their day-to-day work. They then demanded the closure of the best restaurant in Djibouti, from which one could watch the most wonderful sunsets. This was because it overlooked the port where the Americans would be working. Their next action was to claim and close off the best beach in Djibouti, the one we used to go to each weekend. A large, barbed wire fence was built over the entrance road with a gate and a guard.

Finally, they decided to claim the beach by the French Foreign Legion's training camp for themselves as well. A posse of American soldiers in large military vehicles left Djibouti town heading for this beach, but the date and the time that they were going to do this had been leaked. They arrived at the defile between two hills leading to the beach, and there they found a Foreign Legion tank right in the middle of the road and blocking the access. The American commander sent one of his men to tell the tank to move out of the way. The French tank driver told the soldier who was sent to talk to him that he was an officer and that he would only speak to someone of officer rank. If the American commander would care to come and talk to him, he would listen, but he would listen to nobody else. He retired into the tank and closed the hatch. Eventually, the American commander of the posse came to the tank and called out to the officer in charge. He said that he had orders to move in and secure the beach for the sole use of the personnel of the American army. The tank commander told the American that about 30 years ago, the French army had secured the beach and the whole of the surroundings for the use of the French Army and to train its foreign legion. The American shouted at the French officer and said that they were coming through. The Frenchman told the American that it would be a mistake, as the gun on the tank could go off by mistake. He also asked the American to look at the slopes of the two hills forming the defile; both sides of the mountain were covered with Foreign Legion troops. The French officer then retired into his tank and closed the hatch. The American commander said that he would hear more about this and left.

They never came back, and the Foreign Legion continued to welcome all and sundry to their beach. Everybody knew that the Americans were there. There were frequent take-offs and arrivals of American flights. Ships came and went, but the Americans themselves were rather like milkmen in the UK. You go to bed, and nothing is on your front step, and then you wake up to find that there are now 3 one pint bottles of milk there, so there must be milkmen around somewhere.

On the last weekend of our time in Djibouti, we were summoned to a reception. By this time, the minister of health had changed and was now a graduate of a German university with a PhD in veterinary science. During the few weeks we had worked together, I was told that his door was always open to me if I had any problems, and in fact, I found this to be true. The reception took place in our Arhiba clinic, but he had invited everybody who was anybody in Arhiba, plus other ministers and dignitaries from the government. There was an excellent spread of the usual government celebratory food, sticky cakes, and Fanta to drink. He gave a long and warm speech expressing the gratitude of the country for what Peta and I had done, showing the way forward to a more effective and caring health service. I was then presented with a document sent and signed by the Prime Minister, expressing the gratitude of the people and government of Djibouti. The reception, along with the speeches by the government minister and myself, was reported in full as a main item in the Djibouti Times the following day.

This also gave me the opportunity to introduce to all who mattered, the doctor who was replacing me. She was a young Hungarian woman doctor, and I take off my hat to celebrate her courage in taking this on. She always carried a small flute in her top pocket. It was larger than a piccolo but smaller than a full-sized flute. If ever she got into a tight spot, she had a standard reaction: pulling the flute out of her top pocket and playing a little tune. It always seemed to work, perhaps out of astonishment, people who had been shouting and being aggressive stopped what they were doing and quietened down.

Finally, it was time to go. We had spent two years with an immensely diverse team of extremely brave and effective fellow Christians. There were tensions within the team, but these were dealt with. We hung together and carried on helping desperate people survive and develop skills that would lead to sustainable lifestyles. We made it clear that our motivation was to show the love to others God had shown us. If people asked, we told them about how God came to earth to save individual people and to form a loving community. Among the Afar people we had been working with, there had only ever been seven people who had been Christian believers. Six months after we left, another ten Afar people were baptised one early morning on a beach outside of Djibouti town.

We were collected from our flat, taken to the airport, and embarked on an Air France flight. The plane was just as rickety as the one we came out on, and if possible, the food was even more inedible. We arrived at Charles De Gaul Airport in Paris and were told that the flight to take us to London had been cancelled, and there was no seat available on any other flight. They were awfully sorry and left it at that. That behaviour might have washed with a plane full of French people, but there was a revolt among the Brits trying to get home. Eventually, with an enormous sigh, Air France put us on the Eurostar to London. They did not arrange or pay for our train journey from the airport to the Eurostar terminal in Paris, nor did they pay for the transport to take people from St Pancras Station to Heathrow to pick up their cars. Peta and I were not offered any debriefing from the Red Sea Mission in London, but another mission learning what had happened came and saw us and debriefed us.

And Now?

For the last year of our time in Djibouti, we had lent our house to some friends who had bought an old house in Bedford. The house was beautiful but was utterly decrepit and had been used as a squat for the preceding year. Our friends used our house as a store for their furniture and their home while they rebuilt their new home. When we came home from the Horn of Africa, their house was unfinished, so we lived in our French home for four months while their building work was completed. This was a wonderful time of rest and reflection when we could go and shop in the markets, get up late, and go for walks in the forest surrounding our house. We suddenly felt tired and flat. Our French friends were wonderful, inviting us to anything that was happening and quietly caring for us. Just before Christmas, we returned to our home and tried to settle back into British life.

A couple of days after returning, Peta visited Sainsbury's. She found herself in an aisle with approximately 20 different types of breakfast cereals. Walking around the end of the shelves, she came face-to-face with what seemed like a mile of various, well-prepared meat. There was enough to indulge in premium meat for every meal of the month. Overwhelmed, she rushed out of the supermarket and collapsed, eventually vomiting. After dedicating two years to assisting countless mothers without resources to find sustenance for their children and prevent their demise, she found it unbearable to confront such excess.

How does one reconcile the swift transition to Western living, moving from daily encounters with 100 malnourished and dying individuals to a society of overweight, demanding adults indulging in opulent food? How does someone adapt after spending years surrounded by walking skeletons and six-month-old infants weighing a mere three to four kilogrammes, displaying the unmistakable signs of severe malnutrition? Initially, Peta couldn't even bring herself to go grocery shopping. However, after a few days, she discovered that entering a supermarket at its 7.00 am opening with a predefined list, rapidly gathering only the essentials, and returning home for a strong cup of coffee usually provided her with a tenuous sense of coping. She wisely persevered in mastering these strategies over the next three months. Surprisingly, the adjustment to life in Djibouti, and the tasks we set out to accomplish, posed fewer challenges than returning home and confronting the UK's glaring overconsumption and greed in light of our past experiences.

We gradually rebuilt our lives in our community and our village. The French we had been speaking in Djibouti was African French with an appalling accent and very odd grammar, so we decided to go back to our Parisian language school for 6 weeks to brush up on our European French. This was an enjoyable experience and very useful for our language development, which we needed to be full members of the community around our French home. This convinced us to engage in doing an Open University French degree, one of the best decisions we have ever made.

After about a couple of years and when we completely recovered, we started praying about what God had for us to do in the future. At this time, I met up with some people I had known previously who were now working in Whole Person Medicine. For decades, the conventional approach of doctors involved receiving patients in their consultation rooms, gathering medical histories, conducting examinations, and occasionally conducting tests. Following these steps, the doctor would formulate a diagnosis, prescribe a treatment, provide instructions, and say goodbye. The patient was largely a passive being during all of this, presenting facts, accepting diagnoses and obeying instructions. Yet, a shift was occurring, with research programs increasingly demonstrating that involving patients in their healthcare journey led to significantly improved outcomes. By engaging patients, understanding their perspectives on their illnesses, addressing their fears and aspirations, sharing investigation results alongside potential management options, and seeking their input on the next steps, the outcomes were very much better. A group had grown up around a visionary Christian doctor, John Geater, who was promoting this method of medical management. They were promoting their view through the "Doctors' Dilemmas" courses run by the Christian Medical Fellowship and by carrying out further research.

Close relations developed between this group and the Royal College of GPs, of which several members of the group were senior members. Some overseas doctors started attending the Doctors' Dilemmas courses, and requests for help came from doctors' organisations all over the world. An international branch of the organisation was set up as a charity called Partnerships in International Medical Education (PRIME). I went along as a junior on one or two trips to overseas countries. Then, a request for help arrived from the Christian Medical Fellowship in Moldova, the poorest country in Europe. John and I made a visit in the middle of winter and experienced what winter feels like in Central Europe.

The organisation that had invited us was based around a large Baptist Church in Chisinau, the capital. We had a week of discussions with the project director and agreed that I would lead the project. Then, there was a period during which we developed the curriculum and the physical programme to teach the curriculum over a two-year period. Our main focus would be engaging with rural GPs who had received only the basic medical education and no postgraduate training. They were at the absolute bottom of the medical ladder and were not respected. Many of them moved to towns, leaving the countryside without doctors. We had agreed that we would try to replace the doctors' salaries during the time they attended the course so their families would not experience hardship. There was no charge to the doctors for the course, which would lead to a considerable increase in respect and possibly income.

I received a call from the Moldovan director of the course about three weeks before we were set to begin, informing me that the organisation had decided rural doctors would only attend the course if they were paid the equivalent of the salary of a training-grade doctor in the UK. This amount was about five times more than their current salaries, and given Moldova's economic situation, it would have had significant purchasing power. We found this demand outrageous, as it essentially meant the doctors would only participate in the course if they were paid an income that would make them very wealthy, despite the course being offered to them for free. We tried to negotiate over this, but they would not budge, so at the last moment, the whole project was cancelled, and a large amount of time and money was wasted.

After recovering from this setback, we tried once again. We learned that World Vision was in search of a couple with medical and nursing backgrounds, as well as experience in project management, to work in Herat, Afghanistan. We applied for the job and were called to an interview in Milton Keynes at the headquarters of World Vision. We were separated at the door, and both had the most thorough interview we had ever experienced, which was very impressive. The separation aimed to determine whether both of us felt a divine calling to this work. Given that we were heading to a sensitive and unstable part of the world, the interview also assessed our resilience and attitudes toward Muslim people and our preparedness for living in a completely Islamic environment.

At the end of the day, we were offered the jobs. We said, as we always do in this sort of situation, that we were delighted, but we needed to pray for a few days about the move and what we had learned, and we looked forward to getting God's affirmation for going forward with the job. The next day, we were phoned up by a very apologetic senior person at World Vision to say that due to an administrative oversight, at the same time as we were being interviewed, somebody else was also being interviewed in South Africa. He had also been offered the job and said yes immediately to the opportunity. Thus, our opportunity also fell through. We experienced a mix of disappointment with World Vision and a sense of confusion about what God was saying to us. We sought to understand the message He might be conveying, expressing our feelings of abandonment and frustration. His response took several months to reach us.

Egypt

About three months later, Peta and I were having our evening meal when the telephone rang. I picked it up, and a voice said, "Hello Edwin, this is Keith. We have not met before, but I thought that I would give you a ring to tell you that the Bishop is waiting for you." I replied, "Thank you, Keith. Good to hear from you, but what Bishop is waiting for me? Where and for what?" Keith laughed and told me that Bishop Mouneer, who was Bishop of Egypt, Ethiopia, Djibouti, Somalia, Tunisia, Algeria, Libya, and Morocco, in fact, Bishop of almost everywhere where there was trouble, was going round everybody and telling them that Edwin and Peta Martin were coming to Egypt. They were going to turn around the Harpur Hospital in Menouf. The only people he had not told, let alone asked, were Peta and me!

The history was that at the beginning of the twentieth century, an Irish missionary called Harpur, working in Cairo, had decided to take medical care to the isolated areas of the Delta of the Nile. He had acquired a large Nile Felucca and had moored this in the centre of the Delta near a town called Menouf and ran a clinic from the boat. Eventually, as the work had grown, a hospital was built in Menouf as a mission hospital. The hospital had grown, and a surgical team started doing operations. At the time, this was just about the only competent medical treatment available to the peasant farmers in this area. The locals were delighted and considered this as their hospital and became very protective of it.

Not everybody was pleased. The local Imam was unhappy that it was the Christians who were developing the medical care of the neighbourhood. He declared a Fatwa against the hospital, declaring that anybody who was found still working there after a month should be killed. The Director at that time, a young Egyptian doctor, thought and prayed about this and the next morning called together the whole team working in the hospital. He told them about the threat made against the hospital and those who worked there, then said that God had called him to the task of caring for the sick in this area, and until He told him otherwise, he would continue with his work in the hospital. He said that if any of his colleagues were afraid, they should stop working at the hospital and stay home. The work at the hospital continued without any interference. During the month, the Imam developed severe abdominal pain. He consulted all the doctors in the town and received treatment to no avail. Eventually, late one night, when it was dark, he consulted the hospital director. He prayed for the Imam, did a minor operation, and he was cured. Just before the end of the month, the Imam proclaimed another Fatwa. This time, he declared that if anybody impeded the working of the hospital in any way, they would be killed. Clearly, killing played quite a large role in this man's thoughts.

Menouf Hospital had grown in favour with the population over many decades, earning a noble history of providing care for impoverished individuals who would otherwise struggle to afford medical treatment. They also cared for the people with leprosy. That is until recently. In the past few years, the hospital's atmosphere has been far from cheerful. A number of doctors seemed to have lost their sense of purpose, though there remained dedicated physicians who willingly accepted substantially lower earnings compared to private practice, all in the service of their patients. Yet not all doctors were content. They were rude to patients, and there was a lot of backbiting among the staff. The medical care was slipshod, the medical records were non-existent, the doctors did no postgraduate study, and better care could, in some cases, be found outside the hospital.

Bishop Mouneer had, on a visit, seen our work in Djibouti and decided that we were the people to "put the hospital right", but it appeared that he had forgotten to tell us. After discovering more about the project, we agreed to go out to Egypt but made it clear that we would only be free for one year. In many ways, this series of episodes was like the Apostle Paul's experience on one of his missionary journeys described in the Bible in Acts chapter 16. He wanted to preach in Asia and was stopped from doing that. Then he decided to go to Bithynia, and he and his companions were stopped from doing that, too, so they went to Troy. There, Paul had a vision of a man calling them to go to the Greek province of Macedonia. So, he set out for Macedonia and landed in Philippi. There, he set up one of the most effective churches described in the New Testament. This was our Macedonian call.

Once we had agreed to spend a year working in Egypt, we started writing emails to the hospital we would be working in and to the diocese that would be employing us (though, as always when we were working abroad, with the exception of in Fiji and Saudi, we would be self-funding), and to people we knew. We quickly discovered a crucial fact about Egypt: it is exceedingly challenging to obtain information about current events or planned activities. People either take an extended period to respond to emails or disregard them altogether. We did not receive any responses from the Director of the Harpur Hospital prior to our arrival. However, his wife, Mary, did reply to our emails and provided us with valuable insights regarding the living conditions and essential items to bring.

We decided that Dominic would live in our house in Biddenham. One of our cars would be left on our drive, and one would be lent to a Christian single mum who did not have enough money for her own car. Our house was insured with an insurance company for the over-fifties, but they agreed to cover Dominic staying there for a year because he was our son, and this was a temporary arrangement. We extended the insurance on our car to include the person who would be using it.

A week before we moved out to Egypt, our house insurance company phoned us to say that they would not be able to cover Dominic after all. They gave us no reason, so we had to reinsure our house. Three days before our departure, the insurance company covering our car contacted us, stating that they would not insure the person to whom we had lent the car. Consequently, we had to reinsure the car. They provided no reason for this denial. Two days before our scheduled departure, we received a call from the gendarmerie at our home village in France. They informed us that our house had been broken into and that I needed to return to France to fill out all the necessary paperwork for the committed crime. This situation could have potentially postponed our journey to Egypt by at least a week. These occurrences deeply unsettled us. In response, we reached out to Sidney, an older Christian brother whom we trusted. We expressed our uncertainty about proceeding with our plans to go to Egypt due to the series of events that had transpired. We considered the possibility that God might be signalling for us to reconsider this project. Sidney prayed alongside us and conveyed his conviction that these obstacles were the work of the devil rather than God's intention to deter us. He encouraged us by emphasising that if the devil was so threatened by our decision to go to Egypt, it was likely that God was preparing to accomplish significant things through us there. We came home, and shortly afterwards a gendarme from France phoned us and said that he had heard that we worked with Doctors Without Borders (MSF). We told him that we did work in very unstable places but not with MSF. He said that, in any case, he was prepared to fill in all the papers for us and whether we would mind if he forged our signature. Things like that do not usually happen in France, and we thanked God for finding us a gendarme with a soft heart so we could go to Egypt as planned.

We travelled to Cairo by BA, arriving at midnight, and were warmly greeted by a delegation from the hospital. We were then taken to the guest house at the Cathedral and collapsed into bed since we were exhausted after the drama of the last few days. On waking, we explored the guest house. The manager was a fearsome older Australian lady called Shirley, who ruled the Sudanese refugees and ran the place like a military encampment. To begin with, we were terrified of her, though later she became an extremely good friend. The guesthouse itself was a delightful throwback to the 1940s. There were three rooms with ensuite bathrooms, but the guests in most rooms had to use shared facilities. Everything was sparklingly clean, though the water supply could be a problem, and the fans creaked a bit. The air conditioners were certainly not around in the 1940s, but one had the impression that the ones fitted were the first ones on the market and wheezed and creaked.

Breakfast was served as occasionally was supper if you booked it. It was worth going to meals at the guest house as you met a wide range of interesting people there. Perhaps a Catholic priest from Hargeisa in Somaliland, a Rwandan Anglican priest from Benghazi in Libya or a surgeon who was working in a desert hospital in Mauritania. It was a bit like staying in the mess of one of the hubs of the colonial service in the bad old days and extremely enjoyable. The next day, we were taken to the Harpur Hospital in Menouf by the hospital driver on the hospital bus.

A journey like this underlines the fact that Egypt historically has had a large population strung out along the banks of the Nile as it passes through the Sahara Desert. The population density is very high indeed. The breadth of the strip of population has widened over the years due to irrigation using canals, Watering the desert from aquifers has made it fertile, but it is still clear that this is a desert. Also, the density of the population has led to huge air and land pollution. As you come over a low hill to enter Cairo, it is as if the valley ahead is covered with a thick grey blanket of air pollution, with the occasional skyscraper poking through it. The soil has a very high level of pollution by heavy metals.

As we headed north into the Delta, there were frequent dusty small towns with streets lined by jerry-built houses, flats, and small shops, many of which were selling the same range of goods. The street vendors of fruit were ubiquitous. There was always noise, and everybody seemed to shout. Occasionally, one can see a person telephoning somebody else further down the road. One wonders why they are using their phone because the volume of their bellowing would probably mean that their correspondent could hear with no electronic aids. The only problem was that everybody else was bellowing, too, and one had to distinguish which bellow belonged to your friend. Music is always playing at full volume, and the lights are on night and day. Many of the shops seem to be open most of the night, and one wonders whether a characteristic of the Egyptian population is sleep deprivation. As we got to know our colleagues later, we found that they often stayed up until 2 or 3 am, which might explain the fact that they were always late and that the after-lunch siesta was an absolute imperative for them.

The traffic behaviour on the way to Menouf was different, to say the least. Apart from a few motorways, many roads were narrow and in a poor state of repair. One of the main principles of Egyptian road building seemed to be that there was to be a sleeping policeman at least every 50 metres and that they should be unmarked. These seemed to be craftily built so that everybody and everything in the car or bus hit the roof hard if you hit it at any speed. Having said that, drivers drive fast, and as they get to know the roads, they remember which part of the sleeping police officers are the lowest so one can drive over them at speed. Everybody heads for these areas at speed on whichever side of the road they occur on and whichever way one drives. So, one sees vehicles weaving from side to side of the road heading for the same area of the humps from both directions. The weak ones blink first and give way, the rash ones hit the vehicles coming in the other directions and have an almighty crash and the smart ones head for the second lowest place on the hump and drive away before all the rest.

The drivers don't use their lights at night for unknown reasons. The idea is that if one sees another driver driving at you full speed, then you flash your lights at him, and if he is not listening to the radio or having an animated conversation with somebody else and using his hands to illustrate a point, he swerves violently, and a crash is avoided, but only if all those factors come into play. Nobody wears seat belts. On either side of the road, there was a continual stream of pedestrians, donkey carts, bicycles, light motorbikes, and tuck tucks, all going in both directions on both sides. The death rate here is an incredible 32 times as high as on the British roads.

Much of the transport on Egyptian roads is by small minibuses. These buses are bought by Egyptian entrepreneurs using loans at very high-interest rates. The only way the drivers can pay for the monthly payments is to drive hell for leather to-and-fro along their routes for about 16 hours a day with twice the proper number of people onboard. There is no time for marginal requirements such as getting the bus serviced or the brakes checked. Inevitably, crashes are very common, and one often passes a mangled bus with bodies neatly placed in rows under blankets for a lorry to pick up. We often used these vehicles as there was no alternative if one wanted to go from Menouf to Cairo. It was an experience that seemed to promote prayers. Even when doing this, we used to peer through our fingers to judge whether we would make it to the low part of the hump before the bus came in the opposite direction without a crash.

Finally, on the hospital bus, we arrived at Menouf, a much safer option, though not a truly safe one. We never felt safe when being driven by an Egyptian driver in Egypt. We crossed the level crossing at the station, weaved our way through the traffic, a bit less dense than Cairo, but not much so, and arrived at the hospital gate. The hospital was a concrete structure surrounded by a garden that must have been dramatic at some stage. It was now overgrown and neglected, but there were still plants with a wonderful scent in season and the lapwings busily scratched for bugs among the rampant weeds. The hospital, too, was gently crumbling.

The bus stopped outside the outpatient department, and we had a great welcome from the staff, including the Director and his wife, Mary. Mary was unfailingly helpful throughout our time in Menouf and was a lifeline for us, particularly during the difficult times. During our welcome, we noticed a man up one of the trees pruning it, so it did not encroach on the outpatient buildings. Suddenly, as we were talking, there was a thump, and the man had fallen out of the tree and was lying unconscious. He was unceremoniously picked up by three doctors without having any examination for broken bones or neck injury and carried without a stretcher into the outpatient building an action that could have paralysed him for life if his neck had been broken. This rang alarm bells for us, indicating a basic lack of understanding of managing a patient who had fallen from a height and was unconscious.

We were taken up two flights of stairs onto the top floor of the building and shown into a large two-bedroom flat. There was a large sitting room with a huge ornate sofa covered with a silky brocade, but it was filthy and was falling to bits, as were the chairs. This was not, in fact, surprising as the brown desert dust got everywhere, and the sofa was old. If one dusted a surface in the morning, it was again covered in a thick layer of dust by the evening. Things were made worse by the windows not fitting the space in the wall in which they were fixed. One could see the light between the window frame and the sides of the aperture. The front door also had numerous cracks in the wood through which one could see light, which led to a continual and significant wind blowing through the flat. The bedrooms were basic but adequate.

The kitchen was spartan with a sink and draining board, a fridge and a gas cooker with the gas bottle attached to the cooker by tubing which was 6 years out of date. The bathroom had a basin, a toilet and a shower without a shower base. There was a drain for the water to drain into, but the floor had been put in at the wrong slope, and instead of draining into the drain, it drained into the corridor outside the kitchen.

One of the hospital porters brought our luggage to our flat, and after a short period, we were left to sort ourselves out. We looked around and then sat down in the sitting room, noticing that the covering of the settee was slightly sticky and "reviewed the situation". Finally, we decided that if we were going to be missionaries in this place, then we had to live in the conditions that our fellow believers lived in. We rapidly learned that the living accommodations of our colleagues were much the same as ours.

Our colleagues kindly filled our fridge with some basic supplies, but we decided to stock up from shops in the town. We left the hospital and turned up a road with the hospital on one side and a school on the other. At the top of this street was the main road of the town. Everywhere, street vendors were selling flat bread or fruit and vegetables of various sorts; some of these were small and hand-drawn, and some were larger and drawn by a donkey.

At the roadside were men selling Ta'ameya, a broad bean curd fried in oil and served with salad and flatbread. We never saw these men replacing the oil, only adding to it. It was great fun to buy this extremely tasty street food. Nobody in Menouf spoke English, so everything was done using sign language. One approached the frying stand and caught the eye of the man who was shouting to his mate about 6 shops down the road. He nods, and you convey that you want some Ta'ameya using your hands, grunts, facial contortions, and any other way of communicating you can think of. He grabs a handful of the curds and throws it into the hot oil, provoking much sizzling and spurting all around. Meanwhile, he keeps up the bellowing to his friend along the way. Just behind you is the chaos of the road and the cars all hooting and trying to overtake each other.

Many of these cars looked vaguely familiar, but one could not exactly identify what make they were. Suddenly, it becomes clear they are all multiple makes. Perhaps one will have the front of a 1950s Austin Cambridge, the body of a Fiat and the boot of an ancient Peugeot, all of which have been cobbled together to make one vehicle. These seem to transport people around relatively efficiently apart from when they break down. Goodness knows what engines are providing locomotion. The only vehicles that seemed to usually be all of one make were the Ladas. These cars may be horrible to drive, worse to ride in, produce clouds of smoke and frequently break down, but they do seem to survive as individual cars. Many of the Ladas were taxis, and people seemed to hire them even to go 200 yards down the road.

To get back to our noble cook, he seems to be getting on well. His hands look suspiciously grubby, and he sneezes into one hand. There is no sign of any sink to wash in. He coughs in all directions, including over his cooking. The dish is ready. He pulls it out of the oil, wraps it in paper, grabs a flat loaf, and adds a little salad, and we have a meal. After all the excitement, we decided to leave it at that for today and get the rest of the shopping done tomorrow. When we get home, we look at the salad and think perhaps that can go into the bin, and we eat the flatbread and ta'ameya. It is delicious, as we have frequently found, food made under the most insanitary conditions often is.

Eventually, when we had found our way around the town of Menouf, often with Mary's help, we found that if you knew where to go, you could find almost everything you needed, often from a whole series of small shops. The chocolate was disgusting, but the halva and pistachio nuts and when we were feeling brave, the ice cream was very good. We found the people of Menouf universally welcoming and warm. Many of the children would come up to us and say, "Welcome to Egypt," and if people realised that we were lost, they would try hard to help us back to the hospital.

To our surprise, as we were in the back of Beyond, we found that the government had appointed an armed man to guard us. He was dressed in Kaki, and I am unsure whether he was in the army. If he was in the army, he must have been in Dad's army and reminded us very much of Private Godfrey. He was old, had very few teeth and was always disappearing to go to the loo or pray. He always left his gun leaning against a tree when he disappeared, and it did cross my mind that he was providing the weapon if anybody wanted to kill us. However, we were reassured to learn that all the banks and various other buildings had armed guards about the same vintage. The story has it that one bullet was provided for all the guards around the town, and they each took it, in turn, to have the bullet once a week. It is an unlikely story but one that our Egyptian colleagues swore to be true.

Peta was asked to spend time with the nursing staff each week. Nurses in Egypt were very different people from nurses in the West. Firstly, in a Muslim culture, their job was counted as dishonourable as they had to deal with bodily excretions, dead people, and men in an unsupervised environment. In a Christian hospital, the stigma of being a nurse was much less, but the general culture was to despise these girls. Three-quarters of the nurses were from a Christian culture, which did not mean they were believing Christians. A quarter of the nurses were Muslim, drawn by the comparatively improved treatment of women in this environment.

Girls who wanted to be nurses applied after taking the school leaving exam and had 4 weeks of training, then they were on the wards. Not surprisingly, they had no idea of sterility or, in many cases, cleanliness. They frequently kept their lunches in the drug cupboards and had no idea of doing dressings, doing injections correctly or managing intravenous infusions. The doctors almost always did these procedures. The nurses rarely washed their hands, and the wards were not kept clean. Often, they were grubby and a danger to anybody who had had an operation. This situation was little different from that in the government hospitals.

Peta was asked to do some training first in basic cleanliness, but as this was not something counted as important either in the Harpur Hospital or any other hospital around, there was no motivation to change or pressure from the doctors to drive change. Why should these people change their ways when a white foreign woman came and told them to do so when even their doctors did not want change?

When I started working in the hospital, I decided not to do any consulting but instead to sit with the staff doctors to discuss patients and their care and to ask why they did what they did. American doctors, mainly surgeons, had come to the hospital from an organisation called "World Medical Mission" for many years. These people felt that God was calling them to do medical care in the Harpur Hospital. Before they arrived, the fact that they were going to work at the hospital had been advertised, and many people turned up to be operated on by the American surgeon, earning a lot of money in fees for the hospital.

They would arrive with boxes full of sophisticated medical equipment with which to work. They would plug it all in; sometimes they worked, and sometimes they didn't because of the daily chaotic electricity supply with multiple surges. They then worked their way through a list of patients with various ills, and after three or four weeks, they packed up and went home secure in the conviction that God was happy with them as they had done their regulation mission that year. The amount of training they did in procedures that could be safely done in the economic situation of Egypt was minimal. Looking at what notes there were, and in many cases, there were none, there was no behavioural change detectable attributable to these visits individually or over time. The largest obvious effect was a degree of de-skilling and a conviction that Egyptian doctors would stay second-class doctors compared to the wonderful, highly skilled American Christian doctor brothers.

We found the doctors individually to be well-meaning, committed Christian doctors. The fact that they agreed to work in the Menouf Harpur Hospital meant that they would be poorer than if they worked as government-employed doctors. The main reason for this was that they were not allowed to do private practice, which was the major source of income for government doctors. In fact, this caused widespread abuse in government hospitals. The government-employed doctors told me that of the 400 doctors employed in the Menouf city hospital, almost all would book in in the morning, but by 11:00 am, two-thirds of them would have moved to their private practices or private hospitals in the town. One long-standing surgeon at the Harpur Hospital was unwilling to abide by the no private practice rule.

The hospital day started at 8:00 a.m. with the hospital morning service and then moved on to clinic ward rounds and surgery. However, less than 20 % of the staff attended the service, and less than 10% of the medical staff. The doctors were late getting to their clinics. Medical records were almost non-existent. Usually, something was written on the back of the duplicate of the prescription given to a patient about the condition that had been treated, and this was filed, but if one tried to ask for this record to be produced at a subsequent consultation, this was almost always found to be impossible. The records room consisted of a chaotic mess of piles of scraps of paper and folders in no order. Relations between doctors were not good, with gossip and backbiting happening. Some doctors, not the majority but a significant number, were rude to patients, particularly Muslim patients.

The only regular postgraduate education, if that is the right word to use, was carried out by drug reps who came to talk about their drugs and brought a meal with them. What they said was often untrue and, at times, dangerous, but the doctors valued the free meal. There were no up-to-date books in what passed for a library, and none of the doctors I met ever read a medical journal. Some departments were positively dangerous, with doctors using outdated, illogical treatments that were useless or damaging treatments. One American nurse who came to work in one of these departments came to see us in tears soon after starting because of what she had seen and rapidly left her post.

Having said that, there were some doctors who were fighting a battle to improve matters, and there were some who cared and went the extra mile for their patients. The hospital had lost its way. There was no pride in the standard of care, and people had given up. The Director was also a full-time clinician with little time for administrative tasks. He had probably by this time lost the motivation to develop plans by consensus, to challenge bad practice, and at this stage was deeply depressed. One thing that typified the malaise of the hospital happened a few months after we arrived. Our church in England provided a new library so that anybody with the motivation could read up on the basic principles of their discipline. The Director decided that these books were very valuable, so he locked them all up in a cupboard. If anybody wanted to read them, they would have to go and find the Director and ask him for the key to the cupboard, which he often did not have on him. So, nobody read the books, and they remained in mint condition and unused.

When I was sitting in with the doctors, it soon became clear that there was little understanding, let alone tolerance of psychiatric conditions. A patient came in clearly a deeply depressed state and was given some medication as a sort of tonic. When I enquired with the doctor I was accompanying about the man's condition, he told me that this individual should return home, gather his strength, and actively seek employment.

I found that there was no agreed protocol in the hospital for managing common diseases such as hypertension and diabetes. Hypertension was very common among the patients we saw, and I noticed that if a very high blood pressure was found, they were often referred to a nurse who would take the blood pressure again over perhaps three more times, and that was it. The procedure had been done, and nothing was done about the continuing very high blood pressure.

We were uncertain whether all this was because the doctors had never been taught how to care for patients properly or whether they were just slipshod. So, we invited the doctors once a week to our flat for an evening of study and seminars and decided to build a protocol for managing diabetes with them. We did this, put it all together and published it, sending a copy to everyone in the hospital. The entire group that had participated in developing the protocol felt a strong sense of pride. However, conducting an audit after two months revealed that it had not made the slightest difference in altering the doctors' behaviour.

We became more and more depressed. Although they were delightful, and their praise was fervent when they were in church, which took place in the outpatients' department of the hospital, there seemed to be little appetite for change. They also became more and more irritated by us continually asking if there might be a different way of doing things. Realising that this was happening, we invited the doctors to our flat for meals and prayed with them, and they very hospitably invited us back.

We arranged conferences helped by PRIME involving some of the most talented teachers in the UK. The local university asked us to run teaching sessions for their students and conferences for students at the surrounding medical schools. We did this too, and at one of the conferences we arranged, we had faculty present from 15 of the 17 Egyptian medical schools, but the whole laisse-faire attitude of "We are doing fine" remained. The bishop was talking about closing the hospital down, though happily, only briefly. We were even co-opted onto the central hospital management board in Cairo. By the time we left to take our three-week midterm holiday, we were in despair and wondered whether to return.

We spent our leave in France and thought and prayed about Egypt. We concluded that we had been called to this job, and until God indicated to us that we had done what He called us to, we should continue. We arrived back to an altogether different situation. Some of the doctors in the hospital had caught the vision of what could happen if changes were made. The leader in this move was a young physician with a specialty in Hepatology. The faithful few who had always had a clear vision of the possibility of the hospital as being a beacon of light came on board. This project was now "locally owned," and the difference was enormous. Instead of feeling like we were pushing a heavy rock up a steep hill, our local colleagues were in the driving seat. A few people left the hospital at this stage, and the Director, realising that he was trying to do an impossible task, moved on. We were sad to see him go, particularly as he was not well and many other people missed him, particularly the young doctors.

We continued acting as resource people, running seminars in the hospital and in the University of Menoufia. Otherwise, we were able to take far more of a back seat and watch what God was doing through our colleagues. One droll fact was that whereas our efforts were not much appreciated before, certain local doctors now complained that we were spending too much time in the University and not enough time in the hospital. The local doctors set up an organisation called "Doctors With A Mission" (DWAM) to promote good practice and show God's love through medical practice locally and wider in Egypt and internationally in the Middle East.

We now had much more time and energy to get to know the town and surroundings better. We developed a close relationship with one vegetable seller called Om Ramadan (the name means mother of Ramadan, her son). She had a small stall, which she set up daily on top of a huge manhole cover over a junction of several sewage channels just down the road from the hospital. She had a reliable supply of fresh vegetables, which her husband brought in. They must both have been in their 60s, though they looked much older. Once having brought the vegetables in, the husband seemed quite happy to spend the day sitting under the stall. It was quite amusing that Om Ramadan periodically needed his help and shouted at him, whereupon a head appeared from under the stall, and he went to do his wife's commands. During our time in Egypt, we learned about 2-300 words of Arabic, which allowed us to shop and have relatively simple conversations. When we got to know Om Ramadan well, we asked them one day if we could take a photo of her and her husband. They agreed, and we printed and framed the photo and gave it to them. They were absolutely over the moon and took the photo all up and down the road to show all the other stall holders.

During our time in Egypt, some of our clothes started looking very worn because of the continual burden of trying to get the ubiquitous brown desert dust out of them, so we asked how we bought new clothes. Things were not quite as simple as they are in the UK. First, one must choose the material one wants the clothes to be made of.

There were numerous cloth shops, and one wandered from one to the next, often feeling a bit dazed. If there was somebody around who spoke English, they would probably give you some advice that everybody in sight would immediately countermand. Once we had bought the material, we then had to find a tailor and explain to him (and it usually was him) what we wanted made. Many people did this by taking pictures. We decided that the best thing to do was to take along the worn-out shirt or dress or whatever we would replace. After about three days, the garment was ready. Perhaps the clothes were not tailored to West End standards, but they were durably made, and fifteen years later, I am still wearing some of the shirts. Looking at the clothes made for us in Menouf, the overwhelming difference between the shirts seemed to be governed by our mood when we bought the material. Many of my shirts were properly sober, though I have one shirt that my sons tell me makes me look like a pizza delivery man and another that makes me look like I am wearing some curtains.

We walked widely around the town and got to know the railway station, the area where the daily hired workers congregate each morning waiting to be hired, just like in the Bible. We worked out which were the best pastry shops and where the best helva and olives were sold. Most people get around by taxi. A journey of just 3-400 yards would often be accomplished by taxi, and the rigmarole of getting one and then paying them, and the fare was pence, would take longer than walking the distance. This was because, culturally, it was a disgrace that an older person or a person of any standing was seen walking. As well as the taxis, there were horse-drawn carriages drawn by skeletal horses. We were told that using one of these was a surefire way of getting fleas, so we never tried them out. The one thing that Menouf did not have was any restaurants. There were tea houses galore but not a single café of any sort.

There was one shop in town, which was a Muslim bookshop run by a somewhat morose man who did not seem to have a brisk trade. In fact, we never saw anybody buy anything from his shop. I decided one day to pop in to see him and have a short chat with him. He did not seem over the moon about seeing me. One day, I met him on the street about half a mile from the hospital. He looked particularly threatening on this day. But I thought that it was only right, if we were trying to reach the Muslims with the love of God, to accept the invitation to tea in his flat. As I entered the block of flats and went into his basement flat, I remember looking up at the sky, wondering whether I would see it again, and committing myself to God's keeping. My anxiety was not assuaged when I noticed him locking the door after us. He served me bread, salty cheese, helva and tea. I was somewhat reassured because I knew that in Arab culture, one could not harm a man to whom you had given hospitality for 3 days after one had received him for a meal. However, I noticed that he kept a large, pointed kitchen knife grasped in his right hand throughout the meal. We chatted about prayer, the mosque peace, and other similar subjects, which was not easy as we communicated largely with sign language.

After about three hours, he suddenly threw the knife across the room, and it went under a sofa and told me that I could go. However, the door was locked, and when I pointed this out to him, he gave me about twenty keys. I struggled to find the right one when he pushed me aside, opened the door, and allowed me out. Walking down the road home, I looked up at the sky and thanked God for delivering me. I hoped he understood that some Christians do not shun Muslims but sincerely wish to get to know them. When I shared my encounter with our friends at the hospital, they informed me that two years prior, this man had killed a woman passing by his shop, whom he believed had been dressed inappropriately. Grateful for my safety, I thanked God for my deliverance, and from then on, he became known as 'Freddie the fundamentalist' within our family.

The area around Menouf in the western part of the Nile Delta is intensively farmed. Rainfall is extremely sparse, and almost all of the land is irrigated by canals starting in the Rosetta branch of the Nile. The average size of a farm is less than a hectare, but because of the temperature and sunlight, it is quite possible to produce three harvests a year from this land. All the canals have walkways and sometimes rough tracks beside them, and the farmers often build their houses along these canals. As we grew accustomed to life in Egypt, we spent a lot of time walking miles into the countryside along these canal tracks.

People who were not local were rarely seen along these tracks, and white people from the West almost never, so the residents were intrigued to find out who we were and what we were doing. Happily, they all knew and appreciated the Harpur hospital because they said that overall, they were treated better there than in the government hospitals. As we walked, we realised that it was not only farmer's houses along the canals, but there were also bakers, woodcarvers, mechanics who mended the light motorbikes used by everybody and the donkey carts, which were the main transport of the small farmers. People were universally hospitable.

One day, we walked about 4 miles into the countryside and came on what looked like an igloo made of mud. We stop and look at this, wondering what it is and a lady of about 40 greets us. Using our very limited Arabic, Peta asks what it is, and the lady shows her the bread she made in it. It is a mud bread oven. She says that she is about to make some bread, so Peta goes off with her into her home, a jerry-built brick structure. I sit under the shade in the animal shed, much like the one where Jesus was born just a few hundred miles northeast of here. I commune with the two buffalos there and occasionally say hello to the goats and chickens, who wander in and out. The lady and Peta reappear with tea and bread, and we chat in sign language. Her husband turns up and sits down. He is a silent sort of chap.

We finish our tea and walk about another mile past houses where the children stop their play by saying "Welcome to Egypt" and, having got that over, giggle and go off to play again. Eventually, we get to the home of some wood carvers who produce carved heads for beds and whom we have often met over the months we have been walking this way. We had got to know this family well and had occasionally brought them a small gift. We have another cup of tea sitting on their house's entrance step. Mohamed, another brother, arrives with a donkey cart full of animal manure for the crops on his farm. After a while, we realise that he is slightly mentally challenged. We are introduced to the younger carver's fiancée when she brings our tea. About two months later, he got married, we were invited, and I was invited to dance with his bride at the wedding. This is a huge honour and is rarely seen in this culture.

When our colleagues in the hospital learned what we were doing, they were horrified. They said that this is just not done, whatever that might mean. We talked and thought about this and realised that this was probably the reaction of a small, persecuted minority who always felt threatened when they were out of their minority group. In fact, we might well have been taking risks in doing this, but we never felt any aggression or any sense of risk from the people we met and got to know.

As well as exploring the town of Menouf, we travelled quite widely around Egypt. One of the surgeons, Dr Samir Wadie, was extremely kind to us and took us under his wing. He and his family were believing and faithful members of the Coptic church, and he took us to several of their monasteries. The monastic movement here started way back at the beginning of the Christian era, and the first monasteries in the world were built in Egypt. At the start of the Islamic period in Egypt, the Muslims often used to protect the monks from attack by the marauding bands of brigands.

One visit particularly stuck in our minds. The monastery was on the coast of the Red Sea. Just as we entered the monastery, our grandson telephoned us and asked where we were. We told him we were just on the shore of the Red Sea. There was a pause, and Jonathan said, “Don’t be silly, Grandpa. The sea isn’t red; it’s blue.” It took a bit of time to tell him that while the sea is blue, this blue sea is called the Red Sea. I think that he thought that we must be in a very weird part of the world if they call blue things red there.

When we got into the monastery, we met a young monk who said he would like to show us the icons. My heart dropped a bit. However, he went from picture to picture, explaining from these icons the story of God's dealing with mankind, from creation to slavery in Egypt to Canaan to the birth and then the death of Jesus. He explained sin, the consequences of sin, Jesus' salvation on the cross, the church's work, and the final picture of the heavenly city we are traveling to. This was superbly done, and nobody could say that they did not know about God's creative brilliance, His hatred of sin, His kindness and grace and the work of the church and the individual Christian after such a tour. It struck us that this was the original purpose of these icons in a period when almost nobody could read.

We were always given a meal when we went to any monastery, which usually consisted of grains, pulses, and eggs. In Menouf, the whole town was dry, and one could not get any alcohol of any sort anywhere in the town. However, on the way back home, Dr Samir knew all the hidden shops where one could buy alcoholic drinks and very often, we would arrive back at the hospital with a bottle of Arrack, hidden in a paper bag. This is an aniseed aperitif. Occasionally we bought a bottle of Egyptian made whisky, which one only knew that it was whisky because of the label on the bottle.

We also went on some journeys with the church pastor in Menouf. He was a South Korean and managed to lead the church despite not speaking Arabic and having bad relations with the Bishop of Cairo. He took us to St. Catherine's monastery in the Sinai Peninsula. This was the first monastery in the world and was situated right at the base of Mount Sinai, where Moses received the law and the Ten Commandments. We climbed the mountain, all 7260 feet, the winding track and 4200 steps. On the top, where Moses received the tablets of the law, was a platform and a small chapel. Here, we were higher than any of the surrounding peaks and looked out over an arid and utterly wild landscape. From there, we went north to the Israeli border, which I am certain was in a regulated area, and we ought not to have been there.

Driving from there, Pastor Joshua pulled into a nondescript petrol station and was greeted warmly by the owner. He was a Bedouin, and he ran his own enterprise, which took people into the white desert, spent a night sleeping in the desert and had a desert barbecue. We set off driven by his son, who was 22 years old and in a Toyota Landcruiser, older than its driver by two years. All went well for about 6 hours while we were being driven through a completely trackless desert. Then we became stuck in some soft sand. Despite trying everything to free ourselves, our efforts were in vain. We found ourselves approximately 90 miles deep into the wild and desolate stretches of this Sahara region. Puzzled, we turned to our driver for guidance. With no mobile phone signal available and lacking a satellite phone, he simply said, "We wait." Naturally, we enquired, "Wait for what?" His response was cryptic: "You'll see."

We waited for about 45 minutes until, unexpectedly, two modern Land Cruisers emerged over the sand dune on our right and skilfully pulled us out. After rescuing us, they vanished as mysteriously as they appeared. We questioned our driver about how these individuals knew of our predicament and location. His reply was intriguing: "The Bedouin know absolutely everything that happens in the desert." That was the extent of his explanation. The following evening, after enjoying a night of eating and sleeping beneath the desert sky, we returned to the petrol station. Despite the unexpected turn of events, we had had an incredibly memorable experience.

In addition to our journeys with friends and colleagues, we also ventured into Cairo for a weekend every third week to maintain our sanity. Whether these trips fulfilled their purpose depends on the person you ask. The consensus suggests that the goal was, perhaps, hopeless in the first place. Nonetheless, we bravely caught a minibus into the bustling city, fully aware that our lives were in our hands. The trip was very good for renovating our prayer life and testing how fast our hearts could beat without bursting. Once in Cairo, we took a taxi to the diocesan guest house, where they always found us a bed. The problem was that no taxi driver in the whole of Cairo seemed to have any idea of what or where the diocesan guest house was. Eventually, we realised that if we wanted to arrive at our destination, the only thing to ask for was to ask for the Cairo Marriot. This was just down the road from the guest house.

On arrival, we made our way down the road to the guest house opposite the cathedral entrance and just opposite the hut for the armed guard. We gave the guard a cheery wave as he was, as always, standing having an animated conversation with anybody who would agree to have an animated conversation with him, leaving his gun propped up against the guard's hut. We recuperated the key from the gate office and entered the guest house.

There are 6 floors in the building, starting with the first two floors occupied by the bishop. It struck us that two floors of a relatively grotty tower block were rather different living accommodations from the bishops' palaces in England. The guest house is on the 3rd and 4th floor, and there was an extremely rickety lift that groaned mightily every time you travel in it. For some time, we thought it best to send the cases up in the lift and walk up the stairs. Then a new lift was installed, a lift where the doors closed and what is more, music played when you used it, American country music from about the sixties. After about three months, the singer sounded slightly drunk and then after about another month, it sounded like an off-key, very drunken singer. If the quality of the music was that poor, it crossed our minds to consider the lift mechanism's quality. We started climbing the stairs again, which made us feel safer and probably did wonders for our health.

One felt immediately at home with the 1940s boarding house ambience we found there and the great welcome we always received. After checking into our room, whatever time it was, we always made a beeline back to the Marriott Hotel. This hotel is constructed around the palace that was originally built to accommodate Princess Eugenie for the inauguration of the Suez Canal. Between two standard tower blocks, the palace stands as the centrepiece—a true marvel. Adorned with ornate ceilings, elegant chandeliers, and original-looking damask-covered chairs, the palace exudes magnificence. The meticulously maintained oriental garden retains its original charm. The tables, sunshades, and chairs are thoughtfully arranged amidst beautiful flowers. On Fridays, the scene transforms, with elegantly attired Egyptian locals, adults and children enjoying a day out. The children were usually looked after by Filipino nannies. The clientele range from serious businessmen to individuals like us—seeking a respite from the clamour, poverty, dust, and oppression of the outside world, if only for an hour, before rejoining life's challenges.

Menouf was a dry town, so the first thing we always did was to order a drink. I always chose a locally brewed Stella beer, which tasted much better than the drink brewed in Europe. Peta would perhaps choose an Obelisk. This was an Egyptian red wine, but the problem was that one had to have a certain level of blood alcohol even to recognise it as wine, so we had to order two glasses of it, and of course, I had to help Peta with the second glass. If there was a dust storm or during the winter if it was cold, there was the piano bar inside the palace where the seating and tables rose in tiers from a grand piano. Here students at the Cairo conservatoire would earn a little cash to help with the accounts by playing anything from Mozart to Gershwin while the waiters brought you your chosen tipple. The light was low, and one almost expected Humphrey Bogart to appear from the wings.

We arrived at the Marriot at all sorts of times to have a drink and sometimes a meal when we felt rich. The latest we turned up was one occasion when the bishop had offered to bring us from Menouf after one of his visits. The bishop likes to talk, and we did not arrive in Cairo until 3.00 am. We still made our pilgrimage to the Marriott, found the piano bar in full swing and duly ordered our Stella and Obelisk before tumbling into our beds. We found this hotel an oasis of beauty and peace in the middle of a hot, dusty, noisy city.

The next morning, we would get up late and go to an excellent pizza bar, Maison Thomas, run by a French woman and her Egyptian husband for lunch, and then perhaps go for a walk along the Nile. There was a knack for walking anywhere in Egypt. The roads were 6-lane dual carriageways. The cars drove at high speed and stopped for nothing. In many places, the traffic would grind almost to a stop because of a snarl-up. Everybody hooted all the time and headed for that tiny gap that five other people were heading for simultaneously. They might now be driving slower, but they still stopped for nothing. There were no proper crossing points, so if one wanted to get to the other side of a road, one took one's life in one hands. However, we eventually learnt how to cross safely. First, you had to find a pregnant woman. Then, you would follow her until she wanted to cross the road and position yourself on the opposite side of her, facing away from the direction of the traffic. As she crossed, you would cross on her lee side. The one person that cars would not drive into and would stop for was a pregnant woman. Often, pregnant women were seen crossing roads with a long line of people crossing with them.

In the evening, we would often go to an excellent restaurant located just a five-minute walk from the guesthouse. To get there, one entered through an archway that displayed several companies' names at the entrance, but there was no mention of any restaurant. Inside, there was a hall with an even more dangerous-looking lift than the one where we were staying, so we opted to climb the stairs. Upon reaching the first floor, a frieze of carvings adorned the exterior of a large wooden door. Upon pushing the door, we found ourselves in an excellent restaurant that mainly served French cuisine. The place was usually bustling with youngish people engaged in lively conversations, and the waiters were efficiently and friendly. They claimed to offer a view of the Nile, and I'm inclined to believe that there might have been a single table where, if one were to stand on a chair and crane their neck, a glimpse of water could be seen.

On Sunday, we made our way either by taxi or underground to the luxury suburb of Mahdi, where the Cairo International Church met.

This church had a meeting under canvas on the grounds of an Anglican church, once on Thursday night and twice on Friday. There were about 500 people present at each meeting. The style of the church meeting was free evangelical, but due to its very diverse congregation, it was not affiliated with any denomination. At an average meeting, there could be anything from 20 to 35 nationalities present, and the meetings were run in English. Because of this arrangement, it was a very exciting place to attend, and one met and heard about people in all sorts of work, lay and Christian from all over the globe. Having worked in many countries, we sometimes met people from other countries that we had not met for years and who either were working in Egypt or staging through using this country as a hub for the Middle East. For example we met a missionary sent out from our son's church in Hackney, whom we had last seen at dinner in our home in Biddenham. There had been regular threats against this meeting by fundamentalist groups in the area, so for this reason, the Egyptian government provided a very heavy guard of soldiers armed with submachine guns. These men were posted all around the perimeter every three metres. The guards were the same men each week, which meant that not only did we get to know them, but they got to know many of the hymns and choruses. If we were late and the service had started when we arrived, we would often see the soldiers singing along with the hymn being sung inside. It was a somewhat bizarre sight to see a row of heavily armed Egyptian soldiers singing "Shine Jesus Shine," using their guns to keep time on an otherwise quiet suburban road in Cairo.

On a late Sunday night, we made our way to the minibus terminal to find the bus back to Menouf. None of the busses were marked, so one had to make enquiries about which of 35 white Toyota minibuses was heading for Menouf. An even bigger problem was that morc people were trying to get to Menouf than places inside even the most crowded busses. Once the bus arrived, people would pile in, sometimes even climbing in through the windows. Usually, after a time, somebody would take pity on two older white people who were mad enough to risk life and limb going by bus to Menouf and would find two small crannies for us, moving the bus from the grossly overcrowded category to the jam-packed one. One almost had to breathe in a rota.

Our time was coming to an end, and we were turning our thoughts to moving back to Biddenham. The hospital was still in a fragile state. Many things needed changing, but the local doctors had the change in hand and had a plan to change the hospital for the better. One very encouraging change that occurred was that when drug salespeople came from the pharmaceutical companies to make sure that their drugs were used in the hospital, the doctors used to read up in respected journals about the evidence for benefit from the drugs and what were the side effects. The drug representative was allowed to give his talk, and then the "facts" he produced were challenged by the evidence in the mainline journals. The drug rep would then try and deny this evidence by quoting from other journals, but usually, these journals were produced by the drug company itself, and the articles were neither peer-reviewed nor statistically sound. I have seen the reps gathering their papers and fleeing when faced with people who knew how to assess bogus claims. Happily, if they did this, they always left the meal they had brought for the doctors behind. Rumour had it that the visit to the Harpur Hospital in Menouf among drug reps had become the most difficult and scary one in Egypt because the doctors could discern when they were lying.

We were happy about the changes that were happening and the people who were making these changes. We were, however, asked to come back to Egypt after our departure to run teaching sessions for the doctors not only in Menouf but also from all the Christian hospitals in Egypt. We were happy to do this as the state medical education system frequently excluded Christian doctors from postgraduate education. We arranged postgraduate sessions using some of the best-known teachers in Cardiology, Psychiatry, Gastroenterology, Endoscopy and Endocrinology, among other specialties. We returned three times in the first year after we went home, twice in the second year and about yearly thereafter. Our last programme before I retired at 79 was to work with students in their last year of medical school and for the first year after graduation, trying to fill in gaps in their education. We had a team of three men from the UK and an inspirational woman doctor from New Zealand who was at that time working in Qatar. We found that the biophysical knowledge of our students was overall excellent, but their understanding of Psychiatry and particularly of Whole Person medicine was very poor. The whole idea of patients being not only informed about their treatment but also being given choices about that treatment was a totally foreign concept. However, what was outstanding was their motivation to show the love of Christ to their patients.

The doctors in charge of DWAM, the new organisation for change in Menouf, met up with an Arabic Christian doctor who had emigrated to the USA. He had made a very large amount of money and had a teaching post in a well-known American medical school. He was also very well-connected, coming from a powerful political family in Lebanon. He had decided that God was calling him to use his money and skills to improve medicine and to spread the Christian gospel in the Middle East. With DWAM, he set up an umbrella organisation, Health Outreach Middle East (HOME) with the aim of improving medical standards and Christian outreach in Middle Eastern countries. This doctor's input made a huge difference to the Hospital in Menouf and set up and renewed projects running into the sand in Lebanon, Syria, Iraq and Mauritania.

Eventually, this all led to rebuilding the hospital in Menouf and setting up a surgical training system run by an American surgeon experienced in Africa. This programme was accredited by PAACS (the Pan African Association of Christian Surgeons) and the medical school at Duke University, an Ivy League university in America. The Family Medicine Department was accredited by the international department of Edinburgh University. We were involved in all of this to sow the very first tiny seeds. Our church at the time, Christchurch Bedford, paid for building the first postgraduate medical education centre and paid part of the money for the renovation of the Menouf Anglican church. The real transformative work was done by local dedicated Christian doctors doing their daily clinical work and working half the night as well to reform medical practice.

One of the outcomes of this renewal of the commitment of Christian doctors to provide high quality to their patients was the setting up of a yearly conference under the auspices of DWAM and HOME to which all Christian doctors were invited. About 500 young, enthusiastic Christian doctors attended these gatherings, and we were invited to speak at several of them. They lasted over 3 days, were residential, and usually took place at conference centres deep in the desert run by the Coptic Orthodox Church. The mornings were taken up with presentations from the front, and the afternoon was taken up with break-out groups looking at clinical subjects or how Christian doctors should react to their patients and the community in general. This was an important issue because, in Egypt, it was rare for Christian doctors to be offered any postgraduate teaching after their basic qualification. The well-known cardiac surgeon at Harefield Hospital in the UK, Dr Magdy Yacoub, passed out at the top of his year at Assuit Medical School. However, because he was a Christian, he was denied any further training and had to come to Britain to advance in his career. In the evening, there was worship.

It was an inspiring and humbling experience to stand addressing 500 young doctors who had come to see what God was leading them to do. It was also encouraging to see many of our students there, too. These conferences were also forums where many doctors found a believing Christian wife or husband. We know of two of our students whom God called to go and serve in difficult non-Christian environments. One young doctor called Beauty went to live and work at Wadi Haifa in Northern Sudan. This industrial desert town was known for its poverty and violence. She ran a 120-bed hospital with both surgical and medical wings as the only doctor for 5 years. The town had such a bad name that no other doctors would work there other than in expensive private practice. She had always to be guarded but was very much loved. While she was working there, the Sudanese government closed all mission hospitals except this one. Beauty was so loved and was performing a task that nobody else would be prepared to do that the government did not dare to close the hospital.

The other doctor worked in a similar situation in Mauritania, where mission hospitals are forbidden. However, the only people prepared to run a hospital in a desert town were Amanda from the USA and Michel from Egypt. Other doctors were inspired to enter careers in Psychiatry, the most despised of the medical specialties with a very low income, because they wished to confront the large incidence of female abuse and rape, which was very much brushed under the carpet.

Having said all that, many doctors enjoyed the time at the conference, but it did not change their career plans or lifestyle. That, of course, is common all over the world. Intellectual consent to the faith is fine as long as it does not affect your lifestyle.

During this time, Egypt went through political convulsions and a great increase in persecution of the Christians. There was a revolution, particularly by the young people of Egypt, against President Mubarak's corrupt and cruel rule. Hundreds of thousands of people came out on the streets to demand the retirement of the president and elections for a new president. This was associated with the Arab Spring movement all over the Middle East. The revolution was met with gross brutality, particularly in Cairo. The revolutionaries congregated in the central square, Tahrir Square, which they occupied, setting up an encampment. This was met with gunfire using live ammunition. The soldiers and police also drove into the crowds, killing people under armoured vehicles' wheels and using poisonous gas against the protesters. There were many casualties and deaths.

There is a large church on the border of this square called the Kasr El Dobara evangelical Church, of which a medical friend of ours was a member. She got permission from the church council to take out all the pews and seats from the church and set up a casualty clearing station there. As it became known that this was happening, doctors and nurses appeared from all over the city, both Muslim and Christian and the doctors brought equipment and supplies from the hospitals where they normally worked. Many lives were saved. There was a tremendous sense of comradeship across the normally difficult divide between Muslims/Christians. On Fridays, the Christian demonstrators guarded the Muslims as they prayed in the square and on Sundays, the Muslims protected the Christians as they had their services.

Mubarak was deposed eventually, and there was a great feeling of excitement and hope in the country. At a free election, President Morsi, a member of the extreme Muslim Brotherhood, was elected. This time was a dangerous one in the city as the police had been totally discredited by their brutal actions during the revolution, so there were no forces of law and order in the city and thefts and robberies were common. We visited not long after Mubarak fell, and a friend took me to see Tahrir Square. There was still a tent city in the square. As we skirted the area, we found a roundabout with about 30 young people on it with placards jumping up and down and shouting. I asked my friend what was going on, and he told me that these were people from the church in the square with placards saying Muslim brothers and sisters, we love you, and God loves you too. We value our partnership in building a new Egypt.

Sadly, Morsi proved to be a totally incompetent president. The Muslim Brotherhood made sure that everything he did would lead towards an exclusively Muslim state, and chaos ensued. Relations between the Muslims and Christians broke down, and Christians experienced a large increase in persecution. Babies and young women were kidnapped. In a particular region of the country, an Arabic symbol, 'N,' signifying 'Christian' or 'Nazarene,' was painted on the doors of Christian families' homes. These households faced violent attacks, resulting in burned houses and injured individuals. On a single day, a shocking incident unfolded where 36 churches and 7 church social service centres were systematically burned down, leading to significant destruction, and tragically, two Christian pastors lost their lives. During this unsettling time, a distressing event occurred involving a bus transporting members of a large church to a meeting at another church. The bus was intercepted, and all passengers were instructed to disembark. Each individual was then questioned individually, asked whether they would renounce their faith in Jesus and convert to Islam. Remarkably, they all remained steadfast in their faith and declined the offer, resulting in tragic consequences as they were all fatally shot. Likewise, another tragic incident involved a bus carrying 35 members of a Christian youth group. The bus came under machine gun fire, leading to the loss of many young lives.

The reaction of the Orthodox Pope was: "Our churches can be rebuilt, and what you have done to our pastors and our church members has sent them into the presence of their Lord and Master Jesus Christ. We bear you no ill will and will serve you where you have the need as much as we have the strength."

At about this time, I was on the speakers team of one of the large DWAM conferences, and one afternoon, I was to lead a breakout session on Whole Person Medicine, giving the patients the right to choose their treatment and how they react to illness. About 30 young doctors turned up and told me they did not want to carry out the scheduled programme. Instead, they wanted to write a new constitution for their country stating what they would undertake to do from now on. The constitution reads:

The Egyptian Christian Constitution

We, a group of young Christian Egyptian people, declare that:

1) Muslim people are precious souls for whom Jesus died, and they are loved by God.

2) There should never be any discrimination against Muslim people.

3) They are not enemies. They are trying to please God but are misled when they use violence. God shows us that we should pray for them when they act against us.

4) We should feel for them when they have troubles.

5) We should greet them with a smile.

6) We should always be ready to give them practical help.

7) We should pray for them regularly and present the love of God to them.

8) We should remember that when one of our churches was bombed and many people killed at the last New Year, many Muslims helped us.

9) We must keep loving them even if we have been wounded by them.

10) If we live close to the Lord, He will give us the grace we need to do all this.

11) We must never ever take revenge, whatever they do to our community.

This was written when the whole community was hurting and frightened after the most terrible attacks. We stood and still stand in awe of our Egyptian brothers and sisters.

Yemen

A couple of months before we left Egypt, we received a call from Peter Crooks, the vicar of the only Anglican church in Yemen, located in Aden. This church had been granted a fatwa by the chief imam of the country, recognising it as a legitimate centre of Christian worship, free to function without hindrance. The granting of the fatwa was conditional upon the church establishing a clinic to provide treatment for the poor and the blind. Named Christ Church Aden, the construction of this church had been funded by Queen Victoria during Aden's time as a British colony, serving as the garrison church. Subsequent to Aden's independence, under a communist government, the building was transformed into a gym and then stable for horses. Following the overthrow of the communist regime, the church was reconsecrated, and a clinic was established on its grounds. Situated in an impoverished area of Aden, near the well-known landmark of Steamer Point in Aden Harbour, the church and clinic were enclosed by a tall wall, with access through a high steel gate. The church itself featured a ground floor divided into a worship space, a meeting room, offices, and a kitchen. A first floor had been built inside the church, consisting of bedrooms and bathrooms used by many members of the various NGOs working in the country when we first engaged with this work. It was also used t o house stranded seamen. Ruthless ship owners, particularly those from Somalia or certain African countries, used to engage crews on six-month contracts to run their ships and then after five and a half months, they used to call into Aden and throw the crew off the boat so that they did not have to pay them. This sometimes left these men with no salary or even passports, far from home and penniless. These people were taken in by Christ Church, and the vicar, wearing his hat as a local rep for the Mission to Seafarers, would try and negotiate with the embassies of wherever they had come from to repatriate them. The British Embassy in Sanaa recognised the Church and the clinic as part of development work in

Yemen and occasionally made some small grants. Most of the money for running the project came from the Anglican diocese of Cyprus and the Gulf.

All the medical staff in the clinic were Muslim, and the great majority were women. When we were there, one of the nurses was a Christian Pakistani girl, and one was from the Netherlands. Her husband oversaw the maintenance. All the maintenance workers were Ethiopian refugees living in Aden. Due to a conflict between the Amharic and Oromo tribes in Ethiopia, a significant number of Ethiopian refugees sought shelter in Yemen. The violence prompted many Oromo individuals to flee to Yemen out of fear for their lives. Among these refugees was a large community of practising Christians. The church held regular Sunday services, drawing attendees from local Christian NGOs, businesses, and government agencies, representing various organisations. The congregation boasted a diverse composition, including members from Russia, Pakistan, the United States, Ethiopia, the Netherlands, and Sweden. Conducted in English, the services catered to a wide range of attendees. However, as a considerable portion of Oromo Christians were not proficient in English, and their numbers were substantial, they established their own separate church. This new congregation had its own pastor and conducted services independently from the main group. The relationship between the two congregations remained harmonious and cooperative. Additionally, throughout the week, various Christian meetings were held.

To the right of the main door of the church was a courtyard and then the clinic buildings. These consisted of a reception office that held the patients' notes, two consulting rooms, a laboratory, a pharmacy and operating suite for eye surgery, and a recovery room. The waiting room was the courtyard, which had a wide shady veranda. The first two consulting rooms were used for a family medicine practice. When one registered with this unit and paid a set fee, that covered all costs and all drugs for a year. The other side of the compound consisted of living accommodation for the expatriate staff.

The large entrance gate was guarded by a guard employed by the Yemeni branch of G4S. Weapons were ubiquitous in Aden and carried quite openly, but our guard only carried a metal bar. In fact, this was plenty of protection as the local community in Tawahi, our area of Aden, was intensely proud of "their" church clinic and very protective if there was any disturbance.

As well as working in the Church compound, the medical staff did sessions in the camp that the UNHCR had set up for Somali refugees and did operating sessions at Mocha, a port some miles along the coast to the east. The equipment was piled inside an incredibly old, battered, decrepit Landcruiser and set off. Decrepit it might have been, but it never let them down.

Over all this ruled our director and administrator, Mansour. Mansour was a big man in all ways: tall, extremely well-built and well-connected. His wife was the secretary to the Governor of the town. Despite his devout Muslim faith, Mansour demonstrated remarkable respect towards the Christians and their beliefs. Renowned for his unwavering honesty, he efficiently managed the entire unit, especially during times when expatriates needed to leave the country.

The town of Aden has a certain degree of faded glory about it. There is a statue of Queen Victoria in a somewhat overgrown park. On the hill is Little Ben, a smaller version of Big Ben. It still works but does not strike. There is still a promenade along the sea, though the bars have disappeared. The fish market has been rebuilt, and one can wander down there to pick the fish you would like to eat that evening. Until the civil war, there was a mall selling all sorts of glitzy handbags and shoes.

The setting is wonderful! The town is built around the craters of three volcanoes. Two of these are flooded and have become one of the best harbours in the Middle East, and the third is a crowded suburb of the town called, unoriginally, Crater. This was the site of some of the most bitter fighting in the war, which accompanied independence.

Murder Mile, the street where so many British soldiers were killed, is now a normal main road. It is also notable for having the only restaurant where one can buy a beer with a meal. It is run by a Chinese family. All over town, there were many excellent restaurants, but none of the others sold beer. Just outside the town is a Commonwealth Graves Commission graveyard in which the casualties of the war were buried. Sadly, many of the graves have now been desecrated. All the crosses on the graves have been smashed. Just along the road from the Anglican Church was a functioning Catholic church, and just along the coast was a settlement of the Sisters of Mercy, who belonged to the same foundation as Mother Theresa. Sadly, during the war, the Catholic Church was burned down, the Indian priest was kidnapped, and the Sisters of Mercy, nuns from the Philippines, were killed.

Peta and I, along with a series of colleagues from PRIME, were involved in overseeing quality maintenance and postgraduate education for the eye hospital. The medical school expressed interest in being part of this initiative, and we integrated them into the teaching we conducted both in the clinic and within the university itself. During a visit to the dean's office, I encountered an experience unlike any I had encountered elsewhere in the world: passing by armed guards stationed outside the dean's office within the university buildings. With the assistance of PRIME, the University faculty eventually established their own organisation to teach Whole Person Medicine in a Yemeni setting. We even brought some of the faculty members to the UK for training in this approach.

We never stayed for any length of time in Aden. The situation was always brittle, and there was always an undertone of violence. It was considered that having more Westerners staying in the compound might endanger the permanent staff and reduce the solidarity with the local community. We did, however, sponsor a dear and godly Arabic friend of ours whom we had worked with in Egypt, who came and lived and worked with the clinic.

After a few months, it became clear to him that the work in the clinic was not what God was calling him to do. Instead, he started working with a Canadian colleague in an organisation set up to promote peace among warring factions in the country. They would bring the leaders of various factions and tribes who were fighting each other together in one room. Not infrequently at first, while they were meeting, their followers would be firing guns at each other in the streets outside. They used to concentrate in their meetings on how they both saw the future. Initially, the two factions wouldn't communicate except to exchange threats. However, the staff began using large sheets of paper, which they spread on the floor. They then formed several groups, ensuring an equal representation of people from both sides, and provided crayons to draw their vision of the next five years. This activity engaged them in a task they genuinely enjoyed. By the end of the two-day session, both factions were conversing with each other as if they were close friends. Remarkably, even their followers had ceased shooting at each other on the street below. Undoubtedly, achieving this was the primary objective of the project. Frequently, after these sessions, participants returned home and resolved at least some of the issues that had divided them. All individuals involved in this endeavour were Christians, though not overtly so. The government was deeply impressed by their accomplishments, leading to their appointment to oversee peace maintenance and conflict resolution throughout South Yemen.

Our Egyptian friend was also a good friend and pastor to the underground Christians in Aden. The expatriates were allowed to worship in the Anglican church, but Islam was very much part of the identity of the Yemenis, and anyone who professed faith in Christianity was in a dangerous situation, liable to violence or even being killed. Because of this, the Yemeni believers were very scared of meeting with each other in case one person in the group was a spy and informed on them, leading to them and their families being shot. There were about 20 Christians in the town.

Our Egyptian friend's father-in-law was a dedicated Christian in Cairo. He also had severe heart failure. Despite this, he felt God was calling him to go to Yemen and to meet with and encourage the Christians to meet. He came from Cairo to Aden via the airline Yemenia (the most dangerous airline in the world at that time) and met individually with all the Christian families in Aden. The Yemeni Christians and the older Egyptian man met together and read the Bible together, and then, as the Yemeni believers grew in their faith, they gained enough confidence to meet.

Our friend hired a house in the suburbs surrounded by a high wall on the corner of two roads with a gate in each road so that if anybody was watching on one road, the Christians could go round the corner and enter by a different gate. They met weekly for worship, prayer and teaching. The church started increasing in confidence and joy and realised that somebody in the neighbourhood might hear them praising the Lord, so they put the radio outside each time they met and turned it up loud. They also asked the children to play outside as noisily as they could. The church grew as new people became believers. At this stage, our friend's father-in-law thought his work was done and returned to Cairo. When he arrived, he had a great evening with his wife, during which he told her that he felt that his work for God in this world was now finished. He gave his wife a kiss and went to bed. He did not wake up the next morning and died in his sleep. His work was over, and he was promoted into the presence of his Lord.

We made about one or two visits a year to Aden, teaching in the clinics, running conferences, teaching at the university, and most importantly, listening to the plans and hopes of our staff. It was sad to see the security situation becoming more and more fragile as the political situation became more unstable and the president was deposed. We always took advice from Mansour before going to Aden, but several times, we went when there were Foreign Office warnings against going. We were able to do this because an insurance company that covered missionaries, journalists and NGO workers in war situations was ready to cover us for a large premium. We were always met at the airport by Mansour and ushered through immigration and customs. On the way out at the end of our visits, we were searched before we entered the airport before we went to the boarding gate, before we left the terminal and if we were travelling with Royal Jordanian Airlines again at the top of the stairs by a man with a gun in a holster who travelled on the plane with us. Things were very much more relaxed when flying with Yemenia Airlines. As this is supposed to be one of the most dangerous airlines in the world, they probably thought that you were probably more likely to die in a crash than by terrorism, so why bother?

During this period, we arranged a meeting of our Yemeni hospital staff and an equal number of Egyptian staff from the diocesan medical services for a medical conference in Cairo specifically slanted towards ophthalmology and ophthalmic surgery. A dear friend of ours, an eminent eye surgeon and the head of the Egyptian Ophthalmic Quality Maintenance Committee, played a significant role in this conference. He is a Christian and has remained a bachelor to be able to serve his Lord better. This time, together with our Egyptian colleagues, had a profound effect on our Yemeni staff. Our friend accepted the continuing role of overseeing quality maintenance and education at our hospital in Aden. Even when the civil war erupted, he persisted in visiting Aden and providing unwavering support to our staff throughout these challenging times. His presence became particularly valuable after our other friend was forced to return to Egypt. This visiting surgeon also took on the responsibility of supporting the imperilled underground Christian community. This responsibility arose when the resident pastor of the underground church had to depart due to the threats they faced.

Things were relatively relaxed in the town during the first few years of our engagement in Yemen, and we often went out for meals in restaurants. On one occasion, we walked downtown to the fish market to choose a large fish that had been caught that afternoon. We then walked across the road dodging the wrecks of cars, which, like in Egypt, were often made up of bits of several cars and which probably had little braking ability. We sat right down on the beach at a long wooden trestle table. The fish was delivered from the market and was given to the cook. The table was covered with a strong transparent plastic sheet, which served as both the tablecloth and the plates. We sat chatting in the warmth of a spring evening, looking out on the bay of Aden. The lights around the beach and the families surrounding us on an evening out made a calm, peaceful scene. There was no wind. A friend of ours who worked in an office in Aden arrived and sat down, greeting everybody and apologising for being late. Peta remarked that the lights around the bay reminded her of gazing out over the bay at St. Tropez. He looked outside and replied, "Yes, it is peaceful, isn't it? Aden is a beautiful place, but one must put that into the context of life here. Recently, when I was out of my office, terrorists broke in, injured three of my secretaries, and then left. That's just how life is here." Silence enveloped the table briefly, and then conversations gradually resumed. Incidents like this were simply a reflection of the everyday existence in Yemen.

Because the security situation in the country was fast deteriorating and bombs were being made in Yemen and planted on planes coming to the UK, the British government tightened their regulations. All postal services between the two countries were stopped. Mansour's son was studying to be a pilot in Sheffield at this time and had his visa cancelled in the middle of his course. He was told to go home and apply for a new visa from Yemen. However, at that time, the visa section of the British Embassy was closed, and anybody wanting a visa had to go to Addis Ababa in Ethiopia. Mansour and his son filled in all the forms and presented them to the British Embassy several times. There was always a problem, and the cost of multiple visits mounted up. This seemed a pity in such an Anglophile family who had done so many years of faithful service in a British institution. Mansour's son was also a young man known at his university as being sober and hardworking. Happily, I was able to contact the Foreign Office minister in charge of the Middle East, who was a long-time friend of ours and had a personal interest in Yemen at that time. After an investigation, we were given a code to put on the application for a visa. At the next visit, it was issued to him immediately.

I developed prostate cancer at about this time and was no longer insurable to go to Aden, which was a real blow to me. Also, at this time, Our Egyptian friend and his wife became more and more worried about the security of their family. The children went to a Turkish-run school right next door to the offices of one of the main daily newspapers. This paper published an article to which the people in power took offence, so they brought up a tank and shelled the building while the building next door was teaching a large group of children. Happily, none of the children were hurt, but they were considerably shaken. At this point, our friend and his wife decided to return to Egypt. The two children were very happy to be back where they could see their grandparents and childhood friends.

After about two months, they went together to see their parents and asked them how long they would stay in Egypt. Their parents told them that they would not be going back to Yemen, as it was too dangerous to live there now. The children thought about this for about a week and then returned to their parents and asked, "What about our Yemeni friends? Where are they, and what is happening to them?" Our friend and his wife explained that their friends had nowhere to escape to, so they were back in Aden. The children pondered this for a while, then returned to their parents and expressed that they felt it was wrong to run away from all their friends like that. After all, Jesus didn't run away when he was in danger. If their friends could cope with the situation, why couldn't they as a family? Our friend and his wife went to see their pastor and shared this with him. He asked them if they thought that God was speaking to them through their children. They decided to return and continue their work, returning to the same house with a high wall all around it. While frequent fighting occurred in their part of the town, the wall protected the house's ground floor. They could not sleep upstairs or even go upstairs as bullets frequently passed through the windows. During the time after their return, they were able to support the underground believers and prepare them for the very hard time that was to come. The church almost doubled in size during this period, a growth that so often occurs in the face of persecution and danger.

After about 18 months, the fundamentalists made a direct threat against our friend's family and at that time, they felt it was wise to leave permanently. Also, at this time, a colleague of Roy, one of the members of our committee, who worked in the port, was blown up in his car. The security forces phoned this friend of ours and told him not to answer his door or go near the windows. A rescue posse would be coming for him, and he had been given a coded knock that they would use, so he could recognise when they were at his door. After about 4 hours, the knock came, and a group of four heavily armed American men in body armour arrived. They grabbed him and placed him in an armoured vehicle, which then transported him to the airport. From there, he was put on a military plane that flew him to Germany. Evidently, the fundamentalists had planned to kill him that afternoon.

The disorder escalated into a civil war, with Saudi Arabia supporting one side and Iran supporting the other. In other words, two powerful countries were waging a war in a third country to prevent death and destruction from occurring within their own territories. As is often the case, when the Saudis attacked Aden, they initially targeted hospitals, followed by electricity and water purification plants, and then the telephone and internet buildings. Indiscriminate bombing of civilian areas occurred; to our shame, some bombs had British markings. I have seen evidence of this. These bombs had been sold to the Saudis by the British. As the Saudis advanced, they positioned snipers on the roofs of the town, targeting not only soldiers but also people seeking food for their families. Amidst all this chaos, neither Christchurch Aden nor the Ras Morbat Clinic was bombed, possibly due to a superstitious fear of targeting a church compound.

This left our hospital as the sole functioning medical facility aside from the MSF (Doctors Without Borders). The MSF hospital specialised in treating patients wounded below the neck, while the Ras Morbat Hospital handled the more minor of the injuries above the neck. Across the globe, in times of war, both sides generally respect the work done by MSF and take care not to damage their hospitals. However, this was not the case with the Saudis. The MSF facilities had to relocate every three weeks or so to avoid being bombed by the Saudis. Tragically, in another Yemeni town, the MSF hospital remained stationary for too long, resulting in a Saudi bombing that claimed the lives of 150 doctors, staff, and patients.

Throughout the war, except for a single month when our staff couldn't access the church compound due to roads blocked with rubble and burning tyres, our hospital continued to function as normally as possible amidst the chaos. During lulls in the fighting, the hospital performed cataract surgery on Yemeni men. The significance of this procedure was immense – if a husband and father couldn't see due to cataracts, he couldn't work, leading to his wife and children suffering from lack of food or starvation. Despite the constant threats of bombing, snipers, and criminals flourishing under these conditions, our staff made their way to the hospital daily from their homes. Occasionally, groups of men attempted to loot the hospital. In such instances, the local residents of Tawahi rallied and confronted the youths with steel bars.

During one of the lulls in the fighting, Al Qaeda came to visit. Sixteen armed young men on sixteen motorbikes arrived at the gates and demanded entry. Mansour, who is a big man and an elder of the local Islamic society, came out of the compound unarmed, sat down with the men and asked them what they wanted. They said they had come to destroy the clinic and burn the church. Mansour asked them if they had ever read in the Quran that it is an absolute requirement of the Muslims to care for the poor and that this is what was happening within the compound. He said that everybody on the staff was recognised as a Muslim, and all the patients were Muslims. After approximately 4 hours of discussion, the group of men insisted that the large metal cross above the gate be taken down. Mansour readily complied with this demand. A much larger cross was prominently situated on the church roof, distinctly marking the location as a symbol of Christian faith. Around the same time, word had spread throughout the neighbourhood that 'their' church clinic was going to be set ablaze. As a result, a majority of the men from Tawahi gathered and encircled the area. They confronted the Al Qaeda members, warning them that any attempt to harm the church would lead to repercussions against their families. The sixteen young men who had arrived on sixteen motorbikes vanished without a trace. Sadly, the two Catholic churches in the town were burned down.

As the fighting reached a stalemate, an unprecedented Cholera epidemic erupted, becoming the largest outbreak the world had ever witnessed. Soon after, the coronavirus struck an already famine-stricken community. Although a handful of medical facilities had managed to reopen in the town, the scale of this catastrophe was insurmountable. Consequently, people returned to their homes and succumbed to the dire conditions. Their deaths went unnoticed, a silent tragedy that the world seemed to overlook.

We struggled to keep in touch with some of our friends amid the chaotic maelstrom. In the midst of it all, we met a couple who had reached Cairo and were staying at the Cairo Marriott Hotel. Witnessing the unfolding of this disaster among our friends became intensely painful, leading us to tears. For once, this wasn't just a news item; it was happening to people just like us, whom we knew and loved. Adding to this, our country is complicit in this crime against humanity. Until recently, I remained a member of the international advisory committee for the hospital. Being involved with a place of healing in the church compound, where people continue to find solace in the name of Jesus, has been inspirational. The church remains beloved by the impoverished suburb of Aden where it stands, and the local population fiercely protects 'Our Church Clinic.' Remarkably, amidst the fighting, bombing, starvation, and death, the community of faithful Christians in Aden and Yemen at large continues to grow. Jesus promises to be with us in the valley of the shadow of death. He doesn't promise to remove us from that dark valley, but His presence amid the explosions and deadly infections is truly wonderful.

Reassessment and Training for The Future

By this time, I had reached the age of 83, and Peta was 80. I had previously battled prostate cancer, and during treatment, everything that could have gone wrong did. I experienced sepsis after the biopsy and substantial bowel damage from the radiotherapy, resulting in persistent moderate bleeding – the treatment for this that was supposedly a "guaranteed" solution, according to my consultant, proved ineffective for me. Additionally, I dealt with a gastric ulcer, while Peta later required a pacemaker. These medical challenges made acquiring travel insurance prohibitively expensive and often unavailable for regions of the Middle East in turmoil. We bid farewell to our students, returned home, and grieved over the loss of our connections with a part of the world deeply ingrained in our hearts. Our visits to our home in France continued, where we typically spent the entire summer and autumn. By this point, we had become members of our local Catholic Church, fully integrated into the French worshipping community. With the consent of the Catholic bishop, we conducted an Alpha Course in French at our home. This provided us with the wonderful opportunity to host many of our neighbours from the hamlet for a weekly supper. It was very enjoyable yet managing to host a meal for 10 French individuals every week for 14 weeks posed a significant challenge for Peta. Our dear friends David and Jessie Boydell, who directed the language school in Paris where we spent a year at the outset of our engagement with the Francophone world, came to assist us during the initial session. For Catholics, becoming a Christian occurs through baptism as infants. While the terminology varied at the conclusion of their engagement with Alpha, many of our neighbours personally realised that they had established a relationship with Jesus Christ as their Lord and Saviour. The responsibility of running the Alpha course was taken over by members of the Catholic Renewal Movement at the cathedral in Cahors, the capital of the department, located 15 kilometres away from our home.

They now organise two courses annually, accommodating 50 participants in each, many of whom make a commitment to Christ as their Saviour. As our neighbours grew more rooted in their faith, we introduced them to the scripture reading notes of Scripture Union. These materials are published in France by the local office of the Scripture Union, known as La Ligue pour la Lecture de la Bible. Whereas in the past, our neighbours would shout at each other when they had a disagreement, they now pray together.

Back in England, for many years, we had attended a large evangelical church in Bedford called Christ Church. We wondered whether we should move and become members of the local church in our village. About 20 years before, we had spent 10 years attending this church, and I was a member of the PCC. The church was very liberal, but there was a group of people who knew and wanted to spread the gospel in the church. There used to be a youth group with 40 members, a bible study group and a Christian men's group. The vicar who had allowed this left, and a new vicar who came closed the youth group. He told me that he did not know why we met the whole time to endlessly read the Bible with members of the congregation; we should be out in the community helping people. In our men's group meeting after the vicar had told us this, we found that almost every man in the group was involved in youth groups in the town, citizen's advice work, with the women's shelter, with support for prisoners at the end of their sentence. We knew of very few members of the congregation who were doing similar work. We were made to feel unwelcome, and we returned to Christ Church.

We decided to return to our village church again. The vicar was a quiet, reserved man who sadly could come across as very rude and put people off. He never seemed to tell people how to make a relationship with God through Jesus dying on the cross in our place. Almost nothing was read in the church from the New Testament apart from the gospels. The epistles and Paul's teaching were hardly mentioned. Soon after we arrived, the post of churchwarden came vacant; I said I was willing to do the job and was elected. I had the privilege to work with a colleague, Laurie Hurn, the other churchwarden, who was a godly man, extremely hard-working and knowledgeable. We reinitiated the Alpha courses and continued the men's group, which I had led in the village for approximately 30 years. This group was now formally affiliated with the church. Unlike in the past, the vicar did not raise complaints or attempt to shut down these initiatives. Three other families joined the church, collaborating with us towards the shared objective of spreading the gospel and nurturing spiritual growth among the parishioners. Our collective goal was to help the community evolve into mature Christians. The vicar eventually retired after around a year, leading us into a period of transition and a subsequent vacancy. Eventually, we selected a new vicar, who marked a stark departure from his predecessor. He was a compassionate individual who excelled in listening. His commitment to individuals in need occasionally caused him to run late for appointments as he prioritised those seeking assistance.

And then the pandemic swept in. It started with a very nasty bug in some city in China that few people had heard of. The main sensation was 'glad it is over there, not over here.' Then suddenly, it was over here, and the world turned upside down. From being a couple of movers and shakers who had roamed the world, asking awkward questions like, 'Why do you do things that way?' we suddenly became extremely vulnerable old dears to be patted on the head, told to sit by the fire, have a nice cup of tea, and not to go out.

We did a bit of a double take and then realised that we were allowed to go out for a walk with the dog if we and the dog promised to be very good. So, we did! I lost weight, Peta lost weight, and even the dog lost weight. Happily, we had planted plenty of vegetables in our garden at the start of this year, as well as giving two neighbours plots in our garden to cultivate. Looking after our patches, bottling and freezing the vegetables, and giving them away became both an enjoyable form of occupational therapy and a way to keep in contact with everyone.

Many older people lived down our road, old ducks like us, so we helped to set up a road WhatsApp group to make sure that nobody was without food or company. The younger people stepped into the breech, and everybody became extremely good friends. The church closed its doors and instead went on Zoom; the consequence was that we had an increase in attendance, and people were able to join in from as far away as the Wirral. The church prayer meeting, discovery bible study group, and Alpha course all went onto Zoom and thrived, as did the gospel.

We were all living with risk, but as we had been living with risk for much of the last two decades, this did not trouble us at all. However, there was one unexpected problem. Peta has always fainted. very easily, usually in restaurants, particularly when drinking red wine Her fainting became more and more of a problem in January and February. Finally, she was diagnosed with a problem with the timing of her heartbeat 2 days before the first lockdown. We were told that her heart could stop, that she could need to be resuscitated at any time and that she needed a pacemaker. However, it was decided that waiting until the surge of Coronavirus infections had died down would be less dangerous than going into a hospital full of people extremely ill with the pandemic virus. She had to be always in my presence until she had her pacemaker fitted in June. The upside of this was that I had my wife all to myself for a good 4 months.

We found that while walking the dog, which we were allowed to do throughout this time, we chatted with all sorts of people we had never previously met. We celebrated my 80th birthday with bottles of champagne on a table in the middle of the road with canapes to which everybody came and helped themselves and then stood in their gardens and talked to (shouted at?) each other. Christmas and VE day were celebrated similarly, with the permission of the police, and we were continually looking for new occasions to celebrate. On a sadder note, one of Peta's best friends had Motor Neurone Disease and gradually got worse and died. We managed to keep her at home until about three weeks before her death. We also had five widowers and three other very poor people we kept an eye on. We were not bored for one moment during the whole time.

As things very, very slowly began to return to some sort of normality, we decided to join an organisation called 'Sanctuary Hosting.' This organisation provides housing and care in people's homes for asylum seekers. These individuals are often destitute and sometimes homeless while their applications for asylum are being considered, including any appeals that may be made in case of refusal. This process can take several years. Their situation is worsened by the fact that they are not allowed to work during this time. Often, there are children involved, and they receive a weekly sum of money that is impossible to survive on. Our guests stay in our spare room and become honorary members of our family. One recent guest we had was a poet; I found myself revisiting her beautifully written poems in the past few days. After her stay, we hosted a Liberian refugee, the sole survivor of an armed attack on his village. Currently, we have been hosting a Ukrainian refugee for more than a year. She is a very courageous lady who was forced to become a refugee in her own country following the annexation of Crimea in 2014, and now she seeks refuge in Britain.

So, at the age of 83, it is time to reflect on a life on the move. We have worked in 10 countries and lived in 7 of these countries. Some have been utterly remote and almost totally cut off from the outside world, while others have been countries where we have been under threat to our lives, normally because of our faith. Some of these countries have been unstable, and the communities have been at the start of civil wars or political upheavals. At times, there have been Foreign Office warnings against visiting these countries, but as we have had work to do, we have gone anyway. We have flown on some dangerous airlines with similar warnings, particularly Yemenia.

Throughout this time, we have known great peace from our God. As it is written in Deuteronomy 32:4, 'He is the Rock! His work is perfect. For all His ways are just, a God of faithfulness and without injustice. Righteous and upright is he.' With such support, we've been blessed with two sons who have grown into the kind of individuals I would have aspired to be at their age. Over the years, in the UK, we've welcomed ten groups of people into our home for stays ranging from 2 months to 10 years. Among these individuals, who now live all around the world, some have become like sons and daughters, grandsons and granddaughters to us. We've proven that if God is for us, who can be against us? Romans 8:31.

Printed in Great Britain
by Amazon

34921351R00209